A Primer of Psychology
According to *A Course in Miracles*

Joe R. Jesseph, Ph.D.

Outskirts Press, Inc.
Denver, Colorado

Permissions

Portions of *A Course in Miracles* © 1975, 1985, 1992 and *Psychotherapy: Purpose, Process and Practice* © 1976 used by permission of the Foundation for *A Course in Miracles*.

Excerpts from *A Vast Illusion: Time According to A COURSE IN MIRACLES*, 3rd Ed. by Kenneth Wapnick © 1990, 2006 used by permission of the Foundation for *A Course in Miracles*.

Portions of *Glossary-Index for A COURSE IN MIRACLES*, 5th Ed. Revised by Kenneth Wapnick © 1982, 1986, 1989, 1993, 1999 used by permission of the Foundation for *A Course in Miracles*.

Portions of "Resistance: How One Studies *A Course in Miracles* Without Really Learning It" by Gloria and Kenneth Wapnick © 1999 used by permission of the Foundation for *A Course in Miracles*.

Excerpts from "Rules for Decision" by Kenneth Wapnick © 1993 used by permission of the Foundation for *A Course in Miracles*.

Excerpts from "True Empathy" by Kenneth Wapnick © 1990 used by permission of the Foundation for *A Course in Miracles*.

All other material quoted herein from other authors and sources is reproduced by virtue of the Fair Use provision of U.S. Copyright Law.

ISBN: 978-1-4327-1673-8
Library of Congress Control Number: 2007939730
Outskirts Press and the "OP" logo are trademarks belonging to Outskirts Press, Inc.
PRINTED IN THE UNITED STATES OF AMERICA

The teachings of *A Course in Miracles* may seem outrageous, preposterous, and too ridiculous to be believed. But in the Course Jesus implores his readers to *look*! Look closely at life as you experience it. Look at what so many of the world's illustrious writers and thinkers have pointed to throughout the centuries. Look at the thought content of your own mind. The Course is not an isolated, crazy bunch of words dreamed up by a hallucinating and delusional woman. It speaks to the core of life. Look! Just look. And as we look, Jesus invites us to consider whether somewhere within us there is at least a whispering suspicion that, "There must be a better way"?

- *A Primer of Psychology According to A Course in Miracles*, Conclusion, p. 245

Contents

List of Figures

Preface

The flame of truth pierces the heart.

I want to make it clear at the outset that I have written this book from the perspective of one who has been a dedicated student of *A Course in Miracles* for over twenty years. I was also engaged in practice as a professional psychologist from the time I received a Ph.D. in 1963 until 1989 and again from 1992 until retiring in 1996, having been licensed in both the states of Wyoming and Minnesota. In this book I have attempted to clearly describe the comprehensive system of psychology that can be distilled from the pages of the Course, and to some extent to compare and contrast that system with various systems and theories of what I term "conventional psychology," which has a history in the West extending over 125 years. While I have attempted to be objective in this undertaking, I must acknowledge that for me the psychology of the Course—what can appropriately be called "Jesus' psychology"—is the most helpful and satisfying set of psychological principles I have ever encountered. It offers a meaningful explanation for all of human behavior, and has given me a most relevant and useful way of understanding myself and life as I experience it. This has been true for me at both the conceptual level as well as the practical level of daily living. Indeed, the Course can be understood as offering both a philosophy of life and a way of life, the central practical aspect of this being its psychology of forgiveness.

Early in my professional career it occurred to me that I could think of no human problem, whether interpersonal or intrapersonal, for which some form of love was not the answer. But while I continue to think that it is vitally important that we humans find our way to love and the shared purposes of brotherhood, I do not think that everyone should adopt the Course's psychology or its way of life, which really cannot be separated out from its metaphysics and theology. The Course itself is clear on that point, stating that it is but one form of the "universal course" of which there are "many thousands" of other forms. I would add that each form has implicit within it a metaphysical foundation, a theology and a psychology. As forms of the "universal course," each represents a path to the same ultimate goal. This reflects the ancient wisdom that sees there are many paths up the mountain, but at the top they merge into one.

No doubt my preference for the Course will be evident in what I have written so that a bias will be apparent, but my bottom line has been simply to make the principles of the Course's psychology clear, and to do so partly by comparing and contrasting those principles with others. Of course, I am not sure how any given reader will respond. Perhaps some will find an invitation in this book; some may find clarification; and others may find much with which they disagree, even very strongly whether they consider themselves a student of *A Course in Miracles* or not. Each reader must decide for himself or herself how to make use of this book. I just want to communicate my lack of interest in proselytizing as well as my respect for every reader of these words, no matter what his or her reaction might be.

The idea for this writing grew out of my years-long participation on an Internet discussion group for students of *A Course in Miracles* hosted on yahoo.com and named "Course Talk." In the late autumn of 2003 I had posted a series of articles to that group which attempted to summarize the basic principles of the psychology of the Course. When I had finished with that effort, it occurred to me that I could probably make up a pamphlet about the psychology of ACIM by pulling those articles together into one small publication. I did not give much further thought to the idea until the spring of 2005 when I moved from Minneapolis to Murrieta, California in order to participate more closely in the activities of the Foundation for *A Course in Miracles* where I had been a staff member for a few years prior to their move from Tennanah Lake in the Catskill mountains of New York to the Temecula, California location. Over the years since I left the Foundation, I had continued to stay in touch and to provide volunteer services, some of which included assisting with the rough editing of certain publications, most notably the "Shakespeare series"[1] of four booklets wherein Ken Wapnick used certain central themes from Shakespeare's four great tragedies to illuminate central ideas in the Course.

When I took up residence in California near the Foundation, I told Ken about my idea for a pamphlet or small book on the psychology of the Course, which at that time I thought could be titled *A Primer of Jesus' Psychology According to A COURSE IN MIRACLES*. (Many will recognize that this title is modeled after Calvin Hall's well-known little book, *A Primer of Freudian Psychology*;[2] a book I had found very helpful as a graduate student.) Ken said that he thought the idea would be worth pursuing, but then my immediate project was to author an index for the second edition of his book *A Vast Illusion: Time According to A COURSE IN MIRACLES*.[3]

---

[1]Wapnick, Kenneth. Life, Death, and Love: Shakespeare's Great Tragedies and A COURSE IN MIRACLES, Temecula, CA: Foundation for A Course in Miracles, 2004.

[2]Hall, Calvin S. *A Primer of Freudian Psychology*. New York: World Publishing Company, 1954.

[3]Wapnick, Kenneth. A Vast Illusion: Time According to A COURSE IN MIRACLES. Third Edition. Temecula, CA: Foundation for A Course in Miracles, 2006

That project was completed in January of 2006 when I again discussed the idea for this Primer with Ken who said he still thought it worth pursuing. I then invited him to co-author the work, but he declined, being too busy with several other projects and, in any case, of the opinion that, "It should by your book, Joe." Actually, I knew that to be the case, but I did not understand why it should necessarily be so. As I proceeded to write, I discovered why! This undertaking was going to constitute an important set of personal lessons for me. First of all, I discovered that my original series of posts would not lend themselves adequately to some simple revisions which could then be cut and pasted into book form. I was chagrined at how inadequate those posts were to my purpose, both in terms of the quality of writing as well as in the depth of understanding they communicated. But more importantly, as I proceeded to write, I came smack up against my own resistance to Jesus' message!

Ken had agreed to help me by reading and commenting upon every chapter as I wrote, and initially I launched into the project with enthusiasm and delight. But then I found myself procrastinating, avoiding the writing, finding all sorts of excuses not to write, becoming too sleepy to write, and strangely unable to think clearly about subjects I had every reason to believe I understood quite well. It took me a while to realize what was going on. It was very subtle, but obviously my own continuing ego identity did not want to understand and write clearly about the Course! The resistance became quite noticeable as I struggled with chapter four on the ego. The ego does not like to lay itself open to examination, which I well knew, but to which I now can attest from even more intense personal experiences than I had previously. For a while it was difficult for me to accept that my problems in proceeding stemmed from my own ego-inspired fear of the mind, not to mention a more clear view of the vicious, self-centered nature of my own ego identity. I was depressed at times, often without realizing how depressed until later. I even began to have suicidal ideas, but I thought that these were just a natural part of the fact that I'm getting older (soon to be 72 at the time) and life in the body is becoming less comfortable. But why so much physical discomfort this year when a year earlier I had been in remarkably good health and physical vigor, given my age? Upon reflection, I had to admit that some of my new-found arthritic symptoms had begun last year and that I had encountered many similar psychological symptoms of resistance when developing the index for Ken's book. The resistance I was experiencing really was not new, but it was more determined.

Once I understood what was happening, I was able to simply watch and let the resistance (fear) have its way. I knew enough to be gentle with myself, and had enough access to right-minded Help so that I took naps, engaged in distractions, waited to see what the next morning would bring, and continued the inward looking without judgment which is a gift from my years of Course study.

As you can see, my body has survived—at least this far—and hopefully able to be in service to our right mind fairly often. I value this writing project for what I've learned, particularly for that learning which has been intimately personal in nature, but also for the additional clarity gained about this remarkable thought system that is *A Course in Miracles*. I hope that my writing, too, has survived in a sufficiently clear and well-documented form that it will give the reader an opportunity to more fully appreciate and understand the astounding, radical nature of Jesus' system of psychology as it is spelled out in the Course. Radical though it may be, it is also a rather simple psychology, whose central teaching is about forgiveness. What makes it complicated is the very resistance that I encountered in writing about it. In other words, what makes the Course and its psychology seem difficult is fear of our mind and of the truth of oneness; fear which is born of the depth and pervasiveness of our ego identity. Our embrace of separation, self and specialness has led us to believe that illusions are the truth and that hatred in disguise is love. As well, we have been deceived about the nature of God and spirit. So, I think it would not be at all unusual if you as reader encountered resistance to Jesus' psychology similar to that which I in the role of writer experienced, even after spending over twenty years as a student and self-practitioner of this very psychology.

The good news delivered in *A Course in Miracles* is that you are not who you think you are. And that is the bad news as well; at least as far as our cherished ego self-identity is concerned.

As I was writing about the inner, nonintellectual resonance that many readers experience upon first encountering the Course, I was amused at the irony of the fact that so many of us respond with intuitive knowing, love and appreciation to a message that basically tells us we have been wrong about everything, and that our fundamental motivations in life have been those of attack amounting to murder. The Voice for Love sings to us from the pages of the Course, but, unless we fall asleep or otherwise blank out,—which almost all readers do fairly often, and upon re-reading, are amazed to discover what they'd missed!—it also confronts us with what amounts to a powerful blow to the head. It was in reflecting upon this irony that the subtitle of this preface came to mind: *the flame of truth pierces the heart.* The truth of oneness is the essence of Love. It offers us a way to rise in peace above the battleground that is human life on this planet, even though it requires of us that we be willing to set aside our dedication to self and self interest. And so we are both wounded and saved by the same pure flame that burns away the dross of ego to reveal the shining Christ that resides in every heart, uniting us all as One. The Call to oneness lives within each of us. But so does the call to self and battle. We have a choice, and that is the central point of Jesus' psychology. I hope that this little book will make that choice and the means of making it more clear and accessible to those who continue to read herein.

Joe Jesseph
July 21, 2006
Murrieta, California

Acknowledgments

I had thought of dedicating this book to Ken Wapnick, but that seemed inappropriate since this is as much Ken's book as it is mine. He is in effect, if not officially, a co-author. I owe my conceptual grasp of the Course to Ken's teachings over the past twenty years, and I have drawn heavily upon his writings here. In addition, he was so kind as to read and comment upon every chapter as I wrote. So I am first and foremost deeply grateful to Ken, not only for his help at the level of intellectual comprehension, but for his shining example as a "teacher of God" who lives the Course in even the most mundane affairs of daily life. In my eyes, Ken has *become* the Course. As time has passed since I first met him in 1987, he has gone from being for me a brilliant academic teacher of the rather difficult ACIM thought system to being my teacher of brotherhood and forgiveness by example. I hope that this book and my own daily life, are fitting expressions of my gratitude and appreciation for him and for the voice that speaks from the pages of *A Course in Miracles*.

I am also most grateful to the many friends and fellow ACIM students who have read, commented upon and made suggestions for the initial manuscript. Some read the draft in its entirety while others read only portions of it, but all made comments that were helpful to me in preparing the final draft. Emy LaBelle was the first to read the whole thing, offering many corrections and suggestions from her perspective not only as a student of the Course, but as one who is a highly skilled proof reader. My old Internet friend and long-time student of ACIM, Martha Street, also read the entire manuscript. Her response was very helpful and encouraging. Likewise, my email friend Melody Vantucci read the entire draft and responded with very supportive comments from the perspective of a relatively new student of the Course. Another old friend with whom I became acquainted on the Internet and later met personally, Richard Mallett, also read the whole manuscript, offering wise and helpful observations from his perspective as an experienced student of the Course.

Dr. Ruth Gillman, another long-time student of ACIM and member of the social work faculty at Temple University kindly took the time from her busy schedule to read the manuscript. Her comments and observations were very helpful as were those of experienced Course student and author Gene Fessenbecker. Also, Tom Leach, MA Divinity, a former member of the FACIM staff and dedicated ACIM student for many years, offered some very helpful observations after an initial, but as yet incomplete, reading. I look forward to hearing more from him as this book goes to press, anticipating that further revisions might be in order. Dr. Rosemarie LoSasso, FACIM Director of Publications, did not have time for a complete reading, but generously went over the Preface with me, as well as discussing certain aspects of formal writing and indexing. Later she carefully skimmed through the pre-publication draft, offering many very helpful suggestions..

I am grateful to Karen Davis, another long-time ACIM student, who generously spent several hours with me in proofing the copy intended for publication as well as offering helpful feedback. Likewise, I am very grateful to FACIM staff members Karla Royer and Emy Massengill who spent considerable time with me in proof reading and made several helpful suggestions along the way.

Barb Beaven, Tom and Mary Farr, Loral Reeves, Lucy Rudnicka, Tom Smith, John Steiner, and Sarah Favret, all read portions of the manuscript and offered helpful feedback by the time I was ready to prepare the first draft for publication. In addition, two other FACIM staff members, Jennye Cook and Virginia Tucker, helped with proof reading for which I am very appreciative.

Finally, I want to thank the Foundation for *A Course in Miracles* for permission to quote extensively from both the Course itself as well as from the works of Kenneth Wapnick.

Only one equal gift can be offered to the equal Sons of God,
and that is full appreciation (T.6.V.A.4.7).

A Key to Citations Using the ACIM System of Annotation

References to *A Course in Miracles* in this book follow the standard notational system for the Second Edition.

Abbreviations Used

T: text

W: workbook for students

M: manual for teachers

C: clarification of terms

In: Introduction

r: Review (workbook)

FL: Final lessons (workbook)

Ep: Epilogue

P: "Psychotherapy: Purpose, Process and Practice"

S: "The Song of Prayer"

Examples of the second edition notation for each book:

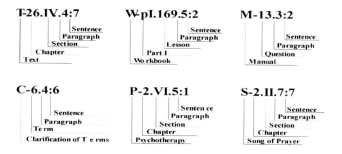

Introduction

Psychology has been described as the science of mind and behavior. A typical dictionary definition is: "The science that deals with mental processes and behavior."[1]

Essentially, it is the goal of psychology to help us understand ourselves: why we behave as we do; think, experience and feel as we do; what accounts for differences among us; and why we have the problems and conflicts that we experience. Hopefully, then, such understanding could help us resolve our conflicts and would be of use to those professionals who attempt to treat persons with what are regarded as psychological problems or disorders.

As a separate scientific discipline, psychology is relatively new in the world, coming on the scene in the late nineteenth century when the eminent German scientist-philosopher Gustav Fechner established that mind, as he understood it, could be studied scientifically, followed by Wilhelm Wundt's founding of a laboratory for psychological experimentation at Leipzig University in 1875, the same year that William James instituted a similar laboratory at Harvard University. Prior to this time, questions relating to mind and behavior had been the province of philosophy, and indeed both Wundt and James were regarded as philosophers though they were instrumental in establishing the science of experimental psychology.

About the same time, Sigmund Freud, who had been deeply influenced by the writings of Fechner, began his study of the human mind as he collaborated with the physician Josef Breuer in treatment of a female patient who began to manifest a series of symptoms with no apparent physiological cause. In 1895 that famous collaboration resulted in the publication of a work entitled *Studies on Hysteria*,[2] a landmark publication in Freud's career as he began to develop his comprehensive theory of psychoanalysis, a theory which he regarded as the basis for a new science of mind.

Experimental psychology has emphasized the study of human behavior and physiology, since such study lends itself to objective observation, quantifiable data, and scientific methodologies. While Freud was trained as a scientist, and regarded his studies as scientific, the object of his study was the inner life of individuals, including himself. His approach has been described as "clinical," distinguishing it from the experimental.

---

[1]The American Heritage Dictionary of the English Language, Fourth Edition. New York: Houghton Mifflin Company, 2000.

[2]Breuer, Joseph and Sigmund Freud, *Studies on Hysteria*. Trans. by James Strachey. New York: U.S. publication by Basic Books, Inc. in arrangement with Hogarth Press, 1957.

Both approaches to psychological study, the behavioral/experimental and the clinical, have produced a wealth of theoretical formulations with their attendant concepts, and *A Course in Miracles* makes use of many of these concepts, while offering a system of psychology that is radically different from anything which has preceded it. It is profoundly different from other psychologies of the world, because it incorporates the spiritual dimension of human experience, and because it is grounded on a non-dualistic metaphysical foundation. At the same time, the Course's psychology is eminently practical, acknowledging that we believe in a dualistic reality and must therefore be helped within the context of what we believe, even though it is not the truth. Forgiveness is the core of this practical teaching, but in order to practice the Course's psychology of forgiveness one must be willing to accept that one's true identity is as spirit of which mind is the "activating agent," and that one is not truly separate from anything or anyone perceived to be other than self. Then, the practice of forgiveness is understood as a spiritual undertaking at the level of mind which requires us to engage in a process of undoing ego identity with its dualistic belief system that conceives of an individual existence separate from God, and of separate individual beings whose differences are quite important and whose goals are often in conflict.

It is no accident that the scribe of the Course and her colleague were professional psychologists who had been schooled in both experimental and clinical traditions, and it is within the framework of traditional psychology that many of the terms and concepts of the Course are found. Indeed, it can be said that the language and conceptual *form* (though not the *content*, or underlying message) of the psychology found in *A Course in Miracles* depends upon the genius of Sigmund Freud and would not have been possible without the hundred plus years of development in western psychological thought that preceded it. However, as with terms and concepts that it draws from religion, the Course offers an understanding that is quite different from the traditional, beginning with the fact that its concept of *mind* is unlike anything attempted in traditional psychology, and no doubt unacceptable to traditional psychologists whose metaphysical premises are those of the ego's dualistic thought system.

Finally, *A Course in Miracles* is a "channeled" work—that is, it is a work whose inspiration and words come from a spiritual source in the mind of its "scribe," Helen Schucman. Schucman herself never used the words "channel" or "channeling" to describe the inspiration that produced the Course through her. Rather, she spoke of a kind of "inner dictation" that was very personal in nature. The personal identity of the inner voice she heard was that of Jesus. But this was a Jesus whose thought system hardly matches that of the Jesus portrayed in the Bible. In fact, the Course itself can be understood in part as representing a critique of, and radical alternative to, traditional Christian thought, which is also dualistic in its premise and has a different understanding of forgiveness.

So, the psychology of A Course in Miracles, which this book is intended to summarize and outline, comes from an authority at the level of spirit and mind. Speaking in terms of Course principles, ultimately all human expressions come from that level—all works are "channeled" or inspired at the level of mind, then to take form, whether as words, music, art, or some other human behavior. The issue of authority, then, is not spirit versus science, or God versus the human intellect. Rather, the issue of authority, from the perspective of the Course, has to do with which thought system in the mind is the source of human activity and expression. And, according to the Course, there are only two thought systems in the mind, of which only one is grounded in truth. Those are the dualistic thought system of the ego, which begins with the false premise that separation from God and from all else is real; and the non-dualistic thought system of the Holy Spirit, Whom Jesus manifests, and which begins with the truth of oneness that separation is impossible. The hope of healing and escape from human suffering that the Course offers lies in the fact that as mind we have a choice between those two thought systems.

The source of A Course in Miracles is ultimately the eternal truth that only Oneness[3] is real, oneness being the essence of Love, or of God. Since, according to the Course, the Mind of God has no awareness of separation, and God did not make the world or the body, the Love of God is not, and cannot be, *directly* present in the mind that dreams of separation. Yet, because God is the only true reality, His essence—His oneness and Love—is ever present and cannot be completely blocked out. So, a *memory* of God and His Love remains in our mind in spite of our dedication to the ego which has led us to dream of an existence apart from Love; separated out from Oneness and hallucinating a world and body.

But God and His Love are without form, ethereal and completely abstract; therefore the Memory which remains in our mind is amorphous. In the Course, that Memory is called the *Holy Spirit* Who can be understood as an abstract Presence of Love in our mind which is able to be sensed and to inform our perceptions in the world of illusions, but which, for most of us, is remote and impersonal. It is therefore very helpful when that amorphous Presence can be symbolized for us in a form that is more accessible—more

---

[3] For our purposes, where the term *oneness* is used as a synonym for God or Heaven it will be capitalized.

personal. In the mind of Helen Schucman, Jesus was that more personal manifestation of the Holy Spirit. Jesus thus serves as the voice whose words speak to us from the pages of *A Course in Miracles*, inviting us to take him as our internal teacher and guide. Recognizing that "The name of Jesus Christ is but a symbol" (M-23.4:1), for convenience throughout this book we will nevertheless freely refer to Jesus as the author of the Course who speaks directly from its pages to the reader.

Speaking in terms of the illusion of linear time, since the Holy Spirit has remained in our mind even while we seem to sleep and dream, Jesus and other symbols of God's Love have always been with us. Thus, as brothers in Christ who share the same mind, when Jesus "arose" (was enlightened and remembered God) we were with him:

> [The Holy Spirit] offers thanks to you as well as him [Jesus] for you arose with him when he began to save the world. And you will be with him when time is over and no trace remains of dreams of spite in which you dance to death's thin melody (C-6.5:5-6; brackets mine).

Because mind is universal, or as the Course often states, "all minds are joined," the message of the Course could have been delivered in any culture, using the language of that culture. The *content* of the message would have been the same since the truth is one and the same for all, but the *form* would have differed according to the symbols of the culture. Indeed, various forms of the same loving content have been manifested in all human cultures throughout the history of mankind. In fact, that message of love resides in every mind, which is why Jesus can invite us to turn to him. Our human problem is that we block out the message of love: we turn away, or do not listen, or refuse to understand, or unconsciously distort what the inner voice of love would say to us.

In Western culture, Jesus is by far the most widely known and influential symbol of the Love of God, however badly that symbol has been misunderstood and misrepresented. In fact, one purpose of the Course is to correct our images of Jesus and of God so that Love is no longer equated with sin, guilt and sacrifice. Thus it is that, for us in the West, Jesus can symbolize the Love of God Whose memory remains in our mind and can serve us in the interest of forgiveness at the dualistic level of human life where we experience pain and believe that there are things and people to forgive.

Jesus represents an ever present source of help for those willing to undertake the Course's path of forgiveness—a path of undoing ego identity. Hence, the system of psychology presented in the Course is Jesus' psychology as is clearly indicated by the paragraphs quoted below from the third volume of the Course, the Manual for Teachers.[4] Regarding the reference to "teachers" in the title of this volume, and the mention of a "true and dedicated teacher of God" in the cited paragraphs, obviously Jesus can be understood as a "teacher of God," but in the Course he invites those who would dedicate themselves to the study of his Course to join him in that function, which does not at all necessarily mean to become a *didactic* teacher, but which most certainly *does* mean to become a teacher of forgiveness *by example*. We do that by implementing the psychological principles of the Course and allowing our minds to join with Jesus' mind.

Ultimately all of us can become a manifestation of the Holy Spirit, like Jesus and others who symbolize the Love of God in this or any culture. That is what is indicated in the second paragraph below by the phrase "laid all limits by;" our limits being our identification with the ego thought system that leads us to identify ourselves as individuals living in bodies which must seek to meet their needs at the expense of other bodies and the environment; thus to be driven by the motivations of what the Course refers to as "specialness". Therefore, we worship the "gods of specialness" that we think can serve our self-centered interests and needs.

The words of the Course itself are presented here by way of closing this introduction. Unlike much of the Course, these words refer to Jesus in the third person. Although they came from the same personified source in Helen Schucman's mind as the rest of the Course, they could be regarded as coming directly from the Holy Spirit. They were initially addressed to Helen Schucman and her scribal colleague, William Thetford, but now in print are addressed to anyone who inwardly resonates to the Course, understanding that this will not be everyone:

> The Name of Jesus Christ as such is but a symbol. But it stands for love that is not of this world. It is a symbol that is safely used as a replacement for the many names of all the gods to which you pray. It becomes the shining symbol for the Word of God, so close to what it stands for that the little space between the two is lost, the moment that the Name is called to mind. Remembering the Name of Jesus Christ is to give thanks for all the gifts that God has given you. And gratitude to God becomes the way in which He is remembered, for love cannot be far behind a grateful heart and thankful mind....

---

[4]Throughout this book, we will refer to the psychological system found in *A Course in Miracles* as "Jesus' psychology."

No one on earth can grasp what Heaven is, or what its one Creator really means. Yet we have witnesses. It is to them that wisdom should appeal. There have been those whose learning far exceeds what we can learn. Nor would we teach the limitations we have laid on us. No one who has become a true and dedicated teacher of God forgets his brothers. Yet what he can offer them is limited by what he learns himself. Then turn to one who laid all limits by, and went beyond the farthest reach of learning. He will take you with him, for he did not go alone. And you were with him then, as you are now.

This course has come from him because his words have reached you in a language you can love and understand. Are other teachers possible, to lead the way to those who speak in different tongues and appeal to different symbols? Certainly there are. Would God leave anyone without a very present help in time of trouble; a savior who can symbolize Himself? Yet do we need a many-faceted curriculum, not because of content differences, but because symbols must shift and change to suit the need. Jesus has come to answer yours. In him you find God's Answer. Do you, then, teach with him, for he is with you; he is always here (M-23. 4:1-6, 6-7).

Chapter 1

The Use of Psychological Terms and Concepts in
A Course in Miracles

As has been said, *A Course in Miracles* makes use of the language and concepts of modern psychology, particularly those concepts developed by Freud. For instance, the Course employs the construct of *ego*, the idea of the *unconscious*, the concept of *defenses*, and particularly the defenses of *denial*, *dissociation* and *projection*. Some aspects of learning theory are utilized as well. However, it is most important in reading the Course to understand that all of these terms and concepts are being applied to a different order of reality than that addressed by conventional twenty-first century psychology which assumes the reality of the body, that consciousness resides in or is somehow a function of the brain, and that psychological healing takes place at the level of the individual person or relationships between persons. Not only does *A Course in Miracles* not accept these assumptions, but, in addition, it gives a different definition for the terms *mind* and *ego*.

So, in the Course the language and concepts of contemporary psychology serve as a set of symbols which is used to help us understand an order of reality with which most of humanity is largely unacquainted, and much of its science unwilling to accept as having any meaningful claim to serious consideration. After all, spirit (therefore mind as the Course uses that term) is intangible, unable to be perceived, and thus not a candidate for operational definition and study in the usual sense. And, as we shall see, the ego thought system seeks to maintain itself by keeping us preoccupied with the body and its world, unaware that we are spirit and mind. Yet, according to the Course, all of human experience is a reflection of what is taking place at the level of mind.

As it turns out, we can employ many of the concepts of psychology along with the kind of observational methodology Freud used, so as to learn a great deal about ourselves as mind, what motivates us at that level, and how to achieve peace within the illusion of the world and body in spite of the turmoil that rages within and in what seems to be without. Thus, the symbols of psychology can help us undertake a necessary journey of observation that honestly looks with non-judgmental objectivity at the processes within our mind. In addition, those symbols provide us with a conceptual framework for making sense of what we discover.

Therefore, employed as they are in *A Course in Miracles*, the language and concepts of psychology offer a symbolic map that can be used to guide self examination and to teach us something about the nature of our true reality, as well as teach us about the dream we think is reality. But those symbols constitute a set of *analogies* rather than an actual description of mind, which ultimately cannot be described. Yet words can point the way to awareness, enabling us finally to discover the power of decision which is ours as mind.

When the Course speaks of concepts such as *ego, learning, denial and projection*, it is speaking of what seems to go on in our mind, using ideas from conventional psychology which intends to understand the brain and behavior of the human body. From the perspective of the Course, that attempt represents an ego undertaking within the framework of its thought system, which begins with the premise that separation between cause and effect (i.e., God and creation) is real, that there is separation between the observer and the observed, and that reality consists of what can be perceived, symbolized and understood intellectually. Jesus, then, without accepting those assumptions, makes use of the symbols of the ego thought system to help us undo our identification with the ego and its belief in separation; a belief which spawns the illusion of a physical universe and all of the conflicts accompanying our perception of differences.

About the limitations of language, the Course states:

> Let us not forget...that words are but symbols of symbols. They are thus twice removed from reality (M-21.1:9).

> This course remains within the ego framework, where it is needed. It is not concerned with what is beyond all error because it is planned only to set the direction towards it. Therefore it uses words, which are symbolic, and cannot express what lies beyond symbols (C-IN 3:1-3).

If one accepts the non-dualistic metaphysical premise of the Course, ultimately all language must deceive, because the truth of oneness, which is the essence of God, cannot be symbolized:

> God is not symbolic; He is Fact (T-3.I. 8:2).

> Oneness is simply the idea God is. And in His Being, He encompasses all things. No mind holds anything but Him. We say "God is," and then we cease to speak, for in that knowledge words are meaningless. There are no lips to speak them, and no part of mind sufficiently distinct to feel that it is now aware of something not itself. It has united with its Source. And like its Source Itself, it merely is.

> We cannot speak nor write nor even think of this at all
> (W-pI.169.5-6:1).

8

Language deceives, because it is necessarily dualistic, based on the belief that there are separate things to be symbolized and interactions between those separate things to be described. Hence, in and of themselves, words convey the idea that separation is real. In other words, language itself has a powerful and pervasive tendency to validate the dualistic ego thought system and its premise of separation, a premise which must be false if oneness is true.

In fact, not only language, but no symbolic system can convey the truth of oneness; not mathematics, music, or artistic expression of any kind. What is infinite cannot be measured; what is eternal cannot be confined within the dimension of linear time; what is completely abstract has no form and cannot be perceived. However, we are confined to the use of symbols for purposes of communication since we are so thoroughly immersed in the ego. And, fortunately, symbols can point to truth even though they cannot directly communicate it.

When Gustav Fechner and Sigmund Freud initiated what they thought was a science of mind, they were studying what the Course regards as an illusion (basically the body). But, for our century, what their efforts have resulted in is both a language and a method which can be used to point us toward an awareness of what is truly mind. Thus, the Course makes use of traditional terms and concepts to help us discover our true Identity wherein lies the hope of rescue from the conflicts which characterize our personal lives; as well as rescue from the bleak despair which has characterized the human condition throughout its bloody history.

Let us, then, proceed to explore Jesus' system of psychology as presented in *A Course in Miracles*, which uses a familiar language, but speaks to us as mind and the Son of God rather than as bodies and separate, individual ego selves.

Chapter 2

The Concept of Mind

What is the "human mind?" Where do thoughts come from? What do we mean when we speak of "my mind?" How is the mind related to the body?

Our human experience is complex. We seem to have a wide variety of sensations: varieties of touch, colors, sounds, smells, shapes, movements; and to be surrounded by beings and objects with which we interact; which we can feel, paint, photograph or describe in words. We experience ourselves thinking: a parade of thoughts seems to accompany our sensations of the outer world, and we find ourselves reacting emotionally as well as intellectually to all of this.

We can ask the question, "What am I?" And we can ask a large variety of other questions such as: "Why do I feel this way?" "What made me do that?" "How does my experience happen?" "Where did I come from?" "Where did this outer world come from?" "What is existence?" "What is reality?" "Is there a God?"

We learn from what others speak or write, and we can question all of what we experience, as well as what we have been taught.

In the center of this human experiencing there seems to be an "I" separate from what is experienced as being "out there"—other than "I." This "I" seems to be more than a body, more than a mere physical being. We may call it "mind" or "consciousness." It seems to be non-physical, but what is it and how does it occur?

Since at least the fifth century B.C. philosophers have attempted to answer such questions, and in the last two centuries psychologists have had to find answers to the questions of "What is mind?" and "How is mind related to the body?" And yet, to this day in the year 2008 there is no universally accepted definition of *mind*, and no universally accepted solution to the question of how the mind and body are related; no universally accepted answer to what has been called "the mind-body problem." Yet every system of psychology posits or assumes answers to these questions.

In general, the term *mind* has been equated with consciousness—with that which makes our human experiencing possible. And in the West especially,

11

it has been assumed that consciousness, therefore the mind, is a function of the brain. As one British philosopher recently put it, rather hopeless of a solution, "Somehow, we feel, the water of the brain is turned into the wine of consciousness, but we draw a total blank on the nature of this conversion."[1]

Generally speaking, there have been two basic answers to the question, "What is mind?" One view asserts that mind is an entity of some sort; that it exists independently of the body, though somehow interacts with it. This view is found in the philosophy of Descartes, can be traced back to Plato, and has been integrated into Christian theology. The other answer stems from Aristotle and asserts that the term *mind* does not refer to anything substantial, but refers to a variety of mental functions which have their origin in the brain; that the concept of mind is one of convenience referring to the brain's ability to be conscious of itself as distinct from what is not itself, as well as to be able to study itself. This is the view implicated in Freud's theory.

Metaphysically speaking, both of these basic answers to the question of mind are dualistic in that they assume either that there are two orders of reality: mind and body, spirit and physicality; or that consciousness is real so that there is a difference between the observer and what is observed; therefore that the perceptual world of separate beings and objects is real, and objective study is possible.

As has been pointed out already, the metaphysical foundation of *A Course in Miracles* is non-dualistic: the Course asserts that there is only one order of reality and that is God, or the *Mind* of God. About his use of the term *mind* in the Course, Jesus says:

> The term *mind* is used to represent the activating agent of spirit, supplying its creative energy. When the term is capitalized it refers to God or Christ (i.e., the Mind of God or the Mind of Christ). *Spirit* is the Thought of God which He created like Himself. The unified spirit is God's one Son, or Christ (C-1.1).

The idea that mind is the activating agent of spirit is simply a way of recognizing that thought is God's means of creation, and that creation takes place *within* His Mind, thus the Mind of His creation, Christ, is not separate from the Mind of the Creator. In the Course, this creation is referred to as the *extension* of God's Thought. But since the Mind of God is not confined to

[1]McGinn, Colin. "Can We Solve the Mind-Body Problem?" *Mind* 98 (1989), pp. 349-66.

the dimensions of time and space, what is meant by *extension* and *creation* in reference to God is unlike anything we can understand in terms of the perceptual world where there is separation between the one who creates and that which he has created, and where the word "extension" is understood in terms of time and space.

It is because of the Course's basic law of mind, *ideas leave not their source*,[2] that the Thoughts of God are not separate from the Mind of God, which is a purely unified oneness, outside of which there is nothing, and within which there is no separation: a completely non-dual, non spatiotemporal reality. The human intellect cannot adequately conceive of this Mind, because our brains are limited to the symbols of duality for the formation of concepts. This is what is meant by the formerly quoted statement: "Oneness is simply the idea God is. And in His Being, He encompasses all things. No mind holds anything but Him. We say 'God is,' and then we cease to speak, for in that knowledge words are meaningless" (W-pI.169.5:1-4).

In another passage, the same idea is reiterated: "Heaven [which can be equated with the Mind of God] is not a place nor a condition. It is merely an awareness of perfect oneness, and the knowledge that there is nothing else; nothing outside this oneness, and nothing else within" (T-18.VI. 1:5-6; bracket mine).

So, regarding the question of "What is mind?" the Course's view is aligned with the Platonic answer, sometimes called the "substantial view," yet the Course makes no metaphysical compromise with dualism: there is no realty other than Mind. Therefore, the Course's answer to the mind-body problem is that the body is not real, but is illusory: a dream figure *in* a mind that has believed in separation, or duality, and has fallen into "the sleep of forgetfulness" (T-16.VII. 12:4). This dream figure is entirely controlled by the mind, fulfilling the mind's wishes, yet the mind which seems to sleep and dream is itself unreal.

Those familiar with eastern spiritualities will recognize this kind of explanation of mind and its relationship to the body. In the West, Ken Wilber is perhaps the leading spokesperson for the non-dual view which he has explored at considerable depth, beginning with his first book, *The Spectrum of Consciousness*,[3] wherein he quotes from a wide range of authors who represent non-dualism both in Western science as well as in eastern spiritual traditions.

---

[2] In the Course, see: T-26.VII, W-pI.132, W-pI.156 and W-pI.167.

[3] Wilber, Ken. *The Spectrum of Consciousness,* 2nd Ed. Wheaton, IL: The Theosophical Publishing House, 1977, 1993.

But Jesus does not simply abandon us to grapple with the metaphysical truth of oneness which we not only cannot fully understand, but which in and of itself is of little help. Because the truth must reach us in a language we can understand and use, the Course makes a practical compromise in favor of the second answer to the question of mind, which has been called the "functional view"—the view represented by Freudian theory and characteristic of most modern systems of psychology. Jesus does not expect us to fully grasp and integrate his non-dualistic metaphysical principles, recognizing that those principles alone would be of no practical value to those who are identified with the body and who believe in the dualistic reality of a world of separation where perception seems to apprehend truth. Rather, he speaks to us in the language of separation, or duality, where there seem to be individual minds which not only seem to be separate from the Mind of God, but from each other. Continuing with the Course's definition of *mind*, we find the following statements about this compromise:

> In this world, because the mind is split, the Sons of God appear to be separate. Nor do their minds seem to be joined. In this illusory state, the concept of an "individual mind" seems to be meaningful. It is therefore described in the course *as if* it has two parts; spirit and ego.

> Spirit is the part that is still in contact with God through the Holy Spirit, Who abides in this part but sees the other part as well....

> The other part of the mind [ego] is entirely illusory and makes only illusions. Spirit retains the potential for creating, but its Will, which is God's, seems to be imprisoned while the mind is not unified. Creation continues unabated because that is the Will of God. This Will is always unified and therefore has no meaning in this world. It has no opposite and no degrees. (C-1.2-3:1; 4; bracket mine).

Speaking to us in terms of an individual mind, the Course's psychology of forgiveness explains dynamic processes which seem to go on within our minds using the language of psychology, as discussed in chapter one. But it is vitally important to recognize that the Course speaks to us *as mind*, not as bodies which house individual personalities, and for whom the personal pronouns "I" and "you" refer to individual consciousnesses. The "you" to whom the Course is addressed is us as *mind*, and in fact a mind that, though it seems separate and individual, is not truly apart from other minds and only dreams of separation from God. We will return to this important point later. Suffice it for now to understand that in the Course the body is an illusion, as is consciousness (awareness of "me" and "not me") itself. But, since we believe that the body, consciousness, perception and individuality are real, Jesus begins with us at that level of belief as he offers us an invitation, and a means, to awaken to an experience of our reality as mind:

What has been given you? The knowledge that you are a mind, in Mind and purely mind, sinless forever, wholly unafraid, because you were created out of Love. Nor have you left your Source, remaining as you were created (W-pI.158.1:1-3; 2:4).

Since you believe that you are separate, Heaven presents itself to you as separate, too. Not that it is in truth, but that the link that has been given you to join the truth may reach to you through what you understand (T-25.I.5:1-2).

A Word about Thought and Thinking

We will return to this point many times, but it is important to be clear about it now before we proceed further to discuss the concept of mind: when Jesus talks about thought and thinking, he is referring to an activity initiated in the mind, not in the brain. The brain, like the rest of the body, is an *effect* of the mind, basically doing as the mind directs. What we regard as thinking is biochemical activity which has its cause not in the body, but in the mind. Both the body and the biochemical activity of the brain are illusions projected *in* the mind by the ego thought system. And in the mind there are only two thought systems which can project effects in consciousness. One is the thought system of the ego, which is the author of consciousness beginning with the mistaken premise that separation from Oneness (God) is real. The other is the thought system of the Holy Spirit which begins with the premise of the truth that separation from Oneness is not possible. When we as mind choose to think with the ego, we produce illusory images of separation—e.g., bodies—which are necessarily in conflict, because they begin with the idea of conflict with Oneness, or God. Such thinking then, according to Jesus, does not represent our "real thoughts," because real thought is of God and reflects His oneness. When we as mind choose to think with the Holy Spirit, our thoughts will reflect reality. Only the thoughts which reflect the truth of oneness are our "real thoughts." Those are basically loving thoughts. So Jesus first of all emphasizes that our brains do not think, but only mirror thoughts in the mind. Secondly, he states that only those thoughts which we think with the Holy Spirit are our real thoughts, because they reflect the reality of God's oneness or Love:

> The Holy Spirit, like the ego, is a decision. Together they constitute all the alternatives the mind can accept and obey. The Holy Spirit and the ego are the only choices open to you. God created one, and so you cannot eradicate it. You made the other, and so you can. Only what God creates is irreversible and unchangeable. What you made can always be changed because, when you do not think like God, you are not really thinking at all. Delusional ideas are not real thoughts, although you can believe in them.

15

> But you are wrong. The function of thought comes from God and is in God. As part of His Thought, you *cannot* think apart from Him (T-5.V. 6:6-16).

Thus, what seems to be thinking apart from God—i.e., separation thinking— is merely an illusion of thought. But we take those illusory thoughts very seriously and have thereby thrown our "arms round the griefs of the ages."[1]

Early in the ACIM Workbook Jesus begins to instruct his students in the distinction between "real thoughts" and what we ordinarily experience as thought. In Lesson 10, titled "My thoughts do not mean anything," he instructs:

> This idea applies to all the thoughts of which you are aware, or become aware in the practice periods. The reason the idea is applicable to all of them is that they are not your real thoughts. We have made this distinction before, and will do so again. You have no basis for comparison as yet. When you do, you will have no doubt that what you once believed were your thoughts did not mean anything (W-pI.10.1).

Later, in Workbook Lesson 45 ("God is the Mind with which I think") Jesus begins to help his students make the distinction between illusory thoughts (idle thoughts of separation) and real thoughts:

> Today's idea holds the key to what your real thoughts are. They are nothing that you think you think, just as nothing that you think you see is related to vision in any way. There is no relationship between what is real and what you think is real. Nothing that you think are your real thoughts resemble your real thoughts in any respect. Nothing that you think you see bears any resemblance to what vision will show you.
>
> You think with the Mind of God. Therefore you share your thoughts with Him, as He shares His with you. They are the same thoughts, because they are thought by the same Mind. To share is to make alike, or to make one. Nor do the thoughts you think with the Mind of God leave your mind, because thoughts do not leave their source. Therefore, your thoughts are in the Mind of God, as you are. They are in your mind as well, where He is. As you are part of His Mind, so are your thoughts part of His Mind.
>
> Where, then, are your real thoughts? Today we will attempt to reach them. We will have to look for them in your mind, because that is where they are. They must still be there, because they cannot have left their source.

---

[1]Thomas, Dylan. "In my craft or sullen art" in *The Collected Poems of Dylan Thomas.* New York: New Directions Books, 1939, 1942, 1946.

What is thought by the Mind of God is eternal, being part of creation (W-pI.45.1-3)

According to Jesus, we, as bodies and separate persons, are not the initiators of thinking. Thought does not come from us as such, but we are images produced by thought! We, as seeming human individuals, do not think, but are "thunk." We do not initiate thinking, but can be witnesses to activities in the brain which have their cause in the mind. So, we, as we experience ourselves in the perceptual world, are the product of thought, not the producers of thought, and further, what we ordinarily have understood to be thinking does not represent what Jesus means by thought at all. Instead of identifying with a body and the illusion that our brain thinks, Jesus invites us to identify as mind. As such, we have the capacity to observe thought and to choose which of the two thought systems in our mind will be our guide to thinking, therefore to perception and behavior within the illusory world that we take for reality.

As we proceed, hopefully these radical ideas and their application will become clearer. For now, it is enough to understand that Jesus has a quite different concept of mind from the conventional one. Thus, he also offers a radically different understanding of thought and thinking. And may we suggest that a question worthy of the reader's contemplation is this:

"Where do my thoughts come from?"

Two Levels of Mind: the Two Teaching Levels of *A Course in Miracles*

One of the many valuable contributions made by Dr. Kenneth Wapnick[1] to the study and practice of *A Course in Miracles* is the recognition that the Course teachings are presented on two levels, which might be termed the metaphysical (Level One) and the practical (Level Two). Both levels of teaching are concerned with mind and are addressed to us as mind; and both levels present their teachings in terms of comparison and contrast. We will draw on Wapnick's material, but for a more complete discussion see Part I of his *Glossary-Index for A COURSE IN MIRACLES*, [2] which is available in the Appendix.

---

[1]President and co-founder of the Foundation for *A Course in Miracles* as well as the most widely published author of works about the Course. For an autobiographical account, see the introduction to his book, *Absence from Felicity: The Story of Helen Schucman and Her Scribing of A COURSE IN MIRACLES*, 2nd Ed., Temecula, CA: Foundation for *A Course in Miracles*, 1991, 1999. (The Introduction to this book may be found on the Web at: www.miraclestudies.net/Absence_Intro.html).

[2] Wapnick, Kenneth. *Glossary-Index for A COURSE IN MIRACLES*, 5th Ed. Revised. Temecula, CA: Foundation for *A Course in Miracles*, 1982, 1986, 1989, 1993, 1999.

We already are familiar with the Level One teaching that God is the only reality and that the essence of that reality is oneness. In turn, the essence of the Love of God is oneness which might be regarded as a unifying principle of Thought within the Mind of God as seen in the fact that the Mind of Christ is one with God's Mind: "... [God] makes no distinctions in what is Himself and what is still Himself. What He creates is not apart from Him, and nowhere does the Father end, the Son begin as something separate from Him" (W-pI.132.12:3-4).

When the Course presents these Level One metaphysical teachings, it contrasts the one Mind with the *seemingly* separated mind. The separated mind *seemed* to arise when the idea of separation was taken seriously in the Mind of Christ; hence separation is the central principle in that mind as compared to the principle of oneness in the Mind of God and Christ: now the "sleep of forgetfulness" appeared to begin, accompanied by a dream that the Son of God could have a mind of his own separate from his Father. The Self which is Christ in the One Mind, is replaced by the separated ego self in the separated mind; the *knowledge* of oneness in the Mind of God is replaced by perception in the separated mind wherein the power of the mind to extend or create is misused in favor of projection, which makes perception and gives rise to the illusion of a separated world. The truth of spirit is replaced by the illusion of the body; the true and eternal life of spirit is replaced by the illusion of a life that dies, hence death replaces life, conflict replaces peace, and guilt/fear replaces love. But the "tiny, mad idea" (T-27.VIII.6:2) of separation, though it may produce the illusion of sleep along with a dream of guilt, fear, conflict and defensiveness, does not have the power to destroy truth. So, the *memory* of truth remains in the seemingly separated mind, and in the Course this memory is called the Holy Spirit. Throughout the Course, the Holy Spirit is characterized as the Memory of God which links the separated mind back to the One Mind. But identification with the ego thought system" of separation serves to effectively block out, or dissociate, that Memory so that it remains as a Presence of love in the separated mind, but one which is unable to help us in the dream until we begin the process of removing the obstacles we have placed in the way of remembering—obstacles which arise from our investment in having a separate ego identity. So, in the introduction to the Course we find this statement about the Course's basic purpose:

> The course does not aim at teaching the meaning of love [i.e., God], for that is beyond what can be taught. It does aim, however, at removing the blocks to the awareness of love's presence, which is your natural inheritance (T-IN.1:6-7; bracket mine).

And later in the Text:

> The Holy Spirit, Who remembers this [what you are and what your Father is] for you, merely teaches you how to remove the blocks that stand between you and what you know. His memory is yours (T-14.IV.9:5-6; bracket mine).

Thus, the separated mind is split between: 1) the thought of separation (the ego); and, 2) the Memory of God represented by the Holy Spirit, Who retains the *knowledge* that separation is impossible. In the Course, these two give rise to two entire thought systems which represent two parts of the split mind: *wrong mind* and *right mind*. As mind, we are capable of observing thought and of choosing between the wrong and right mind as we interpret and react to our experiences in the world.

So the concept of mind found in *A Course in Miracles* asserts the metaphysical truth that in reality there is only the one Mind of God; but, at the same time, the Course addresses us at the level of the illusion of an individual mind so that we can begin to understand that we are mind, and that mind is the cause of the swirling complexity of experience at the center of which is the individual "I" with which we identify. This separated, seemingly individual mind, which is associated with the illusion of a perceptual world and an individual self, is split within itself between the thought system of the ego and that of the Holy Spirit. The Level Two teachings of the Course are addressed to us in terms of that split mind where the key to forgiveness and the resolution of every problem we experience involves learning first of all that we *are* mind, and secondly that, as mind, we have the power to choose between the two thought systems. It is the change from wrong-mindedness to right-mindedness that is the "miracle" that gives the Course its title and which makes forgiveness possible. Forgiveness and the "miracle" are essentially the same, though forgiveness may be thought of as a consequence of the miracle, and the miracle may be thought of as the result of a choice within the mind. Forgiveness is a *reflection* of the Love of God which arises in the split mind through the agency of the Holy Spirit. This all-embracing reflection of the Love of God results from what the Course means by "a miracle," and takes place only in the mind. As long as we seem to be in time and space, there may seem to be worldly consequences of that choice, but the Course is concerned with *cause* (mind), not effect. Effect is whatever seems to take place in the illusory world. That is why Jesus says: "... seek not to change the world, but choose to change your mind about the world" (T-21.IN.1:7).

The summarizing diagram below is a vastly simplified adaptation from Wapnick's diagram which is presented as a part of his discussion of ACIM theory in Part I of his *Glossary-Index*. For further clarification, and a more complete discussion, see that diagram in the Appendix where the theory section of Wapnick's *Glossary-Index* is reproduced.

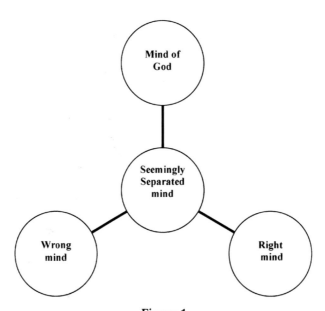

Figure 1

Consciousness and Unconsciousness

Historically, the phenomenon of consciousness has been equated with mind. Returning to *The American Heritage Dictionary*, the first definition given for *mind* is: "The human consciousness that originates in the brain and is manifested especially in thought, perception, emotion, will, memory, and imagination." And the first definition of *conscious* is given as: "Having an awareness of one's environment and one's own existence, sensations, and thoughts;" while the first two definitions of consciousness are: 1) The state or condition of being conscious; 2) A sense of one's personal or collective identity, including the attitudes, beliefs, and sensitivities held by or considered characteristic of an individual or group.

A simple and very useful definition of *consciousness* is: The awareness of "me" and what is "not me." From this concise definition, as well as the others given above, one can see that the sense of self, or "I", is central to the phenomenon of consciousness, which is necessarily dualistic; in other words, which is necessarily an aspect of the separated mind and a component of the ego thought system. Writing within the context of conventional Western science, one author[1] has recently made the cogent argument that consciousness as a function of the brain has arisen evolutionarily from raw sensation, and as a response to the survival requirements of biological organisms to be able to distinguish themselves from their environment.

The idea of consciousness has been elaborated in various ways, recognizing that there are non-ordinary states of consciousness, which William James famously pointed out in his *Varieties of Religious Experience*.[2] But in all of these elaborations, the sense of a separate "I" remains central, except in what has been called "mystical consciousness," where the term "consciousness" really does not apply, because that state (what the Course refers to as an experience of *revelation*) does not involve a sense of separate, personal identity. It is only when the person who has experienced such a state of mind attempts to describe it that personal pronouns must be used; giving the impression that somehow that state was experienced by an "I". However, it is most usual that persons who have had a revelatory experience will acknowledge that it actually cannot be described in words, and in fact transcended the "I" so that there was only an undifferentiated oneness. However, it might later be symbolized in words or some form of art.

---

[1] Humphry, Nicholas. *A History of the Mind*. New York: Simon & Schuster, 1992.

[2] James, William. *Varieties of Religious Experience*. New York: Modern Library Paperback, Random House, Inc., 1999 (originally published in 1902).

21

For instance, in *Alfred Lord Tennyson: A Memoir by His Son*, a letter of Tennyson's is quoted:

> A kind of waking trance I have frequently had, quite up from my boyhood, when I have been all alone. This has generally come upon me through repeating my own name two or three times to myself silently, til all at once, as it were out of the intensity of the consciousness of individuality, the individuality itself seemed to dissolve and fade away into boundless being; and this is not a confused state, but the clearest of the clearest, the surest of the surest, the weirdest of the weirdest, utterly beyond words, where death was an almost laughable impossibility, the loss of personality (if so it were) seeming no extinction, but the only true life.[3]

The Course acknowledges this kind of experience, but does not include it as an aspect of consciousness. Rather, speaking of consciousness the Course states:

> Consciousness, the level of perception, was the first split introduced into the mind after the separation, making the mind a perceiver rather than a creator. Consciousness is correctly identified as the domain of the ego. The ego is a wrong-minded attempt to perceive yourself as you wish to be, rather than as you are (T-3.IV.2:1-3).

> The structure of "individual consciousness" is essentially irrelevant because it is a concept representing the "original error" or the "original sin." To study the error itself does not lead to correction, if you are indeed to succeed in overlooking the error. And it is just this process of overlooking at which the course aims (C-IN 1:4-6).

(The ego idea of separation as sin will be discussed later. Essentially, sin is the belief that separation was actually accomplished, therefore the Oneness that is God the Father would have had to be destroyed—the Father killed by His willful Son hell bent on being a separate individual.)

The astounding implication of the Course's view of consciousness as an aspect of separation is that in the Mind of God (Oneness, Heaven) there is no consciousness! Obviously this must be so, because consciousness as it is typically understood requires that there be an "I" and something that is "not I"—there must be a perceiver and a perceived. To quote again from ACIM Workbook Lesson 169: "[In the experience of oneness there is] no part of mind sufficiently distinct to feel that it is now aware of something not itself. It has united with its Source. And like its Source Itself, it merely is" (W-pI.169.5:5-7).

---

[3]Tennyson, Alfred Lord. "A letter to Mr. B. P. Blood" in *Alfred Lord Tennyson: A Memoir by His Son*, V2. Basingstoke Hampshire, England: Macmillan Publishers Limited, 1899.

When we consider the idea of unconsciousness—or "an unconscious mind" such as Freud explored—in order for this to make sense, there must be consciousness: a conscious mind. So it is apparent that what might be referred to as "the unconscious" is an aspect of the separated mind and a dimension of the ego thought system, which employs denial and repression to keep hidden what threatens it. Thus, in ACIM, what is unconscious is not beyond our ability *as mind* to choose, but is willfully forgotten:

> Defenses are not unintentional, nor are they made without awareness. They are secret, magic wands you wave when truth appears to threaten what you would believe. They seem to be unconscious but because of the rapidity with which you choose to use them. In that second, even less, in which the choice is made, you recognize exactly what you would attempt to do, and then proceed to think that it is done.

> Who but yourself evaluates a threat, decides escape is necessary, and sets up a series of defenses to reduce the threat that has been judged as real? All this cannot be done unconsciously. But afterwards, your plan [i.e., the ego's plan] requires that you must forget you made it, so it seems to be external to your own intent; a happening beyond your state of mind, an outcome with a real effect on you, instead of one effected by yourself.

> It is this quick forgetting of the part you play in making your "reality" that makes defenses [denial and dissociation] seem to be beyond your own control. But what you have forgot can be remembered, given willingness to reconsider the decision…Your not remembering is but the sign that this *decision* [to forget and make unconscious] still remains in force, as far as your desires are concerned. Mistake not this for fact. Defenses must make facts unrecognizable. They aim at doing this, and it is this they do (W-pI.136.3-5; brackets and italics mine)

In summary, with respect to the concepts of consciousness and unconsciousness, *A Course in Miracles* considers both as aspects of the illusion that arose from our willingness to take the "tiny, mad idea" (T-27.VIII.6:2) of separation seriously, thus to identify with the ego and its thought system which defines separation as sin, therefore necessarily includes the idea of guilt and the emotion of fear as basic elements. Thus, consciousness represents a denial of Oneness, which is then equated with a murderous attack on God. Unconsciousness represents a conscious, defensive decision to forget; initially and fundamentally to forget that the sense of an individual self which is at the heart of conscious awareness was achieved at God's expense. In fact—in terms of the Level One metaphysical truth of oneness—God was not destroyed, nor threatened in any way; and the whole ego thought system which defines our sense of being an individual self, and with which we are so deeply identified, is ridiculous.

Hence the sublime assurance found in the introduction to the ACIM Text:

> Nothing real can be threatened.
> Nothing unreal exists.

Herein lies the peace of God (T-IN.2:2-4).

Perception and Knowledge

In the Course, the term *knowledge* refers to the Mind of God or Heaven, and throughout is contrasted with *perception* which is the primary characteristic of the ego's illusory world of separation. Thus, *knowledge* is defined quite differently from its ordinary usage where it refers to what can be taught and learned, and to the information and conceptual understanding stored in human brains, and in their supplements such as books and electronic data systems. As Jesus uses the term in ACIM, *knowledge* refers to the non-dualistic truth which is not accessible to the human senses and central nervous system. And *perception*, which arises from consciousness, may be understood as an attempt to keep knowledge from us; an attempt to replace the truth of oneness with the illusion of duality; an attempt to replace our true Self as Christ, at one with God, with the seemingly separate, individual self which we experience as the center of consciousness, and indeed of our world. In the Course, knowledge is not to be learned, but *remembered* through *un*learning what the ego has taught us.

The meaning of the term *perception* varies in the Course depending upon the level of teaching for which it is being employed. In his *Glossary-Index for A Course in Miracles* [1] Wapnick has provided a comprehensive definition which recognizes the teaching level of usage:

> perception

> > Level One: the post-separation, dualistic world of form and differences, mutually exclusive of the non-dualistic world of knowledge; this world arises from our belief in separation and has no reality outside of this thought.

> > Level Two: comes from projection: what we see inwardly determines what we see outside ourselves; crucial to perception, therefore, is our interpretation of "reality," rather than what seems to be objectively real.

---

[1] op.cit.

wrong-mind: perception of sin and guilt reinforces the belief in the reality of the separation.

right-mind: perception of opportunities to forgive serves to undo the belief in the reality of the separation.

The relationship between projection and perception will be more fully examined later. At this point it is sufficient to understand that, "Projection makes perception" (T-13.V.3:5; T-21.IN.1:1) and is a primary defensive mechanism of the ego as it attempts to divest itself of responsibility for the "sin" of separation. In terms of the Level One teachings, projection involves an attempt to escape the mind where the Memory of God remains and is sensed as a threat. At Level Two, projection is basically an attempt to assign guilt to something or someone perceived to be other than self. Of course, the defense of projection is ultimately unsuccessful because of the basic law of mind that *ideas leave not their source.* Thus, the solution to the guilt and fear which motivate projection is to take responsibility for them and address them at their source within our mind. That is why, again, Jesus tells us: "Seek not to change the world [the illusion that has been projected], but seek to change your mind about the world [i.e., seek to change the projector]" (T-21.IN.1:7; brackets mine).

Like words and other symbols that are required for the ego's form of communication, perception deceives because it depends upon and reinforces the belief in separation. Everything produced by the ego thought system deceives, of course, because deception is its fundamental purpose as it attempts to keep us from knowledge. About this, the Course makes some remarkable observations:

> You have conceived a little gap between illusions and the truth to be the place where all your safety lies, and where your Self is safely hidden by what you have made. Here is a world established that is sick, and this the world the body's eyes perceive. Here are the sounds it hears; the voices that its ears were made to hear. Yet sights and sounds the body can perceive are meaningless. It cannot see nor hear. It does not know what seeing *is*; what listening is *for*. It is as little able to perceive as it can judge or understand or know. Its eyes are blind; its ears are deaf. It can not think, and so it cannot have effects (T-28.V.4).

> ... your idea of what seeing means is tied up with the body and its eyes and brain. Thus you believe that you can change what you see by putting little bits of glass before your eyes. This is among the many magical beliefs that come from the conviction you are a body, and the body's eyes can see.

You also believe the body's brain can think. If you but understood the nature of thought, you could but laugh at this insane idea. It is as if you thought you held the match that lights the sun and gives it all its warmth; or that you held the world within your hand, securely bound until you let it go. Yet this is no more foolish than to believe the body's eyes can see; the brain can think.

It is God's strength in you that is the light in which you see, as it is His Mind with which you think. His strength denies your weakness. It is your weakness that sees through the body's eyes, peering about in darkness to behold the likeness of itself; the small, the weak, the sickly and the dying, those in need, the helpless and afraid, the sad, the poor, the starving and the joyless. These are seen through eyes that cannot see and cannot bless (W-pI.92.1:3-3).

You do not seem to doubt the world you see. You do not really question what is shown you through the body's eyes. Nor do you ask why you believe it, even though you learned a long while since your senses do deceive. That you believe them to the last detail which they report is even stranger, when you pause to recollect how frequently they have been faulty witnesses indeed! Why would you trust them so implicitly? Why but because of underlying doubt, which you would hide with show of certainty?

How can you judge? Your judgment rests upon the witness that your senses offer you. Yet witness never falser was than this. But how else do you judge the world you see? You place pathetic faith in what your eyes and ears report. You think your fingers touch reality, and close upon the truth. This is awareness that you understand, and think more real than what is witnessed to by the eternal Voice for God Himself [i.e., by the Holy Spirit, often referred to in the Course as the "Voice for God" in our right mind] (W-pI.151.2-3; brackets mine).

Summary

At this point some readers may be feeling nonplused, having been exposed to the idea that their brains do not think, their eyes do not see, and that their body, their world, their consciousness and their very self are illusions. Dismay is especially likely for readers unfamiliar with the Course or related thought systems. How can a system of psychology with this kind of understanding of mind possibly be of help to one who is not prepared, let alone able, to accept that he and his world are illusory? The answer to this question has been stated previously, but let us again point out that the practical help of A Course in Miracles lies in its Level Two teachings which, though based on non-dualistic principles, still address us in terms of our dualistic human experience. The center of that help lies in learning how to forgive, or learning how to become what the Course means by "a miracle worker." This *does* involve, however, accepting that all of our perceived problems in the world ultimately derive from the spiritual problem of the belief in separation, and that the only way to address that problem is at the level of mind.

The Course's concept of mind is a spiritual one, and its psychology incorporates a spiritual dimension. The Course itself is religious, though it does not intend to become the basis of an organized, formal religion, which it explicitly characterizes as unhelpful, just as it regards as unhelpful the professional practice of psychotherapy in general. This is not to say that the Course denies the helpfulness of both traditional religion and psychotherapy in many *individual* cases, since any attempt of persons to find a common bond and shared interests is a step in the direction of undoing the belief in separation. However, it is most often the case that human endeavors have just the opposite effect as can be seen in the covert as well as overt warfare among persons of different religious faiths or psychological schools of thought, and in the general lack of long-term success in traditional psychological treatments of all kinds. Obviously, in spite of the longing for love and peace that resides in every human heart, mankind has not yet found its way to either inner peace or brotherly love.

Ultimately, the problem of separation has to do with our relationship to God, or our imagined relationship to our idea of God. The ego idea that there can be an individual life apart from Oneness has inspired a dream of life apart from Love. One has only to look objectively at one's own personal world, as well as the world at large, to see that dream is a hellish nightmare. Those who cannot see this, however dimly, will not be helped by the Course's system of psychology. And the Course does not pretend to be the only source of help, though ultimately all truly helpful attempts to address human problems must in some way address the problem of separation, which the Course asserts is a spiritual problem residing in our mind and must be resolved there.

The chapters to follow will describe more about the nature of this fundamental problem and how it can be resolved through the miracle of forgiveness, which must be an individual undertaking by one who is, at least in some small way, willing to accept his or her identity and responsibility as mind.

> ...the Course can and should stand on its own. It is not intended to become the basis for another cult. Its only purpose is to provide a way in which some people will be able to find their own Internal Teacher.
> -Helen Schucman in the Preface to *A Course in Miracles*, p. viii

Chapter 3

Myth of "The Ladder Separation Led You Down"[1]

Now one might ask: "If I and my world are not real, how come I'm in a body and how did I get here?" This is actually a question asking what the ego is and how do we happen to believe we're separate. And it's not really a question, but a statement which says: "I believe I'm an ego and I want an explanation of my existence." To make the point even more dramatically, one might say: "Cut off your finger and tell me you're an illusion!" Or in the throes of childbirth or the ecstasy of a passionate embrace, one might exclaim to the Jesus of *A Course in Miracles*: "You're telling me this ain't real!? Who are you?!"

This is reminiscent of the oft recounted story about the response of Dr. Samuel Johnson, the famous English literary figure, to the basic philosophical principle of philosopher George Berkeley. Berkeley's prime dictum was: *"Esse est percipi"* ("To be is to be perceived"). He held that we cannot know that the objective world is real, only that it is perceived by a mind. In response, Johnson kicked a large boulder and exclaimed, "Thus I refute him!"

What Johnson failed to understand is that he was merely demonstrating that the stone could be perceived, which includes being sensed by touch as well as having the experience of pain (or pleasure, for that matter). As seen in the series of Course excerpts at the end of the last chapter, *A Course in Miracles* asserts that the brain and sensory system of the body, being aspects of a dream, merely do what the dreaming mind wishes them to do; and under the guidance of our wrong mind, the body becomes an accomplice in the ego's goal of deception by reporting that there is a tangible, physical world and body. The Course goes further than Berkeley in holding that neither perceiver nor perceived are real. The mind that believes in perception is the unreal wrong-minded part of the unreal separated mind.

The Course's Level One answer to the ego's assertion of its own reality disguised in the form of a question ("How did I get here?") is that you are not an ego, you are not *in* a body, and your world is not actually *here*; in fact there is no "here"—no time and space. So, a more sophisticated form of the question would be: "How is it that I came to *think* that I and the world are real and that I'm here in a body?" Or: "If I'm a mind dreaming, how can

---

[1] T-28.III.1:2

29

I know that? Why did I fall asleep and how did the thought of separation occur in the first place?" Again, the Course's Level One teachings say that you are not really a sleeping and dreaming mind:

> God creates only mind awake. He does not sleep, and His creations cannot share what He gives not, nor make conditions which He does not share with them. The thought of death [i.e., illusory life in a body] is not the opposite to thoughts of life [spirit]. Forever unopposed by opposites of any kind, the Thoughts of God remain forever changeless, with the power to extend forever changelessly, but yet within themselves, for they are everywhere.

> What seems to be the opposite of life is merely sleeping. When the mind elects to be what it is not [i.e., a body], and to assume an alien power which it does not have [i.e., the power to separate], a foreign state it cannot enter, or a false condition not within its Source [the Mind of God], it merely seems to go to sleep a while. It dreams of time; an interval in which what seems to happen never has occurred, the changes wrought are substanceless, and all events are nowhere. When the mind awakes, it but continues as it always was....

> Our life is not as we imagine it. Who changes life because he shuts his eyes, or makes himself what he is not because he sleeps, and sees in dreams an opposite to what he is? (W-pI.167.8:8-9:4; 10:2-3; brackets mine)

Before we go on to examine the ego thought system in more depth—the thought system which guides our everyday lives in the illusion and was so carefully observed by Freud—perhaps it will be helpful to summarize the Course's Level Two teachings which address this question of how the world and body seemed to happen; how the mind "seems to go to sleep a while" and dream of physical existence; how the ego seemed to come alive. These teachings can be capsulized in the form of a myth which symbolizes for us what seemed to happen in the non-dualistic mind that has resulted in our dualistic experience of existing in a world of perception and multiplicity.

The following outline of the Course's myth of separation is based on original formulations by Dr. Kenneth Wapnick, and a more thorough treatment of the subject can be found in chapters two through four of his book, *The Message of A Course in Miracles, Volume One: All Are Called*.[2] Of course, the myth outlined here represents a compromise with truth, not only because it is a metaphor utilizing the dualistic symbols of language, but because it speaks as though time and space were real and as though the separation actually happened, taking place in stages.

---

[2]Wapnick, Kenneth. *All Are Called*, Volume One of *The Message of A Course in Miracles*. Temecula, CA: Foundation for *A Course in Miracles*, 1977.

Nevertheless, this can be a helpful way of explaining both the consequences of belief in separation and the role of the Course's psychology of forgiveness in undoing that belief which lies at the core of our ego identity.

The Pre-separation State: Heaven

As we have seen, in the Course Heaven is the Mind of God, Oneness, the perfectly undivided unity of Creator and Creation. Following the basic law of mind that *ideas leave not their source*, the Atonement principle of the Course states that this unity cannot be broken: a Thought of God (His Creation) cannot leave its source in His Mind. Thus in truth sin is impossible, as contrasted with the traditional Christian belief in the reality of sin which must be atoned for through sacrifice. In the Course, nothing has to be done about sin (separation) at the illusory level of the world and body. In fact, nothing *can* be done about it at that level, because the body and world are *effect*, not cause. The Holy Spirit's "Atonement plan" addresses the *cause*, and is accomplished in the *mind*. It involves undoing identification with the ego thought system in favor of accepting the truth of the Atonement principle that separation (sin) is impossible, hence there is no real cause for guilt and fear which are in turn the ego's reasons for projecting the dualistic illusion of a physical cosmos, as we shall see.

Repeating and slightly extending a quote from the previous chapter about Heaven, the Course says:

> The Kingdom of Heaven is the dwelling place of the Son of God, who left not his Father and dwells not apart from Him. Heaven is not a place nor a condition. It is merely an awareness of perfect oneness, and the knowledge that there is nothing else; nothing outside this oneness, and nothing else within (T-18.VI.1:4-6).

And in the second paragraph of the passage quoted at the end of the introduction to this Primer we were told: "No one on earth can grasp what Heaven is, or what its one Creator really means" (M-23.6:1). So, we shall not attempt to go any further in discussing Heaven, but move on to the myth of separation.

There are four main characters in this myth: God the Father, the Son of God, the Ego and the Holy Spirit. These characters are personified with names only for purposes of telling the story of separation and forgiveness. They do not have form and cannot be perceived. They all represent spirit, thought, or aspects of mind; God being the Mind that creates spirit—*All That Is*—within Itself through the extension of Thought.

31

We cannot understand the meaning of the word "God," except to know that it symbolizes the oneness of spirit which is the essence of creation, completely abstract and eternal: the only true reality. The Son of God in truth is Christ,[3] the Thought of Love and the extension of spirit within the Mind of God and not distinct or apart from that Mind. But for purposes of our myth, "Son of God" represents the seeming capacity of mind to choose. The Ego is the villain, representing the thought that separation from God is both possible and desirable, while the Holy Spirit is the Hero Who is the Thought of the Atonement that knows separation from God and His Love is not possible.

The myth proceeds through a series of four stages of splitting within the mind of the Son until the illusion of a physical cosmos is projected. While these stages are described as though they took place over time, it is closer to the truth to say that acceptance of the belief in separation led instantaneously to all of its illusory consequences in the mind, and that these imagined consequences were simultaneously canceled in the same instant by the truth of the Atonement principle. So, none of this actually happened; but it is more practical to say that it seems to happen and be undone in our mind in each present moment: separation happens and does not happen in the present. We either separate from whatever or whoever we perceive in any given moment or we join and forgive. In any given moment, we are either wrong minded or right minded. And in *every* moment we are always mind, not body.

Ontologically, all of the permutations and combinations of the events separation seems to make possible were written and canceled in an instant, which is not a phenomenon of time. As the Course says:

> The time [when the Atonement will be accepted in the mind] is set already....there is no step along the road that anyone takes but by chance. It has already been taken by him, although he has not yet embarked on it. For time but seems to go in one direction. We but undertake a journey that is over. Yet it seems to have a future still unknown to us.

> Time is a trick, a sleight of hand, a vast illusion in which figures come and go as if by magic. Yet there is a plan behind appearances that does not change. The script is written. When experience will come to end your doubting has been set. For we but see the journey from the point at which it ended, looking back on it, imagining we make it once again; reviewing mentally what has gone by (W-pI.158.3-4; brackets mine).

---

[3] In the Course, the terms "Christ" and "Son of God" do not refer exclusively to Jesus, but to all of creation, and "creation" is spirit—the extension of God's being—not anything of form or materiality.

Outline of the Myth

> *Into eternity, where all is one, there crept a tiny, mad idea, at which the Son of God remembered not to laugh. In his forgetting did the thought become a serious idea, and possible of both accomplishment and real effects* (T-27.VIII.6:2, italics mine).

1. The first major rung on the descent down the ladder of separation—the first split—can be understood as the point at which the "tiny, mad idea" of separation was taken seriously by the Son of God. It was then, as we have seen, that consciousness arose and there seemed to be a separated mind: a mind apart from Mind. In that ontologically original instant, the Created seemed to be separate from the Creator, Christ separate from God, the Son separate from the Father and now aware of "me" and "not me"—"I and my Father are not one, but two." What Ken Wilber calls the "Primary Dualism"[1] seemed to arise at this point with the belief that separation was a "serious idea, and possible of both accomplishment and real effects." Or, as the mathematician G. Spencer Brown put it in his *Laws of Form*,[2] the beginning of the universe can be traced back to the primordial decree: "Let there be a distinction." Now it seemed that differences were real and choice possible. And once the thought of separation was put into play, what it had to do, because it is inherent in its nature, was to continue to separate, or split off: to multiply differences, to make distinctions, to continually fragment.

2. On the second rung in our descent, another split occurs. The Son of God, now conscious of self and able to make a choice, decides to believe the ego which basically says: "You pulled it off. You're on your own. Now, follow me!" Given the power to choose, the Son (us as a seemingly separated mind) decides to follow the ego's alluring promise of individuality and essentially becomes the ego. God is perceived as separate and the truth of oneness is forgotten. However, because oneness is the truth, and the mind is fundamentally inextricable from its Source, the *memory* of Oneness—the Holy Spirit—remains in the separated mind although it is denied, dissociated and forgotten. It is a law of mind which applies all the way down the ladder that whatever is split off *from* is forgotten, and whatever is split off *to* becomes the mind's reality—becomes the Son's identity: *our* identity.

Both the ego and the Holy Spirit thought systems cannot remain in the Son's awareness since their premises are diametrically opposed, leading to entirely different conclusions: two different versions of reality. When the Son

---

[1] Wilber, Ken. *The Spectrum of Consciousness*, 2nd Ed., pp.96-106. Wheaton, IL: The Theosophical Publishing House, 1977.

[2] Brown, G. Spencer. *Laws of Form*. New York: Julian Press, 1972.

chooses to follow the ego thought system, which cannot survive in the light of the Holy Spirit's Atonement principle, the Holy Spirit must be forgotten. So it is at this point that unconsciousness develops and the Holy Spirit is relegated to its darkness. The separated mind splits in two: wrong mind and right mind. In essence, the wrong mind is a defense against the right mind; a defense which employs the mechanism of dissociation in order to render the Memory of God unconscious. And now the ego thought system begins to develop logically from its premise of separation, while the Holy Spirit peacefully remains in the Son's mind as a "still, small voice"—a Presence of love.

3. On the third rung down the ladder of separation the Son of God, having chosen to identify with the ego, is now under the sway of ego thoughts which tell the Son: "You've got a life of your own now. Unfortunately you had to destroy your Father in order to get it. That's a very bad thing—a terrible sin in fact—and I'm afraid you're going to be severely punished if you hang around here. The life you've stolen will be taken back."

At this point the full blown ego thought system develops: separation seen as real is defined as sin, with guilt and fear following hard and fast upon its heels. Guilt over the idea that God the Father has been destroyed is grievously enormous, unspeakable, and overwhelming in its sense of self-condemnation, intrinsic wrongness and self hatred. The consequent fear of punishment is intolerable as well, and the alternative to sin—the memory of truth and of God which is the Holy Spirit—has been forgotten. What to do?

To solve the problem of this intolerable sin and guilt, and driven by fear, the ego once again employs its defensive strategy of denial, repressing the ideas of sin and guilt, pushing them down into the darkness of the unconscious along with the Memory of God. Then, sin and guilt themselves become a defensive shield further covering over the buried Memory of Oneness and Love, serving the ego's purpose of making the mind a fearful place where the Son would never dare to look:

> Loudly the ego tells you not to look inward, for if you do your eyes will light on sin, and God will strike you blind. This you believe, and so you do not look (T-21.IV.2:3-4).

(Notice how this ego injunction militates against the very kind of clinical examination of the mind in which Freud engaged. And since this fearful injunction continues to be present in our mind, it is a powerful reason to attempt to discredit not only the process of examining the mind, but the discoveries of anyone who does so. Perhaps this also explains why the phenomenon of Edgar Cayce[3] is not more well known and attended to in scientific circles, since his well documented trance-state work demonstrates not only the reality of mind and spirit, but the truth that all minds are joined.)

The ego thought system continues to develop, becoming almost endlessly resourceful in serving self interest: the special interests of separation. Misusing the power of the mind which we the Son have given it by our choice, and having dissociated the Memory of God, the ego now projects an image of God in the likeness of itself: a God seen as separate, believing in sin and punishment, loving only on condition, selfish, vengeful, and Himself responsible for the separation as seen in the biblical story of the Garden of Eden.

Under the tutelage of the ego, the Son's goal is to keep his special, individual self, but to hold somebody or something else responsible for the consequences. So the God of the ego is a projection which serves the defensive function of assigning responsibility to God in order that the Son can be free of it. Because the ego begins with an insane idea, its thought system is insane; therefore the image of God which it projects—a mirror image of itself—is insane. And this is a very fearful God; one whose presence must be escaped.

Much more could be said about this. The reader who is interested in pursuing the subject is referred to Wapnick's work, *The Message of A COURSE IN MIRACLES,* cited earlier. For our purposes it is sufficient to point out that the major split involved at this stage of our journey down the ladder is between the Son as ego and the ego's image of God. Now in the mind there is a war with God, and this is necessarily a war against our true Self, which is one with God. The whole idea of separation is an attack on Oneness; therefore it is an attack on Who we are in truth. (See Chapter 23 in the ACIM Text, "The War Against Yourself.")

4. On the fourth rung down the ladder of separation, the ego counsels that escape from its image of a fearsome avenger God is both necessary and possible. This actually amounts to the ego counseling escape from itself, but to the ego it is an attempt to escape from the mind where it senses threat. The ego really does not know of the Holy Spirit, but it does know that it is not alone in the Son's mind, and it harbors a sense of unworthiness that invites rejection. It is aware of the power of the Son to choose against it,

[3] Kirkpatrick, Sidney. *Edgar Cayce: An American Prophet.* New York: Riverside Books of The Berkley Publishing Group, a division of Penguin Putnam, Inc., 2000.

and aware that if the Son ever honestly and objectively examined its thought system along with the consequences of believing it, we *would* reject it:

> Spirit in its *knowledge* is unaware of the ego. It does not attack it; it merely cannot conceive of it at all. While the ego is equally unaware of spirit, it does perceive itself as being rejected by something greater than itself (T-4.II.8:6-8; italics mine).

The ego attempts to accomplish its goal of escape by again using the trick of projection which appears to cast ideas outside the mind in violation of the basic law that *ideas leave not their source*. In fact, what happens through this "miscreative use of mind" is that instead of the mind escaping itself—an obvious impossibility—a dream or an illusion of escape is produced *in* the mind. That illusion is the perceptual world of duality seemingly inhabited by separated and competing organisms. It is at this point on the ladder that we, the Son of God, seem to arrive in the world masquerading as unique individuals inhabiting separate bodies.

The projection of illusion at this stage is the Course's equivalent of the "big bang," and the universe that results is one of continuing separation, producing an ongoing "reality" whose fundamental dynamic is fragmentation. So from this point on, the ego's attempt to escape from the mind results in an almost infinite number of lower rungs on the ladder, each composed of separation thoughts. The Course sums this up as follows:

> You who believe that God is fear made but one substitution. It has taken many forms, because it was the substitution of illusion for truth; of fragmentation for wholeness. It has become so splintered and subdivided and divided again, over and over, that it is now almost impossible to perceive it once was one, and still is what it was. That one error, which brought truth to illusion, infinity to time, and life to death, was all you ever made. Your whole world rests upon it. Everything you see reflects it, and every special relationship that you have ever made is part of it.
>
> You may be surprised to hear how very different is reality from what you see. You do not realize the magnitude of that one error. It was so vast and so completely incredible that from it a world of total unreality *had* to emerge. What else could come of it? Its fragmented aspects are fearful enough, as you begin to look at them. But nothing you have seen begins to show you the enormity of the original error, which seemed to cast you out of Heaven, to shatter knowledge into meaningless bits of disunited perceptions, and to force you to make further substitutions.
>
> That was the first projection of error outward. The world arose to hide it, and became the screen on which it was projected and drawn between

36

you and the truth. For truth extends inward, where the idea of loss is meaningless and only increase is conceivable. Do you really think it strange that a world in which everything is backwards and upside down arose from this projection of error? It was inevitable. For truth brought to this could only remain within in quiet, and take no part in all the mad projection by which this world was made. Call it not sin but madness, for such it was and so it still remains. Invest it not with guilt, for guilt implies it was accomplished in reality. And above all, *be not afraid of it* (T-18.I.4-6).

The "one substitution"—the "one error"—is the thought of separation which was intended to replace the *knowledge* of oneness. The "projection of error outward" which seemed to occur at this step down the ladder was the fearful attempt of the ego to divest the separated mind of its responsibility, hence guilt, for separation now made real and seen as sin. The projected thought of separation serves as a screen in the mind upon which separation thoughts take form, thus serving to hide the one thought behind them. Symbolic of this is the *Wizard of Oz* story where the awesome wizard turned out to be a harmless little old man at the controls of an illusion machine. Likewise, a "tiny, mad idea" is behind the "vast illusion" of the entire cosmos.

Everything in the world is "backwards and upside down"[4] because we have substituted perception for knowledge as well as confused cause and effect, believing that cause resides in the physical world while what we regard as mind is an effect of that cause. This is seen in the attempt to make mind somehow a function of the brain, but it is also seen in every other attempt to find causal connections within the physical universe: another way in which the ego thought system keeps us distracted from the true reality of mind. (A friend of the author's and long-time student of the Course once visited Mt. Palomar. Upon seeing that giant telescope she thought to herself, "It's pointed in the wrong direction.")

In later chapters we will further explore the concept of *special relationships* which is mentioned at the end of the first quoted paragraph above. Briefly, a *special relationship* represents the ego's attempt to blame separation (now sin) on someone else, therefore to project its guilt away, as well as to find a substitute for the Love of God. The ego's version of love is called *special love*, because it is an attempt to bring love, whose essence is oneness, into relationships between separated bodies which have the quality of being special because they *are* separate. The most obvious examples of special relationships are our romantic relationships, but specialness can be

---

[4] An allusion to the physiology of vision where images cast on the retina are backwards and upside down.

invested in objects like automobiles and drugs (both prescription and non-prescription, legal and illegal) as well as intangibles like wealth, social status and political power.

At this point on the ladder the split, or projection, amounts to an explosive shattering of the mind so that now there seems to be a myriad of separate minds all housed in bodies inhabiting separate planets in separate solar systems in separate galaxies in an ever dividing and expanding universe, which may be only one of many parallel universes! Each of us represents one fragment of this shattered mind; a fragment that has forgotten what it is, believing it is a living biological organism and that its brain is the mind. And that shattering fragmentation of the mind seems to continue, multiplying differences and distinctions all of which form the distracting stuff of our personal experiences in the world, as well as the objects of our scientific study and mathematical calculations.

The ego's attempt to escape the mind fails, but a very compelling illusion arises through projection wherein we dream of individual lives in bodies apart from God and Heaven. The effect of this dream is to keep us so preoccupied with our self and our self-centered needs and problems that our attention remains focused on what seems to be the outer, never turning within to discover that we are mind; never to discover that as mind we have a choice which profoundly affects our perception of events and situations within the illusion; never to discover our potential to awaken from the dream of separation to the truth of oneness. Thus projection, which "makes perception" (T-13.V.3:5; T-21.IN.1:1), has the effect of rendering the Son mindless; thereby keeping us unaware that we are mind and have a choice between the ego and Holy Spirit thought systems.

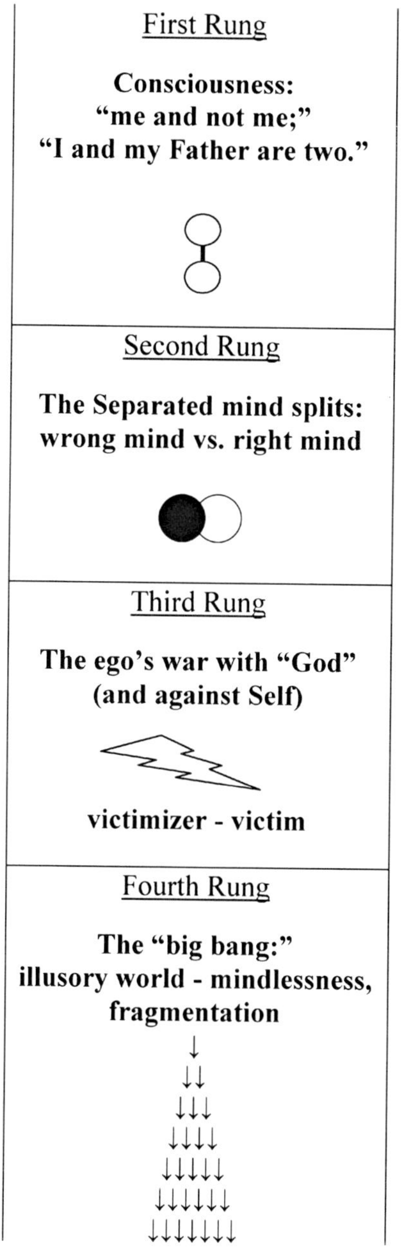

First Rung

**Consciousness:
"me and not me;"
"I and my Father are two."**

Second Rung

**The Separated mind splits:
wrong mind vs. right mind**

Third Rung

**The ego's war with "God"
(and against Self)**

victimizer - victim

Fourth Rung

**The "big bang:"
illusory world - mindlessness,
fragmentation**

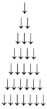

Figure 2

Recapitulation, Summary and Hopeful Conclusion

This myth of separation is a story about what seemed to take place *in the mind*. It is a story about the physical universe only in the sense that the universe is an illusion *in* the mind. Further, the poetic license available in telling a myth has permitted us to speak of "the ego" as though it were some kind of entity. In the next chapter we will give extensive consideration to what the term *ego* means in the Course, and what it means to us personally. But for now it is important simply to recognize that the ego is best understood as a thought system within our mind: the thought system of separation.

As the ladder of separation proceeds downward, the identity of the Son of God changes. In truth, that Identity is Christ, the one Creation of God at one with God in Heaven: a Thought in the Mind of God. That's Who we are in truth, and that Identity remains unaffected by the dream of separation. We just have to wake up to that fact, which is what the Course's psychology of forgiveness is intended to help us do while, in the seeming meantime, allowing us to have a more loving, peaceful dream—a right-minded dream rather than the ego's wrong-minded dream.

On the first rung of the ladder the Son of God identifies as a separate mind. The split at that level is between mind and Mind. On the second rung, the separated mind becomes divided within itself because the Son identifies as ego, dissociating and forgetting the truth of oneness, which is remembered by the Holy Spirit. The split at this level is *within* the separated mind: between wrong and right mind; between the thought system of separation and that of the Atonement. On the third rung, the split is between the Son identified as ego and the ego's image of God. God is now seen as a victimizer and the Son as victim. (Those who do not believe in the idea of God project guilt onto some other "outside force," such as nature, or fate. The point is that, as egos, we attempt to have our separate individuality, but to divest ourselves of responsibility for believing we're separate. Thus, we attempt to avoid the guilt inherent in the separation belief, as well as to escape the fear and suffering which inevitably accompany guilt.)

At the fourth level of separation, what had been one separated ego mind shatters into myriads of seemingly separate minds, and the mind splits off from what appears to be a separate physical universe: mind and body—mind and matter—are now seen as separate. At this level, the mind is effectively split off from itself; we become mindless, lost in fragmentation and physical identity. The Son of God here identifies himself as not only a body, but as billions upon untold billions of bodies. We each, then, represent a case of mistaken identity on the part of the Son. And it is at this level that all of the possible scripts of separated life implicit in the first split are played out in our mind, experienced as our worldly lives. Each life script with all of its subscripts being versions of what it is like to live apart from the Love of God. Just as, at the third rung, guilt was projected onto God, now, in the world of special relationships, guilt is projected onto someone or something other than self which can be blamed for the discomfort brought about by the belief in separation.

The mind is holographic in nature: the whole is contained in each seeming part. Thus, in the world of multiplicity projected on the fourth rung of our descent, each seemingly separated mind contains the same basic elements of wrong mind, right mind and the power to choose between those two. In this important and fundamental sense we are all the same in spite of the illusion of perceived differences. There is oneness in the illusion because all minds are projected by the same separated and split mind. We are all images projected by that mind with the same basic tri-partite content: separation, oneness and decision maker.

Because the mind is holographic and *ideas leave not their source*, guilt and fear have not been escaped by the ego's big bang, but only hidden and disguised through the defenses of denial and projection. The wrong and right mind in each projected fragment has the same basic thought content. The wrong-minded thought system which prevails in the illusion is the home of sin, guilt, fear, and all that attends those basic elements. We will discuss that more fully in the next two chapters.

Thus it is that the world remains a fearful place, not at all the escape promised by the ego; and thus it is that we who identify as separate bodies are in constant need of defenses at all levels: psychological defenses, defenses against illness and disease, defenses against crime, national defenses against other nations, and so on. So it is that we are always at war in one way or another, if not international warfare with blazing weapons, then a war against crime or against disease or against child abuse, against poverty or prejudice, and so on and on. It can be observed that even in our sleeping dreams and waking fantasies, we are usually preoccupied with conflict of some kind. And of course death, conflict, war and murder are the central fascination of our news and entertainment media.

According to the Course, there is no genuine hope in the world, or in attempting to change the world. How could genuine hope lie in illusions?—let alone in an illusion of life apart from love?

41

In the Course we are told that, "the world was meant to be a place where God could enter not" (W-pII.3.2:4) and in fact "was made as an attack on God" (W-pII.3.2:1). That is what separation amounts to: an escape from Oneness as well as an assault upon It. In any case, this dream "world was over long ago" (T-28.I.1:6); the scripts of our lives already written.

In *A Course in Miracles*, Jesus teaches that hope lies in the mind, not in the world. The illusory world is *effect*, not cause. Hope lies in addressing the *cause*. Hope lies in learning how to change our minds about our experiences so that we can see illusions through right-minded eyes, symbolized in the Course by the Holy Spirit and Jesus. But it is not the symbol that is important. What is important is the reality of our right mind and its availability to everyone regardless of race, nation or culture.

In the world perceived through eyes informed by our right mind, there are no victims or victimizers, only guilty, fearful people who need forgiveness, ourselves first of all. There are no villains, only people who are lost in the illusion of separation, feeling absent from love and in one way or another calling out for the love we think we have lost. But we cannot genuinely see ourselves and others through those wise and forgiving eyes without first discovering the reality of mind, and then learning how to utilize our power of decision at the level of mind. It is the mind that is the cause of perception; the cause of how we interpret what we see and experience in ourselves and others. But in order to actually have right-minded perception we have to *be* right minded. Again, it is the goal of the Course's psychology to help us achieve that.

Given the fact that in the practice of our daily lives we demonstrate that we believe in the illusion, whether we intellectually accept the concept of non-duality or not, our problem—the problem addressed by the Course's psychology of forgiveness—is how to begin the ascent back up the ladder separation led us down, because at the bottom of the ladder there is no hope of love or peace. Separation means hatred and war, and it ought to be quite obvious that this is the inheritance we have accepted as egos. Having arrived at the bottom rungs of the ladder of separation, the hope of climbing back which is offered in the Course lies in forgiveness: the undoing of separation, one rung at a time; one situation or relationship at a time.

It is in our special relationships where we find the lessons of forgiveness whereby separation and guilt can be undone if we are willing to accept the right-minded Teacher within. It is through forgiveness that genuine peace can be found in spite of the most terrible of life scripts. It is through forgiveness that guilt and fear are banished from our mind as we learn how to make the change to right-mindedness. Hope lies in forgiveness, and the psychology of the Course addresses itself to that hope. The immediate goal of forgiveness is not Heaven, but harmony and peace of mind within the dream. As we make progress with our forgiveness lessons, we actually are returning Home. Awakening from the dream, however, will take care of itself when our minds are ready.

> There is no need to further clarify what no one in the world can understand. When revelation of your oneness comes, it will be known and fully understood. Now we have work to do, for those in time can speak of things beyond, and listen to words which explain what is to come is past already. Yet what meaning can the words convey to those who count the hours still, and rise and work and go to sleep by them?
>
> Suffice it, then, that you have work to do to play your part. The ending must remain obscure to you until your part is done. It does not matter. For your part is still what all the rest depends on. As you take the role assigned to you, salvation comes a little nearer each uncertain heart that does not beat as yet in tune with God.
>
> Forgiveness is the central theme that runs throughout salvation, holding all its parts in meaningful relationships, the course it runs directed and its outcome sure (W-pI.169.10-12:1).
>
> What waits in perfect certainty beyond salvation is not our concern. For you have barely started to allow your first, uncertain steps to be directed up the ladder separation led you down. The miracle alone is your concern at present. Here is where we must begin. And having started, will the way be made serene and simple in the rising up to waking and the ending of the dream. When you accept a miracle, you do not add your dream of fear to one that is already being dreamed. Without support, the dream will fade away without effects. For it is your support that strengthens it (T-28.III.1).

The myth of the ladder separation led us down addresses the question of how it is that we find ourselves in the situations of our lives at all levels. It serves as background for further understanding the psychology of *A Course in Miracles*, its principles, goals and practical application. Now we are ready to take a deeper look at the pig-in-a-poke that we have bought by deciding to identify with the ego, for in order to make use of Jesus' psychology one must become intimately familiar with one's ego, and be able to observe it in action.

Chapter 4

The Ego

The proverbial phrase, "Don't buy a pig in a poke," cautions against investing in something without examining it first, the word "poke" being an archaic word for "sack" or "pouch." So it might be said that we, as the Son of God, bought a pig in a poke when we took the "tiny, mad idea" of separation seriously and bought into ego identity. We did not open the sack to look inside and examine what separation really amounted to. In terms of the Level One metaphysical teachings of *A Course in Miracles*, if we had done so, we would have found that the sack was empty!

> What is the *ego*? But a dream of what you really are. A thought you are apart from your Creator and a wish to be what He created not. It is a thing of madness, not reality at all. A name for namelessness is all it is. A symbol of impossibility; a choice for options that do not exist. We name it but to help us understand that it is nothing but an ancient thought that what is made [i.e., *not created* but projected or imagined] has immortality. But what could come of this except a dream which, like all dreams, can only end in death?

> What is the ego? Nothingness, but in a form that seems like something... Who asks you to define the ego and explain how it arose can be but he who thinks it real, and seeks by definition to ensure that its illusive nature is concealed behind the words that seem to make it so.

> There is no definition for a lie that serves to make it true. Nor can there be a truth that lies conceal effectively. The ego's unreality is not denied by words nor is its meaning clear because its nature seems to have a form. Who can define the undefinable? (C-2.2:1-2, 5; 3:1-4; bracket mine).

In terms of the Level Two Course teachings about forgiveness, we can still look inside the sack, and must do so, because in each moment we are still buying into ego identity. But we need to look at the malevolence of the ego thought system from a right-minded perspective in order to forgive ourselves—in order to smile at our mistake in making something out of nothing and not feel guilty about it, since the illusion we made is seen to be pretty awful when examined carefully. In a practical sense this involves learning how not to take ourselves seriously, which the Holy Spirit does not do. He knows that a separate self is not possible. So, in looking at the ego, it is important that we not make it seem real simply because we are able to employ words and concepts in the interest of understanding. As quoted above: "The ego's unreality is not denied by words nor is its

45

meaning clear because its nature seems to have a form." But of course, from Jesus' perspective, that is exactly what we all (including Freud and other psychologists) have done: made the meaningless seem meaningful; made the unreal seem real.

The term *ego* was not coined by Freud (in German he used the phrase *das ich*, which translates as "the I"), but it was certainly he who supplied the definition that contemporary Western psychology employs; and he who gave the concept of ego currency in our understanding of ourselves. However, colloquial use often does not mean the term as Freud intended, but in its more archaic sense of being egotistical or egocentric.

Basically, the term *ego* can be equated with consciousness: the awareness of "I" as distinct from "other," but Freud and psychologists who followed him have elaborated on the nature of this "I." In Freudian theory the ego is one of three major components of the human psyche—*id, ego* and *superego*—and the second to develop, being derived from the id. To Freud and modern psychologists in general, *ego* represents the potential saving grace of mankind; and "healthy ego development" is understood as a necessity for living a productive, rewarding life.

Freud clearly saw the murderous motivations that "seethe" at the core of biological existence, and in his structural theory of the human psyche he assigned those motivations to the *id*. He also recognized the pernicious nature of guilt, identifying the judgmental *superego* as its source. In Freudian theory, the ego develops as a survival mechanism out of energy acquired from the id. It has the energy-consuming, fear-driven task of negotiating among threats from all sides: unchanneled id instincts are incapable of survival; the environment is full or threats, both physical and psychological; and the guilty judgments of the superego lead to self destruction unless moderated. In order to fulfill this demanding, anxiety-filled set of tasks—this high wire balancing act of physical life—the ego develops defense mechanisms, which Freud cataloged, and which we will discuss later as they are explained in the Course.

In *A Course in Miracles*, the concept of *ego* includes the murderousness of the *id*, since the belief in separation is the source of ego identity, and separation, if it were possible, would be equivalent to the murder of God: the destruction of true Life, or Oneness. In ACIM it is understood that what drives the ego from its very origin is the seeking to maintain its sense of a separate individual identity at the cost of others who are seen either as competitors and threats or as resources to be exploited in the service of self interest.

The ego does not have relationships in the interest of oneness, but has *special* relationships in the interest of separation and self. Hence, murder is its bottom line, whether acted out or disguised and harbored within.

The ego's world is a "dog-eat-dog" world: it's always *one or the other*, though this basic principle may be cleverly hidden even from one's own self awareness. One has to be able to look with the undaunted integrity of a Freud in order to see this. And one has to be able to look objectively with the right mind (represented by Jesus) in order to see this as a mistake to be corrected rather than as a sin about which to feel guilty and defensive.

A Course in Miracles' concept of the ego also includes the functions Freud assigned to the *superego*. The Course's ego thrives on judgment and is driven by guilt; judgmental condemnation of others being an attempt to divest oneself of guilt, which may take many forms but originates as condemnation of self for the imagined separation from God.

Thus, the Course's *ego* incorporates the functions and dynamics of Freud's *id, ego* and *superego*, but it does not use the terms *id* and *superego*. In the Course, the basic components of the ego thought system are recognized as *sin, guilt* and *fear*, the idea of sin being the belief that separation is real and has been accomplished, therefore a celestial murder must have been committed; or in Freudian terms, one might say that the basic instincts of the id have had their way with God. The belief in sin inevitably results in the idea of guilt (something very bad was done, therefore the separated individual must *be* very bad) and that idea inspires a deep seated sense of intrinsic unworthiness as well as fear of punishing consequences.

The defining content of the Course's *wrong mind* is the ego thought system; and it is the wrong mind that not only projected the illusion of a world, but almost without exception has guided life on this planet. According to the Course, all of our problems stem from the belief in separation and differences, that belief being the foundation of the ego thought system. However, in terms of the Course's metaphysical teachings, because the ego originates out of an impossibility, it is neither truly threatened, nor can what it *makes*[1] be of any real consequence. Therefore, what we need—we who identify with the ego but are in truth the Son of God and brothers in Christ—are not defenses against threat, but to accept the truth held for us in our right mind by the Holy Spirit.

---

[1] In the Course, the verb "make" and its derivatives refer to the *projection* of illusions which produce form at some level, as compared to the word "create" which refers to God and the *extensions* of His Thought which are without form.

And what will contribute most constructively to our ability to negotiate the demands of illusory life in the body is the guidance of love from our right mind, not the defensive strategies of the ego.

Ego Development and Spiritual Development

Given the requirements of the illusion into which we have entered with the birth of the body, *A Course in Miracles* does not deny the necessity of healthy ego development in the *early* years of physical life. However, since the Course teaches that ego identification is the source of human misery, the idea of a "healthy ego" is ultimately nonsensical, *except* as right-mindedness can be understood as consciousness informed by the Holy Spirit: a sense of "I" remains, but is entirely in the service of love and forgiveness.

Paradoxically, spiritual maturity within the mind that believes in separation must await satisfactory ego development. There must be a reasonably strong ego before the process of undoing ego identity can begin. Therefore, the psychology of *A Course in Miracles* is not intended to be practiced by chronological children. Rather, the Course's psychology is for adults who have developed ego strength, but have come to recognize that something is wrong: in spite of what the world might regard as success, they are not satisfied or fulfilled; in terms of inner peace and happiness, the world doesn't work; "there must be a better way," as Bill Thetford and Helen Schucman came to realize. In this sense, while the Course is not for chronological children, it *is* for spiritual children; and in the Course it is clear that Jesus regards most of human kind as spiritually immature.

One characteristic of spiritual immaturity is the belief that peace and happiness can be found in the world on its terms: that the world can somehow work and bodies achieve true happiness. Another is the belief that the physical world—the ego's world of separation—was either created by God or can be changed by God. In other words, from the perspective of the Course, identification with the ego thought system and its dualistic reality is spiritually immature. This immaturity is not "bad" in the sense that it is something to be self-condemning and feel guilty about; it just won't lead to genuine, lasting peace and happiness.

Spiritual maturity, therefore peace and happiness, is possible because our mistaken choice for the ego can be corrected. In the Course, the Holy Spirit's thought system of the Atonement is the correction for the ego thought system of separation: right-mindedness corrects wrong-mindedness. One who seeks spiritual maturity must discover the mind and learn to choose the "better way" of the Holy Spirit. That choice is the Course's "miracle," following which correction and undoing of the ego thought system is the function and responsibility of the Holy Spirit. In our mind there needs to be only a "little willingness" to look honestly within, and then to allow the undoing to take place; a small inclination to set the ego aside. Undoing of separation and salvation from the ego, "asks but a little wish that what is true be true; a little willingness to overlook what is not there; a little sigh that speaks for Heaven as a preference to this world that death and desolation seem to rule" (T-26.VII.10:1). Thus, the Course's path to spiritual maturity requires implementing its psychology of forgiveness in the interest of allowing the Holy Spirit to undo ego identity one step at a time back up the ladder separation led us down.

For evidence of the general level of spiritual maturity in the world, one only needs to look around at the childish, sandbox nature of human life at all levels—personal, family, social and political—where one can observe tug-of-wars about what's mine and what's yours, either materially or symbolically. Of course, within the illusion of time, as the body (which is the ego's "home") matures it becomes capable of acting out the ego's childish self-centeredness and hostility in what we regard as more and more serious ways, including the ability to employ advanced technology in the interest of mass destruction—seemingly a far cry from throwing sand in the eyes of one's antagonists, according to the value relativity which characterizes belief in the illusion of separation.

But Jesus does not accept a hierarchy of illusions:

> It is impossible that one illusion be less amenable to truth than are the rest. But it is possible that some are given greater value, and less willingly offered to truth for healing and for help. No illusion has any truth in it. Yet it appears some are more true than others, although this clearly makes no sense at all. All that a hierarchy of illusions can show is preference, not reality. What relevance has preference to the truth? Illusions are illusions and are false. Your preference gives them no reality. Not one is true in any way, and all must yield with equal ease to what God gave as answer to them all. God's Will is one. And any wish that seems to go against His Will has no foundation in the truth (T-26.VII.6).

> What is not love is murder. What is not loving must be an attack. Every illusion is an assault on truth, and every one does violence to the idea of love because it seems to be of equal truth (T-23.IV.1:10-12).

Clearly, what Jesus is saying here is that everything of the ego is fundamentally murderous. The ego's bottom line is what Freud called the id, thus mature ego development amounts to achieving a successful disguise that covers over the face of cruel intent, allowing us to make thief's bargains in order that we can survive in the jungle of *one or the other*—a survival which ultimately ends in death. This must be the case, since the ego's substitute for the eternal life of spirit is the illusion of finite life in a body: "Whenever you attempt to reach a goal in which the body's betterment is cast as major beneficiary, you try to bring about your death" (T-29.VII. 4:1).

"To the ego the goal is death" (T-15.I. 2:8)

In addition to the so-called "life instincts," Freud recognized that biological life inevitably leads to death: all organisms die. Thus, in his later work, Freud hypothesized a "death instinct," bluntly stating in *Beyond the Pleasure Principle*[1] that, "The goal of all life is death." And the Course agrees with this in terms of the biological existence that is regarded as life within the ego thought system:

> To the ego the goal is death, which *is* its end [i.e., goal]. But to the Holy Spirit the goal is life [i.e., spirit, Heaven], which *has* no end.....The ego wants *you* dead, but not itself. (T-15.I. 2:8-9; 3:3; brackets mine).

The "you" that the ego seeks to kill is our true Self as Christ: the Oneness that is the Mind of God. And the ego can have the goal of survival beyond physical death because it is a thought system in our mind, which does not die with the body. In fact the death of the body is nothing since the only reality is mind. Speaking as though linear time were real, as long as there seems to be an illusion of separation in the mind, the illusion of a body and death continues and the ego survives, as the slaughtering history of mankind so clearly attests.

Regarding death, Jesus states:

> ...nothing is accomplished through death, because death is nothing. Everything is accomplished through life, and life is of the mind and in the mind. The body neither lives nor dies, because it cannot contain you who are life. If we share the same mind, you can overcome death because I did (T-6.V(A).1:2-5).

> There is no life outside of Heaven. Where God created life, there life must be. In any state apart from Heaven life is illusion. At best it seems like life; at worst, like death. Yet both are judgments on what is not life, equal in their inaccuracy and lack of meaning.

---

[1] Freud, Sigmund. *Beyond the Pleasure Principle*. Trans. by James Strachey. New York: W. W. Norton & Co., 1961. (First published in German in 1920.)

Life not in Heaven is impossible, and what is not in Heaven is not anywhere (T-23.II.19:1-6).

Identified with the ego, we are secretly attracted to death (T-19.IV(C)), because to the ego death means life in the sense that it "proves" the body is real and must have lived. One can see this attraction in the widespread fascination with death in literature and in news broadcasts, as well as observe it within oneself. If death were not a common personal preoccupation, there would be no public market for it.

Furthermore, the idea of death validates the seeming reality of the ego, because its "life" had to be achieved upon the death of God: the illusion of a separate life in the body apart from God, therefore apart from Love, requires that Oneness be destroyed, as has been discussed. So the illusion of life that belongs to the ego is part and parcel of the illusion of death, and is central to *fear*, one of the three basic components of the ego thought system. To the ego, which has made up a God in its own image, death is God's ultimate punishment for the sin of separation, insane as that is since in the ego thought system it is never explained how a murdered Oneness rises up to murder in return. The failure to offer such an explanation witnesses to the fact that Oneness cannot be, and has not been, destroyed. But the ego, using its characteristic defenses of denial and dissociation, blots all of this out of awareness.

Thus it is that the God of traditional, ego-based religions in the world is seen as both the loving creator and vengeful destroyer of biological life; His final punishment of death being a threat in every waking moment as "acts of God" threaten to rain down on us out of the heavens in the form of tornados, hurricanes and floods, or rise up to swallow us in earthquakes, or kill us with viruses and toxins that fill the air we breath—not to mention the warfare we wage on one another in the "name of God." And, if nothing else, then the final withering and decay of the body whose life must end in death as ordained by its maker.

In the Course, Jesus flatly denies the ego's image of God. The true God did not create the illusion of a physical universe and biological life, and knows nothing of separation which could never threaten the sublime, eternal peace, joy and Love that are His reality as well as ours in the truth of Who we are as spirit. But to the mass of humanity who remain in the "sleep of forgetfulness" identified as egos, fear most certainly seems warranted while the great burden of our guilt lies buried in the unconscious.

Freud did not know of the alternative to the ego thought system—did not know of the reality of spirit and mind wherein there lies the possibility of a decision for right-mindedness—nor do most human beings who have been deceived and effectively rendered mindless in their embrace of the ego. Yet it is the reality of mind and the power to choose that the Course holds out as escape from the miserable existence required by ego life with its commitment to the ways of separation, guilt, fear and death. In the Course Jesus instructs his students:

> Teacher of God, your one assignment could be stated thus: Accept no compromise in which death plays a part. Do not believe in cruelty, nor let attack conceal the truth from you. What seems to die has but been misperceived and carried to illusion. Now it becomes your task to let the illusion be carried to the truth. Be steadfast but in this; be not deceived by the "reality" of any changing form. Truth neither moves nor wavers nor sinks down to death and dissolution. And what is the end of death? Nothing but this; the realization that the Son of God is guiltless now and forever. Nothing but this. But do not let yourself forget it is not less than this (M-27.7).

Observing the Ego

In order for the Course's psychology to come alive in a practical sense, it is most helpful to be able to observe evidence of the ego thought system at work in one's own mind. In the Course, Jesus gently invites his students to engage in this self observation with him.

> No one can escape from illusions unless he looks at them, for not looking is the way they are protected. There is no need to shrink from illusions, for they cannot be dangerous. We are ready to look more closely at the ego's thought system because together we have the lamp that will dispel it, and since you realize you do not want it, you must be ready. Let us be very calm in doing this, for we are merely looking honestly for truth. The "dynamics" of the ego will be our lesson for a while, for we must look first at this to see beyond it, since you have made it real. We will undo this error quietly together, and then look beyond it to truth (T-11.V.1).

The word "dynamics" is placed in quotes here since, being an illusion arising from an impossible idea, the ego has no power to affect reality. Its only power comes from the fact that we choose to believe it, thus buying into the dream of separation and all of its inherent difficulties. By misusing our power of decision as mind, we make the error of separation seem real. In recognition of the work of Sigmund Freud, it should be pointed out that the paragraph above invites students of the Course to engage in the same unflinchingly honest, rigorous, objective looking beneath the veil of appearances that was the hallmark of Freud's clinical-scientific approach. Kenneth Wapnick has reported that in unpublished personal remarks to Helen Schucman, Jesus told her of his gratitude to Freud, whose ability to "look" was right-minded even though he distrusted anything to do with spirituality. In other words, one could say that Freud did not know of mind as it is presented in the Course, therefore did not know of the alternative to the ego thought system. Wapnick has said that Jesus told Helen, "Freud knew a bad thing when he saw it, but he did not know that bad things don't exist." And Wapnick recounts another story about Freud which is found in the biographical material: Once, walking in the streets of Vienna, Freud said to his daughter Anna, "You see those lovely houses? Things are not so lovely behind their façade." The key to forgiveness as taught in the Course is looking behind the façade.

Before we continue looking behind the façade, a reminder seems appropriate. What we call "the ego" is not a thing, not an identifiable entity of some sort, not even in conventional psychology where there could be a tendency to think that the word "ego" describes some structure in the brain. According to the Course, ultimately the ego is nothing. It is only necessary that we carefully examine it because we have bought a poke without a pig and then attempted to see something real within. What we have attempted to make real in this way is basically our individuality: our separated ego self.

So, in *A Course in Miracles* the term *ego* symbolizes a thought system in the mind, and one that is completely in error leading to a life of error. It is necessary to examine this error because our unhappy human condition results from our having chosen to believe it and continuing to believe it. As an alternative to this unhappy dream, and as a prelude to spiritual awakening, the Course offers a way to correct ego perceptions so that they become "vision" which results in a "happy dream"—a dream of forgiveness and joining rather than of separation and fear. But to do this, we must learn how to access our mind and change the thought system to which we adhere. When seen with *vision*, which is to see through eyes informed by the Holy Spirit, there is beauty in the world and in our brothers. In the Course, Jesus instructs his students about this:

> You cannot lay aside the obstacles to real vision without looking upon them, for to lay aside means to judge against. If you will look, the Holy Spirit will judge, and He will judge truly. Yet He cannot shine away what you keep hidden, for you have not offered it to Him and He cannot take it from you.

We are therefore embarking on an organized, well-structured and carefully planned program aimed at learning how to offer to the Holy Spirit everything you do not want [i.e., learning how to identify and reject the ego in favor of becoming right minded]. He knows what to do with it. You do not understand how to use what He knows. Whatever is given Him that is not of God is gone. Yet you must look at it yourself in perfect willingness, for otherwise His knowledge remains useless to you (T-12.II. 9:6-10:5; brackets mine).

Appearances can but deceive the mind that wants to be deceived. And you can make a simple choice that will forever place you far beyond deception. You need not concern yourself with how this will be done, for this you cannot understand. But you will understand that mighty changes have been quickly brought about, when you decide one very simple thing; you do not want whatever you believe an idol [i.e., the ego] gives. For thus the Son of God declares that he is free of idols. And thus *is* he free (T-30.IV.6; bracket mine).

Further Examination of Sin, Guilt and Fear

Let us now expand upon the definitions of the three basic elements in the ego thought system: *sin, guilt* and *fear*. In doing so, we will make use of the definitions supplied in the *Glossary-Index for A COURSE IN MIRACLES* [1] by Kenneth Wapnick, who has sometimes referred to these as "the unholy trinity." Although Freud did not identify them as such, sin, guilt and fear represent the id content that he observed and described as: "...a chaos, a cauldron of seething excitations..."[2]

1. Wapnick's *Glossary* definition of *sin* is:

the belief in the reality of our separation from God, seen by the ego as an act incapable of correction because it represents our attack on our Creator, Who would therefore never forgive us; leads to guilt, which demands punishment; equivalent to separation, and the central concept in the ego's thought system, from which all others logically follow; to the Holy Spirit, an error in our thinking to be corrected and therefore forgiven and healed.

Sin is basically the idea of separation taken seriously in the mind where it arose.

---

[1] *Glossary-Index for A COURSE IN MIRACLES*, op. cit. (Most definitions from the Glossary can be found on the Web at: http://www.facim.org/acim/glossary.htm, although these definitions lack the cross references to relevant Course passages which are available in the hard copy. We will continue throughout to refer to this work without further footnoting.)

[2] Freud, Sigmund. *New Introductory Lectures on Psychoanalysis*. Trans. by James Strachey. New York: W. W. Norton & Co., 1964, 1965. (First published in German in 1933.)

Had the thought of separation *not* been taken seriously, but discarded with gentle amusement, there would not have been the dream that we take for reality. And since it is *our* dream—our mind in which the idea of separation was taken seriously—we must take responsibility for it. And it is not only in some unremembered past where separation was taken seriously, but in each moment of what we consider to be waking life where we reinforce the idea of separation by taking our ego self seriously, therefore reacting to perceived threats defensively, needily pursuing self interest, and engaging in judgmental condemnation of others.

About the undoing of separation taken seriously and seen as sin, Jesus says in the Course:

> This is the way salvation [i.e., forgiveness] works. As you step back [from taking your ego seriously], the light in you steps forward and encompasses the world. It heralds not the end of sin in punishment and death. In lightness and in laughter is sin gone, because its quaint absurdity is seen. It is a foolish thought, a silly dream, not frightening, ridiculous perhaps, but who would waste an instant in approach to God Himself for such a senseless whim?

> Yet you have wasted many, many years on just this foolish thought (W-pI.156.6:5-7:1; brackets mine).

Thus, the idea of sin amounts to taking our separate, individual ego self seriously. This is the essence of what the course means by *specialness*. When separation is taken seriously, differences between ourselves and others become very important, so we see conflict instead of common interests; we perceive others as having something, tangible or intangible, we ourselves do not have and need; we take offense at perceived attacks rather than seeing the guilt, fear and call for love behind them; we see a world full of threats which require that we be constantly on the defensive. In these ways the ego thought system manifests itself so that we can see it in ourselves in the context of daily life. Thus we are given the opportunity to change our minds at the level of cause (mind) rather than becoming further caught up in effects (illusions: bodies, the world), therefore attempting to resolve problems where they are not.

The ego is a survival mechanism in the sense that it serves to maintain illusions. Once chosen, its primary concern is for the survival of itself as a thought system in our mind. Thus, we find ourselves becoming concerned to the point of obsession with the survival of our separate, individual self.

Recognizing this, the well known spiritual teacher J. Krishnamurti invited his students to examine in themselves their own self-centered ego preoccupations:

> Before we go any further I would like to ask you what is your fundamental, lasting interest in life? Putting all oblique answers aside and dealing with this question directly and honestly, what would you answer? Do you know?
>
> Isn't it yourself? Anyway, that is what most of us would say if we answered truthfully. I am interested in my progress, my job, my family, the little corner in which I live, in getting a better position for myself, more prestige, more power, more domination over others and so on. I think it would be logical, wouldn't it, to admit to ourselves that that is what most of us are primarily interested in—"me first"?[3]

The ego's focus on effects to the exclusion of cause is part of its survival strategy, so we are kept preoccupied with problems perceived in the world and body in order that we remain effectively mindless, unaware that we are mind and as such that we have a choice about how we will perceive (therefore how we will react to) whatever the world seems to offer.

Another part of the ego's self preservation strategy involves the pursuit of specialness, which is equivalent to the desire to be separate, therefore sinful as judged in the ego system which thrives on guilt. Because sin, guilt and fear are inextricably linked together, it is impossible to pursue specialness without incurring and maintaining guilt which results in fear of punishment. Thus, much as Freud saw, though not precisely for his reasons, ego life is fraught with anxiety as we become caught up in a desperate cycle of self seeking which must produce unconscious guilt followed by fear:

> Specialness is the function that you [Son of God as ego] gave yourself. It stands for you alone, as self-created, self-maintained, in need of nothing, and unjoined with anything beyond the body. In its eyes you are a separate universe, with all the power to hold itself complete within itself, with every entry shut against intrusion, and every window barred against the light. Always attacked and always furious, with anger always fully justified, you have pursued this goal with vigilance you never thought to yield, and effort that you never thought to cease. And all this grim determination was for this; you wanted specialness to be the truth (T-24.VI.11; bracket mine).
>
> Specialness is the idea of sin made real. Sin is impossible even to imagine without this base. For sin arose from it, out of nothingness; an evil flower

---

[3] Krishnamurti, J. *Freedom from the Known*, p.39. Ojai, California: Krishnamurti Foundation, 1969.

with no roots at all. Here is the self-made "savior," the "creator" who creates unlike the Father, and which made His Son like to itself and not like unto Him. His "special" sons are many, never one, each one in exile from himself, and Him of Whom they are a part. Nor do they love the Oneness Which created them as one with Him. They chose their specialness instead of Heaven and instead of peace, and wrapped it carefully in sin, to keep it "safe" from truth (T-24.II.3).

What could the purpose of the body be but specialness? And it is this that makes it frail and helpless in its own defense. It was conceived to make *you* [mind, Son of God] frail and helpless. The goal of separation is its curse (T-24.IV.2:1-4; bracket mine).

2. The definition of *guilt* found in Wapnick's *Glossary* is:

> the feeling experienced in relation to sin; its reflection from our minds is seen in all the negative feelings and beliefs we have about ourselves, mostly unconscious; rests on a sense of inherent unworthiness, seemingly beyond even the forgiving power of God, Who we erroneously believe demands punishment for our seeming sin of separation against Him; following the ego's counsel that to look on guilt would destroy us, we deny its presence in our minds, and then project it outward in the form of attack, either onto others as anger or onto our own bodies as sickness. (See: scarcity principle). [Discussed in our next chapter on special relationships.]

Guilt may be understood as a thought or an idea as well as the feeling which accompanies belief in sin. Finally, everything in the mind is thought or idea, but when a thought in the mind is experienced at the perceptual level it takes form, and among the forms that it takes are feelings and emotions. As was pointed out in chapter two, thoughts in the mind are not the same as what we typically regard as thoughts, ideas and thinking which appear in conscious awareness and are assigned to the brain. Because, according to the Course, the brain does not think, what we regard as thought and idea are really *forms* into which thoughts in the mind have been translated. The *feeling* of guilt is therefore one form of the thought of guilt in the mind.

Other forms that thought takes are intellectual concepts and human behavior, not to mention the form of bodies and all that seems to compose the separated world. Again, as we saw in the myth of separation, the world is a projection of the mind—basically a thought in the mind. That is what the Course means when it says: "All thinking produces form at some level" (T-2.VI.9:14).[4]

---

[4] In the Course, the distinction between *form* and *content* is important. Basically, *form* is anything that can be perceived or conceived, therefore is illusory; while *content* refers to thought, is formless and is of the mind.

While sin can be understood as the thought or belief that separation is real, guilt can be understood as the thought or belief that sin is real. If sin is real, then there must be a sinner, the prototype of which is the Son of God who believed he had established a separate identity at the expense of destroying Oneness. Therefore, this idea of being a sinner is inherent in the separated mind and manifest in the wrong-minded thought system of the ego. It is the inheritance of every seemingly separated mind—every seemingly separated Son of God—who identifies with the ego, whether a person consciously believes in sin or not. The guilt that accompanies this idea of sin and sinner is almost never experienced directly in consciousness, but since it is a thought in our wrong mind, when we identify with the ego and its wrong-minded thinking, some form of guilt will be present, however vaguely sensed in awareness. Common forms of guilt include a sense of inferiority, feelings of inadequacy or incompetence, thoughts and feelings of unworthiness, feeling incomplete and needy, and feelings of hopelessness and discouragement about one's future.

Note that the listed forms of guilt have a *feeling* component. It is possible to have a negative assessment of a situation without it necessarily involving guilt. For example, if one has examined the facts and is pessimistic about the prospects of some individual or group undertaking or about the direction of humanity in general, but is not as a result burdened with depression and other negative feelings, then that form of pessimism would *not* be an example of guilt. Instead, it would represent a detached observation. An example of this can be seen in the Course where Jesus tells us: "Learn now, without despair, there is no hope of answer in the world...Seek not another signpost in the world that seems to point to still another road. No longer look for hope where there is none.... Who would be willing to be turned away from all the roadways of the world, unless he understood their real futility?" (T-31.IV.4:3, 5-6; 5:1)

Guilt serves the ego as both a motivating dynamic and a defense which protects the mind from careful examination. The ego has made sin and guilt so horrifically fearful that they must be repressed into the unconscious. In this way, through the agency of fear, we are prevented from looking within to discover our innocence, the truth of oneness, and our true Self Identity. Of course we must fear that Identity with Oneness as long as we value the ego and its story of separation, individuality, physical existence and specialness. In other words, the ego fears the Love of God which means the end of its lie of separation, therefore the end of the ego altogether. And with minds informed by the ego we must share that fear as we cling to our cherished individuality without ever realizing what it costs us.

Remember that the ego is not alone. Its rule is tempered, and its unknown "enemy," [i.e. the Holy Spirit, the Memory of God] Whom it cannot even see, it fears. Loudly the ego tells you not to look inward, for if you do your eyes will light on sin [and guilt], and God will strike you blind. This you believe, and so you do not look. Yet this is not the ego's hidden fear, nor yours who serve it. Loudly indeed the ego claims it is; too loudly and too often. For underneath this constant shout and frantic proclamation, the ego is not certain it is so. Beneath your fear to look within because of sin is yet another fear, and one which makes the ego tremble.

What if you looked within and saw no sin? This "fearful" question is one the ego never asks. And you who ask it now are threatening the ego's whole defensive system... (T-21.IV.2-3:3; brackets mine).

Not only does guilt serve as a defense against examining and uncovering what has been repressed into the unconscious, but the world, which was projected out of guilt and fear, serves as a second, top-layer defense, because it keeps our attention focused on what seems to be outside where we who believe in the illusion of a world and bodies think we can find happiness. Thus, the world serves as a defense against looking within just as the guilt within serves as a defense against awakening to the truth of oneness, the Love of God and our Christ Identity. In the Course, Jesus refers to this two-layered defense as a way in which our decision to be separate and guilty, is "doubly shielded by oblivion" (W-pI.136.5:2).

Freud stated that the goal of psychoanalysis is to make the unconscious conscious. The same can be said of Jesus' goal for those who would study his Course and undertake to practice its psychology of forgiveness. According to the Course, unconscious guilt buried in our mind is the source of all human misery and conflict. This is not different from saying that separation is our only problem, since it is the belief that separation is real that amounts to sin, and the idea of sin that produces guilt. However, both separation and guilt represent a decision that *we* as mind have made—a decision that can be changed—and *that* is the single most serious threat to our identity as egos: "What if you looked within and saw no sin [i.e., no separation]?"

> Once you were unaware of what the cause of everything the world appeared to thrust upon you, uninvited and unasked, must really be. Of one thing you were sure: Of all the many causes you perceived as bringing pain and suffering to you, your guilt was not among them. Nor did you in any way request them for yourself. This is how all illusions came about. The one who makes them does not see himself as making them, and their reality does not depend on him. Whatever cause they have is something quite apart from him, and what he sees is separate from his mind. He cannot doubt his dreams' reality, because he does not see the part he plays in making them and making them seem real (T-27.VII.7:3-9).

> The acceptance of guilt into the mind of God's Son was the beginning of the separation, as the acceptance of the Atonement [i.e., that in truth separation is impossible] is its end. The world you see is the delusional system of those made mad by guilt. Look carefully at this world, and you will realize that this is so. For this world is the symbol of punishment, and all the laws that seem to govern it are the laws of death. Children are born into it through pain and in pain. Their growth is attended by suffering, and they learn of sorrow and separation and death. Their minds seem to be trapped in their brain, and its powers to decline if their bodies are hurt. They seem to love, yet they desert and are deserted. They appear to lose what they love, perhaps the most insane belief of all. And their bodies wither and gasp and are laid in the ground, and are no more (T-13.IN.2:1-10; bracket mine).

And no one who is free of guilt has a need to project guilt, therefore to find in someone else reason for condemnation; reason to attack either overtly or covertly:

> If you did not feel guilty you could not attack, for condemnation is the root of attack. It is the judgment of one mind by another as unworthy of love and deserving of punishment. But herein lies the split. For the mind that judges perceives itself as separate from the mind being judged, believing that by punishing another, it will escape punishment. All this is but the delusional attempt of the mind to deny itself, and escape the penalty of denial. It is not an attempt to relinquish denial, but to hold on to it. For it is guilt that has obscured the Father to you, and it is guilt that has driven you insane (T-13.IN.1).

Without guilt, obviously there is no need of forgiveness. Without guilt harbored in one's own mind, there would be no perception of sin and guilt in others, so that finally forgiveness is forgiveness of one's self; forgiveness of the guilt that stems from one's own belief in separation. And it is that belief which results in ego identification with its subsequent pursuit of specialness at the expense of others.

So, sin and guilt are bound together and largely hidden in the unconscious. No one is aware of the primordial guilt which arose from the "sin" of attacking God when the idea of separation was first taken seriously, but some version of this dynamic is involved in every human undertaking motivated by the ego, especially in what the Course calls *special relationships*, which have been mentioned and will be discussed later in more depth. Fear, too, is inextricably bound up with sin and guilt. Of the ego's three basic elements, fear is the most prominently displayed in our awareness, so it is most easily observed, and we shall now take a further look at it.

3. The definition of *fear* in Wapnick's *Glossary* is:

> the emotion of the ego, contrasted with love, the emotion given us by God; originates in the expected punishment for our sins, which our guilt demands; the resulting terror over what we believe we deserve leads us—through the dynamics of denial and projection—to defend ourselves by attacking others, which merely reinforces our sense of vulnerability and fear, establishing a vicious circle of fear and defense.

A powerful statement about fear can be found in one of Helen Schucman's later inspired works. About two years after the Course had been published she channeled a prose poem entitled "The Gifts of God" which appears in the book of her poetry with the same title. The opening lines read:

> Fear is the one emotion of the world. Its forms are many—call them what you will—but it is one in content. Never far, even in form, from what its purpose is, never with power to escape its cause, and never but a counterfeit of joy, it rests uncertainly upon a bed of lies. Here it will remain where it was born, and where its end will come. For here is nothingness, where neither birth nor death is real, nor any form in the misshapen mind that spawned its seeming life has any meaning in the Mind of God.[5]

Fear follows guilt just as guilt follows the belief in sin; and fear is one of the most frequently discussed topics in the Course, usually in contrast with love. Simplifying things for us, Jesus says: "...you have but two emotions, love and fear" (T-13.V.1:1). "You have but two emotions, and one you made and one was given you. Each is a way of seeing, and different worlds arise from their different sights" (T-13.V.10:1-2). We "made" fear by identifying with the ego, and since it is the ego thought system that projected the illusory world, "Fear is the one emotion of the world." Love, on the other hand, was "given" because it is the essence of oneness and our creation by God.

The original projection of the illusory world was made out of fear. The way we perceive within the illusion continues to depend upon projection, because "projection makes perception." Further, perception always involves *interpretation*, being dependent upon the thought behind the projection:

> There has been much confusion about what perception means, because the word is used both for awareness and for the interpretation of awareness. Yet you cannot be aware without interpretation, for what you perceive *is* your interpretation (T-11.VI.2:5-6).

---

[5] Schucman, Helen. *The Gifts of God*, p.115. Mill Valley, California: The Foundation for Inner Peace, 1982.

> Projection makes perception. The world you see is what you gave it, nothing more than that…It is the witness to your state of mind, the outside picture of an inward condition. As a man thinketh, so does he perceive (T-21.IN.1-2, 5-6).

These statements imply a psychological formula, which can be symbolized as follows:

> thought→ projection→ perception→ reaction (emotion and behavior).

Thus, the thought of fear in our mind projects a world perceived as fearful and demanding of both defense and attack. Wrong-minded perception is fearful because, being separate and vulnerable, our peace and security seem to be in the hands of others. The thought of love in our mind *extends* (the Holy Spirit's form of projection) a world where perceiver and perceived are joined as one and share common interests in spite of superficial differences, and in spite of actions engaged in by others. Right-minded perception comes from the *knowledge* that inner peace does not depend upon anything that others might do. Jesus, who symbolized love in a body 2000 years ago, is an excellent example of this:

> I elected, for your sake and mine, to demonstrate that the most outrageous assault, as judged by the ego, does not matter. As the world judges these things, but not as God knows them, I was betrayed, abandoned, beaten, torn, and finally killed. It was clear that this was only because of the projection of others onto me, since I had not harmed anyone and had healed many (T-6.I.9).

And so he says to us:

> You have probably reacted for years as if you were being crucified. This is a marked tendency of the separated, who always refuse to consider what they have done to themselves. Projection means anger, anger fosters assault, and assault promotes fear. The real meaning of the crucifixion lies in the *apparent* intensity of the assault of some of the Sons of God upon another. This, of course, is impossible, and must be fully understood *as* impossible. Otherwise, I cannot serve as a model for learning. [Implicit in this statement is the principle that minds are joined. In truth there is only one mind which cannot attack itself. Bodies are part of the illusion of separation and differences wherein attack is inevitable.]

> Assault can ultimately be made only on the body. There is little doubt that one body can assault another, and can even destroy it. Yet if destruction itself is impossible, anything that is destructible cannot be real. [This recalls the introductory statement in the Text: "Nothing real can be threatened.

Nothing unreal exists. Herein lies the peace of God."] Its destruction, therefore, does not justify anger. To the extent to which you believe that it does, you are accepting false premises and teaching them to others. The message the crucifixion was intended to teach was that it is not necessary to perceive any form of assault in persecution, because you cannot *be* persecuted. If you respond with anger, you must be equating yourself with the destructible, and are therefore regarding yourself insanely [i.e., with the ego].

I have made it perfectly clear that I am like you and you are like me, but our fundamental equality can be demonstrated only through joint decision. You are free to perceive yourself as persecuted if you choose. When you do choose to react that way, however, you might remember that I was persecuted as the world judges, and did not share this evaluation for myself. And because I did not share it, I did not strengthen it. I therefore offered a different interpretation of attack, and one which I want to share with you (T-6.I. 3-5:5; brackets mine).

Fear too can be understood as an idea: the idea that punishment is inevitable and forthcoming because the separated individual must be a guilty sinner if he is truly separate, as the ego tells us we are; and as we, joined with the ego, continue to tell ourselves we are.

While the ideas of sin and guilt remain mostly unconscious, much of fear rises up to the surface of awareness and gets our attention, if not as raw anxiety, then in some form of conscious discomfort such as anger or a generalized sense of unease and lack of peace. Like guilt, fear takes many forms, some of which are so cleverly disguised that they are not immediately recognized for what they are. An example of fear in disguise is the ego's version of love which in the Course is called *special love*. That is the "love" which is worshipped and pursued in the world, written about, sung about, and celebrated from sidewalk to pulpit. And it is simply fear in disguise, having its origin in guilt and the sense of incompleteness and inner lack that inevitably follows the belief in separation. This form of fear easily turns to hatred, as conventional wisdom recognizes, and hatred is a much more obvious form of fear, though many do not stop to consider that no one hates who is not afraid. And no one needily grasps for special love who is not inwardly guilty and fearful.

Anger and attack thoughts are observed easily enough, but it is not so commonly recognized that the anger one experiences is fear in disguise, or that fear is without justification. But fear of any kind is without a true cause, therefore cannot be justified, because it arises from the mistaken belief in separation, which is why Jesus describes the ego and its fear as illusory.

We make fear real for ourselves, but it is unknown in the Mind of God, therefore unknown in our right mind where the Memory of God resides. Right-mindedness is the solution to fear in any form, legion and cleverly disguised though those forms may be.

Fear serves us as a signal that guilt lurks beneath the surface of awareness where we have accepted the belief in separation. Without that belief and the guilt that follows, there is no fear, even in the face of mortal danger, because the mind that knows its oneness also knows that it is not mortal and cannot be threatened. What any form of fear indicates is that one is in need of forgiveness, which requires the right-minded perceptions of the Holy Spirit or Jesus—forgiveness because one has accepted guilt within. But this requires vigilant self observation, because fear often disguises itself or slips beneath the radar of awareness. When it is recognized for what it is, fear is a certain signal that a change of mind is in order. However, to make constructive use of fear one must both accept responsibility for it as well as cease to attempt to justify it. The Course says:

> Fear is a judgment never justified. Its presence has no meaning but to show you wrote a fearful script, and are afraid accordingly. But not because the thing you fear has fearful meaning in itself (T-30.VII.3:8-10).

> Anger is *never* justified. Attack has *no* foundation. It is here escape from fear begins, and will be made complete. Here is the real world [i.e., forgiven world] given in exchange for dreams of terror. For it is on this forgiveness rests, and is but natural (T-30.VI.1:1-5; bracket mine).

In practicing vigilance for fear, even the slightest clue should not be overlooked, and remember that anger is a form of fear. For instance, in an early ACIM Workbook lesson entitled, "I am determined to see things differently" (W-pI.21), Jesus instructs his student as follows:

> Then close your eyes and search your mind carefully for situations past, present or anticipated that arouse anger in you. The anger may take the form of any reaction ranging from mild irritation to rage. The degree of the emotion you experience does not matter. You will become increasingly aware that a slight twinge of annoyance is nothing but a veil drawn over intense fury.

> Try, therefore, not to let the "little" thoughts of anger escape you in the practice periods. Remember that you do not really recognize what arouses anger in you, and nothing that you believe in this connection means anything. You will probably be tempted to dwell more on some situations or persons than on others, on the fallacious grounds that they are more "obvious." This is not so. It is merely an example of the belief that some forms of attack are more justified than others (W-pI.21.2-3).

Summary

We have seen that there is overlap among the "seething" elements of the ego's "unholy trinity." It is not possible to have one without the other, and they are reciprocal in their causal connection. One leads to another and around they go, so that the ego thought system is self perpetuating until it is observed objectively by that aspect of mind which has the power to choose. This aspect is termed the "decision maker" by Wapnick, also the "observer," and called "the witness" in other spiritual traditions.

The ego is a lie that the Son of God has told himself, hence it is a lie that we all tell ourselves. And if you successfully lie to yourself, how could you ever know it? Something outside of your fixed delusional system would have to intervene. Jesus' *A Course in Miracles* represents such an intervention for those who are open to it. As we continue to explain the psychological principles involved in this remarkable intervention, we will see that not only has the ego made up an illusion of life but, because we believe in that illusion, the ego can be understood as a *way* of life. What Jesus calls *special relationships* are the means by which we pursue the ego way of life. We will next discuss the nature of these relationships at some length.

Chapter 5

Special Relationships

Belief in separation produces the illusion of relationships, so life as we know it is relationships. Perception itself is relational since there must be a perceiver, a perceived and a relationship between the two. And, since a basic principle of the Course's psychology is that there is nothing outside of our mind, all relationships are *in* our mind where perception is subject to either right- or wrong-minded interpretation. When Jesus uses the term *special relationships* in the Course, he is referring to wrong-minded relationships. And since it is our wrong mind—the ego thought system—that first gives rise to perception through projection, all of perception and all relationships *begin* as wrong-minded. In the Course, the ideas of perception and relationship are virtually equivalent, and are derived of the ego thought system whose premise is that separation is real.

So Jesus teaches in ACIM that all relationships begin as *special*, or wrong-minded, relationships because the ego's way of life not only requires relationships, but requires *special* relationships—relationships that are self-serving—in order that the thought system of sin, guilt and fear can be maintained. In a practical sense this means that, until they are corrected by the thought system of our right mind (i.e., the Holy Spirit), all relationships are driven by fear and dedicated to separation, sin and guilt. The ego leads us to have relationships in the interest of self rather than in the interest of true joining and oneness.

Simply put, our lives consist of relationships and, according to the Course, we can participate in them out of fear or love. This depends upon which thought system we, as the maker of decisions in the mind, choose to follow. Special relationships, which are pursued out of fear, are basically hateful; hate being one of the many forms that fear takes in our experience. Though this can be stated simply, it is not so easy to translate into practice, because guilt remains hidden and fear disguises itself as love; and because we cling to ego identification with its "gift" of separation and individuality. That "gift" is accompanied by guilt and fear: fear of oneness, or the all-embracing love that Jesus and the Holy Spirit represent.

In sum, to believe that one is alive in a body is to be in relationship. We are in relationship not only with people, but with everything we perceive; every aspect of our environment: the air we breathe, the earth, the sea, sky, animals, plants, rocks and mountains, our possessions such as clothing,

67

automobiles and houses, etc. We are in relationship with everything we can conceive of, everything we think about: our jobs, social and economic status, politics, our religious beliefs and philosophy of life, ideas about history and culture, scientific theories; indeed, everything we think we know and understand. According to the teachings of Jesus in *A Course in Miracles,* all these relationships begin as special relationships, which are relationships of fear in the service of self-interest and the belief in separation. And all can become relationships of love that serve the truth of oneness.

The particular focus of *A Course in Miracles* is upon the interpersonal relationships that we experience in the dream of separation where forgiveness is both "the key to happiness" (W-pI.121) and the means to awaken from the dualistic dream of separation. But forgiveness ultimately means not only forgiving our special relationship partners, who are in truth merely images of our self we have projected in our mind, but also forgiving our mistaken beliefs about the world and God:

> Forgive the world, and you will understand that everything that God created cannot have an end, and nothing He did not create is real. In this one sentence is our course explained. In this one sentence is our practicing given its one direction. And in this one sentence is the Holy Spirit's whole curriculum specified exactly as it is (M-20.5:7-10).

In Wapnick's *Glossary,* the definition given for special relationships is:

> relationships onto which we project guilt, substituting them for love and our true relationship with God; the defenses that reinforce belief in the scarcity principle while appearing to be undoing it—doing what they would defend against—for special relationships attempt to fill up the perceived lack in ourselves by taking from others who are inevitably seen as separate, thereby reinforcing a guilt that ultimately comes from our believed separation from God: the thought of attack that is the original source of our sense of lack; all relationships in this world begin as special since they begin with the perception of separation and differences, which must then be corrected by the Holy Spirit through forgiveness, making the relationship holy; specialness has two forms: special hate justifies the projection of guilt by attack; special love conceals the attack within the illusion of love, where we believe our special needs are met by special people with special attributes, for which we love them: in this sense, special love is roughly equivalent to dependency, which breeds contempt or hatred.

In this definition, the interrelatedness of various elements in the ego thought system can be seen. The centrality of guilt is emphasized along with the ideas of scarcity and attack, which are important dimensions of the special relationship that we shall discuss later. As always in our discussion of Jesus' psychology, what will make these ideas most meaningful is to be able to identify them in one's own experiences of self and others.

Since it is in special relationships that we act out the ego thought system in our dream lives, these relationships make up the curriculum for the forgiveness classroom which the world becomes when understood from the perspective of *A Course in Miracles*. But again, it must be understood that both the classroom and the special relationships that make up its lessons are in our *mind*, not in the world, which of course is a dream *in* our mind. Forgiveness takes place in our mind and requires a *change of mind*, not an attempt to change behavior without changing the thought system that led to it: "This is a course in cause and not effect" (T-21.VII.7:8). What goes on or does not go on in the dream of relationships among bodies *follows* from thought. To repeat an important point, what we forgive are *images* we have projected *in* our mind, which means that we are actually forgiving aspects of ourselves and the guilt we have accepted into our minds but attempted to be rid of through projection. Projection *is* image making. There is no life outside the mind. There is nothing outside: *ideas leave not their source*:

> There is nothing outside you. That is what you must ultimately learn, for it is the realization that the Kingdom of Heaven is restored to you…Heaven is not a place nor a condition. It is merely an awareness of perfect oneness, and the knowledge that there is nothing else; nothing outside this oneness, and nothing else within (T-18.VI.1-2, 5-6).

In our special relationships, we try to defy this truth of oneness: we believe and act out the ego's basic principle of separation, consequently guilt, largely unknown to us, informs our thinking and drives our behavior, because guilt inevitably accompanies belief in separation. We live lives of fear, but think we love. We seek to find a heaven on earth, but wind up in hell:

> The special relationship is a strange and unnatural ego device for joining hell [separation] and Heaven [Oneness], and making them indistinguishable. And the attempt to find the imagined "best" of both worlds has merely led to fantasies of both, and to the inability to perceive either as it is. The special relationship is the triumph of this confusion. It is a kind of union from which union [oneness] is excluded, and the basis for the attempt at union rests on exclusion [separation: specialness]. What better example could there be of the ego's maxim, "Seek but do not find?"[1] (T-16.V.6; brackets mine)

---

[1] This maxim of the ego is important enough that it is mentioned in several other places throughout the Course. See: T-12.IV.1:4, T-12.V.7:1, W-pI.71.4:2 and M-13.5:8.

69

In the Course, Jesus has a great deal to say about special relationships, but to state the basic point concisely, our primary (and ultimately our *only*) special relationship is with our idea of self: with our separate, individual ego identity. All other special relationship idols, human or otherwise, are sought in order to enhance and support this self by: 1) attempting to obtain from someone or something which seems to be outside of self a substitute for the love the ego says we lost in separating from Oneness; and, 2) by securing a target upon which to project responsibility and blame (guilt) for the separation. Our goal as egos is to have our specialness—our separate, individual self—but not to be responsible for the consequences, which means we must attempt to divest ourselves of the ego's searing guilt over the "sin" of separation, as well as to assuage the pain arising from the seeming loss of love by substituting special love. Essentially, "special love," represents the idea that love can be individual and exclusive rather than universal and *in*clusive of all and everyone; therefore it constitutes an attack on Oneness that amounts to hate.

Specialness, separation and sin are basically equivalent ideas. Speaking in terms of the illusion of linear time and the myth of the ladder separation led us down, the Son's desire to be separate and to have an individual existence apart from Oneness was the original wish to be special. In attempting to fulfill this wish, the Son hoped to establish a special relationship with God, and this desire led to the original authority problem, which Jesus says "*is* 'the root of all evil'" (T-3.VI.7:3). Our authority problem with God is the "root of all evil" because it represents an attempt to establish separation as real; therefore it is both the prototype for all special relationships and the source of all our misery within the illusory world:

> I have spoken of different symptoms [i.e., forms of psychological and physical discomfort], and at that level [of the body] there is almost endless variation. There is, however, only one cause for all of them: the authority problem. This *is* "the root of all evil." Every symptom the ego makes involves a contradiction in terms, because the mind is split between the ego [the desire to be special] and the Holy Spirit [the truth of oneness], so that whatever the ego makes is incomplete and contradictory. This untenable position is the result of the authority problem which, because it accepts the one inconceivable thought as its premise [i.e., the thought of separation], can produce only ideas that are inconceivable. The issue of authority is really a question of authorship. When you have an authority problem, it is always because you believe you are the author of yourself and project your delusion onto others. You then perceive the situation as one in which others are literally fighting you for your authorship [i.e., we perceive others as competing for specialness]. This is the fundamental error of all those who believe they have usurped the power of God. This belief is very frightening to them, but hardly troubles God [Who "does not know of separation," P-2.VII.1:12] (T-3.VI.7-8:5; brackets mine).

Jesus teaches in the Course that every relationship we have in the world derives from the nature of the relationship we consciously or unconsciously imagine we have with God. Even those who deny the existence of whatever they think the term "God" means still have a relationship with God in the sense that they have an *idea* of "God" which they care about. As with our relationship to the idea of Oneness or God, in our human relationships we either perceive ourselves as being separate with different and competing interests, or as being fundamentally the same with shared interests. Some version of the original authority problem always can be found in our special relationships wherein we seek specialness and experience the need for attention which comes from our ego's desire to establish its individuality through special recognition from God.

The original authority problem resulted in the first temper tantrum, according to the Course, because it was not possible for Oneness to grant special recognition—not possible for God to pay attention to us—and so we, as the ego-identified Son who experienced conflict, went to war with God (therefore with our true Self) making up a world of special relationships and a god of specialness:

> You were at peace until you asked for special favor. And God did not give it for the request was alien to Him, and you could not ask this of a Father Who truly loved His Son. Therefore you made of Him an unloving father, demanding of Him what only such a father could give. And the peace of God's Son was shattered, for he no longer understood his Father. He feared what he had made [i.e., a world of separation, differences and conflict], but still more did he fear his real Father [because he felt guilty], having attacked his own glorious equality with Him.

> In peace he needed nothing and asked for nothing. In war he demanded everything and found nothing. For how could the gentleness of love respond to his demands [to be separate and special], except by departing in peace and returning to the Father? If the Son did not wish to remain in peace, he could not remain at all. For a darkened mind cannot live in the light, and it must seek a place of darkness where it can believe it is where it is not. God did not allow this to happen. Yet you demanded that it happen, and therefore believed that it was so (T-13.III.10:2-11; brackets mine).

Oneness could not grant special recognition because to do so would require that God include the idea of separation in His *knowledge*, therefore accord reality to separation and become a perceiver. But in the Mind of God knowledge *is* Oneness: "Perception has no function in God, and does not exist" (W-pI.43.2:2). "God does not perceive at all" (W-pI.193.2:4).

71

Because of the impossibility of establishing a special relationship with God, the ego-identified Son invented a god of his own, as we saw on the third rung of the ladder separation led us down. This was a god in the image and likeness of its maker, the ego: "a jealous god" (Exodus 34:14); a god who gives special recognition and who withholds it as well; a god of vengeance who has temper tantrums and goes on rampages of destruction; a god who wants special favor, who grants special favor and who makes special bargains (covenants) with special people; a god who believes in separation and calls it "original sin," therefore fosters guilt and demands blood sacrifice as atonement for sin. The ego's god is a god of fear and hatred masquerading as a god of love, just as special love is fear and hatred in disguise.

All of the characteristics of the ego's god of specialness can be witnessed in our worldly special relationships within the dream of separation where we seek attention and become angry or depressed when we don't get it; where we seek special love from special people to the exclusion of other people whom we may hate openly; where we make bargains and engage in manipulations to obtain attention and companionship; where we equate love with sacrifice, demanding sacrifice of ourselves and our special love partners, and wreaking vengeance upon those who become our special hate objects (often former special love objects who have disappointed us, frustrating our need to be special).

By way of summarizing our discussion to this point, and before proceeding to examine some corollary elements of the ego thought system found in special relationships, below is presented an extensive series of excerpts from Jesus' discussion of special relationships as found in the Course:

> Because of guilt, all special relationships have elements of fear in them. This is why they shift and change so frequently. They are not based on changeless love alone. And love, where fear has entered, cannot be depended on because it is not perfect. In His function as Interpreter of what you made, the Holy Spirit uses special relationships, which you have chosen to support the ego, as learning experiences that point to truth. Under His teaching, every relationship becomes a lesson in love.

> The Holy Spirit knows no one is special. Yet He also perceives that you have made special relationships, which He would purify [through forgiveness] and not let you destroy [through separation, guilt and fear]. However unholy the reason you made them may be, He can translate them into holiness by removing as much fear as you will let Him. You can place any relationship under His care and be sure that it will not result in pain, if you offer Him your willingness to have it serve no need but His. All the guilt in it arises from your use of it. All the love from His.

Do not, then, be afraid to let go your imagined needs, which would destroy the relationship. Your only need is His (T-15.V.4-5:7; bracket mine).

In looking at the special relationship, it is necessary first to realize that it involves a great amount of pain. Anxiety, despair, guilt and attack all enter into it, broken into by periods in which they seem to be gone. All these must be understood for what they are. Whatever form they take, they are always an attack on the self to make the other guilty. I have spoken of this before, but there are some aspects of what is really being attempted that have not been touched upon.

Very simply, the attempt to make guilty is always directed against God. For the ego would have you see Him, and Him alone, as guilty, leaving the Sonship open to attack and unprotected from it. The special love relationship is the ego's chief weapon for keeping you from Heaven. It does not appear to be a weapon, but if you consider how you value it and why, you will realize what it must be.

The special love relationship is the ego's most boasted gift, and one which has the most appeal to those unwilling to relinquish guilt. The "dynamics" of the ego are clearest here, for counting on the attraction of this offering, the fantasies that center around it are often quite overt. Here they are usually judged to be acceptable and even natural. No one considers it bizarre to love and hate together, and even those who believe that hate is sin merely feel guilty, but do not correct it. This is the "natural" condition of the separation, and those who learn that it is not natural at all seem to be the unnatural ones. For this world *is* the opposite of Heaven, being made to be its opposite, and everything here takes a direction exactly opposite of what is true. In Heaven, where the meaning of love is known, love is the same as union. Here, where the illusion of love [i.e., *special* love] is accepted in love's place, love is perceived as separation and exclusion.

It is in the special relationship, born of the hidden wish for special love from God, that the ego's hatred triumphs. For the special relationship is the renunciation of the Love of God, and the attempt to secure for the self the specialness that He denied. It is essential to the preservation of the ego that you believe this specialness is not hell, but Heaven. For the ego would never have you see that separation could only be loss, being the one condition in which Heaven could not be (T-16.V.1-4; bracket mine).

All special relationships have sin [separation] as their goal. For they are bargains with reality, toward which the seeming union is adjusted. Forget not this; to bargain is to set a limit, and any brother with whom you have a limited relationship, you hate. You may attempt to keep the bargain in the name of "fairness," sometimes demanding payment of yourself, perhaps more often of the other. Thus in the "fairness" you attempt to ease the guilt that comes from the accepted purpose of the relationship [i.e., separation].

And that is why the Holy Spirit must change its purpose to make it useful to Him and harmless to you (T-21.III.1; brackets mine).

Corollaries of Specialness: Ancillary Elements in the Ego Thought System

To state this important point again, according to the Course, the thought system which we as mind and decision maker choose to follow determines our beliefs and attitudes about God, which in turn are reflected in the nature of our worldly relationships. Special relationships are based on the belief in separation—separation from the Love of God—and all that it entails; while forgiveness transforms special relationships into what the Course terms the *holy relationship*[1] which reflects the truth of oneness. Ultimately, there is only one special relationship: our relationship with the ego. When we identify with the ego, all of our relationships are special, and in fact the idea of *relationship* begins with the ego's belief in separation. Likewise, there is really only one holy relationship. When we are right-minded, we identify with Jesus or the Holy Spirit (or identify with spirit and the Love of God, however one understands that). In that right-minded identification the belief in separation is undone and all our relationships become holy, because in truth we *are* one, and relationship is illusion. The love of the Holy Spirit and Jesus leaves no one out of its embrace, so it is not possible to be truly right-minded yet retain any vestige of a special relationship which would exclude something or someone from love.

There are several rather specific ways in which the ego's thought system of separation, sin, guilt and fear is experienced and acted out in our special relationships. Since "all special relationships have elements of fear in them" (T-15.V.4), each of these elements is somehow associated with fear. They are: 1) scarcity-lack-and-deprivation; 2) attack; 3) sacrifice; 4) suffering-victimization, and; 5) judgment. These ego corollaries already have been discussed to some extent, but further discussion of them is in order since, according to the Course, they, along with the three basic elements of the ego system, form the template upon which our individual lives in the illusion are constructed. Thus, in explaining and describing the special relationship and these elements, Jesus is painting a picture of worldly life as it appears when the veil of pretense has been removed. It is not a pretty picture, but Jesus continually emphasizes in the Course that "freedom lies in looking at it" (T-16.IV.1:1). There is no freedom in pretense and self-deception, only perhaps an illusion of freedom which denial attempts to achieve. But denial,

---

[1] In Wapnick's *Glossary* the term *holy relationship* is defined as: "the Holy Spirit's means to undo the unholy or special relationship by shifting the goal of guilt to the goal of forgiveness or truth; the process of forgiveness by which one who had perceived another as separate joins with him in his mind through Christ's vision."

dissociation and even sublimation merely obscure the problem of separation and do not resolve it. Forgiveness, which follows from a change of mind, resolves all seeming problems which stem from the single problem of separation. But before forgiveness really makes any sense, Jesus emphasizes that one must be clear about what it is that needs forgiveness, and just how unsatisfying is a life dedicated to specialness. So in the interest of continuing to see what Jesus would have his students find beneath the ego's veil of deception, we will examine the five corollary elements that accompany sin, guilt and fear.

Scarcity and lack, which were mentioned in Wapnick's definition of *special relationships*, are closely associated with guilt and fear. As we will see, the principle of scarcity is defined as an aspect of guilt. That is because the illusion of separation begins with the idea that we, as the Son of God, are incomplete because we lack specialness (or individuality) which God supposedly withheld for Himself. Then, our seeking to be separate and special puts us in conflict with God, giving rise to guilt. And implicit in guilt is yet again a sense of scarcity, lack and incompletion that must accompany the belief in separation. Guilt basically says: "In separating from Oneness, you have destroyed Love and that is a monumental sin; therefore you have lost your innocence as the Son of God and are unworthy of love." Thus, the idea of love's scarcity, along with a sense of inner lack, goes with the unworthiness and self-condemnation that is guilt.

The illusory body and world are ideas that were projected in an attempt to escape guilt, but since *ideas leave not their source*, that attempt was unsuccessful. As long as ego identity persists with its belief in separation, guilt remains in the mind so the attempt to escape guilt through projection must continue. And now the body becomes both the means of projecting guilt as well as the target of projection. Wapnick has said that the world and all materiality can be understood as crystallized guilt. Likewise, it can be said that the body is guilt personified:

> The body will remain guilt's messenger, and will act as it directs as long as you believe that guilt is real. For the reality of guilt is the illusion that seems to make it [guilt] heavy and opaque, impenetrable, and a real foundation for the ego's thought system (T-18.IX.5:1-2; bracket mine).

> Minds are joined; bodies are not. Only by assigning to the mind the properties of the body does separation *seem* to be possible. And it is mind that *seems* to be fragmented and private and alone. Its guilt, which keeps it separate, is projected to the body, which suffers and dies because it is attacked to hold the separation in the mind, and let it not know its Identity

75

[i.e., sickness, suffering and death are the ego's "proof" that the body, therefore separation, is real; our Identity as spirit and mind is thus denied] (T-18.VI.3:1-4; italics and brackets mine).

Since the idea of guilt is manifested in the body, scarcity is literally incorporated into our bodies at the "gut level" where one form in which it is experienced is hunger. Another form that scarcity takes is seen in the act of breathing where a physiological mechanism is set into motion by a threat posed in the form of a relative absence of oxygen in company with an overabundance of carbon dioxide. In other words, breathing itself is a fear response to a form of scarcity, as anyone who has been deprived of oxygen for even a relatively short period of time can attest. In this fact, we can see an example of why it can be said that, "Fear is the one emotion of the world." We could as well say that fear is the one emotion of the body. And of course sexual motivation is yet another example of the way in which the sense of scarcity and lack in our mind drives behavior within the illusion. All forms of dependency and addiction similarly have their roots in the scarcity belief with its accompanying feelings of emptiness, incompleteness and lack. In Wapnick's *Glossary* the "scarcity principle" is defined as follows:

> an aspect of guilt; the belief that we are empty and incomplete, lacking what we need; this leads to our seeking idols or special relationships to fill the scarcity we experience within ourselves; inevitably projected into feelings of deprivation, wherein we believe others are depriving us of the peace which in reality *we* have taken from ourselves; in contrast to God's principle of abundance.[2]

What could the belief that we are separate from the Love of God produce but a sense of emptiness, incompleteness, inner lack and desperate hunger for love? It is obvious that the principle of scarcity operates in special relationships since an important reason for seeking them is the sense of incompleteness that says something is lacking within. In her own way, Mother Teresa understood this. She often spoke of poverty, not as an absence of money and food, but as spiritual poverty and hunger for love. In June of 1982, Mother Teresa spoke at Harvard University, saying:

> You will, I'm sure, ask me: "Where is that hunger in our country? Where is that nakedness in our country? Where is that homelessness in our country?" Yes, there *is* hunger. Maybe not hunger for a piece of bread, but there is a

---

[2] For purposes of clarification, "God's principle of abundance" only applies to mind and spirit, having nothing to do with the body. The *Glossary* definition of abundance states in part: "God's Son can never lack anything or be in need, since God's gifts, given eternally in creation, are always with him." In the Course, *creation* has to do with Mind, Thought and spirit, while "God's gifts" refer to love, joy and peace.

terrible hunger for *love*. We all experience that in our lives—the pain, the loneliness. We must have the courage to recognize the poor you may have right in your own family.[3]

And she could well have added, as Jesus might say in *A Course in Miracles,* "Have the courage to recognize that poverty and hunger in your own mind and heart." There are many examples of the scarcity principle which can be observed in our lives. One prominent example is seen in the fact that food is a central concern around the world: for some, having enough food is a problem and for others overeating is a problem. One might ask whether there would ever be starvation in the world if humanity operated out of the principle of love and abundance. There is enough food to go around, but not enough people whose minds are free of guilt, therefore of the belief in scarcity with its inner sense of lack, so that they themselves could be generous. Another question one might ask is whether there would be a problem with overeating in the presence of a genuine inner sense of abundance and spiritual fulfillment. It seems evident that both the absence of sufficient food and the problem of overeating come from the inner sense of scarcity and lack which accompany guilt. Likewise, one can see the principle of scarcity at work in concerns about money; concerns which are portrayed in the fear and greed that drive the stock market and produce dishonesty in both government and the world of commerce.

Note how we continue to see here the way in which elements of the ego thought system intertwine and reciprocate. A sense of inner lack accompanies guilt, while fear is implicit in the scarcity belief. The belief in scarcity motivates greedy behavior, so guilt is reinforced; therefore more fear is promoted in the mind, which in turn reinforces a sense of vulnerability, scarcity and lack. Now more fearful, greedy behavior is stimulated, producing more guilt and fear, and so on and around and on.

The principle of *one or the other* again comes into play with the belief in scarcity, not only with the ego idea that in order to *have* one must *take,* but in the thought that if one is somehow incomplete and lacking then someone else must have what is missing. Thus, as the ego seeks to divest itself of responsibility for the consequences of separation, the inner sense of emptiness produces the idea that one's scarcity and lack must come about as the result of someone else's abundance: "There was enough to go around until someone else stole what was rightfully mine." This idea of scarcity caused by the ego way of thinking produces the *principle of deprivation,* which claims that my needs were sacrificed so that another's could be met.

---

[3] Conroy, Susan. *Mother Teresa's Lessons of Love and Secrets of Sanctity,* p.199. Huntington, Indiana: Our Sunday Visitor, Inc., 2003.

I was deprived; therefore I am justified in taking back from others what is rightfully mine. In this way of thinking fear and greed are rationalized while there is complete failure to recognize that the sense of lack and consequent idea of deprivation are the result of one's *own* self-sacrifice in embracing the ego thought system with its belief in separation.

That embrace leads to identification as a body, which the Course calls the ego's symbol (T-15.IX.2:3); and as we have seen, the body is the home of guilt, scarcity, hunger for love, and spiritual poverty—a poverty the body can never resolve and a hunger the body can never satisfy: "Seek but do not find."

> As long as you perceive the body as your reality, so long will you perceive yourself as lonely and deprived. And so long will you also perceive yourself as a victim of sacrifice, justified in sacrificing others. For who could thrust Heaven and its Creator aside without a sense of sacrifice and loss? And who could suffer sacrifice and loss without attempting to restore himself? Yet how could you accomplish this yourself, when the basis of your attempts is the belief in the reality of the deprivation? Deprivation breeds attack, being the belief that attack is justified. And as long as you would retain the deprivation, attack becomes salvation and sacrifice becomes love (T-15.XI.5).

In this paragraph are seen three other ancillary ego elements—victimization, sacrifice and attack—included with a discussion of deprivation which follows from the sense of inner lack or scarcity. This confluence once again demonstrates the intertwining nature of the various ego elements, and is a reminder that the ego thought system is a complete package. Discussing each of its elements is helpful insofar as it permits us to observe in our experience what it is that Jesus is describing when he talks about the ego thought system and the nature of special relationships. However, it should be noted that ego identification carries with it *all* of the elements of the ego thought system along with *all* of the consequences of those thoughts, which consequences will be experienced in some form within the dream of specialness.

As the definition of *scarcity* states, another idea produced by the belief in separation, and associated with the consequent inner sense of lack, is the notion that one must seek completion outside of oneself. In other words, the inner sense of scarcity or lack leads us to seek completion in a special relationship where someone or something other than self is perceived as possessing what seems to be lacking within. Of course what is lacking is love, because the ego system begins with the idea of being separate from love. What the ego would have us seek as a means of completion and replacement for the missing love is specialness. Thus the special love relationship between individuals involves a bargain wherein two people who feel incomplete attempt a negotiation to achieve completeness; a negotiation which cannot succeed, but only reinforces guilt and fear along with sustaining the inner sense of incompletion:

> Most curious of all is the concept of the self which the ego fosters in the special relationship. This "self" seeks the relationship to make itself complete. Yet when it finds the special relationship in which it thinks it can accomplish this it gives itself away, and tries to "trade" itself for the self of another...Each partner tries to sacrifice the self he does not want for one he thinks he would prefer. And he feels guilty for the "sin" of taking, and of giving nothing of value in return. How much value can he place upon a self that he would give away to get a "better" one?
>
> The "better" self the ego seeks is always one that is more special. And whoever seems to possess a special self is "loved" for what can be taken from him. Where both partners see this special self in each other, the ego sees "a union made in Heaven." For neither one will recognize that he has asked for hell [i.e., guilt and fear which must result from the "sin" of separation or specialness] and so he will not interfere with the ego's illusion of Heaven, which it offered him to interfere with Heaven [i.e., true Oneness]. Yet if all illusions are of fear, and they can be of nothing else, the illusion of Heaven is nothing more than an "attractive" form of fear, in which the guilt is buried deep and rises in the form of "love."
>
> The appeal of hell lies only in the terrible attraction of guilt [attractive because the survival of the ego depends upon it], which the ego holds out to those who place their faith in littleness [i.e., the separated self which incorporates the sense of scarcity and lack]. The conviction of littleness lies in every special relationship, for only the deprived could value specialness. The demand for specialness, and the perception of the giving of specialness as an act of love, would make love hateful [because specialness—separation—is hateful, being an attack on God]. The real purpose of the special relationship, in strict accordance with the ego's goals, is to destroy reality and substitute illusion. For the ego is itself an illusion, and only illusions can be the witnesses to its "reality" (T-16.V.7:1-3, 5-7; 8-9; brackets mine).

Here two more ego principles are observed operating in the special relationship bargain. One is the idea of *giving in order to get*. In other words, one has to give up something of self—sacrifice—in order to obtain from another that which hopefully would satisfy the sense of incompletion and lack. This is in contrast to the Holy Spirit's law of oneness that says love is freely given, not exclusive, requires no sacrifice, and increases as it is shared: the more your mind allows love to be extended through it, the more love is in your awareness.

The second ego rule seen operating in the special relationship as discussed in the quoted passages is closely related to the principle of deprivation. This is the principle that, *you have what you have taken* (T-23.II.9:2). In the world this seems to be an obvious truth. In fact, in order to have, you *must* take; hence you must either deprive or be deprived. Therefore, seeking for specialness involves hunting for prey from which to take what one thinks one needs to survive. In fact, all of the means of obtaining food in human cultures—hunting, gathering and agriculture—act out this cannibalistic ego notion based on the idea that one's survival depends upon taking life from something else, whether it be animal or vegetable, microorganism or macroorganism. The same dynamics can be observed in the negotiations and rituals of romantic love and marriage where it seems that one's survival, both psychologically and physically, is dependent upon taking from another. In the special love relationship sacrifice is assumed and "giving to get" is regarded as a healthy relationship practice.

In the myth of separation, the original cannibalism took place when it seemed that the ego-identified Son destroyed God and took His Life: stole specialness from Oneness, thereby destroying It. In contrast to this principle of taking in order to have, the Holy Spirit teaches, "To have, give all to all" (T-6.V(A)). As with all teachings of the Holy Spirit, this applies only at the level of mind or *content* where thoughts are retained and increased by giving, and where love is fundamentally all there is to give and receive. The principle cannot apply at the level of *form*—the level of illusion—because fundamental to that level is the principle of scarcity. In the illusion, generosity depends upon individuals and the particular expression of mind that they might represent. No matter how lovingly motivated, it is not possible for an individual to give all to all at the materialistic level of separation. Even in an ideal world where the love of Jesus and the Holy Spirit would be universal, still there would be some who had more or different *things* than others, but that would not be interpreted in terms of scarcity and deprivation, nor would survival depend upon it. In fact, in the presence of a universally healed mind where the Atonement had been accepted and the principle of oneness ruled, the illusion of separation would dissolve along with the illusion of a perceptual world.

At this point in our discussion, the rapacious nature of the special relationship described by Jesus is starkly apparent. Not only do special relationships operate out of scarcity, lack and deprivation, but they are established by murder, and dedicated to it in the sense that separation, which is their foundation, requires the shattering of Oneness: the murder of God. Figuratively speaking, specialness is ripped in bloody triumph from the slain body of God. And special relationships go beyond murder to what is essentially cannibalism. The voracious and insatiable appetite that accompanies guilt, along with its sense of scarcity and inner lack, demands the sacrifice and consumption of other life. The inner sense of emptiness and lack engendered by separation requires that the life of someone or something else must be sacrificed in order that the life of self can be maintained, whether in physical or psychological terms. In fact, sacrifice is another of the corollary elements yet to be discussed.

One or the other—the law of the jungle, "kill or be killed"—which rules life in the separated world means not only that another must be sacrificed in order for my interests to be served, but that I must consume some portion of the other's life, symbolically or literally, in order to nourish my own: in order for me to have a dollar, it must be taken from someone else; in order for me to eat, something must die; in order for me to have love it must be taken from somebody else and nobody else can have it. Once again, we can see the foundational paradigm for this in the original idea of separation where the oneness of God would have had to be destroyed in order that the Son could have a separate, special identity; and further, that the life of specialness literally must feed off of the Life of Oneness:

> The special relationship must be recognized for what it is; a senseless ritual in which strength is extracted from the death of God, and invested in His killer as the sign that form [illusion, materiality] has triumphed over content [mind, thought], and love has lost its meaning [because love is of the mind, not the body]. Would you want this to be possible, even apart from its evident impossibility? (T-16.V.12:4-5).

Attack has been mentioned frequently in our discussion thus far. It goes hand-in-hand with scarcity and fear as well as with other elements of the ego thought system. It is a common, obvious phenomenon in our perceptual world, not only in behavior, but also in thinking, where it is not unusual to be preoccupied with attack thoughts and fantasies, often in the form of angry criticism and condemnation. According to the Course, this is because attack is implicit in the idea of separation. So it should be no surprise that attack is evident everywhere in the world throughout its history; from international warfare to tribal warfare, family feuds and the sports arena; to the interior of an automobile where we find a most illustrative, everyday example of the ego thought system in operation. Almost everyone who either operates an automobile or has been a passenger at some time or another, if not very frequently, has found himself or herself angry at another driver. The term "road rage" was coined in late twentieth century America because of increasing awareness of this phenomenon along with the increasing frequency and severity of angry incidents between drivers. In the context of our exposure of the ego thought system it is instructive that the term "road rage" actually has a definition in the latest edition of the *American Heritage Dictionary of the English Language*, as well as in the popular Web-based free encyclopedia *Wikipedia*, where one finds the following explanation:

> Road rage (also road violence, road terrorism) is the common name for deliberately dangerous and/or violent behaviour under the influence of heightened anger, by any motor vehicle operator, affecting the safety of one or more other operators or bystanders. Road rage is most usually an egocentric reaction of anger to personal frustration with any road condition or other motorist behaviour which thwarts the personal desires of the road rager.[1]

This definition finds a perfect fit under the category of specialness and special relationships as explained in the Course. It can be understood as an example of the authority problem where we find ourselves competing with others for specialness. This competition begins with the Son's imagined competition with God for the power to create life wherein the desire to be author of one's self involves setting lines of demarcation in the interest of separation; of having boundaries upon which others must not infringe. When other drivers cut us off in traffic, the ego sees a competitor for specialness; a competitor for what the ego regards as a place in heaven. Likewise, when someone else beats us to a parking space, or we can find no parking spaces, frustration is likely to ensue because the ego operates out of the principle of scarcity and deprivation, believing that it is entitled to the special status represented by a parking space which is in short supply: *one or the other*. In any case, whatever the symbolic significance of parking spaces and experiences in traffic, specialness basically says, "me first and damned be he who interferes." That is the essence of attack thinking.

In the interest of understanding the Course's psychology, and of finding practical applications of it in one's own life, it can be fruitful to ask why one would ever experience loss of peace over the behavior of another, whether a fellow motorist or in some other worldly arena, let alone why someone else's mistakes should give us cause for anger, attack, judgmental condemnation, and rejection? And one also might observe how the automobile has become an extension of self so that personal significance (i.e., specialness) is assigned to a mere box made up of plastic and metal, fitted with wheels and a motor, and intended to transport the body. And in connection with the subject of attack, it is interesting to note the popularity in the early twenty-first

---

[1] Wikipedia contributors. "Road Rage," *Wikipedia, The Free Encyclopedia*, http://en.wikipedia.org/wiki/Road_rage (accessed July 10, 2006).

century in the United States of large, muscular looking vehicles which may have a military appearance and which sometimes sport signs and bumper stickers announcing things like: "Attack Vehicle," "Road Warrior," "Truck of Destruction," "Monster Masher," "Dominator," and "Eat My Dust."

Since the ego thought system essentially begins with attack, attack is woven into the fabric of the special relationships which constitute the ego's way of life: "Believing in the power of attack, the ego wants attack" (T-8.IX.6:8). Consequently, the individual personality and its body are always attacking and under attack, if not in relationship to other personalities and bodies, then in relationship to disease organisms, environmental pollution, "natural" disasters, climate and weather, economic and social conditions, and finally in relationship to the withering effects of age. One of the implications of the idea that "fear is the one emotion of the world" is that we are always involved in attack and defense; always at war: at war with one another, but also at war with disease, with poverty, with aging, with crime, and indeed most so-called peace movements amount to being at war with war.

In the context of Jesus' system of psychology, perception itself may be understood as an attack on *knowledge* that attempts to replace the truth of oneness with the lie of differences. In other words, simply perceiving another as a body separate from oneself amounts to an attack. The ego *must* attack in order to maintain its illusion of separation, but Jesus tells us that the Holy Spirit can turn attack into a blessing which sees the truth of sameness beyond the appearance of differences, thus we are not condemned to lives of attack and defense unless we so choose. As has been said, the value of looking carefully at the ego thought system lies in the ability of observation to make another choice possible.

Given Jesus' explanation of the centrality of attack in the ego thought system, the student of *A Course in Miracles* ought not to be puzzled by the widespread social phenomena of warfare and crime, not to mention marital and family discord.

In Kenneth Wapnick's *Glossary*, attack is defined as follows:

> the attempt to justify the projection of guilt onto others, demonstrating their sinfulness and guilt so that we may feel free of it; because attack is always a projection of responsibility for the separation, it is never justified; also used to denote the thought of separation from God, for which we believe God will attack and punish us in return.
> (Note -- "attack" and "anger" are used as virtual synonyms.)

As soon as the idea of separation was taken seriously, the ego defined it as an attack on God, therefore as sin. Guilt and fear followed immediately, and it is fear of the punishment which guilt deserves that motivates attack in our world of special relationships. To repeat a portion of a previously quoted passage: "If you did not feel guilty you could not attack, for condemnation is the root of attack. It is the judgment of one mind by another as unworthy of love and deserving of punishment" (T-13.IN.1:1-2).

As the *Glossary* definition points out, the basis of attack is the desire to be rid of responsibility for separation by projecting guilt onto another and then justifying this projection of blame. We do this by finding all sorts of "good reasons" why others should be condemned and punished. As long as we are unable to make of life a classroom in forgiveness so that we can rise above the battleground which the ego makes of life, we will certainly find "good reasons" to justify our fear, hatred, condemnation and attack. And this effort is helped by the fact that the others in our world, being projections of the same mind, are also busy finding ways to justify their fear, hatred, condemnation and attack. In the dance of guilt, fear and attack there is no room for forgiveness, therefore no way out:

> You who feel threatened by this changing world, its twists of fortune and its bitter jests, its brief relationships and all the "gifts" it merely lends to take away again; attend this lesson well. The world provides no safety. It is rooted in attack, and all its "gifts" of seeming safety are illusory deceptions. It attacks, and then attacks again. No peace of mind is possible where danger threatens thus.

> The world gives rise but to defensiveness. For threat brings anger, anger makes attack seem reasonable, honestly provoked, and righteous in the name of self-defense...The mind is now confused, and knows not where to turn to find escape from its imaginings.

> It is as if a circle held it fast, wherein another circle bound it and another one in that, until escape no longer can be hoped for nor obtained. Attack, defense; defense, attack, become the circles of the hours and the days that bind the mind in heavy bands of steel with iron overlaid, returning but to start again. There seems to be no break nor ending in the ever tightening grip of the imprisonment upon the mind (W-pI.153.1-2:1, 6; 3).

It is actually fear ("the one emotion of the world") that imprisons our mind; and again, the fundamental fear behind attack in our lives is the fear of punishment, which the ideas of sin and guilt demand. Anger and attack are simply forms of fear. They depend upon the perception that the object of our attack is not only separate, but threatening us, and hardly deserving of being included in the embrace of brotherhood. No one who is without fear becomes angry and attacks, because those who are without fear are without the ego's guilt. They know of their own innocence and that of their brothers: they are right-minded.

In the following passage Jesus is speaking to us as mind from the right-minded perspective of the Holy Spirit Who knows that separation is not true, that all minds are joined as one, and that the mind cannot attack itself. Just as separation is illusion, so too is fear. Thus, anger and attack, or the perception of being attacked, are without justification, because they are based on the ego lie of separation:

> The relationship of anger to attack is obvious, but the relationship of anger to fear is not always so apparent. Anger always involves projection of separation, which must ultimately be accepted as one's own responsibility, rather than being blamed on others. Anger cannot occur unless you believe that you have been attacked, that your attack is justified in return, and that you are in no way responsible for it. Given these three wholly irrational premises, the equally irrational conclusion that a brother is worthy of attack rather than of love must follow. What can be expected from insane premises except an insane conclusion? The way to undo an insane conclusion is to consider the sanity of the premises on which it rests. You cannot *be* attacked, attack *has* no justification, and you *are* responsible for what you believe (T-6.IN.1).

The reason that the premises of attack are irrational and insane is that they rest upon the ego's basic premise that separation is real. Without separation, attack is impossible; and we *are* responsible for choosing to believe in the reality of separation.

Further, the *knowledge* that separation is impossible is only available in our right mind. The intellectual concept that fear is without foundation in truth, therefore anger and attack are never justified, may be helpful, but it is not sufficient to bring about the true relief from fear, anger and attack that a change of mind, hence a real change in perception, brings about. Genuine forgiveness and true peace of mind cannot be faked; they do not derive from the intellectual games of manipulating concepts and beliefs, but from a genuine change of mind at the level of spirit.

In order to appreciate fully the teaching that anger and attack are never justified, it is important to distinguish between what is going on in the mind and what seems to take place in the world where people engage in attack behavior. A practical point in understanding the relationship between fear and attack is the realization that one does not *have* to take personally the behavior of another, either in relationship to oneself or to those people and groups with whom one identifies. Therefore, one does not have to *interpret* the behavior of another as a personal attack. Rather, attacking behavior can be seen right-mindedly as coming from guilt and fear, and as calling for forgiveness rather than condemnation. But again, right-minded perception and interpretation are not mere intellectual feats. They depend upon *actually being* right-minded.

Additionally, it must be pointed out that the teachings of the Course are not intended to discredit common sense as long as we believe we are bodies and that the world is real. The purpose of Jesus' psychology is to make us aware that we are mind, not body, and that as mind we have a choice of thought systems which will determine how we perceive and interpret our experiences within the dream of separation. But we are not asked to deny the body and its world. Instead, we are offered a way to be loving and peaceful in a world that is necessarily attacking, because it was born of attack. In practicing Jesus' psychology, one can learn how to access the mind. Then, by choosing to identify with the love that he represents, one becomes a teacher of peace *by example* who does not display or reinforce attack thinking.

In the name of common sense within the illusion, at the level of our belief in the reality of the body and the world one can have a compassionate, forgiving *attitude* of mind yet nevertheless take reasonable steps to protect the body against attack, even appealing to law enforcement and litigation in the process of doing so. Those who are responsible for violating the established laws of society are "guilty" (i.e., accountable) in terms of the law, but need not be condemned as guilty sinners. Laws can be enforced without an attitude of vengeance and attack, and without losing sight of the common spiritual brotherhood we all share. Likewise, one can seek to change the law without an attitude of attack. But again, there is an important difference between simply having these concepts and actually being right-minded.

To repeat, attack is of the *mind* and is inevitable where there is guilt and fear. Since attack is an integral part of the ego thought system, those who accept that thought system must engage in attack thinking, perceiving themselves as vulnerable, subject to attack, and themselves in need of attacking. Once again we can see here the ego's principle of *one or the other* in operation. When we as mind and the Son of God listened to the ego and accepted its thought system as our guide, then our survival as separate individuals became a matter of either God or us. It was a matter of oneness or otherness. In the special relationship this translates into the idea that if I am to be innocent, then someone or something else has to be guilty.

I may form a special relationship alliance with another where we bargain to grant each other specialness while joining in attack upon a third party, but these alliances are unstable and in truth I am interested only in myself, my own safety from attack and my own specialness, which includes the safety and security of the body. Special relationship partners are expendable and replacements can be found.

The attack involved in special love is more subtle than the overt attack that is displayed in special hate. In special love, the underlying attack lies in the unconscious belief that the object of my "love" really does not deserve it, and actually is not innocent, but is guilty of having acquired the innocence and love that I lack and now must take from outside. The principle of deprivation comes into play here, basically saying that the other from whom I seek love, fulfillment and completion must have what I need because he, she, it, they—whomever or whatever—took it from a limited source of supply (limited because I believe in scarcity) that I myself should have been able to take from. Therefore, they basically stole it from me so now I am justified in stealing it back by any means I can employ—by hook or by crook, by seduction or clever bargain disguised—because, after all the other is guilty. Thus it is that special love is a form of special hate which projects blame and guilt onto another. Specialness itself, after all, is hatred because it is basically the idea that separation is real, therefore is a hateful attack upon the truth of oneness; an attack that can succeed in nothing but bringing about a fearful dream of misery full of conflict and anger:

> Whenever you are angry, you can be sure that you have formed a special relationship which the ego has "blessed," for anger *is* its blessing. Anger takes many forms, but it cannot long deceive those who will learn that love brings no guilt at all, and what brings guilt cannot be love and *must* be anger. All anger is nothing more than an attempt to make someone feel guilty, and this attempt is the only basis the ego accepts for special relationships. Guilt is the only need the ego has, and as long as you identify with it, guilt will remain attractive to you (T-15.VII.10:1-4).

Within the ego system, attack invites and justifies counterattack, which is what guilt promised in the beginning: "God will attack you back." Of course in truth God was not and is not aware of being attacked, nor does Love attack or need defense. The Truth is not threatened by what is false. This illustrates the point that Jesus makes about attack not being justified: fear is a fantasy born of separation and guilt, and we always attack some fantasized image of our own making. In essence, we attack ourselves; and this is especially obvious when it is understood that our true Self is Christ, at one with God, so that an attack on Oneness must be an attack on Self. But it is also evident in light of the principle of oneness as it operates within the dream, because according to that principle when we attack someone else, we attack a brother who in truth is one with us; therefore we attack our self. Brothers are of one mind, and there is nothing outside our mind. The ego mechanism of projection was made not only to give the illusion of escape from the mind, but also in order that we could have the illusion of otherness, thus providing images as attack targets for the projection of guilt. But those targets are merely images we have made up. They represent split-off parts of self that first were seen within, judged against and then disowned; therefore projected into what seemed to be without so that they could be blamed, condemned and attacked in an attempt to be free of guilt: free of some aspects of self one has condemned and about which one feels guilty. Sometimes this is obvious so one can recognize that what is irritating about another is some characteristic of one's own that one dislikes or is a source of guilt.

Attack, being an expression of separation, fosters guilt, which in turn demands further projection and attack. And so the mind becomes caught up in a self-perpetuating cycle of guilt and attack similar to what we saw in the dynamics of scarcity, ever burdening itself with the very guilt it hoped to escape by attacking and blaming. This is another example of the ego's maxim: "Seek but do not find." As a practical, personal example of this aspect of Jesus' psychology, it is possible to observe the attack-guilt cycle in one's mind where it may be evident that an outburst of angry and attacking behavior has resulted in feelings of guilt. With this observation, one has available the choice not to continue to attack, defend or justify attack, but to step back from the ego so that Jesus' way of peace may interrupt the cycle. Or, if one proceeds to defend and attack, at least one can be aware of choosing to do so, even in the presence of the alternative, and also aware that one would not need to defend and attack except for the presence of guilt:

> In their angry alliances, born of the fear of loneliness and yet dedicated to the continuance of loneliness, each [special relationship partner] seeks relief from guilt by increasing it in the other. For each believes that this decreases guilt in him. The other seems always to be attacking and wounding him, perhaps in little ways, perhaps "unconsciously," yet never without demand of sacrifice. The fury of those joined at the ego's altar [of the special relationship] far exceeds your awareness of it. For what the ego really wants [i.e., to keep you guilty] you do not realize (T-15.VII.9:3-7; brackets mine).

As we proceed to discuss other ancillary elements of the ego thought system described in *A Course in Miracles*, it should not surprise us that attack and fear are implicated in all of them. We have already seen that the ego thought system is like an interlocking chain wherein each element both stimulates and is stimulated by the other. Once again let us note a central point in the psychology of ACIM: objective observation—the *looking* within that Jesus so often encourages in his course—is the key whereby this chain can be unlocked and escape made possible.

> The ego establishes relationships only to get something. And it would keep the giver bound to itself through guilt. It is impossible for the ego to enter into any relationship without anger, for the ego believes that anger makes friends. This is not its statement, but it *is* its purpose. For the ego really believes that it can get and keep *by making guilty*. This is its one attraction; an attraction so weak that it would have no hold at all, except that no one recognizes it. For the ego always seems to attract through love, and has no attraction at all to anyone who perceives that it attracts through guilt.
>
> The sick attraction of guilt must be recognized for what it is. For having been made real to you, it is essential to look at it clearly, and by withdrawing your investment in it, to learn to let it go. No one would choose to let go what he believes has value. Yet the attraction of guilt has value to you only because you have not looked at what it is, and have judged it completely in the dark. As we bring it to light, your only question will be why it was you ever wanted it. You have nothing to lose by looking open-eyed, for ugliness such as this belongs not in your holy mind....
>
> We said before that the ego attempts to maintain and increase guilt, but in such a way that you do not recognize what it would do to you. For it is the ego's fundamental doctrine that what you do to others you have escaped. The ego wishes no one well. Yet its survival depends on your belief that you are exempt from its evil intentions. It counsels, therefore, that if you are host to it, it will enable you to direct its anger outward, thus protecting you. And thus it embarks on an endless, unrewarding chain of special relationships, forged out of anger and dedicated to but one insane belief; that the more anger you invest outside yourself, the safer you become.
>
> It is this chain that binds the Son of God to guilt, and it is this chain the Holy Spirit would remove from his holy mind (T-15.VII. 2-3:6; 4-5:1).

Next we will examine the element of sacrifice, which is directly related to attack and yet another piece in the ego's interlocking chain of elements which binds the mind:

> In the "dynamics" of attack is sacrifice a key idea. It is the pivot upon which all compromise, all desperate attempts to strike a bargain, and all conflicts achieve a seeming balance. It is the symbol of the central theme that *somebody must lose* [i.e., it's one or the other] (T-26.I.1:1-3).

89

Sacrifice is defined in Wapnick's *Glossary* as follows:

> a central belief in the ego's thought system: someone must lose if another
> is to gain; the principle of giving up in order to receive (giving to get); e.g.,
> in order to receive God's Love we must pay a price, usually in the form
> of suffering to expiate our guilt (sin); in order to receive another's love,
> we must pay for it through the special love bargain; the reversal of the
> principle of salvation or justice: no one loses and everyone gains.

Here again the principle of *one or the other* is seen in operation: someone's
interests must be sacrificed in order for another's interests to be met.
Further, what is sacrificed is considered to be of lesser worth than what is
gained. In the special love bargain what is given up is some aspect of one's
separate individuality—one's self—and, because of the inherent sense of
worthlessness that accompanies guilt, the ego always regards what it has to
offer as being of less value than the self of the other from whom it hopes to
obtain special love. A passage previously quoted in the discussion of scarcity
illustrates this point:

> Most curious of all is the concept of the self which the ego fosters in
> the special relationship. This "self" seeks the relationship to make itself
> complete. Yet when it finds the special relationship in which it thinks it can
> accomplish this it gives itself away, and tries to "trade" itself for the self of
> another...Each partner tries to sacrifice the self he does not want for one he
> thinks he would prefer. And he feels guilty for the "sin" of taking, and of
> giving nothing of value in return. How much value can he place upon a self
> that he would give away to get a "better" one? (T-16.V.7:1-3, 5-7)

Another way of understanding the Course's concept of sin is to recognize
that it amounts to the belief that Love not only can be sacrificed, but has
been sacrificed. Having a separate, special identity housed and "protected"
in a body was regarded as being of more value than oneness, so the Love of
God (the essence of Oneness) had to be sacrificed in favor of individuality:
Self was sacrificed for self. Jesus points out that it is a "sacrifice" of truth—of
our true Self as Christ—to accept the belief in separation and then to identify
with a body, which is both a symbol of the ego and the ego's "home":

> The body is itself a sacrifice; a giving up of power in the name of saving just
> a little for yourself. To see a brother in another body, separate from yours,
> is the expression of a wish to see a little part of him and sacrifice the rest.
> Look at the world, and you will see nothing attached to anything beyond
> itself. All seeming entities can come a little nearer, or go a little farther off,
> but cannot join.

> The world you see is based on "sacrifice" of oneness. It is a picture of
> complete disunity and total lack of joining. Around each entity is built a

wall [i.e., the body] so seeming solid that it looks as if what is inside can never reach without, and what is out can never reach and join with what is locked away within the wall...For if they joined each one would lose its own identity, and by their separation are their selves maintained.

The little that the body fences off becomes the self, preserved through sacrifice of all the rest. And all the rest must lose this little part, remaining incomplete to keep its own identity intact. In this perception of yourself the body's loss would be a sacrifice indeed. For sight of bodies becomes the sign that sacrifice is limited, and something still remains for you alone. And for this little to belong to you are limits placed on everything outside, just as they are on everything you think is yours. For giving and receiving are the same. And to accept the limits of a body is to impose these limits on each brother whom you see. For you must see him as you see yourself.

The body *is* a loss, and *can* be made to sacrifice. And while you see your brother as a body, apart from you and separate in his cell, you are demanding sacrifice of him and you. What greater sacrifice could be demanded than that God's Son perceive himself without his Father? And his Father be without His Son? Yet every sacrifice demands that   they be separate and without the other. The memory of God must be denied if any sacrifice is asked of anyone. What witness to the wholeness of God's Son is seen within a world of separate bodies...? (T-26.I.1:5-8; 2:1-3, 5; 3-4; brackets mine).

Finally, guilt can be understood as involving the belief that God not only demands sacrifice, but that love *is* sacrifice. Within the dream we can see this played out in special relationships where love is equated with sacrifice and subsumed under the principle of *giving to get*. The idea that love is not exclusive, but embraces all and requires no sacrifice is foreign to the ego's way of thinking with which the world is so familiar. Yet in *A Course in Miracles* Jesus makes it very clear that no sacrifice is required of anyone in order that our mind's "natural inheritance" of love might be both given and received. Here another of Jesus' psychological principles comes into play: giving and receiving are the same. Give not to get, but to know that you *have*. This is actually a version of the principle that *ideas leave not their source*. The attempt to project guilt serves to both retain and increase it in our mind. Likewise, as love is projected (extended), it too is both retained and increased: "The cost of giving *is* receiving. Either it is a penalty from which you suffer, or the happy purchase of a treasure to hold dear" (T-14.III.5:8-9).

Jesus teaches that when we decide to set the ego thought system aside, love is increased in our awareness as we are able to *allow* its presence to be extended through us. In our dream this is experienced as the sense that the more love we give, the more we have. Because love is in the mind, not the body, and since the mind is one, love is shared by all. Since love is our "natural inheritance" as the Son of God, it is not scarce, but abundant. We give what we already have in order to experience that we have it. Unlike special love, real love is not scarce and cannot be lost or sacrificed. It is only the *awareness* of love in the mind that is blocked by guilt, not its presence.

Further, real love is not given by one individual to another as the ego's specialness would have us believe. Nor does love depend upon the body which is merely a dream figure—a vehicle of thought within the dream where sex is often confused with love, but is almost always an expression of specialness and a form of sacrifice or attack. Thus it is that the famous four letter English word which means sexual intercourse has become an expletive expressive of violent anger and attack and is often used in phrases indicating that one feels oneself to have been sacrificed or victimized.

The Course is never concerned with the behavior of the body, because the body is a dream figure and its behavior is *effect*, not cause. Rather, the Course is about cause, which means that it is always about our mind and the thought system we choose as our guide. It has already been pointed out that this is basically a choice between being motivated by fear or by love. Another way to understand this choice is to see it as a decision between believing in love as sacrifice or experiencing love that knows no sacrifice:

> So is it that, in all your seeking for love, you seek for sacrifice and find it. Yet you find not love. It is impossible to deny what love is [by believing in separation and seeking special love] and still recognize it. The meaning of love lies in what you have cast outside yourself, and it has no meaning apart from you. It is what you prefer to keep [i.e., separation, specialness, individuality] that has no meaning, while all that you would keep away [i.e., your brothers and God] holds all the meaning of the universe, and holds the universe together in its meaning. Unless the universe were joined in you it would be apart from God, and to be without Him *is* to be without meaning. [The use of the term "universe" here is metaphorical, referring to mind and its oneness, and should not be taken to suggest that the physical universe is real] (T-15.XI.6; brackets mine).

Remember that the unhappy thought system of the ego we are examining presents a picture of what life would be like if it were possible to be separate from God, therefore to live a life of individuality apart from His Love; a life raised up out of the specter of His corpse: a slaughtered Oneness torn apart and feasted upon by the beasts of sin, guilt and fear. Indeed, Jesus tells us that this *is* the life we think we live, but we pretty it up by practicing the ego's arts of deception and denial.

Throughout history there have been those who looked beneath the veil of deception to witness accurately the nature of ego life; not only Freud, but Buddha, Shakespeare, Giuseppe Verdi, Fyodor Dostoyevsky, William Blake, J. Krishnamurti, Thomas Merton, and many, many other authors from ancient times to the contemporary. Based on what is taught in the Course we can assume that the historical Jesus also looked beneath the veil and invited his followers to do likewise, as he does now in *A Course in Miracles.* Perhaps that is why he had to be killed and then symbolically crucified again as his teachings were co-opted in order to be misrepresented in the interests of a dualism comfortable for the ego. Thus it could seem that separation and differences are the truth while conflict, murder and death must either be authored by God or just the way things are in a cosmos which science can explain and where God has no place; where universal love and oneness are mere sentimental fantasies.

Obviously suffering and victimization must accompany fear, attack and sacrifice. They are the next corollary elements of the ego thought system that we will examine in the interest of understanding the nature of specialness and special relationships—relationships authored by the ego as expressions of fear in the form of hatred and then disguised as love. Again, let us be reminded that in explaining Jesus' psychology we are examining the nature of an *illusion* in our mind—a dream that Jesus tells us is in fact a nightmare that we have taken for reality. And again, Jesus' purpose for inviting his students to join him in this looking is that in doing so they are given an opportunity first to awaken to their reality as mind and then to see clearly what it is they, *as mind,* have chosen. Thus, if one chooses to accept Jesus' invitation, one can be in a position to make a better choice—one that corrects the nightmare, replacing it with a happier dream and eventually awakening the mind to awareness of truth:

> Illusion recognized must disappear. Accept not suffering, and you remove the thought of suffering. Your blessing lies on everyone who suffers, when you choose to see all suffering as what it is. The thought of sacrifice gives rise to all the forms that suffering appears to take. And sacrifice is an idea so mad that sanity dismisses it at once.

> Never believe that you can sacrifice [because separation is impossible]. There is no place for sacrifice in what has any value. If the thought occurs, its very presence proves that error has arisen and correction must be made. Your blessing [i.e., forgiveness] will correct it. Given first to you [in the knowledge of the Holy Spirit that separation is not possible and you are not guilty], it now is yours to give as well. No form of sacrifice and suffering can long endure before the face of one who has forgiven and has blessed himself (W-pI.187.7-8; brackets mine).

Suffering and *Victimization* follow from the belief in sacrifice and are important elements in the dismal picture of life that Jesus tells us is painted by the brush of specialness on a background of fear where the colors and hues of scarcity, attack and sacrifice have been employed. In the Wapnick *Glossary* suffering is defined as follows:

> one of the basic ego witnesses to the reality of the body and the non-existence of spirit, since the body appears to experience suffering or pain; to be in pain, therefore, is to deny God, while being aware of our true invulnerability as God's Son is to deny the reality of pain. (Note—suffering and pain are used as virtual synonyms.)

To the ego, our cries of suffering say: "I exist." In the Course we are told that the ego is attracted not only to guilt, but to pain, dying and death, because they seem to stand as witnesses to the truth of separation and the reality of the body (see Text Chapter 19. Sec. IV, "The Obstacles to Peace"). The altar at which the ego's version of love is consecrated is an altar of sacrifice where suffering is seen as a blessing and proof of fidelity, first to the ego and then to the special love partner. To repeat and expand a previously quoted passage:

> Suffering and sacrifice are the gifts with which the ego would "bless" all unions. And those who are united at its altar accept suffering and sacrifice as the price of union. In their angry alliances, born of the fear of loneliness [i.e., the scarcity belief] and yet dedicated to the continuance of loneliness, each seeks relief from guilt by increasing it in the other. For each believes that this decreases guilt in him. The other seems always to be attacking and wounding him, perhaps in little ways, perhaps "unconsciously," yet never without demand of sacrifice. The fury of those joined at the ego's altar far exceeds your awareness of it. For what the ego really wants [i.e., to keep you guilty] you do not realize (T-15.VII.9; brackets mine).

In the Course, suffering and victimization are understood to be aspects of the ego's belief in sacrifice stemming from the idea that separation is an accomplished fact, thus Oneness had to have been sacrificed and God victimized while the Son became a guilty victimizer. But the ego quickly turned the tables, reversing cause and effect so that we could blame our troubles on God, or something perceived as "other," thereby escaping responsibility as decision makers who chose separation in favor of our cherished individuality. The ego's cry of victimization yells out: "IT'S NOT MY FAULT!" And so the ego invented a victimizer god who could be held responsible for separation, exiling the Son from Paradise to become the dualistic father of a dualistic creation where suffering lives. This victimizer god is quite inclined toward vengeance. Rather than a God of Love, he is a god of *special* love: a god of hatred who both practices and justifies killing and hatred; a god who demands sacrifice in the name of special love.

As seen in Jesus' portrayal, the ego's special relationship way of life constitutes a culture of suffering and victimization that requires that there be innocent victims and guilty victimizers. The unconscious foundation for this is the ontological victim-victimizer relationship between God and His Son. Either way, the Son as victimizer or God as victimizer, for the survival of the ego it must be *one or the other*. So once again it can be seen that this principle is incorporated into every aspect of the ego illusion: a dream where individuals compete for specialness and where all living organisms compete with one another for life. Life on earth—and throughout the entire cosmos spawned by the idea of separation—is ruled by the law of the jungle that in order for one to survive victimization is necessary, therefore another must be sacrificed.

Clearly, victimization is closely associated with suffering, attack, scarcity and sacrifice. Wapnick does not define it in his *Glossary*, but the principle of victimization underlies the idea of *crucifixion*, which is defined in the *Glossary* as follows:

> a symbol of the ego's attack on God and therefore on His Son, witnessing to the "reality" of suffering, sacrifice, victimization, and death which the world seems to manifest; also refers to the killing of Jesus, an extreme example that taught that our true Identity of love can never be destroyed, for death has no power over life.

As with the other corollary elements of the ego thought system, manifestations of the thought of victimization are readily observed in the world. Examples are reported frequently in the daily news where vicious acts are described along with the suffering cries of those who have been victimized. As understood by Jesus' psychology, victimizers are driven by guilt and fear, albeit largely unconscious. To repeat an important principle, no one attacks—no one victimizes and abuses—who is free of guilt and fear. But no one who identifies with the ego and believes himself to be a body can be free of guilt and fear. In fact, the choice to identify with the ego and its symbol the body is actually a choice for self-crucifixion:

> Do not underestimate the power of the devotion of God's Son, nor the power the god he worships has over him. For he places himself at the altar of his god, whether it be the god he made [i.e., the ego] or the God Who created him [as spirit, Christ, one within Oneness]. That is why his slavery is as complete as his freedom, for he will obey only the god he accepts. The god of crucifixion [i.e., the ego] demands that he crucify [i.e., attack and

victimize others as well as himself], and his worshippers obey. In his name they crucify themselves, believing that the power of the Son of God is born of sacrifice and pain (T-11.VI.5; brackets mine).

You have nailed yourself to a cross, and placed a crown of thorns upon your own head [by identifying with the ego]. Yet you cannot crucify God's Son, for the Will of God cannot die. His Son has been redeemed from his own [self] crucifixion, and you cannot assign to death whom God has given eternal life. The dream of crucifixion still lies heavy on your eyes, but what you see in dreams is not reality. While you perceive the Son of God as crucified [i.e., as separated and a body], you are asleep. And as long as you believe that you can crucify him [yourself as well as seeming others], you are only having nightmares (T-11.VI.8; brackets mine).

We have seen that guilt may be understood as an inner sense of unworthiness that amounts to self-hatred. Jesus explains that in the attempt to disguise and be free of that hatred it is projected onto someone or something that appears to be other than self. At the same time, in their own attempt to be free of responsibility and guilt, victims point the finger of blame never realizing that their pain comes from within—from the desire to be separate and special. Suffering comes from identifying with the ego. To repeat another principle of Jesus' psychology, peace of mind does not depend upon what others do or what seems to be happening to our bodies. It depends upon which thought system in our mind we have chosen to inform our perceptions, therefore to determine how we will interpret what we perceive and experience.

With minds infected by the ego, victimizers are "made mad by sin and guilt" (W-pI.153.13:1) while victims inwardly cherish their suffering and pain, because it so clearly attracts attention and makes them special, "proves" the body's reality, and provides opportunities for projecting guilt in the form of blame. In contrast, we are invited to think of Jesus on the cross as a model of inner peace in the face of outrageous attempts to victimize him. In spite of what was happening to his body, Jesus refused to be a victim, which means that in his mind he had accepted the Atonement principle that he was not separate from Oneness; therefore not a body, but spirit, invulnerable and the one Creation of God Who remains at one with God. (Note that in the Course, *resurrection* is equated to accepting the Atonement, which takes place in the *mind* and has nothing to do with the unreal body, its illusory life and death.)

Two important statements from the Course apply here:

If you [mind, Son of God] will accept yourself as God created you, you will be incapable of suffering. Yet to do this you must acknowledge Him as your Creator [therefore identify as spirit, not body]. This is not because you will be punished otherwise. It is merely because your acknowledgment of your Father is the acknowledgment of yourself as you are. Your Father created you wholly without sin, wholly without pain and wholly without suffering of any kind. If you deny Him you bring sin, pain and suffering into your own mind... (T-10.V.9:5-9; brackets mine).

To see a guilty world is but the sign your learning has been guided by the world [i.e., the ego thought system], and you behold it as you see yourself. The concept of the self embraces all you look upon [because "projection makes perception"], and nothing is outside of this perception. If you can be hurt by anything, you see a picture of your secret wishes [i.e., to suffer as proof of separation and justification for blame]. Nothing more than this. And in your suffering of any kind you see your own concealed desire to kill (T-31.V.15:6-10; brackets mine).

Both the victimizer who inflicts suffering and the victim who suffers share the same ego thought system, according to the psychology of the Course, and that thought system is one of murder and death. The ego seeks to kill the truth of oneness, therefore to kill us by denying our innocence as the Son of God. The attempt to make guilty is an attempt to murder innocence. The attempt to substitute a bodily self for the truth of spirit is an attempt to murder the life of spirit. So we have the surprising conclusion that both victim and victimizer seek to attack and kill: they seek to make separation real. The victimizer's murderous intent is obvious, while that of the victim is cleverly disguised, just as special love is a disguise for special hate, yet both are simply forms of attack. As always in the system of psychology we are examining, the solution for both victims and victimizers lies in a change of mind from the thought system of separation and guilt to the thought system of innocence and the Atonement that says separation is untrue. The solution lies in discovering through Jesus and the Holy Spirit—or however one would symbolize right-mindedness—that victims and victimizers are one: in truth they are brothers in oneness.

A sick and suffering you but represents your brother's guilt; the witness that you send lest he forget the injuries he gave, from which you swear he never will escape. This sick and sorry picture *you* accept, if only it can serve to punish him. The sick are merciless to everyone, and in contagion do they seek to kill. Death seems an easy price, if they can say, "Behold me, brother, at your hand I die." For sickness is the witness to his guilt, and death would prove his errors must be sins. Sickness is but a "little" death; a form of vengeance not yet total. Yet it speaks with certainty for what it represents. The bleak and bitter picture you have sent your brother *you* have looked upon in grief. And everything that it has shown to him have you believed, because it witnessed to the guilt in him which you perceived and loved.

Now in the hands made gentle by His touch, the Holy Spirit lays a picture of a different you. It is a picture of a body still, for what you really are cannot be seen nor pictured. Yet this one has not been used for purpose of attack, and therefore never suffered pain at all. It witnesses to the eternal truth that you cannot be hurt, and points beyond itself to both your innocence and his. Show this unto your brother, who will see that every scar is healed, and every tear is wiped away in laughter and in love. And he will look on his forgiveness there, and with healed eyes will look beyond it to the innocence that he beholds in you. Here is the proof that he has never sinned; that nothing which his madness bid him do was ever done, or ever had effects of any kind. That no reproach he laid upon his heart was ever justified, and no attack can ever touch him with the poisoned and relentless sting of fear.

Attest his innocence and not his guilt. Your healing is his comfort and his health because it proves illusions are not true. It is not will for life but wish for death that is the motivation for this world. Its only purpose is to prove guilt real. No worldly thought or act or feeling has a motivation other than this one. These are the witnesses that are called forth to be believed, and lend conviction to the system they speak for and represent (T-27.I.4:3-6:6).

Because specialness is separation, it is always fear and attack in some form; therefore victimization is implicit in every special relationship. It can be found everywhere, if not in the criminal acts of individuals and the crippling blasts of war, then in the marriage bed. In victimization, the other side of special love is seen: special hate, which is not different in *content* from special love. Both are means of coping with guilt and fear, one through seduction, manipulation and indirect attack, and the other through overt attack, whether acted out physically or projected as condemnation and blame.

In the face of these harsh observations about the dream of separation and its life of special relationships, again let us not forget that the psychological system we are examining offers freedom from the ego's misery through honest, objective looking at the thought content behind the facades of life. Jesus says to us:

Be not afraid to look upon the special hate relationship, for freedom lies in looking at it. It would be impossible not to know the meaning of love, except for this. For the special love relationship, in which the meaning of love is hidden, is undertaken solely to offset the hate [which is, remember, a form of fear], but not to let it go...You cannot limit hate. The special love relationship will not offset it, but will merely drive it underground and out of sight. It is essential to bring it into sight, and to make no attempt to hide it. For it is the attempt to balance hate with love that makes love meaningless to you. The extent of the split that lies in this you do not realize. And until you do the split will remain unrecognized, and therefore unhealed....

The special love relationship is an attempt to limit the destructive effects of hate by finding a haven in the storm of guilt [i.e., by finding a substitute for Love as well as a special partner upon whom to project guilt]. It makes no attempt to rise above the storm, into the sunlight. On the contrary, it emphasizes the guilt outside the haven by attempting to build barricades against it, and keep within them. The special love relationship is not perceived as a value in itself, but as a place of safety from which hatred is split off and kept apart. The special love partner is acceptable only as long as he serves this purpose. Hatred can enter, and indeed is welcome in some aspects of the relationship, but it is still held together by the illusion of love. If the illusion goes, the relationship is broken or becomes unsatisfying on the grounds of disillusionment (T-16.IV.1:1-3, 5-10; 3; brackets mine).

In recent years in America there have been widely publicized concerns about abuse of all kinds. When understood from the perspective of *A Course in Miracles*, one can see that these concerns are born of the ego's need to have victims and victimizers. And so, for example, we have movements to prevent spouse abuse, child abuse, sexual abuse, abuse of war prisoners, abuse of animals, and abuse of the environment, etc. Jesus does not deny that within the dream people act out the vicious, abusive roles of victimizers. They do indeed; being dream images we have projected in our mind and driven as they are by the ego's insane thought system of sin, guilt and fear. According to the Course, in our world abuse occurs because people are driven by fear which takes the form of hatred, as well as driven by desperate emptiness in the absence of love which their own decision for separation has engendered. As has been discussed, victim and victimizer are cut from the same cloth, only the forms of acting out are different. And so the world is often preoccupied with victimization, futilely attempting to correct it at the behavioral level rather than addressing the true cause, which is in the mind that has chosen the ego as its teacher and guide.

The blunt implications here are astounding to our conventional thinking: no attempts to solve problems at the behavioral level could ever work in the long run; neither at the individual level or at the social and political levels. That is because behavior is *not* the problem. As we have seen over and over again, according to Jesus it is our *mind* that is the problem, because it is the way we think that is the *cause* of how we perceive and therefore how we act. Again, according to *A Course in Miracles* our basic human problem is the belief in separation and guilt, no matter what form they take or what level of importance we assign to those forms. It could as easily be said that our basic problem is specialness, because separation and guilt are the substance and fabric of specialness, therefore of all special relationships. And specialness gets its power not only from the fact that we have chosen it, but from our unwillingness to look honestly upon what we have chosen: our refusal to look behind the deceptive facades of life at the *cause* of every form of misery and unhappiness experienced in the world. Jesus' system of psychology would have us look at the cause to recognize that we have mistaken separation and hatred for love, as well as mistaken illusions for truth. When we look with Jesus from the perspective of our right mind, our mistakes do not become sin: error is not made real, but is dissolved in the light of the Holy Spirit's *reason*.

As stated earlier, and speaking in terms of the Course's Level Two teachings which recognize that we believe the dream is real, when our worldly lives are understood as a classroom for learning and practicing forgiveness, special relationships form the curriculum of that classroom. Through forgiveness, special relationships can become what the Course calls *holy relationships*— relationships which have been given over to the Holy Spirit's thought system of the Atonement rather than being allowed to continue as the ego's arena for acting out separation (specialness), guilt and fear. Jesus assures us that forgiveness requires no sacrifice. We do not have to forego our relationships, but simply allow them to be transformed by right-mindedness. Our problem is that we resist. We cling to specialness, therefore to special relationships, because we believe they offer us something of value and do not recognize what they are costing us; what our ego identity is costing us. In special relationships the ego has us, as the song says, "looking for love in all the wrong places" and attempting to deal with guilt in a way that only continues it: "Seek but do not find." But there *is* a way to seek *and* find: the way of forgiveness that undoes guilt and finds the Presence of love within—the holy relationship alternative to special relationships:

> In this world it is impossible to create. Yet it *is* possible to make happy. I have said repeatedly that the Holy Spirit would not deprive you of your special relationships, but would transform them. And all that is meant by that is that He will restore to them the function given them by God [i.e., love in the form of forgiveness]. The function you have given them is clearly not to make happy. But the holy relationship shares God's purpose, rather than aiming to make a substitute for it. Every special relationship you have made is a substitute for God's Will, and glorifies yours instead of His because of the illusion that they are different.

...Every special relationship you have made has, as its fundamental purpose, the aim of occupying your mind so completely that you will not hear the call of truth [i.e., the Holy Spirit].

In a sense, the special relationship was the ego's answer to the creation of the Holy Spirit, Who was God's Answer to the separation. For although the ego did not understand what had been created, it was aware of threat. The whole defense system the ego evolved to protect the separation from the Holy Spirit was in response to the gift with which God blessed it, and by His blessing enabled it to be healed. This blessing holds within itself the truth about everything. And the truth is that the Holy Spirit is in close relationship with you, because in Him is your relationship with God restored to you. The relationship with Him has never been broken, because the Holy Spirit has not been separate from anyone since the separation. And through Him have all your holy relationships been carefully preserved, to serve God's purpose [i.e., forgiveness] for you.

The ego is always alert to threat, and the part of your mind into which the ego was accepted is very anxious to preserve its reason, as it sees it. It does not realize that it is totally insane. And you must realize just what this means if you would be restored to sanity. The insane protect their thought systems, but they do so insanely. And all their defenses are as insane as what they are supposed to protect. The separation has nothing in it, no part, no "reason," and no attribute that is not insane. And its "protection" is part of it, as insane as the whole. The special relationship, which is its chief defense, must therefore be insane. You have but little difficulty now in realizing that the thought system the special relationship protects is but a system of delusions. You recognize, at least in general terms, that the ego is insane. Yet the special relationship still seems to you somehow to be "different." Yet we have looked at it far closer than we have at many other aspects of the ego's thought system that you have been more willing to let go. While this one remains, you will not let the others go. For this one is not different. Retain this one, and you have retained the whole (T-17.IV.2; 3:3-6:7; brackets and italics mine).

While the *content* is clear in the passages cited above, there are some technical problems of *form* in the use of language that need to be discussed. This is not an infrequent problem in *A Course in Miracles*. The reader may have noticed the contradiction involved where Jesus speaks as though the separation actually happened, that God knows of it, that He knows of us and our relationships, and that He has a purpose for our lives. These apparent contradictions arise from the fact that in the Course Jesus often not only speaks as though linear time were real, but uses metaphor in order to communicate with us, and to reassure us that God is Love wherein there is no thought of sin, guilt and punishment. Remember that the Level Two teachings of the Course are presented in a language we can understand, although it may not accurately represent the Level One metaphysical principles. When the thought system of the Course is grasped in its entirety, it is clear that there is no room for separation in oneness; no metaphysical compromise with duality. The *knowledge* of God does not include dualistic illusions. Therefore, the fact that *knowledge* is the eternal Truth means that it automatically counteracts any possibility of error, making it impossible. Thus, God did not really "create" the Holy Spirit as an "answer" to the separation, which His knowledge does not include. Rather, the word symbol "Holy Spirit" simply stands for the fact that the Truth never can be completely denied in dreams of separation. And often in the Course the word "God" is used when the word "Holy Spirit" would be more accurate, since it is the Holy Spirit that stands as the link between the Mind of God and the mind that dreams of separation; therefore offering us a loving alternative to the ego's sin, guilt and fear. If the ego is understood as authoring a dream with special relationships as a way of life, then Jesus and the Holy Spirit can be understood as offering us an alternative dream with the holy relationship as a way of life. In any case, it is important to remember that we are limited to symbols for purposes of communication, and symbols simply cannot do justice to the Truth. They can only lead us toward it.

And again, it is also important to remember that the "you" being addressed in the Course is not us as separate beings with bodies and unique personalities. The "you" being addressed is us as mind and observer/ decision maker; essentially us as the Son of God who has forgotten Who he is. To repeat this crucial point yet again, the psychology of the Course is about *mind*, not the brain and not the illusory separated personality with its illusory relationships. The personality and its special relationships where victimization and suffering dwell are part and parcel of the ego's dream of separation *in* our mind. They serve us in the interest of forgiveness when we understand them as *effects*—as *reflections*—of what is going on in our mind where a meaningful change at the level of *cause* can be made.

At the level of mind, forgiveness is the responsibility of that Presence of love in our mind symbolized by Jesus and which the Course calls the Holy Spirit. Our responsibility as mind is to learn how to allow that Presence to fulfill Its function through us, thereby making forgiveness our function in the dream of special relationships we call life. Since Jesus is "the manifestation of the Holy Spirit" (T-12.VII.6:1; C-6.1:1), he can be thought of as our teacher of forgiveness and the guide who leads us into direct relationship with the more abstract Presence of love in our mind.

Judgment is another important element in the ego thought system and is the most common form of attack thinking. The kind of judgment most directly addressed in the Course is that which condemns and blames; the type that is involved in the projection of guilt onto another. Judgment is required in the perceptual world, because it is a world of differences where decisions have to be made in even the simplest affairs of life. But it is not these everyday judgments that are of central concern in the Course's psychology of forgiveness, although they too involve attack thinking because they are part of perception which makes separation seem real. Ultimately, the goal of the Course is that all decisions would be made right-mindedly, but the focus of forgiveness is first and foremost upon our interpersonal special relationships, and upon observing the ways in which we separate and attack by judging others. Once we are aware of what we are doing and why, we then can learn to set judgment aside in favor of inner peace and calm acceptance: "Forgiveness…is still, and quietly does nothing…It merely looks, and waits, and judges not" (W-pII.1.4:1, 3).

With regard to the everyday forms of judgment, right-mindedness would see that one's preferences need not be taken seriously, but held lightly and pursued with peace of mind. That is because there is no hierarchy of illusions: "All that a hierarchy of illusions can show is preference, not reality. What relevance has preference to the truth? Illusions are illusions and are false. Your preference gives them no reality" (T-26.VII.6:5-8).

When one considers that, in terms of the Course thought system, what we think of as life is simply a reviewing in the mind of a dream of separation that is already over, it can be understood that ultimately it is not important whether one chooses chocolate or vanilla, classical music or jazz, to spend time with friend A or friend B, to drive a Ford or a Maserati, to eat meat or only vegetables, to live in Paris, Istanbul or Colorado Springs. What makes all of these kinds of decisions seem important, even momentous and therefore burdensome, is specialness. The wisdom of right-mindedness would enable one not to take one's special preferences seriously, just as it enables not taking oneself seriously. There is the prospect of great relief in that!

In the end, undoing the ego thought system means to relinquish all judgment in favor of being guided by the Divine Wisdom of our right mind:

> The world trains for reliance on one's judgment as the criterion for maturity and strength. Our curriculum trains for the relinquishment of judgment as the necessary condition of salvation (M-9.2:6-7).

Judgment, like other devices by which the world of illusions is maintained, is totally misunderstood by the world. It is actually confused with wisdom, and substitutes for truth. As the world uses the term, an individual is capable of "good" and "bad" judgment, and his education aims at strengthening the former and minimizing the latter. There is, however, considerable confusion about what these categories mean. What is "good" judgment to one is "bad" judgment to another. Further, even the same person classifies the same action as showing "good" judgment at one time and "bad" judgment at another time. Nor can any consistent criteria for determining what these categories are be really taught. At any time the student may disagree with what his would-be teacher says about them, and the teacher himself may well be inconsistent in what he believes. "Good" judgment, in these terms, does not mean anything. No more does "bad."

It is necessary for the... [student of *A Course in Miracles*] to realize, not that he should not judge, but that he cannot. In giving up judgment, he is merely giving up what he did not have. He gives up an illusion; or better, he has an illusion of giving up. He has actually merely become more honest. Recognizing that judgment was always impossible for him, he no longer attempts it. This is no sacrifice. On the contrary, he puts himself in a position where judgment *through* him rather than *by* him can occur. And this judgment is neither "good" nor "bad." It is the only judgment there is, and it is only one: "God's Son is guiltless, and sin does not exist" (M-10.1-2; bracket mine).

In his *Glossary*, Wapnick defines judgment according to the different levels of teaching where the term is used in the Course:

level of *knowledge*: strictly speaking God does not judge, since what He creates is perfect and at one with Him; the Course's references to God's Judgment reflect His recognition of His Son as His Son, forever loved and one with Him.

level of *perception*:
> *wrong-mind*: condemnation, whereby people are separated into those to be hated and those to be "loved," a judgment always based upon the past.

> *right-mind*: vision, whereby people are seen either as expressing love or calling for it, a judgment inspired by the Holy Spirit and always based upon the present.

As with every other element of the ego thought system which guides our lives of specialness in the world, according to the Course the origin of judgment has to do with the idea of separation. In the myth of separation, the Son of God listened to the ego's version of the "tiny, mad idea" and *judged* that there was indeed a difference between the Son and the Father; between Creator and Created: "Let there be a distinction."[1] This judgment was part of the first attack, and became a fundamental element in the ego paradigm that shapes the special relationship way of life in the illusion of a separate, perceptual world. Following quickly upon the heels of the judgment of differences came the judgment of scarcity and deprivation: "God has something (i.e., specialness) I do not have and is withholding it from me." This led to the judgment that God was unfair, hence the ontological temper tantrum followed by projection which condemns and blames in an attempt to escape the guilt which comes from accepting differences as real: the judgment which seeks to preserve separation yet be free of the consequences.

So, relinquishing judgment—that form of attack which is carried out continually in our minds, and acted out in our lives—is really the essence of undoing the ego, therefore of forgiveness as Jesus teaches it in his Course:

> A dream of judgment came into the mind that God created perfect as Himself. And in that dream was Heaven changed to hell, and God made enemy unto His Son. How can God's Son awaken from the dream? It is a dream of judgment. So must he judge not, and he will aken. For the dream will seem to last while he is part of it. Judge not, for he who judges will have need of idols [i.e., special relationships and bodies to serve as targets for projection], which will hold the judgment off from resting on himself. Nor can he know the Self he has condemned. Judge not, because you make yourself a part of evil dreams, where idols are your "true" identity, and your salvation from the judgment laid in terror and in guilt upon yourself (T-29.IX.2; bracket mine).

As we have emphasized throughout our discussion, according to Jesus' psychology it is not possible to let go of judgment (attack), therefore to be at peace, unless one identifies as mind rather than body and accepts responsibility for deciding to set the ego thought system aside in favor of the thought system that *knows* the appearance of differences is illusory. The *knowledge* of the Holy Spirit begins with the principle of the Atonement that in truth separation is impossible. This knowledge is the key to our real innocence—our absolute guiltlessness—as the Son of God. Therefore, it is the key to being free of the necessity to project guilt in the form of judgment, and thus free of attack thoughts.

Since in the Course judgment and attack are synonymous, the term "attack" has been inserted after "judgment" for purposes of illustration in the following succinct and pointed excerpt from the Course:

---

[1] *Laws of Form*, op. cit. (See our chapter three.)

You have no idea of the tremendous release and deep peace that comes from meeting yourself and your brothers totally without judgment [attack].

When you recognize what you are and what your brothers are, you will realize that judging [attacking] them in any way is without meaning. In fact, their meaning is lost to you precisely *because* you are judging [attacking] them. All uncertainty comes from the belief that you are under the coercion of judgment [attack]. You do not need judgment [attack] to organize your life, and you certainly do not need it to organize yourself. In the presence of *knowledge* all judgment [attack] is automatically suspended, and this is the process that enables recognition [of oneness] to replace perception [of differences] (T-3.VI.3; brackets and   second italics mine).

Summary and Conclusions

The primary purpose of this and the previous chapter has been to present a description of what the Course means by "the ego thought system," along with a picture of what ego identification entails. An attempt has been made to offer a sufficient number of practical examples so that the reader might be more able to observe this thought system in his or her experiences, both of what seems to be inner life as well as what has the appearance of outer life. As has been repeatedly pointed out, although it is necessary for purposes of communication to speak as though the world of time and space, along with the body and its relationships, were real, it is important to remember that Jesus' psychology is about the *mind* which is not contained in the body or within the dimensions of time and space. Indeed, the psychological teachings of the Course are intended to help its students awaken from the state of *mindlessness*, which is bodily identification and the dream of separation unquestioned, to a state of *mindfulness* wherein one is aware that what is perceived and how it is interpreted is the result of a thought system in the mind; and further, that at the level of mind one has the ability to choose which of two thought systems will be one's guide in the perceptual world. This means that the student of *A Course in Miracles* must be willing to take responsibility for *how* he or she interprets— therefore reacts to—his or her experiences. According to the Course, w*hat* we experience is a dream that is already over, which means that as figures in the dream we are not responsible for what other dream figures do. But as mind we *are* responsible for our perceptual interpretations, which determine our feelings and reactions. To exercise one's power of decision as mind, it is necessary to discover how to step back to the position of a detached, non-judgmental observer. In discovering and assuming this position one is already right-minded, because wrong-mindedness is never willing to observe itself, let alone observe anything without judgment.

In *A Course in Miracles* Jesus invites his students to live an examined life as suggested by the famous Socratic dictum that "the unexamined life is not worth living."[1] And it is a central strategy of the ego to insure that we *do* live the *un*examined life, which is the life of special relationships unquestioned.

Whether or not one accepts that the words "God" and "spirit" symbolize a true order of reality, it ought to be apparent that our relationships are self-serving, or at least that they begin that way, because *we* begin that way: self-centered. As Krishnamurti said to his students, "...it would be logical, wouldn't it, to admit to ourselves that that is what most of us are primarily interested in—'me first'?"

When one stands back to look carefully at the portrait of special relationships presented in the Course, one sees that it is painted on a background of separation, sin, guilt and fear. The colors and their hues have been employed so as to disguise their true nature, which is that of scarcity, attack, suffering, victimization and judgment. The shapes and patterns hidden in the colors portray a picture of rape, murder and cannibalism wherein there is the crimson hue of blood which we believe is essential to life and a symbol of death. Given our examination of this picture, it should not surprise us that its elements are the focus of the news media and the most popular subjects of literature throughout history. Where would literature and art be without portrayals of what Jesus describes as special relationships and all the corollary elements that attain to them!? And why should these portrayals fascinate and horrify us except that they speak to us of a secret inner life we have sought to deny?

Fortunately, Jesus tells us that what our ego fears to have us look upon in the honest light of reason is not real. But before we can *know* that, we *do* have to look. Jesus says to us:

> My brother, you are part of God and part of me. When you have at last looked at the ego's foundation without shrinking you will also have looked upon ours. I come to you from our Father to offer you everything again. Do not refuse it in order to keep a dark cornerstone hidden, for its protection will not save you. I give you the lamp and I will go with you. You will not take this journey alone. I will lead you to your true Father, Who hath need of you, as I have. Will you not answer the call of love with joy? (T-11.IN.4)

---

[1] Paraphrase of a speech quoted in Plato's *Apology*, section 38, where Socrates addresses the court which would eventually condemn him to death for impiety and corruption.

And again:

> No one can escape from illusions unless he looks at them, for not looking is the way they are protected. There is no need to shrink from illusions, for they cannot be dangerous. We are ready to look more closely at the ego's thought system because together we have the lamp that will dispel it, and since you realize you do not want it, you must be ready. Let us be very calm in doing this, for we are merely looking honestly for truth. The "dynamics" of the ego will be our lesson for a while, for we must look first at this to see beyond it, since you have made it real. We will undo this error quietly together, and then look beyond it to truth (T-11.V.1).

Jesus' psychology is practical in that it asks us simply to look at *what is*, rather than attempting to deny our thoughts, feelings and experiences. It does not even expect us fully to be able to look upon the pervasive influence of the ego in our lives without the emotional reactions that accompany judgment and guilt. But it *does* require that we be *willing* to begin the process of setting judgment aside, which is central to becoming right-minded. Further, it is not possible to practice this system of psychology at the level of bodily identification. Once again let us state that forgiveness is of the mind, not the body. What the body does follows from the choice of thought system in the mind, which is the level of *cause*, while the world and body are the level of *effect*. The mind's ability to choose between thought systems is not intellectual and does not represent an intellectual accomplishment. For those who undertake to study *A Course in Miracles*, the intellect is necessary and useful at the *beginning*. Indeed, those for whom the Course is intended *must* begin with the intellect, both because the Course is an intellectual masterpiece and because of the limitations they have imposed upon their mind by identifying with the ego and the body which requires the symbols of separation (e.g., words) in order to communicate. But Jesus would have his students understand that, like other aspects of the body, the data processing and memory storage capacities of the brain were designed by the ego to be an *impediment* to the awareness that we are mind. Intellectualization easily becomes one of the very "blocks to the awareness of love's presence" (T-IN.1:7) which Jesus intends to help his students remove: "You are still convinced that your understanding is a powerful contribution to the truth, and makes it what it is....Forget not that it has been your decision to make everything that is natural and easy for you impossible" (T-18.IV.7:5, 8:1).

Mindfulness ultimately means the foregoing of concepts and intellectualization in favor of that inner silence which permits the "still, small Voice for God" (T-21.V.1:6) to be one's guide. However, as with everything else the ego has made, the intellect can be placed in the service of right-mindedness—in service of Jesus and the Holy Spirit—*if* one is willing.

The material presented in this chapter has been offered not only in the interest of more fully understanding what Jesus means by "the ego thought system," but also in the interest of *looking*, in both an objective and personal way, at the screen of relationship life upon which our projections are displayed.

> The search for the special relationship is the sign that you equate yourself with the ego and not with God. For the special relationship has value only to the ego. To the ego, unless a relationship has special value it has no meaning, for it perceives all love as special. Yet this cannot be natural, for it is unlike the relationship of God and His Son, and all relationships that are unlike this one *must* be unnatural. For God created love as He would have it be, and gave it as it is. Love has no meaning except as its Creator defined it by His Will. It is impossible to define it otherwise and understand it.
>
> ....For the Love of God, no longer seek for union in separation (T-16.VI. 1; 2:3).

Chapter 6

Defenses

> Truth does not struggle against ignorance, and love does not attack fear. What needs no protection does not defend itself. Defense is of your making. God knows it not. The Holy Spirit uses defenses on behalf of truth only because you made them against it. His perception of them, according to His purpose, merely changes them into a call for what you have attacked with them. Defenses, like everything you made, must be gently turned to your own good, translated by the Holy Spirit from means of self-destruction to means of preservation and release (T-14.VII.5:2).

Defenses are of the ego and already have been discussed to a considerable extent, but there is more to say about the Course's perspective on them, and a review may be helpful as well. It is an obvious fact, though perhaps overlooked, that defenses and the attitude of defensiveness are the result of fear. And all defenses are a form of attack; basically an attack on truth. Only those identified with the ego experience fear, and the special relationship is the ego's premier defense against what it most fears: the truth of oneness. Thus, we who identify with the ego must fear that truth, because it threatens our illusion of self; and so we choose the defense of special relationships. In doing so, Jesus tells us that we are insane:

> The ego is always alert to threat, and the part of your mind into which the ego was accepted is very anxious to preserve its reason, as it sees
> it. It does not realize that it is totally insane. And you must realize just what this means if you would be restored to sanity. The insane protect their thought systems, but they do so insanely. And all their defenses are as insane as what they are supposed to protect. The separation has nothing in it, no part, no "reason," and no attribute that is not insane. And its "protection" is part of it, as insane as the whole. The special relationship, which is its chief defense, must therefore be insane (T-17.IV.5).

After all, what else but "insane" might one call a thought system that rejects reality, believes in illusions, is driven by guilt and fear, and can only survive by investing all of its energy in defenses? Kenneth Wapnick has frequently made the pithy observation that the ego's defenses constitute a "maladaptive solution to a non-existent problem:"

> Since the danger is within the mind and *ideas leave not their source*...the world and body can offer no defense against the menacing attack inherent in the ego's thought system, at the same time...they reinforce the sense of

imminent and mortal danger. Thus the ego has successfully protected itself by first establishing a *non-existent problem*—the separation thought system of sin, guilt, and fear—and then making up a *maladaptive solution*—the world, body, and the special relationship. And all the while the true problem—the mind's decision for the ego—remains hidden, virtually inaccessible to the correction of Atonement.[1]

In the absence of fear, there is no need for defenses. When we use our power of decision as mind to choose the Holy Spirit instead of the ego, defenses and the attitude of defensiveness are absent, because fear is absent, thus special relationships can be let go and transformed by love into the all-embracing holy relationship.

The *knowledge* that "There is nothing to fear" (W-pI.48) is implicit in the right-minded thought system of the Holy Spirit, because the Holy Spirit's thought system rests on the Atonement principle, which is the truth that separation is impossible. This principle means that sin, guilt and fear are without foundation in truth, therefore the entire ego thought system is false. Jesus, as a manifestation of the Holy Spirit, demonstrated this through his crucifixion:

> The crucifixion is nothing more than an extreme example. Its value, like the value of any teaching device, lies solely in the kind of learning it facilitates. It can be, and has been, misunderstood. This is only because the fearful are apt to perceive fearfully. I have already told you that you can always call on me to share my decision [to accept the Atonement and identify with the Holy Spirit], and thus make it stronger. I have also told you that the crucifixion was the last useless journey the Sonship need take, and that it represents release from fear to anyone who understands it (T-6.I.2:1-6; brackets mine).

By identifying with the Holy Spirit's loving thought system of the Atonement, and *only* by identifying with that thought system of truth in our mind, whatever name one gives it, we can be free of fear, therefore able to be without defenses. Sanity is restored by identifying with the Holy Spirit. But our world and all that pertains to it is a projection of the ego whose insane thought system with its special relationships goes largely unexamined and unquestioned, hence it is that "fear is the one emotion of the world," and our lives are ruled by defenses and defensiveness. To repeat a portion of previously cited passage:

---

[1] Wapnick, Kenneth. "Identify With Love." *The Lighthouse*, Vol. 16, 3. Temecula, CA: Foundation for *A Course in Miracles*, 2005. (Also available on line at http://www.facim.org/acim/lh051603.htm)

The world gives rise but to defensiveness. For threat brings anger, anger makes attack seem reasonable, honestly provoked, and righteous in the name of self-defense....

It is as if a circle held... [the mind] fast, wherein another circle bound it and another one in that, until escape no longer can be hoped for nor obtained. Attack, defense; defense, attack, become the circles of the hours and the days that bind the mind in heavy bands of steel with iron overlaid, returning but to start again. There seems to be no break nor ending in the ever-tightening grip of the imprisonment upon the mind (W-pI.153.2:1-2; 3:1-3; bracket mine).

Because they were formulated within the paradigm of the ego thought system, neither Freud's psychoanalysis nor any system of psychotherapy ever contemplated being completely defenseless. Instead, in one way or another, the goal of conventional psychotherapy is to strengthen the ego and bring a "reality-based" balance to its defenses, which are seen as necessary for functioning in the world where threat is ever present. In the Course, however, Jesus states that not only are defenses unnecessary, but that they contribute to and support the insanity of the ego, and in fact defenses can never work to bring us true safety and peace:

You think you made a place of safety for yourself [i.e., the world, the body and special relationships]. You think you made a power that can save you from all the fearful things you see in dreams [i.e., defenses]. It is not so. Your safety lies not there. What you give up is merely the illusion of protecting illusions. And it is this you fear, and only this. How foolish to be so afraid of nothing! Nothing at all! Your defenses will not work, but you are not in danger. You have no need of them. Recognize this, and they will disappear. And only then will you accept your real protection (M-16.6:3-14; brackets mine). What can be expected from insane premises [i.e., that we are separate from God] except an insane conclusion [i.e., that we are a body and self-created]? The way to undo an insane conclusion is to consider the sanity of the premises on which it rests. You cannot *be* attacked [because you are mind and spirit; the one Creation of God at one with your Creator], attack *has* no justification, and you *are* responsible for what you believe (T-6.IN. 1:5-7; brackets mine).

As was discussed earlier, the Course is not intended to discredit common sense by advocating the foolish notion that we who still identify as bodies in a world of fear containing all kinds of perceived threats should give up the necessary defenses for negotiating life in the dream. After all, breathing itself is a defense, as are the other defensive requirements of the body, which include food, clothing, clean water and shelter. Exercising "good judgment" in interpersonal relationships, in driving a car, in obeying civil and criminal laws, and in conducting financial affairs, illustrate other forms of ego defenses necessary for "survival" in our dream of special relationships where scarcity and attack seem very real to us.

In the Course Jesus offers a way to be in the world and the body without fear and defenses, which means to be *in* them, but not *of* them—not *of* the ego thought system even though one goes about fulfilling the ordinary responsibilities of daily life in the illusion. For instance, through the practice of forgiveness, which means the undoing of guilt and fear, it is possible to be less and less anxious and defensive in interpersonal encounters. Likewise, it is possible to become less anxious and defensive about financial affairs and one's preferences for types of food and clothing. Through forgiveness, one is more able to live in the present moment free of fears from the past, therefore free of the defenses which those fears bring. Since learning to apply Jesus' psychology of undoing guilt is a *process*, at first the defenseless state of mind is transitory—in the Course it is called the *holy instant*—but the process leads eventually to a consistently right-minded state which in the Course is designated by the term *real world*.[2] Finally, from that fearless and defenseless state of mind spiritual awakening can occur.

Again, for students of the Course Jesus is the best model of what it means to actually live in an egoless, defenseless state—to live out of the *knowledge* that "I am not a body. I am free" (W-pI.199). That is why he describes his crucifixion as representing our "last useless journey," which would be the journey of the body to death. Recall that in the Course, resurrection is of the *mind* not the body. Resurrection, which means to accept the Atonement, is salvation of the mind from the fear and defensiveness imposed by the belief in separation, therefore from the belief that the world and body are real. Resurrection of the mind is salvation from the ego thought system accomplished by the "miracle" of choosing the Holy Spirit's thought system.

In Wapnick's *Glossary* we find the following definition of *defenses* according to both their wrong-minded purpose as well as their reinterpretation by the Holy Spirit for right-minded purposes:

> wrong-mind: the dynamics we use to "protect" ourselves from our guilt, fear, and seeming attack of others, the most important of which are denial and projection; by their very nature "defenses do what they would defend,"

---

[2] Wapnick's *Glossary* defines *real world* in part as: "the state of mind in which, through total forgiveness, the world of perception is released from the projections of guilt we had placed upon it: thus, it is the mind that has changed, not the world, and we see through the vision of Christ which blesses rather than condemns;..."

as they reinforce the belief in our own vulnerability which merely increases our fear and belief that we need defense.

right-mind: reinterpreted as the means to free us from fear; e.g., denial denies the "denial of truth" [i.e., the ego] and projecting our guilt enables us to be aware of what we have denied, so that we may truly forgive it.

In the interest of clarity, it may be helpful to distinguish between defenses and defense *mechanisms*, although the two terms are often used interchangeably. For instance, the special relationship is a primary *form* of ego defense which arises out of the defense *mechanism* of projection, which in turn follows the mechanism of denial. We have seen that included within the special relationship are other *forms* of defenses such as attack and victimization. Illusions themselves are defenses against the truth, but the *mechanisms* underlying these defenses are the same: denial and projection. Thus, the term *mechanisms* could be substituted for *dynamics* in the above definition, while the truth that "defenses do what they would defend" can be seen in the fact that the defense of attack does not alleviate fear, but produces more fear and attack.

It was Sigmund Freud who discovered the ego's mechanisms of defense which he identified and interpreted according to his theory where these mechanisms were seen to be employed in the brain of individuals as their ego struggled to deal with threats posed by id impulses, the environment and the demands of the superego. Later, his daughter Anna, also a psychoanalyst, further developed and elaborated the concept of ego defense mechanisms, and she is usually given credit for doing the major work on the subject, while she acknowledged her father's genius in making the original discovery.[3]

As has been pointed out, in the Course Jesus makes use of Freud's discoveries, but applies them at a spiritual level of mind which was unrecognized by Freud, and no doubt would have been unacceptable to him. Basically, Freud identified the function of defense mechanisms as being that of coping with fear, but capable of doing so irrationally when the mechanisms of defense distort, disguise or deny the truth. Thus, Freud's basic concept of defense mechanisms is applicable for understanding the Course's ego thought system and what is meant by *wrong-mindedness*. While Freud and his daughter identified several defense mechanisms, as the *Glossary* definition indicates, the Course's system of psychology primarily makes use of the mechanisms of *denial* and *projection*, but also of relevance in the Course

---

[3] Freud, Anna. *The Ego and the Mechanisms of Defence*. London: Hogarth Press and Institute of Psycho-Analysis, 1937.

is the mechanism of *dissociation*. We shall discuss all three, beginning with denial which, speaking in terms of the illusion of linear time, was the first defense mechanism the ego made. As with other elements of the ego thought system, we shall see that defenses and defense mechanisms are integral parts of the whole. In fact, the ancillary elements we have discussed serve a defensive purpose, while defense mechanisms themselves are interrelated, drawing upon one another, mutually supportive, and really not distinct though we can speak of them in terms of separate functions serving to maintain the primary defensive function of unconsciousness—the function which effectively keeps us mindless.

An excellent summary discussion of defenses appears in ACIM Workbook Lesson 136, which is specifically concerned with illness as a defense. The title of that very important lesson is: "Sickness is a defense against the truth." In this book's chapter two explanation of the Course's concept of mind, excerpts from that lesson were quoted in reference to the idea of "the unconscious." For the purpose of concluding our discussion thus far, the following excerpted passages repeat and add to some of the previously quoted material. As we proceed, we will be revisiting some of the important points made below. It should be noted that these passages could not reasonably be addressed to the ego self who mindlessly believes in the reality of the body. That self is itself a defense which does not choose, but has been chosen. It results from the mind's decision to embrace the ego thought system. These passages are most meaningful when understood as being addressed to us as *mind*, and specifically as the mind's decision maker who, though having chosen the ego, is capable of assuming the observer position and *looking* objectively within:

> Defenses are not unintentional, nor are they made without awareness. They are secret, magic wands you wave when truth appears to threaten what you would believe. They seem to be unconscious but because of the rapidity with which you choose to use them. In that second, even less, in which the choice is made, you recognize exactly what you would attempt to do, and then proceed to think that it is done.

> Who but yourself evaluates a threat, decides escape is necessary, and sets up a series of defenses to reduce the threat that has been judged as real? All this cannot be done unconsciously. But afterwards, your plan requires that you must forget you made it, so it seems to be external to your own intent; a happening beyond your state of mind, an outcome with a real effect on you, instead of one effected by yourself.

> It is this quick forgetting of the part you play in making your "reality" that makes defenses seem to be beyond your own control. But what you have

forgot can be remembered, given willingness to reconsider the decision which is doubly shielded by oblivion. Your not remembering is but the sign that this decision still remains in force, as far as your desires are concerned. Mistake not this for fact. Defenses must make facts unrecognizable. They aim at doing this, and it is this they do.

Every defense takes fragments of the whole, assembles them without regard to all their true relationships, and thus constructs illusions of a whole that is not there. It is this process that imposes threat, and not whatever outcome may result. When parts are wrested from the whole and seen as separate and wholes within themselves, they become symbols standing for attack upon the whole; successful in effect, and never to be seen as whole again. And yet you have forgotten that they stand but for your own decision of what should be real, to take the place of what is real. (W-pI.136.3-6)

Denial

This defense mechanism is used in the service of a wish to have truth be other than what it is. It represents a decision not to know and to lie, first of all to oneself. Thus, it represents an attack on truth as well as upon oneself as mind. It is the mechanism whereby truth is relegated to unconsciousness and made fearful. In fact, it is the mechanism whereby what is called "the unconscious" is made; and since implicit in denial is threat and fear, the unconscious thereby becomes fearful. It is the ego's purpose to keep it that way: to make what is unconscious so fearful that we never dare to look at it; to render us afraid of our own mind. In this connection, an important function of perception is to support denial by keeping our attention focused "outside," away from the mind where the *knowledge* of oneness, having been denied, is now buried beneath a blanket of guilt and fear.

In the Course we are told: "The ego is a wrong-minded attempt to perceive yourself as you wish to be, rather than as you are" (T-3.IV.2:3). Since it is our ego's wish to be separate and special, the ego begins with the denial of oneness. Thus, the entire ego thought system begins with a defense, which is actually an attack on God, and then becomes an elaborate system of defenses. So our ego lives dedicated to specialness amount to an elaborate system of defenses or, more bluntly, an elaborate system of lies.

The concept of denial as a mechanism of defense is widely recognized in the world, not only in psychological theories of personality and psychotherapy, but in common parlance as well as in the important layman's twelve-step system of dealing with addictions which began with the work of *Alcoholics Anonymous* where the first, fourth, fifth, eighth and tenth steps in the recovery process can be understood as involving the undoing of denial.

Additionally, an important 1973 book by Ernest Becker dealt with the pervasive tendency to avoid facing the subject of death, and was entitled, *The Denial of Death*.[1] Likewise, the practice of denial as it relates to death has received broad attention following the work of Elisabeth Kubler Ross who identified denial as the first of five stages people go through in accepting death, whether their own or that of a loved one.[2]

Given Jesus' teaching that the mechanism of denial is directly involved in the origin and continuing maintenance of the ego thought system, and that that thought system forms the template for the illusion of separated life, it is not surprising that we find the widespread use of denial in our world, which is itself a defense that denies the truth of mind and spirit: "What makes this world seem real except your own denial of the truth that lies beyond?" (W-pI.165.1:1)

As long as we believe we are bodies and that the ego's illusory world is real, we must employ the defense of denial on a moment-to-moment basis or we would be incapacitated by fear. The world is full of threats of all kinds which could kill our body at any moment: earthquakes, lightning, asteroids, hurricanes, automobiles, bullets, bombs, poisonous snakes and insects, viruses and bacteria, to name a few. We may know of these threats, but we must distance ourselves emotionally from them by denying their personal relevance or we would literally be flooded with a crippling level of anxiety.

Wapnick's *Glossary* definition of *denial* recognizes that it has both a right- and wrong-minded use according to the principle that the Holy Spirit's thought system of the Atonement can make loving use of everything the ego has made:

> <u>wrong-minded</u>: avoiding guilt by pushing the decision that made it out of awareness, rendering it inaccessible to correction or Atonement; roughly equivalent to repression; protects the ego's belief that it is our source and not God.

> <u>right-minded</u>: used to deny error and affirm truth: to deny "the denial of truth."

The wrong-minded use of denial as a mechanism of defense means that once the decision has been made to believe in separation and deny oneness, then the fact that separation is a *decision* is hidden from awareness by the

---

[1] Becker, Ernest. *The Denial of Death*. New York: The Free Press, 1973.

[2] Kubler-Ross, Elizabeth. *On Death and Dying*. New York: Touchstone, 1997. (Originally published in 1969.)

ego so that it cannot be evaluated. Of course, fear motivates this denial, and that fear comes from the guilt aroused by belief that separation is real, therefore is a sin punishable not only by death, but by damnation and eternal suffering.

Denial basically says, "Separation is a fact and I am *not* responsible for it." This message not only denies God, but denies the guilt over deciding to believe separation is real, repressing it into the unconscious along with awareness of the mind and its decision-making power. The unconscious now hides from awareness what the ego most fears: the mind and its power of decision along with the truth of oneness. Thus we are rendered effectively mindless—unaware that we are mind—while guilt is kept unconscious in order to preserve it. The ego thrives on guilt, but must keep it and our reality as mind hidden in order to protect itself from being exposed as a choice based on a lie, therefore subject to being evaluated and discarded. Freud discovered that what is denied or repressed in what he called the *psyche* will find a way to surface and be projected, often in the form of a physical or psychological symptom, but also in the form of anger and attack. This dynamic constitutes a law of mind that is incorporated in the Course's psychology. Because it is a law of mind that what is denied will find a way to be expressed, guilt becomes a powerful motivator in the dream. The means by which guilt surfaces is through the mechanism of projection, which produces special relationships: "The ego tells you all is black with guilt within you, and bids you not to look. Instead, it bids you look upon your brothers, and see the guilt in them" (T-13.IX. 8:2-3).

The message of denial that says separation is a fact also makes the world, body, suffering and death seem to be the truth. Thus, the ego becomes the author of what we think of as life and the ego's god of crucifixion and suffering is made real. This can be seen in words from Genesis found in the King James Version of the Bible where the ego's storybook God believes in separation and sin, and then excludes Adam and Eve from His Kingdom of spirit, condemning them to physical lives of sorrow and death:

> Unto the woman he said, I will greatly multiply thy sorrow and thy conception; in sorrow thou shalt bring forth children....And unto Adam he said, ...cursed is the ground for thy sake; in sorrow shalt thou eat of it all the days of thy life; Thorns also and thistles shall it bring forth to thee; and thou shalt eat the herb of the field; In the   sweat of thy face shalt thou eat bread, till thou return unto the ground; for out of it wast thou taken: for dust thou art, and unto dust shalt thou return (Genesis 3:16-19).

Belief in the ego's god of crucifixion, which accompanies denial of the true God of Love, serves as a defense which justifies attack. After all, "If God can attack, victimize and produce suffering, *in the name of God* so can I." In another context within the Course where he discusses the story of his own crucifixion, Jesus says: "...the real Christian should pause and ask, 'How could this be?' Is it likely that God Himself would be capable of the kind of thinking which His Own words have clearly stated is unworthy of His Son?....Persecution frequently results in an attempt to 'justify' the terrible misperception that God Himself persecuted His Own Son ..." (T-3.I.1:8-9; 2:4).

Because we as mind have the power of decision, if we accept Jesus' invitation to look within we can choose to let the Holy Spirit correct the errors of the ego. If we are willing, the right-minded use of denial by the Holy Spirit will undo the denial of God and the guilt which accompanies that denial. Right-minded denial basically says: "No, separation is not real. You are mind and the Son of God with the power to choose, and you have made a silly mistake which can be corrected. There is nothing to feel guilty about and no punishment to fear." Of course, this also denies the reality of the illusion of the world, body, suffering and death:

> Denial has no power in itself, but you can give it the power of your mind, whose power is without limit [in other words, you as mind have the power of decision which will determine what you experience as reality]. If you use it to deny reality, reality is gone for you. *Reality cannot be partly appreciated.* That is why denying any part of it [i.e., judging against and excluding anyone or anything] means you have lost the awareness of all of it. Yet denial is a defense, and so it is as capable of being used positively as well as negatively. Used negatively it will be destructive, because it will be used for attack [i.e. to deny oneness and to enable the projection of guilt onto others]. But in the service of the Holy Spirit, it can help you recognize part of reality [e.g., that you are not separate from a perceived other], and thus appreciate all of it. Mind is too powerful to be subject to exclusion. You will never be able to exclude yourself from your thoughts [by attempting to exclude anyone or anything you perceive, which are in fact projections of the *one* mind we all share] (T-7.VII.1:5-13; brackets mine).

The last two quoted sentences above are saying that the ego's attempt to use denial in order to render us mindless ultimately cannot work. Meanwhile, the Holy Spirit's use of denial "*to deny the denial of truth*" (T-12.II.1:5) restores us to mind*ful*ness and awareness of our true Identity.

Many are afraid of blasphemy, but they do not understand what it means. They do not realize that to deny God is to deny their own Identity, and in this sense the wages of sin *is* death. The sense is very literal; denial of life perceives its opposite, as all forms of denial replace what is with what is not. No one can really do this, but that you can think you can and believe you have is beyond dispute.

Allegiance to the denial of God is the ego's religion...Blasphemy...is *self-destructive*, not God-destructive. It means that you are willing *not* to know yourself...This is the offering your god [of specialness] demands because, having made him out of your insanity [i.e. the ego thought system], he is an insane idea. He has many forms, but although he may seem to be many different things he is but one idea;—the denial of God. (T-10.V.1:4-7; 3:1, 5-8; bracket and second italics mine).

Through an incisive application of logic, Jesus makes an important point about denial, which is that the mind would not attempt to deny something that it knew was untrue. What is false can be left to witness for itself, but if what is true threatens a false idea that one wishes to believe, then denial will be employed. Thus, the ego's denial of God (Love) is actually a demonstration of the truth of oneness and the appeal of Love. The attempt to replace love with fear can be understood as recognition of the reality and appeal of love which is denied because it is threatening to our ego identity:

Son of God, you have not sinned, but you have been much mistaken. Yet this can be corrected and God will help you [through the Holy Spirit], knowing that you could not sin against Him [a statement of the Atonement principle]. You denied Him because you loved Him, knowing that if you recognized your love for Him, you could not deny Him [but neither could you be separate]. Your denial of Him therefore means that you love Him, and that you know He loves you [because love is the essence of oneness]. Remember that what you deny you must have once known. And if you accept denial, you can accept its undoing (T-10.V.6; brackets mine).

Fear and love are the only emotions of which you are capable. One is false, for it was made out of denial [i.e., separation denies Oneness, thus leading to guilt and fear]; and denial depends on the belief in what is denied for its own existence. By interpreting fear correctly as a positive affirmation of the underlying belief it masks, you are undermining its perceived usefulness by rendering it useless. Defenses that do not work at all are automatically discarded. If you raise what fear conceals [i.e., love] to clear-cut unequivocal predominance, fear becomes meaningless. You have denied its power to conceal love, which was its only purpose. The veil that you have drawn across the face of love has disappeared. [In other words, the denial of truth has been undone: "The task of the miracle worker...[is] *to deny the denial of truth*" (T-12.II.1:5; bracket mine).]

121

If you would look upon love, which *is* the world's reality [in the sense that it is the mind's reality—an indirect reference to the concept of the *real world*], how could you do better than to recognize, in every defense against it, the underlying appeal *for* it? And how could you better learn of its reality than by answering the appeal for it [i.e., some expression of fear] by giving it? The Holy Spirit's interpretation of fear [as a call for love] does dispel it, for the awareness of truth cannot be denied. Thus does the Holy Spirit replace fear with love and translate error into truth. And thus will you learn of Him how to replace your dream of separation with the fact of unity. For the separation is only the denial of union, and correctly interpreted, attests to your eternal knowledge that union is true (T-12.I. 9:5-10:1-6; brackets mine).

Dissociation

The mechanism of dissociation works hand-in-hand with denial, serving to split off what has been denied in order to keep it unconscious, thus it involves a conscious decision to forget. But the decision itself is immediately denied and forgotten, which means that dissociation serves the ego's goal of keeping us unaware of mind and our power to choose. This involves an ongoing decision not to look within—to live the unexamined life. Since, in truth, the only real time is now—the present moment—in each moment we continue either to deny and dissociate the truth, or to look within to know ourselves as mind and reclaim our power of decision. The ongoing decision not to look within is basically a statement that says: "I don't want to know about this," which is a statement of fear that keeps fear alive in our mind. Throughout the Course, Jesus tells us that if we will accept his invitation to *look*, we will not find the horror of sin and guilt that the ego subliminally whispers is present in our unconscious mind, but we will be able to look past the ego's defenses to the love that is our true nature and which has not been defiled and denied by the mistaken belief we are separate.

Examples of the mechanism of dissociation are seen in the myth of the ladder of separation, where there are four levels of dissociation or splitting off: 1) the mind of the Son is dissociated from the Mind of God; 2) within the separated mind, the wrong mind (ego) is dissociated from right mind (Holy Spirit); 3) the ego's image of self as victim and God as victimizer reinforces the dissociation between wrong and right mind; 4) the dissociation of mind from itself which leads to the projection of a physical world and bodies, while our identity as mind is forgotten. Wapnick describes this final level in his *Glossary* under the definition of *split*: "the final ontological split wherein the guilt in our minds is denied and projected out, making a separated world of attack and death, a world which appears to be split off from the mind that thought it."

One can simplify an understanding of how dissociation relates to the psychology of the Course by thinking in terms of two basic levels of splitting off. First, would be the level at which God is denied and dissociated so that separation seems to be the truth. At this level, knowledge of our true Self as Christ—the non-separate, loving extension of oneness within the Mind of God—is split off from the illusion of our ego self: Self is dissociated from self; Mind from mind. Because this level of dissociation is equivalent to the belief in separation, guilt and fear are implicated in it and will continue to be implicated at all levels of dissociation.

> The ego is nothing more than a part of your belief about yourself. Your other life has continued without interruption, and has been and always will be totally unaffected by your attempts to dissociate it....The ego and the spirit do not know each other. The separated mind cannot maintain the separation except by dissociating. Having done this, it denies all truly natural impulses, not because the ego is a separate thing, but because you want to believe that *you* are. The ego is a device for maintaining this belief, but it is still only your decision to use the device that enables it to endure....

> Love does not conquer all things [because love does not oppose or attack], but it does set all things right. Because you are the Kingdom of God I can lead you back to your own creations [i.e., extensions of the Thought of Love which come from our function as a creation of God within His Mind]. You do not recognize them now, but what has been dissociated is still there (T-4.VI.1:6-7; 4; 7:6-8; brackets mine).

> Any split in mind must involve a rejection of part of it, and this *is* the belief in separation. The wholeness of God, which is His peace, cannot be appreciated except by a whole mind that recognizes the wholeness of God's creation. By this recognition it knows its Creator. Exclusion and separation are synonymous, as are separation and dissociation. We have said before that the separation was and is dissociation, and that once it occurs projection becomes its main defense, or the device that keeps it going (T-6.II.1-5).

The second basic level of dissociation in our simplified schema is the one with which the Course's psychology of forgiveness is most directly concerned: the dissociation which takes place *within* the separated mind where the ego thought system is dissociated from the Holy Spirit's thought system of the Atonement. This level is emphasized in Wapnick's *Glossary* definition of *dissociation*:

> an ego defense that separates the ego from the Holy Spirit—the wrong mind from the right mind—splitting off what seems fearful, which merely

reinforces the fear that is the ego's goal; the ego's attempt to separate two conflicting thought systems and keep them both in our minds, so that *its* thought system of darkness is safe from undoing by the light.

Dissociation at this level reinforces fear, because its implicit message is that there is something fearful in the mind to be avoided, and because dissociation began with an attack on truth, which is fearful in and of itself. As with all defenses, if there were nothing to fear, the energy required to mount and maintain the defense of dissociation would not be necessary. Thus, the mere fact of dissociation produces an inner sense of tension which signals the presence of fear in the unconscious. Further, the effect of this dissociation within our mind is to produce internal conflict and continuing demand for our ego identity to maintain defenses, because that identity is threatened by the truth of oneness which the Holy Spirit remembers for us. By this dissociation, our mind becomes split, often being referred to in the Course as the "split mind."

The function of mind is thought, and the activity of thought requires that it either be extended or projected within the mind itself.[1] Thus, it is a law of the split mind that it must either wrong-mindedly *project* the thought of guilt or right-mindedly *extend* the thought of love. Therefore, since mind can only project according to its own nature, the split mind projects a split or divided world: a world with conflicting and competing goals, and a world of ambivalent love divided between specialness and forgiveness.

The perception of differences is necessary in order for there to be special relationships with all of their elements; their various forms of attack. In order for the mind to be healed of its split, the Holy Spirit must correct the perception of differences with the *vision* of oneness. This is only possible when we become aware of our identity as mind by accepting the invitation to look within, and then exercise our power of decision so that the two dissociated thought systems can be brought together wherein the ego's thought system of separation and darkness must disappear in the presence of the Holy Spirit's light of the Atonement—the light of love:

> Dissociation is a distorted process of thinking whereby two systems of belief which cannot coexist are both maintained. If they are brought together, their joint acceptance becomes impossible. But if one is kept in darkness from the other, their separation seems to keep them both alive and equal in their reality. Their joining thus becomes the source of fear, for if they meet, acceptance must be withdrawn from one of them. You cannot have them both, for each denies the other. Apart, this fact is lost from sight, for each in

---

[1] Recall the principle: *ideas leave not their source.*

a separate place can be endowed with firm belief. Bring them together, and the fact of their complete incompatibility is instantly apparent. One will go, because the other is seen in the same place (T-14.VII.4:3-10).

In order to demonstrate that dissociation witnesses to truth, Jesus uses the same logic as he employs in demonstrating that denial witnesses to truth. Unless the mind was aware of something, it would not be motivated to split it off. And since what is being preserved is the idea of separation, what must be split off is the truth of oneness. Hence, the act of dissociation, which protects the idea of separation, means that the truth of non-separation must be present in our mind. Further, Jesus points out that we are not really afraid of *what* we have dissociated (the Presence of love; the Holy Spirit), but of the fact that we have engaged in attack, which is always fearful:

> Unless you first know something you cannot dissociate it. *Knowledge* must precede dissociation, so that dissociation is nothing more than a decision to forget. What has been forgotten then appears to be fearful [thus fear is associated with the unconscious], but only because the dissociation is an attack on truth. You are fearful *because* you have forgotten. And you have replaced your *knowledge* by an awareness of dreams because you are afraid of your dissociation, not of what you have dissociated. When what you have dissociated is accepted, it ceases to be fearful....

> To remember is merely to restore to your mind *what is already there*. You do not make what you remember; you merely accept again what is already there, but was rejected (T-10.II.1, 3:1-2; brackets and first two italics mine).

The psychology of the Course aims to undo the defenses of denial and dissociation, which is what is meant in the introduction to the ACIM Text where it is stated: "The course does not aim at teaching the meaning of love, for that is beyond what can be taught. It does aim, however, at removing the blocks to the awareness of love's presence, [in our mind]..." (T-IN.1:6-7). The process of undoing defenses heals the split mind, thus relieving us of the conflict and fear inherent in dissociation. In Lesson 96 of the Course's Workbook one finds an inspiring invitation to this process along with a summary of some important Course concepts. A lengthy excerpt from this lesson serves to conclude our discussion of dissociation.

In reading this, it is important to pay close attention to capitalization, which has very specific meanings in the Course. Capital "S" Self = Christ, our true Identity, while little "s" self refers to the split mind and the conflicted self identity it produces, most usually the wrong-minded ego self. Little "m" mind = split mind. Capital "S" Source = God.

As always, these passages are addressed to us as mind; specifically as the Son of God who is the mind's decision maker:

> Although you are one Self, you experience yourself as two; as both good and evil, loving and hating, mind and body. This sense of being split into opposites induces feelings of acute and constant conflict, and leads to frantic attempts to reconcile the contradictory aspects of this self-perception. You have sought many such solutions, and none of them has worked. The opposites you see in you will never be compatible. But one exists.
>
> The fact that truth and illusion cannot be reconciled, no matter how you try, what means you use and where you see the problem, must be accepted if you would be saved. Until you have accepted this, you will attempt an endless list of goals you cannot reach; a senseless series of expenditures of time and effort, hopefulness and doubt, each one as futile as the one before, and failing as the next one surely will.
>
> Problems that have no meaning cannot be resolved within the framework they are set. Two selves in conflict could not be resolved, and good and evil have no meeting place. The self you made can never be your Self, nor can your Self be split in two, and still be what It is and must forever be. A mind and body cannot both exist. Make no attempt to reconcile the two, for one denies the other can be real. If you are physical, your mind is gone from your self-concept, for it has no place in which it could be really part of you. If you are spirit, then the body must be meaningless to your reality.
>
> Spirit makes use of mind as means to find its Self expression. And the mind which serves the spirit is at peace and filled with joy. Its power comes from spirit, and it is fulfilling happily its function here. Yet mind can also see itself divorced from spirit, and perceive itself within a body it confuses with itself. Without its function then it has no peace, and happiness is alien to its thoughts.
>
> Yet mind apart from spirit cannot think. It has denied its Source of strength, and sees itself as helpless, limited and weak. Dissociated from its function now, it thinks it is alone and separate, attacked by armies massed against itself and hiding in the body's frail support. Now must it reconcile unlike with like, for this is what it thinks that it is for.
>
> Waste no more time on this. Who can resolve the senseless conflicts which a dream presents? What could the resolution mean in truth? What purpose could it serve? What is it for? Salvation cannot make illusions real, nor solve a problem [i.e., separation] that does not exist. Perhaps you hope it can [through special relationships, which are the ego's version of salvation]. Yet would you have God's plan for the release of His dear Son bring pain to him, and fail to set him free? [As we have seen, special relationships are painful and ultimately must fail to find love and peace, or to escape from guilt and fear.] (W-pI.96.1-6; brackets mine).

Projection

Thought is the activity of mind, and in the Course we are told that the mind is very powerful, never sleeps and is quite active (T-2.VI.9:5-6; T-3.IV.5:2). In Heaven—in the Mind of God—the *extension* of Thought is the means of creation, but as noted previously, in this context, and as it is used in the Course, the term *extension* cannot be interpreted according to the definitions and understandings of our perceptual world. In terms of the Course's metaphysics, the process of creation may be called the "non-separate extension of Thought within the Mind of God." But that description must remain fundamentally meaningless to a mind that believes in separation, measurable space, linear time, and has limited its understanding to what can be symbolized in the dualistic brain. The Mind of God is not confined within the dimensions of time and space, nor are time and space dimensions within God. St. Augustine (354-430 A.D.) expressed this incomprehensibility by giving words to an understanding which probably was uttered first by the Greek philosopher Empedocles (490-340 B.C.). He stated that the nature of God is like a circle whose center is everywhere, and whose circumference is nowhere.

Nevertheless, in the Course Jesus uses the term *extension* to indicate the creative activity of spirit via the agency of thought. (Remember, "The term *mind* is used to represent the *activating* agent of spirit, supplying its creative energy," C-1.1:1; second italics mine). In the Mind of God, the active nature of Thought means that it *must* extend. Paralleling this law of Mind, in the separated mind thought *must* project, which represents the ego's *mis*creative use of the power of mind.

> We have said that without projection there can be no anger, but it is also true that without extension there can be no love. These reflect a fundamental law of the mind, and therefore one that always operates. It is the law by which you create and were created. It is the law that unifies the Kingdom, and keeps it in the Mind of God. To the ego, the law is perceived as a means of getting rid of something it does not want. To the Holy Spirit, it is the fundamental law of sharing, by which you give what you value in order to keep it in your mind. To the Holy Spirit it is the law of extension. To the ego it is the law of deprivation. It therefore produces abundance or scarcity, depending on how you choose to apply it. This choice is up to you, but it is not up to you to decide whether or not you will utilize the law. Every mind must project or extend, because that is how it lives, and every mind is life (T-7.VIII.1).

The defense mechanism of projection is central in the Course's explanation of the ego and how it is undone through forgiveness, which requires that we recognize and take back our projections. We have mentioned this defensive strategy frequently. Like all other defenses and elements of the ego thought system, it operates as an integral part of the whole which has the purpose of keeping us mindless while maintaining the belief in separation, yet divesting responsibility for choosing to believe in it by casting guilt away. To do this, the mechanism of projection makes up the illusion of a world outside the mind—a world of perception: "Projection makes perception" (T-13.V.3:5; T-21.IN.1:1)—thus attempting to overturn the basic law of mind that *ideas leave not their source*. Projection involves an ego attempt to escape the mind where loving truth is present, as well as an attempt to get rid of guilt by placing it outside one's self onto someone or something else that can be blamed for the negative consequences of separation. Yet projection reinforces guilt, because it always involves attack:

> We have said before that the separation was and is dissociation, and that once it occurs projection becomes its main defense, or the device that keeps it going. The reason, however, may not be so obvious as you think.

> What you project you disown, and therefore do not believe is yours. You are excluding yourself by the very judgment that you are different from the one on whom you project. Since you have also judged against what you project, you continue to attack it because you continue to keep it separated. By doing this unconsciously, you try to keep the fact that you attacked yourself out of awareness, and thus imagine that you have made yourself safe.

> Yet projection will always hurt you. It reinforces your belief in your own split mind, and its only purpose is to keep the separation going. It is solely a device of the ego to make you feel different from your brothers and separated from them. The ego justifies this on the grounds that it makes you seem "better" than they are, thus obscuring your equality with them still further. Projection and attack are inevitably related, because projection is always a means of justifying attack. Anger without projection is impossible. The ego uses projection only to destroy your perception of both yourself and your brothers. The process begins by excluding something that exists in you but which you do not want, and leads directly to excluding you from your brothers.

> We have learned, however, that there *is* an alternative to projection. Every ability of the ego has a better use, because its abilities are directed by the mind, which has a better Voice. The Holy Spirit extends and the ego projects. As their goals are opposed, so is the result. (T-6.II.1:5-6; 2-4).

Projection is the mind's attempt to get rid of an idea or thought that it does not want; an attempt to dump one's mental trash (guilt in all its various

128

forms) on the roadside where someone else will have to deal with it. But the attempt does not work. Unlike the world, where one can leave one's garbage on the road and drive away, nothing can be discarded from the mind to be left outside, because there is *no* outside: *ideas leave not their source.* Thought begins and ends in the mind. The only way to get rid of our mental garbage of guilt is first of all not to deny it, but to acknowledge it—to *look* at it. Next, we must be willing to accept responsibility for our choice to believe in separation and guilt. Then, finally, our guilt can be released to the Holy Spirit. The Holy Spirit *knows* that guilt is as unreal and impossible as sin, and in the light of His *knowledge* the garbage of guilt is disposed of. One could say that the Holy Spirit is the mind's automatic garbage disposal unit. The garbage disposed of is all our guilty thoughts which we project onto others in all forms of attack, whether acted out overtly, or experienced within as thoughts of rejection and judgmental condemnation. Likewise, we may dump our pail of guilty garbage onto our own heads as we project onto our self; projections which take the form of mental and physical symptoms of any kind, ranging from mild depression to terminal diseases of the body.

Because the highly active nature of thought means that in the separated mind it *must* be projected, and because projection does not rid the mind of its thoughts, projection will continue until the Holy Spirit is invited into the process. Then we can be helped to non-judgmentally examine our guilt and the various forms that it takes. In terms of Jesus' psychology, the only way for our mind to be rid of the thoughts it does not want is for us as decision maker to place thought under the direction of the Holy Spirit Who transforms the ego's hateful illusions of specialness into images of forgiveness. Forgiveness involves allowing the Holy Spirit to transform projection from attack into understanding and acceptance. Projection then becomes a *reflection* of extension, paralleling the activity of Thought in the Mind of God.

The definition of *projection* found in Wapnick's *Glossary* is:

> the fundamental law of mind: projection makes perception -- what we see inwardly determines what we see outside our minds.
>
> wrong mind: reinforces guilt by displacing it onto someone else, attacking it there and denying its presence in ourselves; an attempt to shift responsibility for separation from ourselves to others.
>
> right mind: the principle of extension, undoing guilt by allowing the forgiveness of the Holy Spirit to be extended (projected) through us.

There is no more important principle in the Course than the one which states that "projection makes perception." This principle explains how the illusory world of perception was made *within* the mind where it then becomes a screen permitting the further projection of guilt—the projection of special relationship images which seem to constitute our private lives. In turn, guilt over the "sin" of denying God hides the truth of His Love in a shroud of fear in our mind, while the decision which produced guilt is in turn shielded from awareness by the illusory world which keeps our attention focused away from the mind. The purpose of this double layer of defenses is to prevent us from *looking* within where we could discover the ego's lies and the source of all conflicts, all human problems and all of our unhappiness. Again, that source is simply the *decision* to believe in separation and then to accept the ego's story of sin, guilt and fear.

There are two places in the Course where the principle is stated that projection makes (*not* "creates") perception. Each is of central importance and contains profound implications. So that we can move from the more general to the more specific, we will consider them in the reverse order of their appearance in the ACIM Text:

> Projection makes perception. The world you see is what you gave it, nothing more than that. But though it is no more than that, it is not less. Therefore, to you it is important. It is the witness to your state of mind, the outside picture of an inward condition. As a man thinketh, so does he perceive. Therefore, seek not to change the world, but choose to change your mind about the world. Perception is a result and not a cause. And that is why order of difficulty in miracles is meaningless. Everything looked upon with vision [i.e. perception informed by the Holy Spirit] is healed and holy. Nothing perceived without it means anything. And where there is no meaning, there is chaos (T-21.IN.1; bracket mine).

As has been pointed out repeatedly, the "you" being addressed is us as mind with the capacity to decide. The world we project reflects the thought system we have chosen; therefore what we perceive is a reflection of the content of our own mind. To see a bastard without we first must have seen a bastard within. To see some egregious act as a call for love, we have to have seen that same call within our own mind and heart, which the Holy Spirit and Jesus know, and will show to us. There is in truth no world out there! We see what we want to see, and we first began to see with the ego. Projection originated with the ego thought system, energized by its belief in sin, guilt and fear. So perception is first of all a reflection of the ego wherein we see differences, competition and conflict, cause for hatred and attack, grounds for judgmental condemnation and the necessity that others must suffer and sacrifice if we are to survive. The reason that all relationships in this world begin as special is that projection makes perception and the first projections come from the ego. Additionally, our concepts and images of self come from the ego, and it is these the ego would have us defend at all cost. (Ultimately the cost is to ourselves in the loss of the awareness of love, but the ego would have us believe that the cost is to others, never realizing that the "others" we perceive are but split off aspects of our self which have been projected from our own mind.)

To repeat, "projection makes perception," so what we perceive comes from *within* our own mind: "There is no sight, be it of dreams or from a truer Source, that is not but the shadow of the seen through inward vision. There perception starts, and there it ends. It has no source but this" (W-pI.188.2:6-8). Because of this fact, there is no point in attempting to change what appears as the images of an outside world on the screen of projection in our mind. In order for a meaningful change to occur, we have to change our mind, and then the projections will change; not *what* is projected, but *how* we *interpret* and react to what we perceive. As for the *what*: "This world was over long ago. The thoughts that made it are no longer in the mind that thought of them and loved them for a little while" (T-28.I.1:6-7). The goal of forgiveness is first to change our perceptual *interpretations*, and then to awaken from the dream of perception altogether.

The very nature of perception is separation—differences—because it begins with the ego. From there, perception involves *interpretation*; so how we interpret what we perceive depends upon which thought system we choose. The dynamic of projection is that we wind up keeping what we sought to give away. This reflects another basic Course principle that giving and receiving are the same just as teaching and learning are the same: we give what we want to keep and we teach what we want to learn. This parallels the law of extension in Heaven, that Love is always extending and creating Itself. If we choose the ego and project separation, sin and guilt, we reinforce in ourselves the belief that we are separate, sinful and guilty. Projecting guilt involves attack, so when we justify attack in thought or action, we are attacking ourselves and teaching attack to ourselves and others. Basically this means that we are teaching and learning hatred. Even more basically, it means that we are teaching and learning murder: "What is not love [the *vision* of oneness] is murder [separation]. What is not loving must be an attack. Every illusion [i.e., perception of form and differences] is an assault on truth, and every... [illusion] does violence to the idea of love because it seems to be of equal truth" (T-23.IV.1:10-12; brackets mine).

131

> To the extent to which you value guilt, to that extent will you perceive a world in which attack is justified. To the extent to which you recognize that guilt is meaningless, to that extent you will perceive attack cannot *be* justified. This is in accord with perception's fundamental law: You see what you believe is there, and you believe it there because you want it there. Perception has no other law than this. The rest but stems from this, to hold it up and offer it support. This is perception's form, adapted to this world, of God's more basic law; that love creates itself, and nothing but itself (T-25.III.1).

> Perception seems to teach you what you see. Yet it but witnesses to what you taught. It is the outward picture of a wish; an image that you wanted to be true (T-24.VII. 8:8-9).

One might ask how it is that we can agree upon what we perceive in the world at large. If I am projecting the world I see, why is it that this world seems to be the same as that seen by others? The answer to this question is that first, we all do not see the same world in the sense that we all do not share the same interpretation of what is perceived. One person may think George is a nice guy and another may hate him. However, the fact that we can agree that there's a George out there comes from the fact that we share one mind, and it is that mind which has projected the world at large, making consensual validation possible. But because the mind seems to be fragmented, we seem to have private worlds with private meanings projected from an individual mind. For this reason, Jesus meets us where we believe we are in our dream of separation. It is practical to think in terms of our individual projections, because that is where we must start with the process of forgiveness. This amounts to starting at the bottom of the ladder separation led us down. As we proceed back up the ladder, undoing one projection of guilt at a time, eventually it becomes apparent that what we are perceiving is a huge drama in which we are actors playing out a script mutually written and mutually agreed upon wherein we could have the illusion that we are special individual persons, separate from one another. It has been pointed out already that our individual lives and special relationships represent a few of the myriad permutations and combinations of the thought of separation—subplots of the massive script of specialness that was spun out and corrected only to disappear before it began: "Time is a trick, a sleight of hand, a vast illusion in which figures come and go as if by magic...The script is written...we but see the journey from the point at which it ended, looking back on it, imagining we make it once again; reviewing mentally what has gone by" (W-pI.158.4:1,3,5).

Wise observers through the ages have had a similar perspective, among them Omar Khyyam:

> But leave the Wise to wrangle, and with me
> The Quarrel of the Universe let be:
> And, in some corner of the Hubbub coucht,
> Make Game of that which makes as much of Thee.
>
> For in and out, above, about, below,
> 'Tis nothing but a Magic Shadow-show,
> Play'd in a Box whose Candle is the Sun,
> Round which we Phantom Figures come and go.
>
> And if the Wine you drink, the Lip you press,
> End in the Nothing all Things end in ---Yes---
> Then fancy while Thou art, Thou art but what
> Thou shalt be---Nothing---Thou shalt not be less.[1]

Shakespeare, too, had insight into this vast, shared projection we call life:

> All the world's a stage,
> And all the men and women merely players:
> They have their exits and their entrances;
> And one man in his time plays many parts,...[2]
>
> Life's but a walking shadow, a poor player
> That struts and frets his hour upon the stage,
> And then is heard no more; it is a tale
> Told by an idiot, full of sound and fury,
> Signifying nothing.[3]

And Robert Louis Stevenson had a similar insight:

> The streets are full of human toys,
> Wound up for three score years.
> Their springs are hungers, hopes and joys,
> And jealousies and fears.
>
> They move their eyes, their lips, their hands;
> They are marvelously dressed;
> And here my body sits or stands,
> A play thing like the rest.
> The toys are played with till they fall,
> Worn out and thrown away.
> Why were they ever made at all!
> Who sits to watch the play![4]

---

[1] Khayyam, Omar. *Rubaiyat of Omar Khayyam*, pp.45-47. Trans. by Edward FitzGerald. New York: St. Martin's Press, 1983.

[2] Shakespeare, W. *As You Like It*, II, vii,139-142.

[3] Shakespeare, W. *Macbeth*, V, v, 19.

[4] Stevenson, Robert Louis. "Playthings," in *Elbert Hubbard's Scrapbook*, p. 47. New York: American Book Co., 1943.

The first mention to appear in the Course of the principle that projection makes perception focuses more specifically upon the individual and interpersonal nature of projection as it produces images for purposes of attack in the unsuccessful attempt to be rid of guilt:

> Each one peoples his world with figures from his individual past, and it is because of this that private worlds do differ. Yet the figures that he sees were never real, for they are made up only of his reactions to his brothers, and do not include their reactions to him. Therefore, he does not see he made them, and that they are not whole. For these figures have no witnesses, being perceived in one separate mind only.

> It is through these strange and shadowy figures that the insane relate to their insane world. For they see only those who remind them of these images, and it is to them that they relate. Thus do they communicate with those who are not there, and it is they who   answer them. And no one hears their answer save him who called upon them, and he alone believes they answered him. *Projection makes perception*, and you cannot see beyond it. Again and again have you attacked your brother, because you saw in him a shadow figure in your private world. And thus it is you must attack yourself first, for what you attack is not in others. Its only reality is in your own mind, and by attacking others you are literally attacking what is not there (T-13.V.2-3; italics mine).

What is perceived to be without was first seen within, and giving is the way to keep. Projection does not help us to escape the unhappiness and dissatisfaction with self and others that accompanies guilt. Like the other ego defenses, projection does not work. It makes up a fearful illusion of reality that requires continuing defense and attack, demanding an enormous amount of energy; hence the brain and body require sleep even though the mind never sleeps. Defenses, especially projection, literally wear us out:

> The belief that by seeing... [something you do not want] outside you have excluded it from within is a complete distortion of the power of extension. That is why those who project are vigilant for their own safety. They are afraid that their projections will return and hurt them. Believing they have blotted their projections from their own minds, they also believe their projections are trying to creep back in. Since the projections have not left their minds, they are forced to engage in constant activity in order not to recognize this (T-7.VIII.3:8-12).

Projection in company with denial and dissociation literally makes up the entire perceptual cosmos as well as what seem to be our private lives and relationships. Everything produced by projection is illusion, and the purpose of illusions is to serve as a defense against the Love of God; more specifically, as a defense against our ever becoming aware that we are mind and have the power to decide against the ego—the power to make decisions that will undo guilt and the elaborate structure of ego defenses that constitutes what we have regarded as life. It can be said that the ego thought system itself is a defense against God. Therefore, our ego identity—our very self—is a defense against God. But, although they are fundamentally dedicated to death, we have seen that there is a positive, right-minded use that can be made of the ego's defense mechanisms, and so it is with projection. Under the control of the Holy Spirit—the thought system of the Atonement—projection becomes a *reflection* of Heaven's Love which *extends* an earthly form of love.

And the Holy Spirit has yet another use for projection. Because what is projected shows us the content of our own mind ("the outside picture of an inward condition" (T-21.IN.1:5)), if we are willing to look at that picture with Him, or his manifestation, Jesus (or however one might understand right-mindedness), we can see the forms that our guilt takes. We can thus bring to light what we have denied which then permits it to be forgiven as we look, understand, accept and do not judge our mistaken choice for specialness. In the clear light of the Holy Spirit's reason, the perception of differences and attack in any form cannot be justified. In looking objectively at our projections, we can see what it is in ourselves that needs forgiveness, thus in forgiving others we forgive ourselves. The law of mind that says the thoughts we give we receive comes into play here. What is given and received from our right mind are thoughts of love in the form of forgiveness. Thus projection can be used in the service of that *looking* which puts us in the mental position of the observer/decision-maker, and which is the heart of forgiveness.

To summarize our discussion of defenses thus far, simply stated: 1) all defenses come from fear, constitute an attack on truth and are ultimately unnecessary although some forms of defense have practical utility along the path of spiritual growth within the dream of separation; 2) *denial* represents a decision not to know, especially not to know the mind and its power of decision; 3) *dissociation* is a decision to forget, therefore to keep unconscious, especially to forget and keep unconscious the right mind; 4) *projection* represents an attempt to cast unwanted ideas out of the mind, thus to make up an "outside," and especially to get rid of guilt. Note that each defense mechanism is employed as a result of a *decision* consciously made by us as mind. An important function of defenses is to hide the fact that we are mind and decision maker so that we literally do not know what we are thinking and or why we do what we do.

"Defenses do what they would defend."

This statement quoted from the Course (T-17.IV.7:1) has been mentioned previously, but it is important enough to require some further attention. We have already noted that defenses do not work. What may not be quite so clear is the further fact which Jesus emphasizes that instead of protecting the mind from fear, defenses sustain and promote fear. This means that if we think there is something to defend against, then we are making it real and justifying fear. Remember that the ego's fear begins with the belief that sin and guilt are real; therefore require our death and damnation. So, all defensive strategies, however cleverly disguised, are defenses against guilt, specifically against the awareness that guilt represents a *decision*. This is most clearly illustrated in the defense of projection which blames a perceived "other" for one's loss of peace in any form, seeking to relieve the self of guilt by blaming another, therefore making the other guilty. But that strategy reinforces the belief in guilt by making it seem to be something real that must be escaped. Secondly, the more one projects blame, the more guilty one feels because projection basically is attack, and it is not possible to attack without feeling guilty. Attack in any form reenacts the original idea of separation, which constituted an attack on God. Thus it is that defenses actually make even more real the very guilt they seek to defend against:

> It is essential to realize that all defenses *do* what they would defend. The underlying basis for their effectiveness [according to the ego's strategy] is that they offer what they defend. What they defend is placed in them for safe-keeping, and as they operate they bring it to you. Every defense operates by giving gifts, and the gift is always a miniature of the thought system the defense protects, set in a golden frame. The frame is very elaborate, all set with jewels, and deeply carved and polished. Its purpose is to be of value *in itself*, and to divert your attention from what it encloses. But the frame without the picture you cannot have. Defenses operate to make you think you can (T-17.IV.7).

This paragraph is taken from an extensive discussion of the special relationship as a defense wherein the relationship seems to offer love and safety while in fact it retains the belief in separation, sin, guilt and fear with the necessity to continue investing in the various mechanisms of defense in order to keep the relationship going. And to keep the special relationship going not only keeps the ego thought system in place, but serves the ego's basic purpose of rendering us mindless. In terms of our discussion in this chapter, we can apply this principle that defenses do what they would defend as follows: 1) *denial* hides guilt in the unconscious, therefore retaining it along with fear in the form of an inner sense of threat; 2) *dissociation*, too, serves to maintain the ego's thought system of guilt and fear, keeping it hidden from the right-minded light of reason and supporting fear of the unconscious, therefore making the mind fearful, and; 3) projection reinforces the very guilt that it tries to get rid of, as well as promoting fear, therefore further need of defenses.

A lesson in the ACIM Workbook speaks to this same point. It is entitled: "If I defend myself I am attacked" (W-pI.135). Two further points about defenses are made here: 1) defenses attest to a concept of the self as weak and vulnerable; 2) that concept comes from the mind having confused itself with a body—from the fact that *we* have mistakenly confused our identity with a body. Following is an extensive selection of passages from this Workbook lesson:

> Who would defend himself unless he thought he were attacked, that the attack were real, and that his own defense could save himself? And herein lies the folly of defense; it gives illusions full reality, and then attempts to handle them as real. It adds illusions to illusions, thus making correction doubly difficult. And it is this you [mind/decision-maker] do when you attempt to plan the future, activate the past, or organize the present as you wish.

> You operate from the belief you must protect yourself from what is happening because it must contain what threatens you. A sense of threat is an acknowledgment of an inherent weakness; a belief that there is danger which has power to call on you to make appropriate defense. The world is based on this insane belief. And all its structures, all its thoughts and doubts, its penalties and heavy armaments, its legal definitions and its codes, its ethics and its leaders and its gods, all serve but to preserve its sense of threat. For no one walks the world in armature but must have terror striking at his heart.

> Defense is frightening. It stems from fear, increasing fear as each defense is made. You think it offers safety. Yet it speaks of fear made real and terror justified. Is it not strange you do not pause to ask, as you elaborate your plans and make your armor thicker and your locks more tight, what you defend, and how, and against what?

> Let us consider first what you defend. It must be something that is very weak and easily assaulted. It must be something made easy prey, unable to protect itself and needing your defense. What but the body has such frailty that constant care and watchful, deep concern are needful to protect its little life? What but the body falters and must fail to serve the Son of God as worthy host?...

> The "self" that needs protection is not real. The body, valueless and hardly worth the least defense, need merely be perceived as quite apart from you,

137

and it becomes a healthy, serviceable instrument through which the mind can operate until its usefulness is over. Who would want to keep it when its usefulness is done?

Defend the body and you have attacked your mind. For you have seen in it [the mind] the faults, the weaknesses, the limits and the lacks from which you think the body must be saved. You will not see the mind as separate from bodily conditions. And you will impose upon the body all the pain that comes from the conception of the mind as limited and fragile, and apart from other minds and separate from its Source [i.e., from the belief in separation and the ego's concept of self]....

Defenses are the plans you undertake to make against the truth. Their aim is to select what you approve, and disregard what you consider incompatible with your beliefs of your reality. Yet what remains is meaningless indeed. For it is your reality [as mind and spirit] that is the "threat" which your defenses would attack, obscure, and take apart and crucify....

Your present trust in... [the Holy Spirit] is the defense that promises a future undisturbed, without a trace of sorrow, and with joy that constantly increases, as this life becomes a holy instant, set in time, but heeding only immortality. Let no defenses but your present trust direct the future, and this life becomes a meaningful encounter with the truth that only your defenses would conceal (W-pI.135.1-4, 8-9, 17, 19; brackets mine).

"In my defenselessness my safety lies."

The title of Workbook Lesson 153 which serves as the heading for this section makes an extraordinary statement, given the common sense of the world at large. The statement could be rephrased as: "In my *egolessness* my safety lies." The world's "common sense" reflects the ego thought system and its elaborate defensive structure. To the ordinary person as well as leaders at all levels of industry and government it must be a completely absurd idea that safety lies in defenselessness! Yet Jesus offers this idea as a statement of truth which represents the only way to experience peace and happiness in our nightmare dream of separation with its never-ending conflicts; conflicts which must result from perception of differences and pursuit of specialness. However, one might be tempted to reply to Jesus' invitation to defenselessness: "Easy for you to say."

In Workbook Lesson 153 of *A Course in Miracles*, we have his response:

You who feel threatened by this changing world, its twists of fortune and its bitter jests, its brief relationships and all the "gifts" it merely lends to take away again; attend this lesson well. The world provides no safety.

It is rooted in attack, and all its "gifts" of seeming safety are illusory deceptions. It attacks, and then attacks again. No peace of mind is possible where danger threatens thus.

The world gives rise but to defensiveness. For threat brings anger, anger makes attack seem reasonable, honestly provoked, and righteous in the name of self-defense. Yet is defensiveness a double threat. For it attests to weakness, and sets up a system of defense that cannot work. Now are the weak still further undermined, for there is treachery without [i.e., threats perceived in the world] and still a greater treachery within [i.e., the concept of a weak and vulnerable self housed in a body and identified with the ego]. The mind is now confused, and knows not where to turn to find escape from its imaginings....Defenses are the costliest of all the prices which the ego would exact. In them lies madness in a form so grim that hope of sanity seems but to be an idle dream, beyond the possible. The sense of threat the world encourages is so much deeper, and so far beyond the frenzy and intensity of which you can conceive, that you have no idea of all the devastation it has wrought.

You are its slave. You know not what you do, in fear of it. You do not understand how much you have been made to sacrifice, who feel its iron grip upon your heart. You do not realize what you have done to sabotage the holy peace of God by your defensiveness. For you behold the Son of God as but a victim to attack by fantasies, by dreams, and by illusions he has made; yet helpless in their presence, needful only of defense by still more fantasies, and dreams by which illusions of his safety comfort him.

Defenselessness is strength. It testifies to recognition of the Christ in you... choice is always made between Christ's strength and your   o   w   n weakness, seen apart from Him. Defenselessness can never be attacked, because it recognizes strength so great attack is folly,...

Defensiveness is weakness. It proclaims you have denied the Christ and come to fear His Father's anger. What can save you now from your delusion of an angry god, whose fearful image you believe you see at work in all the evils of the world? What but illusions could defend you now, when it is but illusions that you fight?... (W-pI.153.1.1-2, 4-7; brackets mine).

This book is being written in the long shadow of the events of September 11, 2001. Those events, and all that has transpired in relationship to them, stand on the world's stage as one of history's many stark witnesses to our captivity in the prison of the ego thought system, with its ever mounting and self-defeating fortifications of defense and attack. In considering those events it might be useful to speculate about what a right-minded attitude of defenselessness and love could have offered in contrast to what seems a stark example of wrong-mindedness on all sides. What difference might it have made to see the attacks of 9-11 as expressions of fear and a call for love?

What difference might it have made if any of the political leaders involved had a vision of universal brotherhood which overrode the perception of "enemy"? What difference might it have made if some leaders sought to find a way of communicating about hatred and fear without resorting to overt, armed attack on behalf of any of the political interests involved? What difference might it have made if any one of the people most directly involved had been able to recognize hatred as fear, and then to question that fear rather than justify it?

The projection of guilt seems obvious in the events of 9-11 and its aftermath wherein one side sees the image of Satan to be attacked and destroyed while the other sees "evil doers" to be exterminated: each side projecting and perceiving the face of sin and guilt in the other, unwilling to look within where the real "culprit" could be found. This is reminiscent of the wisdom of cartoonist Walt Kelly who gave these words to his character Pogo: "We have met the enemy and he is usn'."[1]

Considering the example of 9-11 in relationship to our discussion of Jesus' system of psychology will not be useful if one regards it in the context of a misguided effort to bring peace to the world. Recall Jesus' words: "... seek not to change the world, but choose to change your mind about the world" (T-21.IN. 1:7). "Learn now, without despair, there is no hope of answer in the world...No longer look for hope where there is none" (T-31.IV.4:3, 6). Peace is not possible *in* the world. Peace is only possible *in* our mind. The best use to be made of any vast drama of human conflict, whether played out on Shakespeare's stage or the stage of world history, is to regard it as a mirror which can show us the contents of our own mind. Thereby, we can be in a position to pursue the change of mind that leads to *inner* peace. Though our concern is not with the illusory outer world, inner peace will manifest outwardly as long as there seems to be an "outer." But the point is to see the perniciousness of defenses and the authority of terror in ourselves. Love does not go to war against the inner terrorist who resides in our mind. However, the Presence of love in our mind will shine away the dark terrorism of the ego and its vicious cycle of fear-guilt-attack-defense-fear-guilt, etc.

One could take the questions posed earlier in a more personal sense: What difference might it make for me to see attack as an expression of fear and a call for love? What difference might it make if I had a vision of brotherhood

---

[1] Kelly, Walter Crawford Jr. This quote apparently evolved in Kelly's writings. One version appeared first in the forward to his book, *The Pogo Papers*. New York: Simon and Schuster, 1953. The final version quoted here appeared in 1971 in his famous cartoon strip entitled, "Pogo."

that overrides the perception of an enemy (for instance, the next time another driver cuts me off in traffic)? What difference might it make for me to find a way of communicating about anger and fear without resorting to attack on behalf of self-interest? What difference might it make if I am able to see my anger as an expression of fear and then question whether it is justified?

Throughout the Course, Jesus' message about the unnecessary and destructive nature of defenses is given repeatedly, along with his invitation that we would join our minds with his—that we would find our way to right-mindedness. We close this chapter on defenses with one statement of that invitation:

> My brother, you are part of God and part of me. When you have at last looked at the ego's foundation without shrinking you will also have looked upon ours. [i.e., Looking at our wrong mind puts us in the presence of our right mind]. I come to you from our Father to offer you everything again. Do not refuse it in order to keep a dark cornerstone [guilt] hidden, for its protection will not save you. I give you the lamp and I will go with you. You will not take this journey alone. I will lead you to your true Father, Who hath need of you, as I have. Will you not answer the call of love with joy? (T-11.IN.4; brackets mine).

141

Chapter 7

Motivation

"Why did you do that?"

In one form or another, this question which asks about the "why" of behavior lies at the heart of psychology, as was indicated in the introduction to this book. In the science and practice of psychology, the study of motivation is both a traditional and complex subject which is of interest as a field of scientific investigation, as well as in such areas of applied psychology as education, therapy and human resources management. Hundreds, if not thousands, of books and scientific papers have been written on the subject of motivation. While Jesus' psychology is not directly concerned with the body and its behavior, but with mind and spirit, the Course does offer a way of answering the "why" question. Perhaps the reader will be relieved to know that Jesus simplifies this subject so that we will not have to attempt a wide ranging, complicated discussion of it. But before we summarize Jesus' approach to motivation, which the reader may well understand at this point, let us take some time to appreciate how others have regarded this important topic, and how complicated it has become.

Examples from the Traditions of Conventional Motivation Study

The AllPsych.com Web site[1] contains a well-developed and widely-used *Psychology Dictionary* wherein we find the following definitions:

> *Motivation*: The process that energizes and/or maintains a behavior.

> *Motive*: Internal states that provide direction for one's behaviors.

Also found on the AllPsych.com site is a discussion of motivation. A brief abstract of that material follows:

> There are several distinct theories of motivation... Some include basic biological forces, while others seem to transcend concrete explanation... the five major theories of motivation are: Instinct Theory, Drive Reduction Theory, Arousal Theory, Psychoanalytic Theory [e.g., Freud], and Humanistic Theory [e.g., Maslow].

---

[1]AllPsych Online, The Virtual Psychology Classroom, http://allpsych.com/dictionary/m.html

The College of Pharmacy at the University of Texas in Austin offers instruction for its students interested in the clinical teaching of pharmacy. In that program, the subject of motivation is considered, as it is in many other college and university courses having to do with professional education. On their Web site[2] a useful, and typical, summary/definition of the subject as regarded by educators is offered. Following is an abbreviated version:

> Motive is any condition within a person that affects that person's readiness to initiate or continue an activity.
>
> Motivation is difficult to define but most psychologists who are concerned with learning and education use the word to describe those processes that can:
>
> - arouse and instigate behavior.
> - give direction or purpose to behavior.
> - continue to allow behavior to persist.
> - lead to choosing or preferring a particular behavior.
>
> Motivation is that certain something which gives an individual the desire to perform some activity, e.g. listening to a patient's story, going to the gym to exercise, visiting a nursing home, or searching for a journal article.
>
> Six Major Factors Have a Substantial Impact on Learner Motivation: Attitude, Need, Stimulation, Affect, Competence, and Reinforcement.

An example of how the subject of motivation is approached in the context of human resources management can be found in material published by *Accel-Team*, a British organization concerned with advancing employee productivity. The following is excerpted from a manuscript entitled *Employee Motivation in the Workplace* which is available on the Accel-Team Web site:[3]

> The job of a manager in the workplace is to get things done through employees. To do this the manager should be able to motivate employees. But that's easier said than done! Motivation practice and theory are difficult subjects, touching on several disciplines.

---

[2] College of Pharmacy, University of Texas at Austin, material dated August 4, 2004, http://www.utexas.edu/pharmacy/general/experiential/practitioner/effective/motv.html

[3] Accel-Team.com: http://www.accel-team.com/productivity/index.html, (Advancing Employee Productivity: "...draws on the extensive experience and knowledge of improving productivity of human and others resources. This experience and knowledge base emanates from a diverse management services project portfolio in a number of industries, both here in the UK and South Africa."

In spite of enormous research, basic as well as applied, the subject of motivation is not clearly understood and more often than not *poorly practiced*. To understand motivation one must understand human nature itself. And there lies the problem!

Human nature can be very simple, yet very complex too. An understanding and appreciation of this is a prerequisite to effective employee motivation in the workplace and therefore effective management and leadership.

Our articles on motivation theory and practice concentrate on various theories regarding human nature in general and motivation in particular. Included are articles on the practical aspects of motivation in the workplace and the research that has been undertaken in this field, notably by Douglas McGregor (theory y), Frederick Herzberg (two factor motivation hygiene theory,) Abraham Maslow (theory z, hierarchy of needs), Elton Mayo (Hawthorne Experiments) Chris Argyris Rensis Likert and David McClelland (achievement).

A scholarly example of the scientific approach to the study of motivation is found in statements excerpted from a paper authored by William Revelle, PhD[4] of Northwestern University:

Over the past 17 years, my colleagues and I have examined how personality traits   combine with situational manipulations to produce motivational states that in turn affect cognitive performance. For organizational purposes, these effects can be conceived as affecting information processing at several different, possibly overlapping, stages....

Fundamental questions of motivation are concerned with the direction, intensity, and duration of behavior. Within each of these broad categories are sub-questions such as the distinctions between quality and quantity, effort and arousal, and latency and persistence. Cutting across all these questions are the relative contributions of individual differences and situational constraints to the level of motivation and of subsequent performance.

One of the most popular formulations about human motivation, referenced in some of the material above, was developed by Abraham Maslow and published in his book, *Motivation and Personality*.[5] Maslow synthesized a large body of theory and research in the field of human motivation to develop

---

[4] Revelle, William. "Individual Differences in Personality and Motivation: 'Non-cognitive' Determinants of Cognitive Performance." In *Attention: Selection, Awareness and Control: A Tribute to Donald Broadbent*. Baddeley, A. & Weiskrantz, L., eds. Oxford, UK: Oxford University Press, 1993.

[5] Maslow, Abraham. *Motivation and Personality*, 3rd ed. New York: Addison-Wesley, 1987. (Originally Published in 1954 and revised in 1970.)

his comprehensive theory of the "Hierarchy of Human Needs." According to this hierarchical view, motivation could be understood as responding to two basic categories of need: 1) deficiency needs, and; 2) growth needs. His basic idea was that lower order needs had to be met before a person would be motivated to fulfill higher order needs. His hierarchy is outlined as follows:

Deficiency Needs
1) *Physiological*: hunger, thirst, food, elimination, sleep, temperature regulation and bodily comforts in general
2) *Safety/Security*: physical, financial, emotional
3) *Love/Belonging*: family, sexual intimacy, friendships, social affiliation and acceptance
4) *Esteem*: approval and recognition from others, competence and achievement leading to self-esteem

Growth or Being Needs
5) *Cognitive:* to explore and seek, to know, to understand
6) *Aesthetic:* to experience beauty, order, balance, symmetry
7) *Self-actualization:* to find self-fulfillment, to realize one's potential, to grow and expand the self
8) *Self-transcendence:* to connect to something beyond the self, to join with others in shared interests, spiritual enlightenment

In Maslow's "deficiency needs," one can see clearly the presence of what we have discussed as the ego's sense of scarcity and lack which lead to the pursuit of specialness and special relationships. This same ego dynamic is also seen in the first three of his "growth or being needs." In the final need for self-transcendence, Maslow contributes a spiritual dimension to the psychology of motivation, and many regard this as his most important contribution in addition to the value of bringing together into one, comprehensive schema the various threads of motivational research and theory.

It is to be noted that all of the above examples focus on the body and its behavior. Again, in the Course Jesus is never concerned with the body and behavior, which are simply part of our dream of separation, but is concerned with *mind*. While behavior is not the issue, he nevertheless reassures us that right behavior will follow from right-mindedness. And, since we believe and experience ourselves to be separate individuals inhabiting bodies, Jesus addresses us at that level, speaking in terms of our experience and using it for purposes of example and communication, but inviting us to identify as mind and actually addressing us as mind. As far as the body and behavior are concerned, they are ultimately irrelevant, because they are not real. However, they constitute our classroom in forgiveness as long as they are the focus of our dream experiences. But the final goal of forgiveness is that we would awaken from the dream of perception and physicality to our reality as mind, which in truth has never separated from the One Mind. As a general commentary on the above examples, and by way of prefacing further discussion of the subject from an ACIM perspective, the following two paragraphs from the Course are pertinent. Remember, these comments were first addressed to two professional psychologists:

> The analysis of ego-motivation [in others] is very complicated, very obscuring, and never without your own ego-involvement. The whole process represents a clear-cut attempt to demonstrate your own ability to understand what you perceive. This is shown by the fact that you react to your interpretations [of others' motivations] as if they were correct. You may then control your reactions behaviorally, but not emotionally [i.e., inwardly, one engages in judgment and how one behaves is not consistent with how one thinks and feels]....

> There is but one interpretation of [anyone's] motivation that makes any sense. [Again, he's talking about the level of *mind*.] And because it is the Holy Spirit's judgment it requires no effort at all on your part. Every loving *thought* is true. Everything else is an appeal for healing [i.e., forgiveness] and help, regardless of the form it takes. Can anyone be justified in responding with anger to a brother's plea for help? No response can be appropriate except the willingness to give it to him, for this and only this is what he is asking for. Offer him anything else [e.g., judgment, criticism], and you are assuming the right to attack his reality by interpreting it as you see fit. Perhaps the danger of this to your own mind is not yet fully apparent. If you believe that an appeal for help is something else you will react to something else. Your response will therefore be inappropriate to reality as it is, but not to your perception of it (T-12.I.2-3; brackets and italics mine).

Jesus' Psychology of Motivation: Cause and Effect

We have seen that in the Course Jesus answers the "why" question by stating that *mind* is the cause of all we perceive, and that human behavior follows from perception. Recall the formula: thought→ perception→ reaction (emotion and behavior). Recall also that everything of perception is illusion, including forgiveness, which is corrected perception, and which the previously quoted material is really addressing. We have to begin with illusions and their forgiveness, because we believe in illusions. However, again, the goal of forgiveness is to arrive at a state of mind free of guilt and fear so that awakening to oneness is possible.

At the level of mind there are basically only two categories of motivation or cause: 1) the ego's thought system of separation, sin, guilt and fear, and;

2) the Holy Spirit's thought system of non-separation and forgiveness. Jesus thus simplifies the question of motivation in the same way that he simplifies the subject of emotions. In fact, the two emotions fear and love also represent two basic categories of motivation. Since fear comes from believing in the ego's illusion of separation, when we respond from fear, as most of us do most of the time, we have chosen to believe in unreality. It is fear, for instance, that would have us interpret another's motivations and behavior as attacking rather than as a call for help and forgiveness. And again, lives motivated by fear—lives of specialness apart from love—are meaningless, as are the perceptions (interpretations) which characterize them.

> The ego can be completely forgotten at any time, because it is a totally incredible belief, and no one can keep a belief he has judged to be unbelievable. The more you learn about the ego, the more you realize that it cannot be believed. The incredible cannot be understood because it is unbelievable. The meaninglessness of perception based on the unbelievable is apparent, but it may not be recognized as being beyond belief, because it is made *by* belief. [Belief does not create reality, but it does make illusions. The motivations of the world are based on illusions and intended to sustain illusions.] The whole purpose of this course is to teach you that the ego is unbelievable and will forever be unbelievable (T-7.VIII.6:2-7:1; bracket mine).

According to the Course, everything that conventional psychology posits in an attempt to explain motivation is not a true cause of anything, but is the *effect* of what goes on within the causal dimension of mind that is beyond the body, indeed beyond time and space; and those effects are illusions. In attempting to understand motivation by studying the body and its behavior, psychologists are studying illusions and effects, not reality and cause. Neither the physical environment nor the physiological functioning and status of the body are a cause of human behavior according to Jesus' psychology where motivation is of the *mind*, not the body; and where bodily experiences offer us "the outside picture of an inward condition" (T-21.IN.1:5), which is directly relevant to forgiveness. In the Course, the body is not truly alive, but is merely a puppet whose strings are pulled by the mind; and whose activities, including the thinking perceived to be in the brain, is the result of *thought* which takes place at the level of mind. The ego personality which characterizes our body, and with which we identify, is merely a characteristic of that puppet whose cause is a thought in the mind.

Neither does the Course support the idea of a hierarchy of needs. According to Jesus there is no hierarchy of illusions: "All that a hierarchy of illusions can show is preference, not reality. What relevance has preference to the truth? Illusions are illusions and are false. Your preference gives them no reality" (T-26.VII.6:5-7).

Obviously right-mindedness does not depend upon having all of the specialness needs of the wrong mind satisfied. Enlightenment does not depend upon a full belly: truth is not dependent upon illusion. There is, however, one way in which the lower order needs on Maslow's hierarchy interfere with the goal of mindfulness and spiritual awakening: preoccupation with them serves as a distraction which keeps us unaware of mind and the possibility of enlightenment. Again we see that the body serves the ego's purpose of sustaining its thought system in our mind, which requires that we remain unaware of mind.

Nor does it make sense in Course terms to talk about motivating one's behavior or that of others. We are *always* motivated. The question of importance has to do with which thought system in the mind will be our source of motivation. Jesus' psychology is concerned with motivation for changing our mind, which represents fundamental change. We need not be concerned with what follows from right-mindedness; only with placing our mind under the guidance of love and then being willing to follow it:

> All good teachers realize that only fundamental change will last, but they do not begin at that level. Strengthening motivation for change is their first and foremost goal. It is also their last and final one. Increasing motivation for change in the learner is all that a teacher need do to guarantee change. Change in motivation is a change of mind, and this will inevitably produce fundamental change because the mind *is* fundamental (T-6.V(B).2).

(In this paragraph, Jesus is not only offering wise counsel to his students, but is also describing his own role and the approach he models as the teacher of *A Course in Miracles*.)

Further, it is not necessary, nor is it really possible, to judge from the behavior of another which thought system is the operant motivator for them. All that is necessary is that we learn for *ourselves* the change of mind that permits us to perceive through right-minded eyes, and in doing so we are automatically motivated to respond in whatever way is most loving. The implication of this for parents, teachers and managers is that their concern should be with their own mind. The concern for motivating others really amounts to a concern for how to manipulate others to do what one wants them to do. There are effective ways of accomplishing such manipulation within the dream. Traditional psychologies of motivation and learning offer understanding and techniques to that end. Those methods of manipulation come under the category of what is referred to as "magic" in the Course, and we shall address that subject a bit later. But what Jesus would have us be concerned about is that whatever we do, we do it from the guidance of the right-minded place of love in our mind rather than from the place of specialness and self interest.

149

Guilt as easily motivates what the world calls success as it motivates what is called failure, because both can serve the purpose of specialness. According to Jesus' psychology, someone who says they want to break a "bad" habit, but needs to be motivated to do so, would best be advised to understand that they *are* motivated, and then to examine the nature and purpose of that motivation. "Bad" habits serve the purpose of sustaining guilt in the mind. Ironically, the ego loves not only the guilt, but the special attention which a "bad" habit brings, whether it is attention brought to a problem child, to a repeating violator of the law, or to one who consistently overeats and is therefore overweight. One could say that we all have a "bad habit," and the ego (i.e., specialness and guilt) is it. Recall Walt Kelly's wisdom: the enemy is us. In light of this fact, Jesus' advice to us about motivation is that we always should question our *purpose* in anything.

Jesus' Psychology of Motivation: Purpose

One of the most important aspects of the Course's approach to motivation has to do with the question of *purpose*. There are only two purposes to be served by anything we undertake in any of our roles and relationships within the world: 1) the ego's purpose of separation and specialness; 2) the Holy Spirit's purpose of oneness and forgiveness. So, Jesus urges his students to recognize that purpose is of fundamental importance and always to question their purpose. This is really another form of his invitation to *look* within:

> Preoccupations with problems set up to be incapable of solution are favorite ego devices for impeding learning progress. In all these diversionary tactics, however, the one question that is never asked by those who pursue them is, "What for?" This is the question that *you* must learn to ask in connection with everything. What is the purpose? Whatever it is, it will direct your efforts automatically. When you make a decision of purpose, then, you have made a decision about your future effort; a decision that will remain in effect unless you change your mind (T-4.V. 6).

> Hallucinations [i.e., illusions] disappear when they are recognized for what they are. This is the healing and the remedy. Believe them not and they are gone. And all you need to do is recognize that *you* did this. Once you accept this simple fact and take unto yourself the power you gave them, you are released from them. One thing is sure; hallucinations serve a purpose, and when that purpose is no longer held they disappear. Therefore, the question never is whether you want them, but always, do you want the purpose that they serve? This world seems to hold out many purposes, each different and with different values. Yet they are all the same. Again there is no order; only a seeming hierarchy of values.

Only two purposes are possible. And one is sin [i.e., separation, specialness, and guilt], the other holiness [i.e., forgiveness; oneness]. Nothing is in between, and which you choose determines what you see. For what you see is merely how you elect to meet your goal. Hallucinations serve to meet the goal of madness. They are the means by which the outside world, projected from within, adjusts to sin and seems to witness to its reality. It still is true that nothing is without. Yet upon nothing are all projections made. For it is the projection that gives the "nothing" all the meaning that it holds (T-20.VIII.8-9; brackets mine).

Magic

Wapnick's *Glossary* contains the following definition for the term *magic* as it is used in the Course:

> the attempt to solve a problem where it is not, i.e., trying to solve a problem in the mind through physical or "mindless" measures: the ego's strategy to keep the real problem -- the belief in separation -- from God's Answer [i.e., the Holy Spirit]; guilt is projected outside our minds onto others (attack) or our bodies (sickness) and sought to be corrected there, rather than being undone in our minds by bringing it to the Holy Spirit; referred to as "false healing" in "The Song of Prayer"[1] (bracket and footnote mine).

The conventional study of motivation and attempts to apply principles of motivation in practical settings such as schools, businesses and various forms of medical and psychological treatment are examples of "magical thinking," in that they represent attempts to understand the body and manipulate its behavior without recognition of, or concern for, the causal level of mind. "Magical thinking" assumes that the body is its own cause: i.e., that the answer to motivation lies in the body and that the source of its illnesses is physical in nature and can be cured with physical means. All of this assumes the reality of the illusion of separation which the world and body symbolize, but within the world this kind of approach certainly seems to work to a limited extent at least. Aspirin seems to relieve headaches and surgery seems to be a cure for many ills. Positive reinforcement (reward) seems to be effective in motivating both students and employees. Magic seems to work because we *believe* in it, and we believe in it because it serves the ego's purpose of keeping us mindless.

Now, Jesus is not against the use of magic just as he does not expect his students to renounce common sense in conducting the affairs of worldly life. The point of importance is to understand that mind and spirit are our true reality.

[1] *The Song of Prayer: Prayer, Forgiveness and Healing: An Extension of the Principles of A COURSE IN MIRACLES* © 1978 by the Foundation for Inner Peace, Mill Valley, CA 94942

When we accord reality to the body, which the use of magic usually does, we are identifying with the ego and serving its purposes. From the point of view of the Course, a better use of intelligence and scholarship would be to question our beliefs about the nature of reality and the most basic cause of our difficulties rather than to strengthen the ego's hold on us by attempting to understand the body and the world on their own terms, making them seem real in the process.

As for magic, like the body, in and of itself it is neutral: neither good nor bad; nor holy or evil. What is important is the *purpose* for the use of magic—right-minded or wrong-minded. Using professional medical practice as an example, one can practice magic in the form of medical treatment from a right-minded motivation that expresses love and the brotherhood of shared interests. Ultimately it will be the love that heals, not the magic. The same can be said of the professions of teaching and human resources management, as well as of parenting. The right-minded guidance of the Holy Spirit or Jesus can make loving use of our bodies and of the forms and practices of magic. In terms of Jesus' psychology, the goal is not to heal the body, but to heal the mind; not to manipulate the body's behavior through motivational techniques, but to ourselves be motivated to choose right-mindedness in all things.

> The body is merely part of your experience in the physical world. Its abilities can be and frequently are overevaluated. However, it is almost impossible to deny its existence in this world. Those who do so are engaging in a particularly unworthy form of denial. The term "unworthy" here implies only that it is not necessary to protect the mind by denying the unmindful. If one denies this unfortunate aspect of the mind's power [i.e., to make illusions through projection], one is also denying the power itself.
>
> All material means that you accept as remedies [and explanations] for bodily ills are restatements of magic principles. This is the first step in believing that the body makes its own illness. It is a second misstep to attempt to heal it through non-creative agents. It does not follow, owever, that the use of such agents for corrective purposes is evil...it may be wise to utilize a compromise approach to mind and body, in which something from the outside is temporarily given healing belief. This is because the last thing that can help the non-right-minded, or the sick, is an increase in fear [and what *does* help is an expression of love in a form that can be accepted and understood] (T-2.IV.3:8-4:1-7).

Summary

In every heart there is the longing for love which, however hidden and dimly sensed, remains in our mind under the care of the Holy Spirit and Jesus (or any symbol that one can relate to which stands for "love that is not of this world," M-23.4:2).

In his identification of the "self-transcendent need," Maslow recognized this call for love and the memory of our true Identity as one spirit. Among the most important contributions of *A Course in Miracles* is the message that the love we seek lies within, as does the *knowledge* of our true Self; and that we have not been deprived of these except by our own choice, which comes from our motivation to be separate and to protect our separate individuality in special relationships. In the Course, Jesus invites his students to examine their motivations, their choices, and their purposes.

As far as motivation is concerned, Jesus' psychology is simply based on the idea that what is most important is that we learn how to be motivated by love rather than fear: to be right-minded. He invites those who resonate to his words in the Course to take him as their teacher and as their model for purposes of motivation and learning:

> I have enjoined you to behave as I behaved, but we must respond to the same Mind to do this. This Mind is the Holy Spirit, Whose Will is for God always. He teaches you how to keep me as the model for your thought, and to behave like me as a result. The power of our joint motivation is beyond belief, but not beyond accomplishment. What we can accomplish together has no limits, because the Call for God is the call to the unlimited. Child of God, my message is for you, to hear and give away as you answer the Holy Spirit within you (T-5.II.12).

Chapter 8

Memory

In considering the subject of memory, we must also consider the concept of time as well as the phenomenon of forgetting. We have seen already that in *A Course in Miracles* time and space are part of the illusion of separation and that forgetting is intentional, being the result of the ego-guided decision to employ the defense mechanism of dissociation in order to keep unconscious what it has denied. Furthermore, in ACIM memory is not regarded as an attribute of the brain, but is a function of the split mind, and is only important because of denial and dissociation. In the Mind of God, nothing is forgotten because there is no dissociation in *knowledge*; therefore the concept of memory is irrelevant in Oneness, which, in any case, is timeless: eternal.

As with the topic of motivation, the conventional psychological study and theory of memory is quite complex. We will not take the time to present a series of examples, but in the interest of continuing to compare and contrast conventional psychology with Jesus' psychology, a rather brief summary may be of use.

Conventional psychology regards memory as a capacity of the brain, whereas in Jesus' psychology the brain, like the rest of the body, simply does what the mind instructs it to do. Forgetting and remembering represent decisions made at the level of mind and then programmed into the brain, much as a computer programmer gives instructions to a computer.

In conventional psychology, it is understood that memory involves three processes or functions, similar to what is required of a computer: *encoding, storage,* and *retrieval.* Additionally, it is typically understood that there are three kinds of memory: *sensory memory, short-term memory,* and *long-term memory.* Sensory memory then is divided into subcategories, depending upon the sensory channel that is the source of input; e.g., *iconic memory* for visual stimuli, *echoic memory* for aural stimuli, and *haptic memory* for tactile stimuli. There is then the necessity for explaining how short-term memory transfers information to long-term memory, while long-term memory is divided into subcategories depending upon the nature and function of the data stored. In the illusory world, this kind of understanding has practical utility, just as information about the body's physiology has practical application in the profession of medicine. But from the point of view of the Course, all of this comes under the category of magic, and what is ultimately important from Jesus' perspective is whether the concepts and understanding of psychology will be used right-mindedly in the spirit of shared interests, love and forgiveness; or used wrong-mindedly in the interest of specialness, separation and guilt. The latter use basically would be to employ psychological concepts and understanding for purposes of attack; that is, for purposes of projecting guilt. Indeed, from a Course perspective, to the extent that psychology teaches that we are a body and that our behavior and problems are caused at the physical level, psychology is attacking our true Identity as spirit and, like much of science, has become an instrument of the ego. Of course the vast majority of human beings, as manifestations of the same ego thought system, also share in this attack on their true Identity by their belief in the reality of the body and a separate, special, individual self.

The Concept of Time

In order to understand the teaching-learning plan of salvation, it is necessary to grasp the concept of time that the course sets forth. Atonement [i.e., the *process* of forgiveness which undoes belief in separation, sin, guilt and fear] corrects illusions, not truth. Therefore, it corrects what never was. Further, the plan for this correction was established and completed simultaneously, for the Will of God is entirely apart from time. So is all reality, being of Him. The instant the idea of separation entered the mind of God's Son, in that same instant was God's Answer given. In time this happened very long ago. In reality it never happened at all.

The world of time is the world of illusion. What happened long ago seems to be happening now. Choices made long since appear to be open; yet to be made. What has been learned and understood and long ago passed by is looked upon as a new thought, a fresh idea, a different approach. Because your will is free [i.e., as decision maker, you have the power of choice between thought systems] you can accept what has already happened at any time you choose, and only then will you realize that it was always there. As the course emphasizes, you are not free to choose the curriculum, or even the form in which you will learn it. [This is mentioned in the Text introduction: "Free will does not mean that you can establish the curriculum. It means only that you can elect what you want to take at a given time." It is also related to the idea of not seeking to change the illusory world, but to change our mind about the world; change how we interpret our worldly experiences.] You are free, however, to decide when you want to learn it. And as you accept it, it is already learned.

Time really, then, goes backward to an instant [of seeming separation] so ancient that it is beyond all memory, and past even the possibility of remembering. Yet because it is an instant that is relived again and again and still again, it seems to be now (M-2.2-4:2; brackets mine).

Without belief in linear time, the conventional idea of memory has no meaning. Memory assumes a past, present and future: an ongoing, linear process of experiencing with perceptual data inputs to be stored and retrieved. This process is commonly understood to go in only one direction, from the past through the present to the future. It is one of the most radical and difficult-to-grasp concepts of the Course that in truth there is no linear time! So much for the importance of memory! However, as with all other aspects of the illusory world of perception spawned by belief in separation, there is a loving use for the illusion of time and the idea of memory, as well as for the associated idea of forgetting. But before we get to that, let us first discuss a little more about the origin of linear time and its relationship to the ego thought system.

It should be obvious that separation, perception and the appearance of differences—a differentiated, separated reality—are necessary in order for there to be a concept of space. Space represents distance between separated things. That distance can be measured in quantifiable units that permit the application of mathematics, therefore the pursuit of objective, consensually verifiable scientific investigation. Time represents one dimension by which space can be measured: the greater the distance, the longer the time it takes to traverse that distance, assuming a constant rate of speed. The time constant used in astronomical measurements is the light year, which is the distance traveled at the speed of light in one earth (or solar) year. In our everyday experience, the distance between two cities is often expressed as the average amount of time it takes to drive between them. Of course, the concepts of time and space have been, and continue to be, the objects of sophisticated scientific investigation and theory as scientists and philosophers continue to raise questions about the nature and reality of time and space, or what may be called the "space-time continuum." In the Course, we find Jesus making the following statements:

> ...time and space are one illusion, which takes different forms. If it [the illusion of separation] has been projected beyond your mind you think of it as time. The nearer it is brought to where it is [i.e., in the mind], the more you think of it in terms of space (T-26.VIII.1:3-5).

According to the Course, the concepts of time and space are of the ego's making, and are essentially equivalent to the illusion of separation. And that aspect of separation which is time is particularly central to the ego thought system, which it both supports and serves to protect from the truth of timelessness—the truth of eternity or God. This works as follows: time begins with the idea that separation is real and *has been* accomplished: in the past something happened to God (Oneness), and we did it.

157

Thus, there is a *past*, which automatically requires a *present*, and a present different from the past where change occurred. Somehow the changeless Truth of God was changed. The ego says that the change which happened in the past was necessary so that we could have a separate life of our own, but unfortunately it meant that Oneness, Whose essence is Love, had to be destroyed. Furthermore, the change (separation) which took place in the past is over and done. According to the ego thought system, what happened in the past cannot be changed. The "big bang" took place, shattered Heaven, and that's it. In fact, since time is linear, proceeding in an irreversible sequence of events from past to future, the sin of separation continues to recede, lost in the eons of cosmic history. In that distant past, in order that we could be who we think we are, we committed an unspeakable and unforgivable *sin* which destroyed our Father. So we are *guilty now*, in the *present*, and there's no way around it, we must sacrifice and suffer; if not us, then someone, whether a spouse, a foreign enemy or a crucified savior. Even worse, since guilt ultimately demands that we be punished, our past sin will eventually catch up with us in the *future*, so we have every reason to be afraid. The future essentially becomes *fear*. Of course, the universal punishment and source of fear for those who believe they are a body is death. We don't know when it will happen, but death is in our future, and the Bible's gospel of Paul makes this ego statement quite precisely: "the wages of sin is death" (Romans 6:23). The ego continually whispers some version of this story in every human heart: we have sinned in the past and destroyed our Father, which left us without His Love and protection, alone in a body subject to "time's fell hand"[1] and "the heart-ache and the thousand natural shocks that flesh is heir to."[2]

To recap this story of linear time: according to the ego thought system, we sinned in the past, we are guilty in the present, and in the future we shall be punished. This is equivalent to saying that change is real; there is no timelessness, no changeless eternity, no Oneness; the God of Love is dead and has been usurped by a god of fear; eternity has been destroyed and replaced by time—replaced by change and death. Now belief in time, accompanied by the beliefs in sin, guilt and fear, replaces the truth of oneness. The ego's formula for linear time is:

$$\underline{past = sin} \rightarrow \underline{present = guilt} \rightarrow \underline{future = fear}$$

Just as the ego thought system makes perception seem real, so does it make linear time seem real. In truth, both are merely illusions in the mind, but

[1] Shakespeare, W. *Sonnet 64*, l.1

[2] Shakespeare, W. *Hamlet*, III,i,62

both serve the ego as witnesses to the "reality" of separation (duality). In addition, the ego uses time to anchor that "reality" in the past which is beyond the reach of correction, and where it seems to be a cause of both the present (guilt) and the future (fear).

According to Jesus, the mind is not confined within any measurable dimension; therefore it is not located anywhere in time and space. Yet it is ever present, though we are not aware of it. Therefore, just as our ego identity intends, we are effectively mindless. We are like fish that swim in the sea which sustains their life, yet are unaware of the vast life-giving sea around them; or, more apropos of our case, unaware of the vast illusion-giving mind which sustains our image of life and self. Time and space are illusions in the mind which keep us unaware of mind; basically forms of the illusion of separation or duality which support the deception that there is something outside the mind, a measurable, separated reality, part of which we think is us.

Mind cannot be perceived or measured, yet by its very nature it is always present. It is not in the past or future, it is *now*. Therefore the decision to believe in separation is *now*. The power of decision is *now*, and so the ego fears the present, which is why, when there is observation of the thinking that appears in awareness, one finds an ongoing process of judgmental preoccupation with past and future, and great difficulty entering that place of silent, non-judgmental observation that is the present—that state of mind referred to by J. Krishnamurti as "choiceless awareness" [3] (by which he meant non-judgmental observation). In fact, the mind cannot enter that state by our conscious striving—the willful exertion of effort—but it can be *permitted* through our willingness to passively observe without judging, which automatically puts the mind in the place of decision maker, as well as in the presence of the right mind as alternative to the ego's wrong mind.

The ego's strategy for time is discussed in two important paragraphs from the ACIM Text:

> The ego has a strange notion of time, and it is with this notion that your questioning might well begin. The ego invests heavily in the past, and in the end believes that the past is the only aspect of time that is meaningful [because that is where it's origin in separation is supposedly located]. Remember that its emphasis on guilt enables it to ensure its continuity by making the future like the past, and thus avoiding the present. By the notion of paying for the past in the future, the past becomes the determiner

---

[3] Krishnamurti, J. *Choiceless Awareness: A Selection of Passages from the Teachings of J. Krishnamurti.* Ojai, CA: Krishnamurti Foundation of America, 1992 (Revised, 2001).

of the future, making them continuous without an intervening present. For the ego regards the present only as a brief transition to the future, in which it brings the past to the future by interpreting the present in past terms.

"Now" has no meaning to the ego. The present merely reminds it of past hurts, and it reacts to the present as if it *were* the past. The ego cannot tolerate release from the past, and although the past is over, the ego tries to preserve its image by responding as if it were present. It dictates your reactions to those you meet in the present from a past reference point, obscuring their present reality. In effect, if you follow the ego's dictates you will react to your brother as though he were someone else, and this will surely prevent you from recognizing him as he is [now]. And you will receive messages from him out of your own past because, by making it real in the present, you are forbidding yourself to let it go. You thus deny yourself the message of release that every brother offers you *now* (T-13.IV.4-5; brackets mine).

A very helpful discussion of these paragraphs, which is pertinent for our purposes, is found in Kenneth Wapnick's book, *A Vast Illusion: Time According to A COURSE IN MIRACLES.*[4] This book was based on a tape recorded class. Below are some extensive excerpts from his line-by-line exegesis, including consideration of a student's question. As in Wapnick's book, quotes from the Course are in bold face for ease of distinguishing them from commentary. Ellipses are mine.

The ego has a strange notion of time, and it is with this notion that your questioning might well begin.

As Jesus does in many other places in the Course, he is asking us to *look* at the ego's thought system with him....

In this particular set of passages Jesus is asking us to examine the ego's manipulative use of time through guilt and fear. Once we understand these dynamics and realize guilt's purpose, we can step back and realize we are not guilty for the reasons we think. All that has happened is that we played the ego's tape rather than the Holy Spirit's, having rooted ourselves in a belief that guilt and fear were real and justified. The problem is never what we think we are guilty or fearful of, but rather that we have *chosen* to become a slave to time's guilt and fear. Thus, understanding the ego's use of time allows us to make another choice, and this then allows us to take a major step towards becoming free of the imprisoning nature of the ego's thought system....

The ego invests heavily in the past, and in the end believes that the past is the only aspect of time that is meaningful. Remember that its emphasis

[4] Wapnick, Kenneth. *A Vast Illusion: Time According to A COURSE IN MIRACLES*, 3rd ed. Temecula, CA: Foundation for *A Course in Miracles*, 2006.

on guilt enables it to ensure its continuity by making the future like the past, and thus avoiding the present. By the notion of paying for the past in the future, the past becomes the determiner of the future, making them continuous without an intervening present. For the ego regards the present only as a brief transition to the future, in which it brings the past to the future by interpreting the present in past terms.

... "Continuity" according to the ego is the linking of past and future, which becomes a defense against the "true" continuity of the present which leads continuously to Heaven. The ego's continuity, on the other hand, is *its* Heaven, which is merely hell. The more prominent psychological theories, almost all ultimately derived from Freud, are examples of this. Such theories typically maintain, in one way or the other, that the child is the father of the man; i.e., what happens in the past imprisons us and determines what the future will be. It is as if our past experiences carved out our future in stone, whose core can never be changed, simply dressed up differently. Everything then is perceived through the filter of our guilty past.

"Now" has no meaning to the ego. The present merely reminds it of past hurts, and it reacts to the present as if it *were* the past. The ego cannot tolerate release from the past, and although the past is over, the ego tries to preserve its image by responding as if it were present.

The reason of course that "now" has no meaning is that in the holy instant, that is now, we let go of the guilt of the past and the fear of the future that had obscured the ongoing presence of the Holy Spirit. Thus, saying that the ego is not able to tolerate the release from the past is no different from saying the ego is afraid of love, or that the ego is afraid of forgiveness. The attraction of guilt then becomes the way in which the ego protects itself from the Holy Spirit's Love, for our acceptance of that Love does mean the end of its thought system.

It [the ego] dictates your reactions to those you meet in the present from a past reference point, obscuring their present reality. In effect, if you follow the ego's dictates you will react to your brother as though he were someone else, and this will surely prevent you from recognizing him as he is.

The opening statement foreshadows later discussions of specialness, and especially the section "Shadows of the Past" in Chapter 17. Once we see through the filter of the past, we cannot see the light of Christ that shines in others. Rather, we shall see around them only a shadow of the guilt which *we* have put there. We put it there because we have projected it from our minds as a magical attempt to escape from the guilt of *our* past. An example of this is people who have unresolved problems with their fathers, and with authority figures in general, who then see any authority figure as if that person were their father. The ultimate origin of the authority problem of course is our belief in the separation from God, the only Authority....

161

And you will receive messages from him out of your own past because, by making it real in the present, you are forbidding yourself to let it go. You thus deny yourself the message of release that every brother offers you now.

The "message of release," which is the message of forgiveness, is that there is no past because there is no sin and no guilt. That is the crucial factor because it is guilt that holds the ego's system of time together. Therefore, in my choice to see another is my choice to see myself: guilty or innocent, imprisoned or free.

Q: The brain probably has been programmed over eons of evolution to constantly react to the past. In fact, all thought seems to deal with that. What method could we use to over-come this pattern of action-reaction?

A: Krishnamurti frequently spoke about that. The first step is to recognize, at least intellectually, exactly what the purpose of time is from the ego's point of view. On a practical level, when we start getting angry, which means that we are already caught in the midst of the ego's thought system, we should step back as quickly as we can and look at ourselves being caught. This is what the "little willingness" is about; there is really no other way. The idea is to try and stop the ego reaction as close to its starting point as possible.

This process, incidentally, is similar to the Buddhist practice of stepping back and watching our thoughts, and is extremely helpful as an exercise. We are not trying to stop the thoughts, but simply stepping back and watching them. Consequently, the power of those thoughts is diminished because their power lies in *not* looking at them. If we are stepping back and watching ourselves becoming upset, the part of us that is watching cannot be the part that is upset. This initiates the process of weakening our identification with the ego. *A Course in Miracles* explains that we have no choice but to choose *either* the ego or the Holy Spirit as our guide. There are no other alternatives, and we cannot *not* to choose....[5]

In sum, the ego is the author of the illusion of time, and is concerned primarily with the past and future, as anyone who has practiced any form of meditation can readily attest. The ego fears the present, both because it can be undone in the present where it knows there is a "power greater than itself" (T-4.II.8:8); and because of guilt, which it teaches us to fear and does not want examined, but from which it has our mind seek an illusory escape through projection. Yet we have seen that projection only acts to retain and increase guilt, which serves the ego's secret purpose, since guilt is necessary for the ego's survival in our mind where guilt fosters special relationships.

---

[5] Ibid, pp.168-71

The Uses of Time

For the ego, time is of crucial importance. Like everything else of the ego, time is purposeful. It was made to serve two ego goals: First, the goal of reinforcing the belief in duality, since time is "one illusion" joined with the idea of space, and speaks directly of separation. Thus, the mere experience of linear time attests to separation as real, therefore attests to the ego as real. Second is the goal of maintaining the belief in separation as a fact accomplished in the past and whose consequences of guilt and fear cannot be escaped. Our personal memories of past regrets and grievances attest to the ego's ontological guilt and are shadows of the ancient time of separation which we continue to choose to believe and reenact in the present, thus fomenting guilt and fear.

> Each day, and every minute in each day, and every instant that each minute holds, you but relive the single instant when the time of terror took the place of love. And so you die each day to live again, until you cross the gap between the past and present, which is not a gap at all. Such is each life; a seeming interval from birth to death and on to life again, a repetition of an instant gone by long ago that cannot be relived [according to the ego]. And all of time is but the mad belief that what is over is still here and now (T-26.V.13; bracket mine).

The Holy Spirit also has a purpose for time, as He does for everything the ego has manufactured. While the ego's purpose for time is basically to sustain itself by retaining guilt in our mind (i.e., *our* purpose as egos is to sustain the illusion of self by holding on to guilt through special relationships), the Holy Spirit's purpose for time is forgiveness. We are speaking here in terms of the Level Two teachings of the Course which are presented in the context of the illusion of separation and as though perception and linear time were real. In that context, forgiveness seems to proceed linearly, one step at a time: one rung at a time back up the ladder separation led us down. And the process of the "Atonement plan" in time is gentle, asking no more of us than we are willing to give in any situation, respecting our fear of surrendering the illusion of a separate, special identity, however painful:

> It is evident that the Holy Spirit's perception of time is the exact opposite of the ego's. The reason is equally clear, for they perceive the goal of time as diametrically opposed. The Holy Spirit interprets time's purpose as rendering the need for time unnecessary. He regards the function of time as temporary, serving only His teaching function, which is temporary by definition [since His goal is to undo the illusion of separation, therefore of time]. His emphasis is therefore on the only aspect of time that can extend to the infinite, for *now* is the closest approximation of eternity that this world offers. It is in the reality of "now," without past or future, that

the beginning of the appreciation of eternity lies. For only "now" is here, and only "now" presents the opportunities for the holy encounters [i.e., meeting others free of the shadow images from our personal past] in which salvation [i.e., forgiveness] can be found.

The ego, on the other hand, regards the function of time as one of extending itself in place of eternity, for like the Holy Spirit, the ego interprets the goal of time as its own. The continuity of past and future, under its direction, is the only purpose the ego perceives in time, and it closes over the present so that no gap in its own continuity can occur. Its continuity, then, would keep you in time, while the Holy Spirit would release you from it. It is His interpretation of the means of salvation [i.e., the illusion of time in the service of forgiveness: the *process* of the "Atonement plan"] that you must learn to accept, if you would share His goal of salvation [i.e., forgiveness] for you(T-13.IV.7-8; brackets mine).

The Uses of Memory

Most often when Jesus speaks of *memory* in the Course, he is speaking of remembering God Whom the ego has led us to deny and dissociate. However, since the idea of linear time begins with the ego, so too does the function of memory. While the belief in time is a defense against the truth, memory both depends upon the belief in time as well as sustains it. Therefore, memory sustains a defense against truth. Memory is the ego's mechanism of time; and what it would have us continually remember is that we are sinful because we destroyed Oneness, therefore punishment is to be feared. And the ego actually relishes punishment, pain, suffering and death because those experiences seem to validate its thought system.

By using memory as time's spokesman for retaining the ideas of sin, guilt and fear in our mind, the ego serves to replace God as First Cause, essentially making us believe that we, as ego, are our own cause. And so scientists go about searching for cause within the body and the perceivable universe.

At the level of our everyday inner experience, we can easily observe this function of memory as it constantly keeps the past alive in our awareness. Under the influence of ego thinking, we literally worship the past, both its painful as well as pleasant memories, because our image of self as special must have a history. And specialness does not care whether that image and its history is full of remorse or prances narcissistically with self congratulation. All forms of self image have guilt as their source, whether guilt is denied, as in reaction formation (protesting ones goodness too much), or displayed as depression and self condemnation. In this way, memory serves the ego's need for continuity of its basic elements (sin, guilt and fear), both at the metaphysical level where memory retains the belief in duality, as well as at the personal level where memory retains the idea of a separate, special self. At both levels, the ego uses memory to remind us of our past sins, thereby reinforcing guilt in the present and justifying fear of the future.

A practical example of this dynamic at the personal level can be observed in the angry thoughts and images which arise out of the past in our awareness, perhaps from actively recalling them, or seemingly without one's bidding. In terms of Jesus' psychology, these thoughts serve a purpose, and we can ask the rhetorical question: "Why else would they appear except for guilt which seeks to find a means of projection in the form of 'justified' anger and attack?" These angry thoughts and images are examples of how the ego uses memory to hold on to the past for its purposes: i.e., how *we* use memory for purposes of reinforcing our self concept and as a means for projecting guilt which inevitably leads to holding on to guilt and fear, therefore retaining the thought of victimization and justifying attack.

The ego uses time to make separation seem real; and the ego uses memory to keep guilt alive and well, therefore to keep special relationships alive and sick—sick because the special relationship is the home of guilt and fear; sick because the special relationship is the queen of defenses that "do what they would defend," thus they make fear seem real, usually transforming it into hate. Every attack we launch upon a brother, whether in the form of inward judgment or outward assault, announces the presence of guilt and fear in our mind, reinforcing them as real until we are willing to question our motives. Every attack comes from the ego's *memory* of guilt which demands projection upon images from the past, and this serves to keep the ego in business:

sin (past) → guilt (present) → fear (future).

Enthusiasm for "historical preservation" is another example of the ego's worship of memory to serve the purpose of maintaining its continuity as the prevailing thought system in our mind. The point of this example is not to disparage people's interest in history, art and architecture, but simply to illustrate the ego thought system at work in our lives. Looking backward and bringing the past with us is a way to preserve the illusion of time, hence the illusion that we are separate, since time and separation are "one illusion."

Another example of the way in which memory serves the ego is in its keeping the idea of death "alive" in our mind. Perhaps there is no better illustration of the association between memory and the ego than in the worldwide presence of war memorials which historically began as celebrations of triumphant attack, but in recent history have become places for honoring the dead who are said to have *sacrificed* their lives in the name of warfare; i.e., in the name of those ego hallmarks, *victimization* and *attack*. Surely the worm of guilt crawls in the foundation of every war memorial which speaks not only for guilt and fear, but for the ego's illusion of life that dies; speaks for the ego's denial of God as well as its worship of the body:

> Death is the symbol of the fear of God. His Love is blotted out in the idea, which holds it from awareness like a shield held up to obscure the sun. The grimness of the symbol is enough to show it cannot coexist with God. It holds an image of the Son of God in which he is "laid to rest" in devastation's arms, where worms wait to greet him and to last a little while by his destruction. Yet the worms as well are doomed to be destroyed as certainly. And so do all things live because of death. Devouring is nature's "law of life." God is insane, and fear alone is real.
>
> The curious belief that there is part of dying things that may go on apart from what will die, does not proclaim a loving God nor re-establish any grounds for trust. If death is real for anything, there is no life. Death denies life. But if there is reality in life, death is denied. No compromise in this is possible. There is either a god of fear or One of Love. The world attempts a thousand compromises, and will attempt a thousand more. Not one can be acceptable...because not one could be acceptable to God. He did not make death because He did not make fear. Both are equally meaningless to Him.
>
> The "reality" of death is firmly rooted in the belief that God's Son is a body. And if God created bodies, death would indeed be real. But God would not be loving...Death is indeed the death of God, if He is Love. And now His Own creation must stand in fear of Him. He is not Father, but destroyer. He is not Creator, but avenger. Terrible His Thoughts and fearful His image. To look on His creations is to die.
>
> "And the last to be overcome will be death." Of course! Without the idea of death there is no world [i.e., no ego thought system]. All dreams will end with this one. This is salvation's final goal; the end of all illusions. And in death are all illusions born. What can be born of death and still have life? But what is born of God and still can die? The inconsistencies, the compromises and the rituals the world fosters in its vain attempts to cling to death and yet to think love real are mindless magic, ineffectual and meaningless. God is, and in Him all created things must be eternal. Do you not see that otherwise He has an opposite, and fear would be as real as love? (M-27.3-5:3; 5:5-6:11; brackets mine).

To summarize, memory, which depends upon the illusion of time, is the means the ego uses to ensure its continuity by keeping the lie of separation fixed in the past and retained in our mind. Memory is the way *we* ensure *our* continuity as separate, special individuals. Our self concept is rooted in the idea of a personal history made up of images from the past; images which establish our differences from perceived others as well as our claim to grievances. Likewise, our perception of others is rooted in memory and made up of images from the past. These images of self and others prevent us from living in the now, which Jesus tells us is really the only time there is:

> The present now remains the only time. Here in the present is the world set free. For as you let the past be lifted and release the future from [the memory of] your ancient fears, you find escape and give it to the world. You have enslaved the world with [your memory of] all your fears, your doubts and miseries, your pain and tears, and all your sorrows press on it, and keep the world a prisoner to your beliefs. Death strikes it everywhere because you hold the [the memory of the] bitter thoughts of death within your mind (W-pI.132.3; brackets mine).

The belief in separation is the original thought of death which led to the ego's image of a god of death. Separation is not true, but it is held in the mind by memory and the belief there is a past. Separation did not happen. There is no past, and there is no time. Time is a lie: "a trick; a sleight of hand." Therefore memory is a lie that sustains a lie.

It is in the present moment when the truth of God and oneness can be found, because that truth is held in our right mind by the Holy Spirit, Who is ever present in the *now*, and often referred to in the Course as "the Memory of God."

"The Present Memory" (T-28.I)

Jesus uses the curious, thought-provoking and pregnant phrase, "present memory" to indicate the important principle that the only real time is *now*; and that it is in the now where we decide whether to join with the ego or the Holy Spirit. If we choose the ego, we elect its version of time which uses memory to anchor us in the past, trapping us in linear time, which is to be trapped in its thought system of sin, guilt and fear. However the Holy Spirit—the memory of God—is in our mind regardless of our ego illusions. Therefore, in the present moment we can choose the Holy Spirit, which means to choose His version of time, thus to be freed of the ego's linear-time prison; freed from the lie that separation happened in the past and is the cause of our reality; freed from the burdens of guilt and fear with their illusions and demand for defenses—defenses which include the world and the body. Essentially the Holy Spirit's *knowledge* replaces perception and offers us the truth of timelessness and our Identity as spirit. By choosing the right-minded thought system of the Holy Spirit *now*, we can forget what the ego taught us to remember, and remember What it had us forget.

At this point we are going to invite Kenneth Wapnick to be a guest author for purposes of concluding this chapter with an extensive set of excerpts from his line-by-line discussion of that section in the Course entitled "The Present Memory" (T-28.I). This discussion constitutes a sizeable portion of chapter four in Kenneth's book, *A Vast Illusion: Time according to A Course in Miracles*. For our purposes, some sections of that chapter have been deleted and citations have been inserted for material quoted from the Course. Dr. Wapnick's treatment of this material serves not only as an excellent summary and elaboration of the Course's concepts of time and memory, but as a review and further explanation of many subjects discussed in this book so far.

In the excerpts to follow, the reader will need to understand an analogy that Dr. Wapnick uses to clarify the Course's concept of time, which basically says that what we think of as past, present and future has already happened; that our lives constitute a series of dramas in separation or specialness which were corrected before they began; and that we are actually "reviewing mentally what has gone by" (W-pI.158.4:5). By way of explaining this remarkable and uncommon view, Wapnick uses an analogy which employs the familiar experience of watching a video taped movie. With respect to the movie of our lives, there are basically two versions of the video: the ego's and the Holy Spirit's. At any time we can press a button on our remote control in order to view one or the other of these versions. It is this analogy that Wapnick refers to in the following selections when he speaks of tapes, videos and pushing buttons.

Further, we are now at a point where it will be helpful for the reader to have in mind some additional definitions of concepts and terms used in the Course, since they are central to Jesus' thought system and will be referred to in Dr. Wapnick's discussion. We have already discussed some of these, but have not taken the time for a more thorough explanation.

First, it is important to understand that the Course's *miracle* has nothing to do with the usual idea that miracles change physical phenomena. All "physical phenomena"—everything that can be perceived in form or even conceptualized in the symbolic systems we use for communication—are *effect*, not *cause*. They are illusions. The Course's miracle is about changing the cause, which is our mind; specifically changing the thought system in our mind with which we perceive and interpret what we perceive. The miracle is not enlightenment (metaphorically referred to as "God's last step"), but sets the stage for enlightenment through forgiveness, to which it is roughly equivalent. Wapnick's *Glossary* definition of *miracle* is:

> the change of mind that shifts our perception from the ego's world of sin, guilt, and fear, to the Holy Spirit's world of forgiveness; reverses projection by restoring to the mind its causative function, allowing us to choose again; transcends the laws of this world to reflect the laws of God; accomplished by our joining with the Holy Spirit or Jesus, being the means of healing our own and others' minds. (Note: not to be confused with the traditional understanding of miracles as changes in external phenomena.)

It can be said that the miracle involves accepting the "Atonement principle" that the separation never happened since that principle is the foundation stone of forgiveness and the Holy Spirit's right-minded thought system. In the Course, the term *Atonement* refers both to this principle and to what is called "God's plan" or the "Holy Spirit's plan" for undoing the belief in separation (i.e., sin). Here again, Jesus is using metaphor to communicate with us, and elsewhere in the Course points out that in truth God does not plan, nor does it make sense to speak of a "plan" in terms of the Holy Spirit's *knowledge*, which includes the truth that there is no future to plan for, nor any past which could inform an effort to plan. All that the miracle and Atonement do is restore to our minds the eternal truth that the ego had us dissociate. So, neither the miracle nor the Course's Atonement "do" anything. They simply remove the barriers to the memory of God and our true Identity that was always present. The idea of an "Atonement plan" simply refers to the *seeming process* of forgiveness in time—a process that in truth is already over and was never necessary in the first place, however simply understanding that does us no good as long as we identify as bodies, pursue specialness, and believe both time and perception are real. Rather, within the illusion of linear time, we need the help of the Holy Spirit or Jesus Who bridge for us the gap between *knowledge* and perception as we undo our self-imposed barriers to knowledge. *Atonement* is defined as follows in Wapnick's *Glossary*:

> the Holy Spirit's plan of correction to undo the ego and heal the belief in separation; came into being after the separation, and will be completed when every separated Son has fulfilled his part in the Atonement by total forgiveness; its principle is that the separation never occurred. [Note: this definition is presented in the context of the Course's Level Two teachings where Jesus speaks to us in terms of our experience that linear time is real.]

Three other related definitions from Wapnick's *Glossary* follow. They are sufficiently self-explanatory that we will not discuss them further:

> *memory of God* – the Atonement's final stage, which follows seeing the face of Christ in all our brothers and precedes the last step, taken by God Himself; we remember God through forgiveness, undoing all beliefs in separation that obscured His Presence to us.

> *face of Christ* - symbol of forgiveness; the face of true innocence seen in another when we look through Christ's vision [i.e., the Holy Spirit's perception], free from our projections of guilt; thus it is the extension to others of the guiltlessness we see in ourselves, independent of what our physical eyes may see. (Note: not to be confused with the face of Jesus, nor with anything external.)

> *last step* [i.e., God's "last step"] - this step, belonging to God, occurs when the Atonement is complete and all ego interferences have been removed; when nothing remains to separate us from God, He takes the last step, raising us unto Himself; strictly speaking God does not take steps, and the term actually refers to *our* experience of returning to our Source Which we never truly left.

Now we can proceed to Dr. Wapnick's extensive commentary on time and memory, which also includes an excellent overview and summary of the material found in this book, and of the basics of the ACIM thought system.

> We turn now to "The Present Memory," and recall to mind that time is not linear. Events are not happening now nor are they yet to happen. Everything has already happened, and time is seen within a holographic rather than a linear model. The Holy Spirit's use of memory, the "present memory," refers to our remembering right here and now, with the help of the Holy Spirit, that we have never left our Father's House. The ego's use of memory, on the other hand, is to remind us of our past sins to reinforce our guilt, causing us to be afraid of the future. But the faculty of remembering is used by the Holy Spirit to undo our belief in the past, so that we can recall that ancient memory, "the forgotten song" referred to in the section of the same name (see above, p. 59), and remember that we never left God. Now we begin with "The Present Memory" (T-28.1).

> **The miracle does nothing. All it does is to undo. And thus it cancels out the interference to what has been done. It does not add, but merely takes away. And what it takes away is long since gone, but being kept in memory appears to have immediate effects. This world was over long ago. The thoughts that made it are no longer in the mind that thought of them and loved them for a little while. The miracle but shows the past is gone, and**

what has truly gone has no effects. Remembering a cause can but produce illusions of its presence, not effects (T-28.1.1).

As *A Course in Miracles* frequently emphasizes, the miracle (as well as the Atonement, forgiveness, or salvation) does not do anything, since there is nothing that needs to be done. Rather, it corrects (or undoes) the ego's belief that there is a problem (i.e., our guilt) that needs defense (i.e., the world and the body) and atonement (i.e., sacrifice and suffering). The ego holds on to that ancient memory of our belief in having separated from God, and it was that separation thought that became the cause of the world of the body, suffering, and death. In our experience of individual lives, whenever we feel pain, or accuse someone else of victimizing us, we are actually reliving that ancient moment, saying, "Look at the misery of my life; my sin against God has had very real effects." And the ego tells us, even if we are not conscious of it, that this pain ultimately is our punishment because of what we did against God.

"What it takes away is long since gone": the miracle takes away the cause and effect connection. It helps us realize that these terrible effects we believe are real, are not so, and if they are not real—if they are not effects—they cannot have a cause. If something is not a cause it does not exist, which is the Holy Spirit's way of teaching us that sin is an illusion: it never really happened. That is why it is imperative when working with *A Course in Miracles* to recognize that it teaches that the world is an illusion. If we acknowledge the world, and therefore the body, as real, we are saying sin has had effects. If we believe the body is eternal, or resurrects and therefore has died (which of course means that it once lived), we are saying the body has a reality, and therefore that sin has had an effect and must be real as well.

A Course in Miracles is teaching us that the body is not real because the world is not real. They are illusory because they came from the illusory belief that we have sinned against God. "The thoughts that made it are no longer in the mind that thought of them and loved them for a little while": the Holy Spirit has already undone the illusory thought that made the world; the mistakes have already been corrected.

All the effects of guilt are here no more. For guilt is over. In its passing went its consequences, left without a cause (T-28.2:1-3).

This is another way of saying what was discussed above. Guilt is over because sin has been undone. The seeming separation from God which led to our guilt was corrected in that same instant, which meant it did not have any effects. And so the world, which is the effect of guilt, is over as well, with all the seeming consequences of pain, suffering, and death. And yet we still sit in front of the screen replaying the ancient scripts, as if it all were happening today, as if our sin and guilt were real and had real effects.

Why would you cling to it in memory if you did not desire its effects? (T-28.2:4).

The thought expressed here has important implications for psychological theory and psychotherapy. The past does have an effect on us, if we choose in the present to hold on to it. Strictly speaking, if I continue to believe that my parents abused me and did not love me, then I will see my adult sufferings as a direct effect of that abuse. And I will be able to say: "Yes, the reason I am like this is because I was mistreated when I was a child." All of this is true within the illusory nature of the ego's world, a belief upheld by many personality theorists. The real truth, however, is that I am choosing in the *present* to hold on to that memory. If I change my mind in the present, then no matter what my parents did or did not do, it would have no effect. And I choose to hold on to the bitter memory because I desire its effects of pain now, but wish to deny my responsibility for choosing it. Instead, the responsibility is projected onto the past and specific figures in it, and so I put on the "face of innocence" (T-31.V.2:6).

The same is true of the larger picture. We believe our suffering in this world is a direct result of our sin against God, and so we cling to the past as if it were still here. And that is only because we are choosing now to hold on to the past; the pain belonging to it is what sustains the ego's existence. We are choosing, as the observer, to hear the ego's voice. So we play the ego's tapes, which are tapes of separation, misery, suffering, anxiety, guilt, depression, sickness, and death. Furthermore, we are choosing to play those tapes because that relives for us the seeming reality of the time of separation. We are not aware at all that the problem is not what we believe we are experiencing or observing; the problem is that we are choosing, from the point of view of the observer, to make it real for us now, even though that "now" no longer exists, being a defense against the true now of the holy instant. As the Text states:

> Once you were unaware of what the cause of everything the world appeared to thrust upon you, uninvited and unasked, must really be. Of one thing you were sure: of all the many causes you perceived as bringing pain and suffering to you, your guilt was not among them (T-27.VII.7:3-4).

Remembering is as selective as perception, being its past tense. It is perception of the past as if it were occurring now, and still were there to see (T-28.2:5-6).

Perception, as the Course teaches us over and over again, is a choice. A section called "Perception and Choice" (T-25.III) teaches that what we see comes from our desire to see a specific thing, a desire which is then projected out. Consequently we see something, not because it is truly there, but because we *wish* to see it there. Remembering works in the exact same way;

the only difference is that perception, as we experience it, occurs in the present. I am perceiving you right now. If I remember something you did yesterday, then obviously that is in the past. But the past and the present in the split mind are different forms of the same illusion....

Q: So is the idea then that healing does not ask that you do anything, but rather simply to recognize that a mistake was made, ask the Holy Spirit for a corrected perception, and then let it go, trusting that by letting it go the "wrongs" that took place would be healed?

A: That is exactly the idea. If we then feel guided by the Holy Spirit to go and talk to the person, this would have to be done from a corrected perception which would lead to a different attitude if the healing were to occur. But what most of us do is feel guilty for something, and then feel we have to make up for it to the person, or we deny the guilt altogether, and continue going on as if nothing happened, but the guilt of the past remains deep within us. So either way, the ego's atoning or denying serve the ego's purpose of making the past real.

Memory, like perception, is a skill made up by you to take the place of what God gave in your creation. And like all the things you made, it can be used to serve another purpose [the Holy Spirit's], and to be the means for something else. It can be used to heal and not to hurt, if you so wish it be (T-28.2:7-9).

We made up memory because memory obviously implies a linear view of time, past and present, and so time becomes a substitute for the eternal present, which is the closest we can come to the state of reality. And yet, despite its ego purpose of attack, time can be used by the Holy Spirit to help us...the Holy Spirit uses what we made for the purpose of separation or attack, as a means to join and heal....

Nothing employed for healing represents an effort to do anything at all (T-28.3:1).

In other words, in our right mind (which is the only place healing can occur) we do not do anything, for nothing *has* to be done; a miracle does not do anything, it simply undoes—that is how the section began. Whenever we experience ourselves as expending effort—which is different from our *bodies* behaving in certain ways—we know that our egos have gotten in the way. When Lesson 155 tells us to "step back and let Him lead the way" (W-pI.155), it is making the same point as when the Course elsewhere tells us to undo the interferences that prevent the Holy Spirit's Love and healing from extending through us. Love simply *is;* it does nothing at all.

It is a recognition that you have no needs which mean that something must be done (T-28.3:2).

If I believe I have a need, then obviously I have to do something about it; the idea behind the miracle (or healing) is that nothing has to be done. This of course does not mean that our bodies do not do things in this world, but simply that we recognize that it is the Holy Spirit's Love that is "doing" it through us. Our only need, therefore, is to remember that we have no needs. The Course states that

> the only meaningful prayer is for forgiveness, because those who have been forgiven have everything.... The prayer for forgiveness is nothing more than a request that you may be able to recognize what you already have (T-3.V.6:3, 5).

And so, to state it once again, the miracle simply undoes our faulty belief system, which then inevitably leads to the memory of our one need—the Love of God.

It is an unselective memory, that is not used to interfere with truth (T-28.3:3).

I can have memories of the past, but I do not need to judge them. I do not think "this is a good thing, or a bad thing; this is a good person, or a bad person"....

Therefore, instead of judging what my memory holds, I am to realize that these were lessons *I* chose to re-experience, so that I could learn the ultimate lesson of accepting the Atonement.

All things the Holy Spirit can employ for healing have been given Him, without the content and the purposes for which they have been made. They are but skills without an application. They await their use. They have no dedication and no aim (T-28.3:4-7).

...everything the Holy Spirit will use has already happened. Specifically, if there is a relationship that has really been a terrible one, it is given to the Holy Spirit, but without the ego purpose of specialness it was made to serve. Thus, the relationship becomes an instrument of salvation. This theme is restated later in the Text in a powerful passage that expresses the Holy Spirit's reinterpretation of our specialness:

> Such is the Holy Spirit's kind perception of specialness; His use of what you made, to heal instead of harm....The specialness he [the Son] chose to hurt himself did God appoint to be the means for his salvation, from the very instant that the choice was made (T-25.VI.4:1; 6:6).

The form remains the same—the relationship itself—but the content has been shifted from the special one of guilt, murder, and separation, to the holy one of forgiveness, love, and joining. All things in the world are neutral—"My body is a wholly neutral thing" (W-pII.294)—awaiting a purpose to be assigned to them. As the Course says: "The test of everything on earth is simply this; 'What is it *for*'" (T24.VII.6:1). Things either serve the ego's or the Holy Spirit's purpose, as the mind elects.

The Holy Spirit can indeed make use of memory, for God Himself is there. Yet this is not a memory of past events, but only of a present state. You are so long accustomed to believe that memory holds only what is past, that it is hard for you to realize it is a skill that can remember *now* (T-28.4:1-3).

This is a totally different view of memory, and basically points to that very important notion of the observer...There can be no memory of past events, for there *are* no past events. There is only a decision made in the present by the observer to hold on to the memory of the thought of separation that is no longer there. Memory is a skill that will help us to remember ultimately that our true reality is the one we never left. Thus the ability to remember that the ego made to imprison us in the memory of our sin of separation, can now be used by the Holy Spirit to remember our present state with God, in which the sin of separation never occurred.

The limitations on remembering the world imposes on it are as vast as those you let the world impose on you. There is no link of memory to the past. If you would have it there, then there it is. But only your desire made the link, and only you have held it to a part of time where guilt appears to linger still (T-28.4:4-6).

We are so totally identified with the world's view of linear time, that it seems impossible for us to believe that time can be anything else. In truth, of course, the illusory world is powerless to impose anything on us, for, in fact, it is simply the power of our own minds that places such limitations upon us. The statement that there is no memory link to the past refers to what was mentioned earlier about holding on to painful memories of the past. What we remember in the present has nothing to do with the past. It really is but a choice in the present to hold on to our guilt and the belief that the separation is real. Remembering the bad things my parents did to me thirty or forty years ago is just an excuse that the ego uses to achieve its aim of hiding its foundation thought of separation from awareness.

The Holy Spirit's use of memory is quite apart from time. He does not seek to use it as a means to keep the past, but rather as a way to let it go. Memory holds the message it receives, and does what it is given it to do. It does not write the message, nor appoint what it is for. Like to the body, it is purposeless within itself (T-28.5:1-5).

This is an important idea in *A Course in Miracles,* and it appears quite a few times. The body does not do anything; it merely carries out the messages the mind has given it. This theme of messages and messengers is found also in "The Attraction of Guilt" in Chapter 19, which emphasizes that the problem is the *messengers* we send out, not the *messages* that are brought back. The messengers simply do what we told them to do. Similarly, regarding the world, the Course states:

> The world you see is but the idle witness that you were right. This witness is insane. You trained it in its testimony, and as it gave it back to you, you listened and convinced yourself that what it saw was true. You did this to yourself. See only this, and you will also see how circular the reasoning on which your "seeing" rests (T-21.II.5:1-5).

And if it [memory] seems to serve to cherish ancient hate, and gives you pictures of injustices and hurts that you were saving, this is what you asked its message be and that it is.

The problem is not the specific form of past hurts we are recalling to mind, but rather that we have chosen *in the present* to look only upon those past hurts, those ancient hates. Thus, it is not the specific event or person that is the cause of our distress, but rather the split mind (or more properly, the decision maker) that chose to be upset in the first place. Once that choice to be upset is made, the mind then uses the "pictures of injustices" to justify a feeling for which it does not want to accept responsibility. It is an insidious and particularly vicious form of relating to others, though never recognized as such because our guilt prevents us from ever looking at what the ego tells us is the horrible truth about ourselves. Indeed, as we have seen, when we finally are able to look, we see that the ego's emperor has no clothes on, that its "truth" is simply non-existent...

Committed to its vaults [the ego's vault of its memory], the history of all the body's past is hidden there. All of the strange associations made to keep the past alive, the present dead, are stored within it, waiting your command that they be brought to you, and lived again (T-28.5:7-8).

...The body's past is hidden, not in the body or its brain, but in the *mind* of the decision maker. Recalling our image of the observer sitting in front of the television screen with the remote control, we press a button and that is what we see, what we have recalled from our video library, our "memory banks." The ego lives only in the past, because that is where it believes sin is, while the Holy Spirit's Love, containing the memory of God, lives only in the present, untouched by the sin, guilt, and fear that is the ego's "life." Thus, this present cannot be experienced by a body (brain), but only by the mind that has chosen to remember God, in what *A Course in Miracles* refers to as the holy instant.

And thus do their effects appear to be increased by time, which took away their cause (T-28.5:9).

In this sentence, "effects" refers to the body, whose number certainly appears to increase as time goes on. And the world of time and space, with which we so identify, has effectively done its job of concealing from us the world's cause, which is the thought of separation now buried in the vaults of our mind.

This non-linear conceptual scheme is totally and radically different from what we usually hear presented. The model of the world used by scientists has been a linear one for the most part. The quantum physicists are increasingly moving away from this, although they would most probably not accept the kinds of statements the Course is making. Einstein's relativity theory of course was a major shift in terms of how we look at time. However, I do not think these physicists apprehend *A Course in Miracles* ...understanding that the thought in back of the universe of time and space, that was its seeming cause, is also illusory, being a thought of guilt.

Yet time is but another phase of what does nothing. It works hand in hand with all the other attributes with which you seek to keep concealed the truth about yourself (T-28.6:1-2).

This refers to the ego, the thought of separation which contains the ancient cause of sin. Yet, this thought does nothing; it has had no effect. Therefore, since the thought of separation is nothing, all that results from it, such as time, is also nothing: "Ideas leave not their source." Time, thus, is just another device the ego uses—obviously, a very powerful one, as is its use of death, space, and the body—to keep concealed the truth about ourselves. This truth of course is that we are eternal spirit. The ego would have us believe that our identity is our body bound by time and space. Thus, this body serves as a most effective smokescreen, distracting our attention from the mind, where we truly are.

Time neither takes away nor can restore. And yet you make strange use of it, as if the past had caused the present, which is but a consequence in which no change can be made possible because its cause has gone (T-28.6:3-4).

This of course is the traditional psychological point of view. For example, take again someone who believes he is having trouble as an adult because he was abandoned as a child. In effect, the basic premise here closes off all possibility of change because the cause is gone. No hope of healing can exist because the deed is done and the past cannot be changed. Within the dream, the abandonment did in fact happen. And so since the past cannot be undone, the man is stuck: the innocent and hopeless victim as an adult of what went wrong in his childhood. And so there is actually nothing that he can do about his situation. Psychoanalytic theory is inherently pessimistic, because it teaches that there is no way out: the past cannot be changed. The best one can do is try to become "free" of some of the blocks (hurtful and painful memories). However, we still remain within a closed system in which the past does have real effects.

That same model also holds on an unconscious cosmic level, where we say that our sins against God are real, and there is nothing we can do about it. That is the central stone in the ego's foundation: there is nothing we can do about our sinfulness. We cannot change what the ego has made to be reality; we cannot change our individual bodies, the laws of nature, the laws of the world. We are, for all intents and purposes, totally powerless.

This hopelessness is the context of the Manual's references to the dreariness of the world and the weary march of time (M-1.4:4-5). We feel as if we are stuck in a prison house, the cause of which is now gone, and so cannot be changed. Listening to the ego's voice, we believe that the past has caused the present, and that the present now is the effect of the past. So in this larger metaphysical view, the ancient past of our sin of separation against God has caused all the problems of the present. It caused this world, the body, and all the attendant problems. And so this world is the consequence or effect, and no change is ever possible because the cause is gone: it has already happened in the past.

Finally, when *A Course in Miracles* says that the cause or the past is gone, it means something quite different from what the ego means. The past is gone because it never happened; it was never there in the first place. This is the major difference between these two approaches, and within it lies the difference between Heaven and hell.

Yet change must have a cause that will endure, or else it will not last. No change can be made In the present if its cause is past. Only the past is held in memory as you make use of it, and so it is a way to hold the past against the now (T-28.6:5-7).

If there is going to be change, and ultimately the mind is the only place where we can have true change, it must be on the level of the cause. The ego tells us that the cause is already finished. You cannot change the cause that has already happened, so therefore you are stuck with the consequences or the effect. On the other hand, Jesus is teaching us that the only way we can change something is by changing the cause, the belief that we have separated from God. That change can occur only within the mind, because that is where the belief "resides," and it is this *belief* that is the problem. *A Course in Miracles* helps us make another choice by returning us to that ancient moment when we chose to believe we could be separate from God. We do that in the context of our relationships with each other, precisely because it is within this context that we relive that ancient moment over and over again.

Remember nothing that you taught yourself, for you were badly taught. And who would keep a senseless lesson in his mind, when he can learn and can preserve a better one? (T-28.7:1-2)

This is another way of looking at the Course's fundamental purpose of teaching us that we have learned senseless lessons that make us suffer, and that our suffering comes about, not because it simply has happened to us, but because we have *chosen* to suffer, to learn these senseless lessons. But there is another Teacher in our minds who will teach us different ones. Ultimately this means that there is a Teacher in our minds who will remind us that we should choose His tapes. This theme of choosing another Teacher appears frequently in *A Course in Miracles*. I like to combine a phrase from this passage with an earlier statement in the Text (T-12.V.8:3), so that it reads thus: "Resign now as your own teacher, for you were badly taught."

When ancient memories of hate appear, remember that their cause is gone. And so you cannot understand what they are for (T-28.7:3-4).

Jesus is now telling us that whenever we feel ourselves getting angry at someone, the anger and the hatred are really coming from this ancient hatred that we are just re-experiencing over and over again. All we have to remember is that the cause is gone. The cause was the sin of being separate and that thought has already been undone. In terms of our experience, this translates into my no longer seeing you as an enemy who is separate from me; I see you as my brother and friend, joined with me. As the Text says earlier:

> In separation from your brother was the first attack upon yourself begun. And it is this the world bears witness to (T-27.VII.6:4-5).

Therefore, it is when we share the common interest of salvation and join with our brothers, originally perceived as separate from us, that we undo the cause of separation.

Let not the cause that you would give them now be what it was that made them what they were, or seemed to be. Be glad that it is gone, for this is what you would be pardoned from (T-28.7:5-6).

The "cause" is the reliving of that ancient instant of being separate, and "them" refers back to the ancient memories. In other words, Jesus is asking us not to make the error of separation real. We would be pardoned from, or forgiven for, our sin of being separate. Whenever we are upset we are really bringing to mind this ancient memory which is inherently causeless; its cause was undone in that very instant when it seemed to happen.

And see, instead, the new effects of cause accepted *now*, with consequences *here*. They will surprise you with their loveliness. The ancient new ideas they bring will be the happy consequences of a Cause so ancient that it far exceeds the span of memory which your perception sees (T-28.7:7-9).

... The "cause accepted *now*" would be the Holy Spirit's Atonement principle, with consequences of joy and peace experienced now. It is what *A Course in Miracles* refers to as the forgiven or real world, which contains such loveliness in it....

This loveliness, of course, is not anything external, but rather comes from the *inner* experience of the loveliness of Christ, our Identity and all our brothers as well. The "new" ideas, such as peace, joy, and love, are ancient because they reflect the Atonement principle, which occurred in that one instant. Thus they reflect the eternal nature of Heaven. They are new only because they *seem* to be such in our experience; new to our remembering, although in truth they were always there.

This is the Cause [the capitalization tells us that this is God] the Holy Spirit has remembered for you, when you would forget (T-28.8:1).

When we forget God and find ourselves becoming upset, for example, we can remember to ask the Holy Spirit to be *present* to us. At once—in whatever form the experience would speak to us—we feel His gentle hand tapping us on the shoulder, saying: "My brother, choose again. There is no need to continue to see yourself as separate, and attack someone else; you no longer have to protect your guilt by projecting it onto another. There is no cause of guilt within you, as the thought of sin has already been undone." Thus do we let the Holy Spirit awaken us from the dream, as we welcome God's Love back into our forgetful mind. The *cause of* our upset—the separation from God—has been undone through our joining with His Love through the Holy Spirit, and through that joining are all the effects undone as well.

It [the Cause] is not past because He let It not be unremembered. It has never changed, because there never was a time in which He did not keep It safely in your mind. Its consequences will indeed seem new, because you thought that you remembered not their Cause (T-28.8:2-4).

The state of being with God is always present because the Holy Spirit has never let it leave our memory, as He is in truth this memory of God's Love. The memory is within our minds, and because it is, there is a part of us that does remember that we have never really left our Father's House. Even though our split minds may continue to dissociate this Love and play only the ego tapes, still are the Holy Spirit's within our minds as well. His Love patiently awaits the time when we accept what He has already accepted for us. When we suddenly have an experience of God's Love, it will seem to be totally new. Yet all that has happened is that we were suddenly able to release our fingers from the ego's wrong-minded button, and finally play a tape in which God's Love would appear. That tape was always held for us by the Holy Spirit. This thought parallels an earlier one in the Text, where Jesus says that he has saved all our loving thoughts and kindnesses and kept them for us in their perfect radiance (T-5.IV.8:1-4). The experience will thus appear new to us even though it really is not. *Nothing* is new.

Yet was It never absent from your mind, for it was not your Father's Will that He be unremembered by His Son (T-28.8:5).

The Father's Will is manifested in our mind through the Holy Spirit, and that is the link back to Him. Thus, there is always a part of our minds—the decision maker—that can choose to remember what the Holy Spirit is holding for us. God's Will is simply the expression of the truth of His Being, and Christ's Being joined with His: Father and Son, God and Christ, can never be separated, nor forgotten one by the other.

What *you* remember never was. It came from causelessness which you confused with cause. It can deserve but laughter, when you learn you have remembered consequences that were causeless and could never be effects (T-28.9:1-3).

The "you" here is the decision maker or observer in our minds, which has chosen to identify with the ego. The ego would have us remember all the sins of the past, which never were to begin with. Thus, what we remember—pain, sorrow, and misery—are the effects of their cause, sin. We are now being taught, however, that sin has had no effects, being without a cause. Sin merely came from a silly thought—"a tiny, mad idea"—in our minds that was undone the instant that it seemed to occur.

The cause-effect idea, simply stated again, is that if something is not an effect it cannot have a cause, and if there is no cause it cannot exist. Our experiences in this world consist of our continual attempts to teach ourselves that sin is real, a cause with the very real effect of misery that proves that sin is so. But we could just as easily play a different tape in which happiness instead of misery is the effect, showing us that sin had no effects at all. Another way of stating this is that the world is causeless. The seeming cause of sin was undone and corrected in the same instant in which it seemed to come into existence. Thus, the idea that we could actually sin against our Source is so preposterous, that we could only laugh at the silliness of it all...

> Together, we [Jesus and ourselves] can laugh them [the separation thought and its seeming effects] both away, and understand that time cannot intrude upon eternity. It is a joke to think that time can come to circumvent eternity, which *means* there is no time (T-27.VIII.6:4-5).

Thus, at last, with Jesus' love beside us we do remember to laugh.

The miracle reminds you of a Cause [God] forever present, perfectly untouched by time and interference. Never changed from what It is. And you are Its effect, as changeless and as perfect as Itself. Its memory does not lie in the past, nor waits the future. It is not revealed in miracles. They but remind you that It has not gone. When you forgive It for your sins, It will no longer be denied (T-28.9:4-10).

Once again, the miracle does nothing. It does not bring to us the Love of God, because His Love is already in us. The miracle simply reminds us that, in truth, there is no real interference—i.e., sin—to the Love of God, and so we, as extensions of that Love, have never changed from our reality as Christ. In a wonderful early passage, Jesus makes the same point speaking of the Holy Spirit's role:

> The Voice of the Holy Spirit does not command, because it is incapable of arrogance. It does not demand, because it does not seek control. It does not overcome, because it does not attack. It merely reminds. It is compelling only because of what it reminds you of (T-5.II.7:1-5).

You who have sought to lay a judgment on your own Creator cannot understand it is not He Who laid a judgment on His Son (T-28.10:1).

This is another way of saying that because we are so guilty we cannot begin to understand that it is not God's Will that we suffer. This is succinctly expressed in this statement closing a section on specialness: "Forgive your Father it was not His Will that you be crucified" (T-24.III.8:13). It is impossible for our ego selves to conceive that God does not choose to crucify or punish us, and of course this is what our egos hold against our loving Father. Our belief that we have sinned against Him leads us, due to the dynamic of projection, to believe He must attack us in return. It thus becomes impossible for us to believe that our sin, guilt, and fear of punishment is just a bad dream that we have made up. Since we have judged against Him in the dream, we must believe He will judge us too.

You would deny Him His Effects, yet have They never been denied (T-28.10:2).

A Course in Miracles states that God is First Cause and all of us, as Christ, are the Effects of this First Cause. Moreover, as we have already seen, there is nowhere where God ends and we begin. However, the intent of that tiny, mad idea of separation was to deny that God was First Cause, and that we ourselves were His Effects. Thus the Son of God has become the self split off from its Source, his own origin as it were, with cause and effect now the same:

> The ego believes it is completely on its own, which is merely another way of describing how it thinks it originated.... The ego is the mind's belief that it is completely on its own (T -4.II.8:1, 4).

There was no time in which His Son could be condemned for what was causeless and against His [God's] Will. What your remembering would witness to is but the fear of God. He has not done the thing you fear. No more have you. And so your innocence has not been lost (T-28.10:3-7).

How can God condemn us for the thought of separation, which the Atonement principle states clearly has never happened? The truth remains that we are still as God created us, and that His Will and ours are one. It was our split mind that made up the drama of the separation and the emotion of fear. The ego would have us believe that we have really accomplished the impossible by separating from our Source. This is what the ego thought system witnesses to, and if we identify with the ego we will fear God's retaliation. What Jesus reminds us of here is that we are innocent, the drama is make-believe, and therefore we have nothing to fear.

You need no healing to be healed. In quietness, see in the miracle a lesson in allowing Cause to have Its Own Effects, and doing nothing that would interfere
(T-28.10:8-9).

That most important teaching with which this section opened, and which appears many other times in the material, is restated here: the miracle does not do anything; healing does not do anything; neither does forgiveness nor salvation. They merely correct the mistaken *belief* in separation, restoring to our minds the awareness of what always was and is. Thus, we do not have to be healed because we *are* healed. There has never *been* anything in us that needed healing. Our belief in sin was nothing more than a bad dream. Thus, "allowing Cause to have Its Own Effects" and not interfering, means acknowledging that the ego in all its grandiosity has never, and *can* never usurp God as First Cause. Therefore we still remain as God created us—His Effect forever and forever. In the quietness of our minds we remember our Cause—"The memory of God comes to the quiet mind" (T-23.I.1:1). The ego's raucous shrieking is finally chosen against, and the interference to remembering our Creator is gone....

Born out of sharing [joining with others in forgiveness], there can be no pause in time to cause the miracle delay in hastening to all unquiet minds, and bringing them an instant's stillness, when the memory of God returns to them. Their own remembering is quiet now, and what has come to take its place will not be wholly unremembered afterwards (T-28.11:4-5).

Elsewhere the Text talks about *our belief* that an enormous amount of time is necessary between the time we choose forgiveness and when our minds are finally healed (T -15.I.2:1; T 26.VIII.1:1; 3:1-2). Thus, Jesus is reiterating that the miracle occurs in an instant. It does not take any time because there is no time, but it appears to do so because we are still trapped in the illusion. In reality, however, in the instant that we forgive, all minds are joined and healed with us. Because our minds are already joined, all that we have done is remove the barrier to the awareness of that reality. That is why it occurs in an instant, when the decision maker makes another choice. Once we have experienced what it feels like to join truly with someone, rather than continually to attack, we can never totally lose that experience. No matter how we may try to fight it, the fact that we have had the experience of true peace that comes from forgiveness means that we can nevermore choose the ego one hundred percent of the time, despite our fear of identifying with God's Love: His Love will nevermore be "wholly unremembered"....

How instantly the memory of God arises in the mind that has no fear to keep the memory away! Its own remembering has gone (T-28.13:1-2).

Here, time is spoken about differently from its more common usage in the Text. The main point in this passage is that the entire ego world can disappear in one instant. When we totally forgive, all illusions—our veils of guilt—will disappear at the same time. At that point the memory of God's Love dawns upon our minds. The purpose of all fear, of course, is to prevent this memory from returning to us. Without fear, everything that constitutes ego thinking in the mind has vanished. Once the observer in our split minds chooses to identify with the Holy Spirit, there is no longer any purpose in remembering the ego's thought of separation, which we now know never was. Thus the thought disappears, as *A Course in Miracles* says in another context...back into "the nothingness from which it came" (M-13.1:2).

There is no past to keep its [remembering's] fearful image in the way of glad awakening to present peace. The trumpets of eternity resound throughout the stillness, yet disturb it not. And what is now remembered is not fear, but rather is the Cause that fear was made to render unremembered and undone. The stillness speaks in gentle sounds of love the Son of God remembers from before his own remembering came in between the present and the past, to shut them out (T-28.13:3-6).

With fear gone, all that remains in our minds is the memory of God, held there for us by the Holy Spirit, and at this point we begin to hear the "trumpets of eternity resound." It is really the heralding of our return home, now that our fear has been undone and we have let go of all bitter memories. What is left, again, is the memory of God. As we have seen, the purpose of fear and guilt is to be a defense, smokescreen, or distraction that keeps from us the memory of our real Cause, God. The ego tells us that our real cause is the ego itself, and what keeps us believing its lies is the idea that God is to be feared. This is how the ego uses memory, reminding us of our sins and justifying the guilt and fear that keeps the Love of God away from us. In the midst of that painful memory, the Holy Spirit was "placed" to retain for us the memory of our true thoughts of the Love of God: "In crucifixion is redemption laid" (T-26.VII.17:1). Now that fear is gone, all that remains is the Love that the Holy Spirit has held for us.

**Now is the Son of God at last aware of present Cause and Its benign effects
(T-28.14:1).**

This contrasts the Holy Spirit's use of memory, which focuses only in the present, with the ego's use of memory, which is focused only on the past. The Cause, *our Cause*, is in the present....

What has been lost, to see the causeless not? And where is sacrifice, when memory of God has come to take the place of loss? What better way to close the little gap between illusions and reality than to allow the memory of God to flow across it, making it a bridge an instant will suffice to reach beyond? For God has closed it with Himself (T-28.15:1-4).

From the ego's point of view, something indeed has been lost—a belief which is the origin of the scarcity principle—and we shall never retrieve it. In truth, all we have lost is the *awareness* of the innocence of Christ, to which our sinfulness testifies, we believe. We then believe that we must atone through sacrifice for that loss, brought about by our sin. Thus, sacrifice becomes a special bargain with God to win back His Love. When the memory of God dawns upon our minds, which is now washed clean by forgiveness, all pain and loss disappear and we perceive the causeless no longer....

His memory has not gone by, and left a stranded Son forever on a shore where he can glimpse another shore that he can never reach. His Father wills that he be lifted up and gently carried over. He has built the bridge [the Holy Spirit], and it is He Who will transport His Son across it. Have no fear that He will fail in what He wills. Nor that you be excluded from the Will that is for you (T-28.15:5-9).

...What carries us across the bridge are the forgiveness lessons that the Holy Spirit teaches us through the miracle...[1]

---

[1] Ibid, p. 73ff

185

Chapter 9

Learning

A Prefacing Statement: From Jesus to His Students

You have learning handicaps in a very literal sense. There are areas in your learning skills that are so impaired that you can progress only under constant, clear-cut direction, provided by a Teacher Who can transcend your limited resources. He becomes your Resource because of yourself you cannot learn. The learning situation in which you placed yourself is impossible, and in this situation you clearly require a special Teacher and a special curriculum. Poor learners are not good choices as teachers, either for themselves or for anyone else. You would hardly turn to them to establish the curriculum by which they can escape from their limitations. If they understood what is beyond them, they would not be handicapped.

You do not know the meaning of love, and that is your handicap. Do not attempt to teach yourself what you do not understand, and do not try to set up curriculum goals where yours have clearly failed. Your learning goal has been *not* to learn, and this cannot lead to successful learning. You cannot transfer what you have not learned, and the impairment of the ability to generalize is a crucial learning failure. Would you ask those who have failed to learn what learning aids are for? They do not know. If they could interpret the aids correctly, they would have learned from them.

I have said that the ego's rule is, "Seek and do not find." Translated into curricular terms this means, "Try to learn but do not succeed." The result of this curriculum goal is obvious. Every legitimate teaching aid, every real instruction, and every sensible guide to learning will be misinterpreted, since they are all for facilitating the learning this strange curriculum is against. If you are trying to learn how not to learn, and the aim of your teaching is to defeat itself, what can you expect but confusion? Such a curriculum does not make sense. This attempt at "learning" has so weakened your mind that you cannot love, for the curriculum you have chosen is against love, and amounts to a course in how to attack yourself. A supplementary goal in this curriculum is learning how *not* to overcome the split that makes its primary aim believable. And you will not overcome the split in this curriculum, for all your learning will be on its behalf. Yet your mind speaks against your learning as your learning speaks against your mind, and so you fight against all learning and succeed, for that is what you want. But perhaps you do not realize, even yet, that there is something you want to learn, and that you can learn it because it *is* your choice to do so.

You who have tried to learn what you do not want should take heart, for although the curriculum you set yourself is depressing indeed, it is merely ridiculous if you look at it. Is it possible that the way to achieve a goal is not to attain it? Resign now as your own teacher. This resignation will not lead to depression. It is merely the result of an honest appraisal of what you have taught yourself, and of the learning outcomes that have resulted. Under the proper learning conditions, which you can neither provide nor understand, you will become an excellent learner and an excellent teacher. But it is not so yet, and will not be so until the whole learning situation as you have set it up is reversed. Your learning potential, properly understood, is limitless because it will lead you to God. You can teach the way to Him and learn it, if you follow the Teacher Who knows the way to Him and understands His curriculum for learning it. The curriculum is totally unambiguous, because the goal is not divided and the means and the end are in complete accord. You need offer only undivided attention. Everything else will be given you. For you really want to learn aright, and nothing can oppose the decision of God's Son. His learning is as unlimited as he is (T-12.V.5-9).

ACIM and the Psychology of Learning

Since *A Course in Miracles* comes in an educational format—Text, Workbook for Students and Manual for Teachers—obviously it concerns itself with learning but, as will be clear to the reader by now, not the same kind of learning which has been a central preoccupation of traditional psychologists and educators. The subject of learning has a very long and distinguished history in the western world. Anyone who has taken an introductory course in psychology will recognize the names of Ivan Pavlov, John B. Watson, Edward Thorndike, B. F. Skinner, and Jean Piaget, to mention some of the more historically prominent researchers and theorists in the field. The focus of this tradition has been upon understanding behavioral changes in humans and animals, and upon how to bring desired changes about. In addition, it has been assumed that learning takes place in the nervous system, primarily the brain and central nervous system.

A simple definition of *learning* is found in the AllPsych.com *Psychology Dictionary*: "A relatively permanent change in behavior due to an interaction with the environment."[1] In the on line *Encyclopedia of Psychology* is found a cogent statement about learning as adaptive behavior authored by the brilliant young German biologist Björn Brembs who has pursued research in learning, memory and evolution:

> The brain's primary objective is to carry out certain adaptive behaviors. It is fine-tuned by evolution to safely govern its carrier through life and to

---

[1] AllPsych On Line Dictionary: http://allpsych.com/dictionary/l.html

achieve successful reproduction. There are two alternatives to accomplish this task: by innate behavior programs (e.g., reflexes, stimulus-response chains, etc.) adapted by evolution; or by acquired behavioral traits, adapted by experience.[2]

Of course, as with the subjects of emotion, motivation and memory, the subject of learning has become complex, involving various categories, subcategories, theoretical formulations and hypothesis for scientific research. And the fruits of all this labor over the decades have been useful in such fields of "magic" as formal education, military training, training dogs and other animals, human resources management and psychotherapy.

As with Freud's discoveries, many of the concepts from the psychology of learning have been adapted in the Course to apply at the level of mind. In his course, Jesus not only discusses some aspects of learning theory, such as reinforcement and generalization, but incorporates those aspects into the very curriculum which the Course represents. The most important teaching-learning principle represented by Jesus in the Course is loving respect for the learner; both for his strengths and weaknesses.

In *A Course in Miracles* Jesus tells us that his course is not about the brain and human behavior, but about "mind training." (T-1.VII.4; W-pI.IN.1). Although his students may at first think that this has to do with the traditional kind of learning to which they have become accustomed, it ought soon to become apparent that this is not the case. The mind is not the brain, and we saw in chapter two that Jesus explicitly states our brains do not think, nor do our senses sense. Instead, the body is an instrument of the mind which does at it is told, thinking thoughts that either support the illusion of separation, or the truth of oneness; likewise seeing in a way that endorses illusions as truth, or looks beyond the appearance of separate forms to the unity of spirit. This apparent contradiction of, on the one hand being invited to study a sophisticated intellectual work, and on the other hand being told that the eyes which read don't see and the brain does not think (nor does it learn), amounts to a kind of Zen koan. Faced with this conundrum, the student of the *A Course in Miracles* might well ask, "What's going on here? If my eyes don't see and my brain doesn't think, what's the point of reading this damned book?!"

There is a lot to be learned from contemplating this riddle, but a somewhat satisfactory answer comes from remembering that the Course communicates with its students at two different levels.

---

[2] Encyclopedia of Psychology: http://www.psychology.org/links/Environment_Behavior_Relationships/Learning/

On Level One, the metaphysical level, separation never happened, "not one note in Heaven's song was missed" (T-26.V.5:4), and there is no need of learning anything. The One Mind of God needs no training. But at Level Two, the level of the split mind and our dualistic experience as bodies, perception seems to show us what is real, and what seems to be real is made up of differences that lead us into constant conflict. At our level, which began with the idea of change, it is starkly apparent that some kind of change is in order. We ought somehow to be able to learn the ways of peace and brotherhood. But Jesus tells us that it is not us as bodies and brains that can accomplish that learning. At our level—Level Two, the level of the split mind, the level of illusion—there is a need for "mind training," or mind *changing*, which, as we have discussed, is the essence of the *miracle*. Mind training is really about educating us as the mind's observer/decision maker so that we can exercise our power to choose, thus become "miracle workers." Fortunately, at our level, the body, even limited as it is, can be an instrument of that learning which Jesus means by "mind training":

> ...the body is a learning device for the mind. Learning devices are not lessons in themselves. Their purpose is merely to facilitate learning. The worst a faulty use of a learning device can do is to fail to facilitate learning. It has no power in itself to introduce actual learning errors (T-2.IV.3:1-5).

> It should be emphasized again that the body does not learn any more than it creates. As a learning device it merely follows the learner, but if it is falsely endowed with self-initiative, it becomes a serious obstruction to the very learning it should facilitate. [For instance, there is a strong tendency to overvalue the intellect, thus making of intelligence an impediment to learning rather than an asset.] Only the mind is capable of illumination.

> Spirit is already illuminated and the body in itself is too dense. The mind, however, can bring its illumination to the body by recognizing that it [the body] is not the learner, and is therefore unamenable to learning. The body is, however, easily brought into alignment with a mind that has learned to look beyond it toward the light (T-2.V.6; brackets mine).

> The body thinks no thoughts. It has no power to learn, to pardon, nor enslave. It gives no orders that the mind need serve, nor sets conditions that it must obey. It holds in prison but the willing mind that would abide in it. It sickens at the bidding of the mind that would become its prisoner. And it grows old and dies, because that mind is sick within itself. Learning is all that causes change. And so the body, where no learning can occur, could never change unless the mind preferred the body change in its appearances, to suit the purpose given by the mind. For mind can learn, and there is all change made (T-31.III.4:2-8).

As long as we believe in perception, change and linear time; learning to change our mind is both necessary and possible, all be it illusory. But then, eating and breathing are illusory, too! It is possible for our mind to awaken from its "sleep of forgetfulness" (T-16.VII.12:4), and when it does, the truth of Level One will dawn as an *experience* that ends all doubt. The puzzle about how the illusory body can be used in mind training will no longer be of interest:

> There is no need to further clarify what no one in the world can understand. When revelation of your oneness comes, it will be known and fully understood. Now we have work to do, for those in time can speak of things beyond, and listen to words which explain what is to come is past already. Yet what meaning can the words convey to those who count the hours still, and rise and work and go to sleep by them?
>
> Suffice it, then, that you have work to do to play your part. The ending must remain obscure to you until your part is done. It does not matter. For your part is still what all the rest depends on. As you take the role assigned to you, salvation comes a little nearer each uncertain heart that does not beat as yet in tune with God (W-pI.169.10-11).

In a line-by-line commentary on the Text section entitled "Setting the Goal" (T-17.VI), Kenneth Wapnick elaborated upon this issue of learning and the intellect:

> This is not a course that you can master on an intellectual level. There is no question it is written on a high intellectual level, and it is meant to be studied and thought about. But if you think that the understanding comes from your thinking about it, you are going to miss the whole point. Your understanding will come *in spite of* your thinking about it. What makes this such a powerful spiritual tool is that it seems to be doing *one* thing, when it really does the exact opposite. It is written, again, on an intellectual level, and is meant to be studied over and over again. Jesus told Helen and Bill: "Study these notes"...he wanted these "notes" to be studied just as a text in college is studied. But as you study, you will begin to realize over a period of time that you are learning the exact opposite of what you think you are doing. This is a course that will lead you beyond your intellect and your brain to an experience of love. And so as you go through the process of studying and practicing it, and doing exactly what it says, you will be lead on a journey that is the exact opposite of what you think you are doing. This is a journey that will lead you, by its very nature, to the heart of the problem, which is your mind.

That is why when people try to change this Course around (e.g., come up with a different way of doing the workbook or a different way of studying the text), they are not aware that they are tampering with the very heart and soul of this book, because the curriculum is to do exactly what Jesus says here: study the text as he gives it, do the workbook as he says you should do it. The very fact that you do it that way would automatically lead you on the journey with him as your guide. When you change it around, when you write abridged versions and shorten it, what you really are doing is attacking this Course and its author by saying: "I can do this better than he did. You don't need 365 lessons; you need x amount of lessons. There are shortcuts to studying this text. You don't have to wade through all this -- after all it is only the same stuff over and over again." What you are really doing is subverting the pedagogical process which again is the meat of the Course. The shortcut to this Course is that there is no shortcut! You should do it exactly the way it is given. Why would you want to do it differently, unless you thought you could do a better job than he [Jesus] could? It is not sinful if you do it differently. It is not sinful if you do the workbook lessons backwards; it is just another reflection of your authority problem. You won't be punished for it, but you won't find peace or truth either. One of the best ways of learning this Course is to observe how subtle your ego will be in trying to subvert it, change it, distort it, and make it into your own image, rather than growing into the image that he gives you.

Doing the Course the way he gave it is the way that you will "unlearn" your ego. And you don't have to understand how that happens—it will happen in spite of your seeming understanding. There is that wonderful line in the text: "You are still convinced that your understanding is a powerful contribution to the truth, and makes it what it is" (T-18.IV.7:5). That is another line the ego hates, because we are always trying to understand. The way to understand this Course is to do what it says, which is to look at your specialness and your guilt with the love of Jesus beside you. *That* is how you will understand this Course. Understanding is not achieved through intellectual mastery of its principles. You can spout back the Course perfectly and not have a clue as to what it says. You don't have to distort the Course by changing what it says intellectually: you can give back exactly what it says intellectually, but you won't understand what it is saying, because you have not become part of the process. The intellectual mastery of the Course is the stepping stone towards the experience the Course will give you. This is a very carefully conceived and well-thought-out curriculum: don't try to change it. Simply do what it says as best you can. The learning and the understanding will come from another part of your mind -- it certainly won't come from your brain.[3]

Let us again point out that what seems to be going on with the body and its relationships is an "outside picture of an inward condition" (T-21.IN.1:5), the "inward condition" being the thought *content* of the mind.

---

[3] Wapnick, Kenneth. "Rules for Decision." Temecula, CA: Foundation for *A Course in Miracles*, 1993. (This recorded workshop has been transcribed and can be read on line at: http://facim.org/excerpts/rfdseries.htm For these particular comments and their context see Part IX of that series.)

The "outside picture" is *form*, which has no meaning in and of itself, but which is given meaning according to the thought system in the mind: the meaning that is assigned by either fear or love. So the body offers us a reflection of what is taking place within the mind, thus the body can serve the purpose of looking within. As Ken Keyes wrote, "A loving person lives in a loving world. A hostile person lives in a hostile world. Everyone you meet is your mirror."[4]

The usefulness of the body is further explained by Jesus: "The body was not made by love. Yet love does not condemn it and can use it lovingly, respecting what the Son of God has made and using it to save him from illusions" (T-18.VI.4:7-8). In other words, our illusions of separation and specialness can be used to restore our mind to sanity, saving us from the pain of our illusions, assuming that one has given up the practice of denial enough to have recognized the pain. To this end, using "the language that... [our] mind can understand, in the condition in which it thinks it is" (T-25.I.7:4), Jesus says:

> This is a course in mind training. All learning involves attention and study at some level. Some of the later parts of the course rest too heavily on these earlier sections not to require their careful study. You will also need them for preparation. Without this, you may become much too fearful of what is to come to make constructive use of it. However, as you study these earlier sections, you will begin to see some of the implications that will be amplified later on. (T-1.VII.4).

And in the introduction to the Workbook:

> A theoretical foundation such as the text provides is necessary as a framework to make the exercises in this workbook meaningful. Yet it is doing the exercises that will make the goal of the course possible. An untrained mind can accomplish nothing. It is the purpose of this workbook to train your mind to think along the lines the text sets forth (W-pI.IN.1).

The Course itself illustrates the use of some important principles of learning. It represents a masterfully well conceived learning program which invites students into a series of profound encounters with themselves while balancing the need for structure with the freedom necessary for students to take responsibility for their own learning. For instance, there is no specific instruction about which of the three volumes a student might choose to begin his or her study. This is made clear in both the Preface (viii) and the Manual for Teachers (M-29.1-2).

---

[4] Keyes, Ken Jr. *Handbook to Higher Consciousness*. Coos Bay, Oregon: Love Line Books.

The Workbook is divided into two major parts and can be thought of as a series of meditative exercises which are given direction by discussion of a particular theme to be contemplated each day. These lessons proceed from moderate structure in the early lessons to a more highly structured format in the later lessons of the first part of the Workbook. This increased structure is explained as follows:

> The use of the first five minutes of every waking hour for practicing the idea for the day has special advantages at the stage of learning in which you are at present. It is difficult at this point not to allow your mind to wander, if it undertakes extended practice. You have surely realized this by now. You have seen the extent of your lack of mental discipline, and of your need for mind training. It is necessary that you be aware of this, for it is indeed a hindrance to your advance.
>
> Frequent but shorter practice periods have other advantages for you at this time. In addition to recognizing your difficulties with sustained attention, you must also have noticed that, unless you are reminded of your purpose frequently, you tend to forget about it for long periods of time. You often fail to remember the short applications of the idea for the day, and you have not yet formed the habit of using the idea as an automatic response to temptation.
>
> Structure, then, is necessary for you at this time, planned to include frequent reminders of your goal and regular attempts to reach it. Regularity in terms of time is not the ideal requirement for the most beneficial form of practice in salvation. It is advantageous, however, for those whose motivation is inconsistent, and who remain heavily defended against learning (W-pI.95.4-6).

Clearly, Jesus knows his students. He knows that fear of the mind training which leads to relinquishment of the ego will give rise to resistance; resistance which can be so seemingly insignificant as becoming drowsy while reading, failing to comprehend a single word or sentence, allowing time pressure to force skimming rather than reading with care and contemplation, or forgetting the lesson which one is asked to remember periodically throughout the day.

Throughout the first part of the Workbook there is encouragement to let go of the hierarchy of values typically assigned to illusions in favor of generalizing with the understanding that: "Illusions are illusions and are false" (T-26.VII.6:7). Then, in the second part of the Workbook, structure is reduced to a minimum and words themselves become less and less important in favor of entering a place of inner silence where the Presence of love may be experienced.

The introduction to the second part begins this way:

> Words will mean little now. We use them but as guides on which we do not now depend. For now we seek direct experience of truth alone. The lessons that remain are merely introductions to the times in which we leave the world of pain, and go to enter peace (W-pII.IN.1:1-4).

No one is able to do the year-long Workbook program perfectly, and there is a valuable lesson to be learned from this inability. It is an important part of Jesus' curriculum that his students would come to recognize the very strong ego attachment (i.e., attachment to specialness) that such failure represents. Indeed, because few appreciate the pervasiveness and strength of their ego identity, it can be said that one of the most important leanings from study of the Workbook is that which comes from failure to do its lessons or achieve its goal within the specified time period. That is why at the end of the Workbook the student is told: "This course is a beginning, not an end" (W-E.1:1).

Finally, before we proceed to look at some of the more traditional principles of learning which Jesus has adopted for the purpose of "mind training," it should be pointed out that there is a third level at which the Course communicates with its readers and teaches them. This is a non-intellectual level, which might be said to speak to the heart through the medium of artistic expression. Much of the Course is written in iambic pentameter and employs other lovely poetic forms. The structure of the Text is not that of an academic tome, but resembles a great symphony with two major themes, several minor themes and repeated variations upon those themes. The Course literally sings to its reader and many who have read it comment upon their first encounter as one in which something from within resonated to the music of the words they were reading in a way that told them they were in the loving presence of truth.

A Course in Miracles is far more than a course. The "miracle" of which it speaks has to do with love, and in this world it ought to be apparent that any genuine expression of love qualifies as a miracle. The Course represents a spiritual path in twentieth century form, utilizing a sophisticated language and set of psychological principles applied at the spiritual level of mind in company with a non-dualistic metaphysical foundation. And all of this is presented in poetic and symphonic form, yet also constitutes a very practical learning curriculum. We shall now proceed to examine some of its more practical aspects.

Defining the Goal

In formal education with human beings, defining and clarifying the goal of learning is an important element in effective teaching. Consistent with this principle of goal setting, throughout the Course Jesus defines various goals which are part of a process of learning that leads to the final goal of awakening from the dream of separation when the mind fully knows that it is not a body and there is no world. These various goals are different facets of the same overall goal, but depending upon the context they are identified as accepting the Atonement, forgiveness, inner peace, escape from fear, vision, learning to distinguish truth from falsity, and learning that giving and receiving are the same. All of these goals are related to the goal of right-minded identification with the Holy Spirit which, when it is fully accomplished, prepares the mind to awaken. The truth of oneness then takes "the last step" in the sense that the mind is now prepared to accept it without fear.

The Preface for *A Course in Miracles* makes an important statement about its goal, and does so in a context that clarifies some other issues. In this case, the statement of purpose, which we already have cited at the end of chapter one, was not channeled, but written by the Course's scribe, Helen Schucman:

> . . . the Course can and should stand on its own. It is not intended to become the basis for another cult. Its only purpose is to provide a way in which some people will be able to find their own Internal Teacher (viii).

This is a practical, Level Two statement. Of course, the goal of the Course can be stated in a more abstract fashion, recognizing that the "student" is not really a person, but a mind, and specifically what we have called the "decision maker." The "Internal Teacher" spoken of is What Jesus calls the Holy Spirit of Whom he is a manifestation; therefore, the figure of Jesus represents our right mind and can also serve as one's inner teacher. But there are some other implications of this statement that are important.

Generally speaking, for the kind of learning that the Course represents, it is important to respect the integrity of the thought system being studied, assuming that the goal is to understand and implement that particular system. Saying that "the Course can and should stand on its own" means that it is a complete learning program and system of thought unto itself. To echo Kenneth Wapnick's remarks quoted above, the Course needs no alteration, either by addition or subtraction. Although it shares much in common with other spiritualities, it is not intended to be combined with any of them and, in fact, it is a mistake to do so if one truly wants to be a student of *A Course in Miracles*. Those who attempt to add to, subtract from, condense, simplify or combine with other systems wind up with something that might be useful to them, but which is not Jesus' *A Course in Miracles*. The Course is carefully designed and constructed to meet its stated goals. It makes these statements:

> You cannot lay aside the obstacles to real vision without looking upon them, for to lay aside means to judge against. If you will look, the Holy Spirit will judge, and He will judge truly. Yet He cannot shine away what you keep hidden, for you have not offered it to Him and He cannot take it from you.

> We are therefore embarking on an organized, well-structured and carefully planned program aimed at learning how to offer to the Holy Spirit everything you do not want. He knows what to do with it. You do not understand how to use what He knows (T-12.II.9:6-10:3).

> This course will be believed entirely or not at all. For it is wholly true or wholly false, and cannot be but partially believed. (T-22.II. 7:4-5)

> To learn this course requires willingness to question every value that you hold. Not one can be kept hidden and obscure but it will jeopardize your learning (T-24.IN. 2:1-2).

Dr. Schucman's prefacing statement, which says "it is not intended to become the basis for another cult," means not only that the Course is not intended to become the basis for another formalized religion (the definition of *cult*[1] includes religions and religious worship groups), but that it is not intended to be the basis for any *special*, exclusive and formally structured organization with the usual trappings of credits, grades, degrees and/or certificates. This includes educational institutions as well as schools of psychology and psychotherapy or centers for charismatic healing. The Course has only *one* student, who is the Son of God, and as long as the Son seems to be fragmented then it is up to any given fragment ("person") to decide whether he or she will become a dedicated student of *A Course in Miracles*.

---

[1] Partial definition of "cult" from *The American Heritage® Dictionary of the English Language*, 4th ed.:

1. a. A religion or religious sect generally considered to be extremist or false, with its followers often living in an unconventional manner under the guidance of an authoritarian, charismatic leader.

   b. The followers of such a religion or sect.

2. A system or community of religious worship and ritual.

3. The formal means of expressing religious reverence; religious ceremony and ritual.

5 a. Obsessive, especially faddish, devotion to or veneration for a person, principle, or thing....

6. An exclusive group of persons sharing an esoteric, usually artistic or intellectual interest.

The question of importance then becomes whether the self-identified student is going to learn and practice the Course for himself or herself. As Jesus says to psychotherapists in the supplementary *Psychotherapy Pamphlet*,[2] "He who needs healing must heal. Physician, heal thyself. Who else is there to heal? And who else is in need of healing?" (P-2.VII.1:3-6). In this regard, it is notable that in the Course Jesus never advises his students to form study groups or to seek out or become *formal* teachers of the Course. Groups and teachers may or may not be helpful, but when the Course speaks of "teaching" and "teachers of God" it is not talking about an organized effort at educating others, but about oneself learning the ways of the miracle and forgiveness, and then being a *teacher by example*. Teaching by example means that one's thoughts, perceptions and behavior would be coming from that place in the mind represented by the "Internal Teacher."

When Dr. Schucman identifies the goal of the Course as the finding of one's own "Internal Teacher," the phrase "some people" indicates that the Course is not intended for everyone. Jesus makes that very clear:

> This [course] is a manual for a special curriculum, intended for teachers of a special form of the universal course. There are many thousands of other forms, all with the same outcome (M-1.4:1-2; bracket mine). [Note that the word "special" in this context refers to a unique, coherent thought system and teaching program, but not one that is exclusive in the sense of the ego's specialness. The Course is open to all, but it is not expected that all will or should be drawn to it.]

> This course has come from ... [Jesus] because his words have reached you in a language you can love and understand. Are other teachers   possible, to lead the way to those who speak in different tongues and appeal to different symbols? Certainly there are (M-23.7:1-3; brackets mine).

In addition to never suggesting the development of study groups and instituting didactic teachers of his course, neither does Jesus ever encourage his students to proselytize for *A Course in Miracles*. When he uses the term *witness*, he is most often speaking of the various ways in which the ego uses perception to witness for its thought system. But sometimes, he speaks of his students witnessing in the sense of teaching forgiveness by example. In this regard, it is important to read the Course in its larger context so as to distinguish between the *content*, or meaning, of certain words and the mere form of words with their ordinary definitions and connotations. An example of what Jesus intends by the idea of "witnessing for Christ" follows. Note that this does not mean preaching on a street corner, or from a pulpit, nor

---

[2] *Psychotherapy: Purpose, Process and Practice, An Extension of the Principles of A Course in Miracles.* Mill Valley, CA: Foundation for Inner Peace, 1989.

does it mean that one would necessarily even mention Jesus by name, talk about the Course, or use holy and spiritual sounding words. This does not mean that right-mindedness would never lead to any of those behaviors, but the point is not to get the cart before the horse: i.e., not to give behavior preeminence over mind and the miracle. In fact, *no* words are necessary at all in this kind of witnessing for Christ, which is essentially to be right-minded. The ideas of "speaking" and "hearing" are used metaphorically here. Basically, this is a statement about what the Course means by forgiveness, which has to do with *content*—the mind—not form:

> Every brother you meet becomes a witness for Christ [our true Identity as spirit and the creation of God] or for the ego, depending on what you perceive in him. Everyone convinces you of what you want to perceive, and of the reality of the kingdom you have chosen for your vigilance. Everything you perceive is a witness to the thought system you want to be true. Every brother has the power to release you, if you choose to be free. You cannot accept false witness of him unless you have evoked false witnesses against him. If he speaks not of Christ to you, you spoke not of Christ to him. You hear but your own voice, and if Christ speaks through you, you will hear Him (T-11.V.18; brackets mine).

In sum, a basic point is that achieving the goal of the Course's curriculum is an individual responsibility pursued in the context of the Level Two teachings that speak in terms of an individual mind, since initially that is how we are able to understand forgiveness and the miracle. The idea is to take responsibility for finding one's own "Internal Teacher;" one's own right mind. The Course is a program for spiritual development wherein the student is invited to enter into an intimate relationship with the mind of its teacher whose voice speaks from the pages of the Course itself, thus is the student invited into a relationship with his or her own right mind. The Course is a curricular package which includes a teacher as well as books for study and a classroom, which is the student's worldly life. If one is going to make use of human teachers and study groups, first of all those should be seen as another classroom in forgiveness, and secondly the best that they could offer is help that permits the student to understand and make use of the Course for himself or herself.

The goal of the Course's curriculum is relevant to every moment of the student's experience, because our life experiences make up the curriculum. In other words, every moment is a learning situation, which means that in every moment one is both teaching and learning. This is especially clear in human relationships. In the section of the Course entitled "Setting the Goal" (T-17.VI), Jesus points out the necessity of having a clearly identified goal so that one's purpose for learning will determine the outcome of learning situations for the mind. The mind asleep and dreaming—the student who is unaware of mind and identified with the ego—does not set a goal for learning, but lets situations happen and then decides what they meant according to the ego thought system, which the mind has already learned and whose goals are not questioned. The ego evaluates everything in terms of self interest and specialness: was this good for me or not? But the mind of the student who would follow the Course must accept the goal of the Course ahead of time, and then let that goal give meaning and direction to the situation, which would always be understood as a lesson in forgiveness. The goal of forgiveness can be variously stated as, for instance: to identify as mind not body; to be at peace regardless of the worldly situation; to be right minded and under the Guidance of one's Internal Teacher; to undo the blocks to awareness of love and the truth of oneness; to allow the Holy Spirit or Jesus to replace perception of differences with the vision of oneness, etc. And the ultimate goal of forgiveness is to awaken from the dream of separation, so with this goal in mind, each moment becomes an opportunity to practice the mindfulness that leads to awakening.

To restate and emphasize an important point about Jesus' approach to setting the goal for learning, the idea is that nothing which happens in the world needs to be given the power to affect one's peace of mind or ability to forgive. If the goal of peace or truth is accepted ahead of time, for instance upon awakening each day, then everything that happens, no matter how the ego would evaluate it, is understood as a lesson in forgiveness, *as long as that goal is kept in mind.* Inner peace is the unfailing result of applying this goal for learning. But of course, the learning process involves forgetting the goal and continuing in the old habits of the ego's self-centeredness, victimization and refusal to accept responsibility. But with Jesus' curriculum in mind, one is more and more able to catch these lapses, to observe them for what they are, and to learn from them. Thus, the goal which is forgotten can also be remembered. As the student comes to understand the curriculum and its goal, more and more often any lack of peace is a signal that the goal of right-mindedness has been forgotten. Therefore, it is remembered and can then be implemented to give the Holy Spirit's meaning to any situation.

As for the ultimate goal of awakening from the dream, the ego is terrified of that! We who harbor the ego in spite of a small willingness to have it undone must therefore also be terrified of awakening to the truth of non-separation, because that means the end of specialness—the end of self. But here again, being mindful of the goal puts one in the observer position where it is possible to observe and learn from one's resistance. It is not necessary to do more than observe, because the very act of objective looking is part of the process of awakening. The very act of looking at the activities of one's own mind without judgment is an act of mindfulness and a step out of the darkness of mindless ego dreaming. Likewise, accepting the goal of the Course and being willing to apply it ahead of time is a step toward achieving that goal, which could be called mindfulness as well as forgiveness or right-mindedness:

> In any situation in which you are uncertain, the first thing to consider, very simply, is "What do I want to come of this? What is it *for?*" The clarification of the goal belongs at the beginning, for it is this which will determine the outcome [i.e., not the worldly outcome, but the state of mind]. In the ego's procedure this is reversed. The situation becomes the determiner of the outcome, which can be anything. The reason for this disorganized approach is evident. The ego does not know what it wants to come of the situation. It is aware of what it does not want, but only that. It has no positive goal at all [i.e.: The ego is entirely negative because it begins with the negativity of denying God, therefore Love. What appears to be a positive ego goal—pursuit of special love—is actually attack designed to rid the mind of guilt at the expense of another mind] (T-17.VI.2; brackets mine).

Learning and Unlearning

Certain conditions had to be met in order for the idea of separation to have developed into a full-blown thought system which could *seem* to beguile the mind with the illusion of perception, a world to be perceived, and a body as the mechanism of perception. The first condition was that the idea would be taken seriously as a worthy goal, and continue to be taken seriously. That we continue to take it seriously is obvious, but Jesus tells us that at the very beginning (speaking within the context of the illusion of linear time): "the Son of God remembered not to laugh. In his forgetting did the thought become a serious idea, and possible of both accomplishment and real effects" (T-27.VIII.6:2-3). Undoing the ego thought system which followed can be understood as learning to laugh at the impossibility of separation. But in taking the idea of separation seriously, the ego's goal for learning was set, and this involved the very idea of learning itself. In the Mind of God learning is unknown and irrelevant: "Where learning ends there God begins, for learning ends before Him Who is complete where He begins, and where there *is* no end" (T-18.IX.11:4). Learning involves change, and separation *is* change; therefore learning is implicated in the thought that separation is "possible of both accomplishment and real effects." So, learning was set in motion by the ego at the very beginning. It is inextricable from the idea of separation and the thought system that builds upon that idea. Thus learning itself becomes yet one more invention of the ego that the Holy Spirit must use to undo the ego.

In the introduction to the Course Jesus says that: "The course does not aim at teaching the meaning of love, for that is beyond what can be taught" (T-IN.1:6). This is essentially saying that what Jesus means by *knowledge* cannot be taught, since *knowledge* is of the Mind of God and love is its essence. In the eyes of the world, this must be a strange course! If it does not aim to teach knowledge, what can one learn from it? The answer lies in the sentence which follows the one quoted above: "It does aim, however, at removing the blocks to the awareness of love's presence, which is your natural inheritance" (T-IN.1:7). In other words, the Course is not about learning as the world knows it, but about *unlearning* a thought system in the mind. This involves undoing the blocks to love's awareness which the world has taught. No matter what its guises, the education of the world has been the ego's teaching, and it has taught separation. It teaches separation at all levels of formal and informal education, and in almost every aspect of scholarly and scientific enterprise. To say this another way, the world depends upon and teaches perception in a myriad of ways, and it is perception that stands as a primary block to the awareness of *knowledge*, the essence of which is love. And love is our "natural inheritance," therefore is *already present* in our mind.

Because the world teaches separation, it teaches guilt and fear; and those fundamental ego elements are also primary blocks that stand in the way of remembering our "natural inheritance." Perception speaks of the reality of separation, therefore seeks to deny knowledge. Denial is the ego's purpose for the world of perception. Therefore, it is not possible to believe in the reality of perception without feeling guilty and fearful, because not only does it serve to block awareness of knowledge, it is an attack upon it—an attack upon God: Oneness, Love.

The reader who has some background in philosophy may recognize this approach of unlearning so that knowledge may be revealed in the mind. It is the approach that Plato taught, and is directly related to the "examined life" of his teacher, Socrates. Not only does the Course have strong Freudian roots, but it has strong Platonic roots as well.

In the Course, therefore, Jesus' teaching is directed toward self examination so that our mind can recognize the ego for what it is and remember what the ego had us deny and dissociate. However useful the teachings of the world might be in practicing magic and surviving in the ego's loveless hell of guilt, fear, attack and defense, still the world's teachings are intended to keep us unaware of truth, with knowledge remaining forgotten and unconscious.

Another way to speak of the unlearning goal of the Course is to say that it is enlightenment, whereas the ego's goal—the goal we have accepted for ourselves in pursuing the learning of the world—is darkness. Fortunately, the eternal nature of Truth ordains that there be a "light in darkness" (T-15.XI.2) which can make use of the inventions of darkness—e.g., teaching and learning—as temporary expedients for clearing away the obfuscating clouds of darkness; a light to guide the way until the dawning of God's Light:

> Love is not learned. Its meaning lies within itself. And learning ends when you have recognized all it is *not*. That is the interference; that is what needs to be undone. Love is not learned, because there never was a time in which you knew it not. Learning is useless in the Presence of your Creator, Whose acknowledgment of you and yours of Him so far transcend all learning that everything you learned is meaningless, replaced forever by the knowledge of love and its one meaning (T-18.IX.12).

The Love of God (knowledge) cannot be taught or learned because it is formless; completely abstract and unable to be symbolized. It is an indivisible totality which cannot be analyzed. Knowledge is beyond the grasp of perception and all its tools of learning which the world employs. However, the Holy Spirit stands in our mind between the thought system of perception and that of knowledge, and is able to translate perception into knowledge through forgiveness. This is another example of how the Holy Spirit can use everything that has been fabricated by the ego for purposes of undoing the ego:

> Complete abstraction is the natural condition of the mind. But part of it is now unnatural. It does not look on everything as one. It sees instead but fragments of the whole, for only thus could it invent the partial world you see. The purpose of all seeing is to show you what you wish to see. All hearing but brings to your mind the sounds it wants to hear.

> Thus were specifics made. And now it is specifics we must use in practicing. We give them to the Holy Spirit, that He may employ them for a purpose which is different from the one we gave to them. Yet He can use but what we made, to teach us from a different point of view, so we can see a different use in everything (W-pI.161.2-3).

> Perception is not an attribute of God. His is the realm of knowledge. Yet He has created the Holy Spirit as the Mediator between perception and knowledge. Without this link with God, perception would have replaced knowledge forever in your mind. With this link with God, perception will become so changed and purified that it will lead to knowledge. That is its function as the Holy Spirit sees it. Therefore, that is its function in truth.

203

> In God you cannot see. Perception has no function in God, and does not exist. Yet in salvation, which is the undoing of what never was, perception has a mighty purpose. Made by the Son of God for an unholy purpose, it must become the means for the restoration of his holiness to his awareness. Perception has no meaning. Yet does the Holy Spirit give it a meaning very close to God's. Healed perception becomes the means by which the Son of God forgives his brother, and thus forgives himself (W-pI.43.1-2).

There is a familiar Zen proverb which says, "Before enlightenment, chopping wood and hauling water. After enlightenment, chopping wood and hauling water." It is like that with the Course. As we have seen, the Course is practical. It does not ask its students to reject the world of perception, but to allow the Holy Spirit to make use of it for them in the interest of unlearning the ego's blocks. The fact that the ego's purpose for perception is to deny knowledge and block out awareness of love does not mean that in order to learn from the Course one must try to somehow not perceive or to abandon worldly responsibilities. Again, to the Holy Spirit, the world is a *classroom in the mind*, and so can it be for Jesus' students who are offered the opportunity of learning "to be in the world, but not of it" (1 John 2). One may continue to chop wood and haul water, but with a different attitude: worldly activities are no longer seen as matters of survival—matters of life and death driven by fear and its *one or the other* thinking. An example of how Jesus helps his students strike a balance between unlearning the world and living in the world can be found in the ACIM Workbook:

> Thus what you need are intervals each day in which the learning of the world becomes a transitory phase; a prison house from which you go into the sunlight and forget the darkness. Here you understand the Word, the Name Which God has given you; the one Identity Which all things share; the one acknowledgment of what is true. And then step back to darkness, not because you think it real, but only to proclaim its unreality in terms which still have meaning in the world that darkness rules.

> Use all the little names and symbols which delineate the world of darkness. Yet accept them not as your reality. The Holy Spirit uses all of them, but He does not forget creation has one Name, one Meaning, and a single Source Which unifies all things within Itself. Use all the names the world bestows on them but for convenience, yet do not forget they share the Name of God [i.e., the Identity of Oneness] along with you. (W-pI.184.10-11; brackets mine).

Teaching

In the Course, teaching and learning are about *content*, not *form*. Regardless of the many forms that teaching takes in the world, there are only two contents which can underlie them, because there are only two thought systems in the mind. We have seen that there are many ways to characterize those two thought systems, but they can be simplified as representing and teaching either love or fear. Early in the Text Jesus makes a statement which has led to the title of a book[1] as well as being one of the most frequently quoted lines from the Course: "Teach only love for that is what you are" (T-6.I.13:2). This is not referring to the Love of God, but to a *reflection* in the split mind of that Love. It is not possible for the Love of God to reach directly into the world, because God did not make the world. The mind that projects a world believes itself separate from the Mind of God, and has substituted illusion for truth; perception for knowledge. Since God did not make the world, He does not know of it—it is not included in His *knowledge*—nor does He perceive or teach, but His Love can be *reflected* in the mind that made the world; reflected through the Holy Spirit or Jesus. In the Course the Holy Spirit is sometimes referred to as "God's Teacher."

Because the ego fears the Love of God, we whose minds are identified with the ego cannot be taught about that Love directly. So, the Holy Spirit must teach indirectly, which is what is involved in using what the ego has made (i.e., the body, perception and learning) to undo the ego. Forgiveness is an indirect way of teaching the Love of God which cannot reach directly into the fearful, separated mind that has produced the illusion of perception. Thus, forgiveness can be understood as corrected perception, but it is not knowledge. Jesus explains the necessity of this indirect approach:

> Any direction that would lead you where the Holy Spirit leads you not, goes nowhere. Anything you deny that He knows to be true you have denied yourself, and He must therefore teach you not to deny it. Undoing *is* indirect, as doing is. You were created only to create, neither to see [perceive] nor do [behave]. These are but indirect expressions of the will to live, which has been blocked by the capricious and unholy whim of death and murder that your Father does not share with you. [The point here is that the body has been projected by the mind that believes in separation. It is the body which seems to perceive and behaves, but these are illusions and only indirect expressions of the will to create and live as known in the Mind of God.] You have set yourself the task of sharing what cannot be shared [i.e., separation]. And while you think it possible to learn to do this, you will not believe all that *is* possible to learn to do [i.e., forgive; undo separation, guilt and fear; accept the Atonement].

The Holy Spirit, therefore, must begin His teaching by showing you what you can never learn [i.e., love, oneness]. His message is not indirect, but He must introduce the simple truth into a thought system which has

---

[1] Jampolsky, Gerald G. *Teach Only Love: The Seven Principles of Attitudinal Healing.* Revised. Hillsboro, Oregon: Beyond Words Publishing, Inc., 2000.

become so twisted and so complex you cannot see that it means nothing. He merely looks at its foundation [i.e., separation] and dismisses it. But you who cannot undo what you have made, nor escape the heavy burden of its dullness [i.e., the body and the perceptual world] that lies upon your mind, cannot see through it. It deceives you, because you chose to deceive yourself. Those who choose to be deceived will merely attack direct approaches, because they seem to encroach upon deception and strike at it (T-14.I.4-5; brackets mine).

What Jesus is talking about by encouraging us to "teach only love" is forgiveness:

Forgiveness is an earthly form of love, which as it is in Heaven has no form. Yet what is needed here is given here as it is needed. In this form you can fulfill your function even here, although what love will mean to you when formlessness has been restored to you is greater still. Salvation of the world [i.e., undoing the ego thought system and its illusions] depends on you who can forgive. Such is your function here (W-pI.186.14:2-6; brackets mine).

When Jesus tells his students to teach only love (forgiveness) he is saying that no matter what the form of your teaching in the world, the underlying content in your mind should be that of the Holy Spirit. And, love is "what you are," because in truth our mind is of the one Mind, which the Holy Spirit knows and which informs His teaching. In turn, He can guide our "teaching" in the illusion. Of course, the same is true of Jesus. He says: "I will teach with you and live with you if you will think with me," (T-4.I.6:3). And then he goes on to say that any good teacher seeks to make himself unnecessary. In this case, that means that the student would graduate into that same right-minded state which Jesus represents. To be consistently in that state of mind is to be in the "real world" where perception is continually informed by the Holy Spirit, Who then becomes the student's "Inner Teacher." Thus, like Jesus, the student can become a manifestation of the Holy Spirit and an "advanced teacher of God".

So, whatever the form of worldly teaching—be it parenting, classroom teaching, friendship, marriage, giving instruction in trash collecting or in astrophysics—Jesus urges us always to teach from that content of love in our mind which he represents and models for us by the nature of his teaching in the Course. In fact, it is the content of love in the Course that appeals to many of its students, whether they actually understand the concepts being taught or not. Which brings us to a further point: ultimately it does not matter whether the form of teaching is successful at the intellectual and behavioral level. What matters is whether the teaching came from the content of love, and if it did, *that* teaching is what will make a difference to the student.

An effective teacher models what it is that he or she seeks to teach; in other words, teaches by example. Since a primary goal of the Course is teaching forgiveness, it should be no surprise that throughout the Course Jesus is remarkable for his loving consistency in manifesting a forgiving attitude toward his readers and students. This is even more remarkable for the fact that, while serving as an inspiring model of forgiveness, Jesus is at the same time presenting a powerfully confronting message.

The subjects of teaching and learning are among the most frequently discussed in *A Course in Miracles*. One of the most important points Jesus makes in this regard is that these two functions of our mind are not really different; furthermore, we not only learn what we teach, but we teach what we *want* to learn. That means that most of humanity most of the time is teaching the ego thought system of separation, sin, guilt and fear and we would not be teaching those thoughts unless we *wanted* to learn and reinforce them in our own mind. That is, we teach specialness because we are dedicated to the pursuit of specialness, believing that it will bring us what we want. Teaching and learning represent a choice, but the mindless do not recognize that they have made a choice nor do they accept responsibility for what they teach and want to learn, usually not even recognizing the thoughts that they are learning, or that they *are* in fact *teaching*. Parenting is an excellent example of this, one with which everyone is familiar. Parents often verbally teach one thing, but behave in ways that silently teach the opposite. That is because the parent actually believes something different than what is verbalized and wants to hold on to that belief. In parenting and other worldly relationships the words "I love you" are almost always dishonest, because the world does not *know* of love—does not have *knowledge*—and because the ego thought system, which is the template for the world, is fundamentally a thought system of hate that substitutes special love for love. As we have seen, special love is hatred in disguise because it fosters attack and teaches guilt, knowing nothing of the oneness that connects all minds, and *not wanting to know* of that oneness.

In the Course Jesus talks about four kinds of teachers: 1) the ego might be called the first teacher and is the inventor of teaching and learning; 2) the Holy Spirit, Who is "God's Answer" to the ego, thus "God's Teacher; 3) Jesus is a manifestation of the Holy Spirit and offers himself as a teacher, both through the medium of his words as found in the Course and in our mind as a more identifiable form or symbol of the Holy Spirit; 4) ourselves as teachers; either teachers of the ego or "teachers of God" in any given moment. The Holy Spirit is spoken of as that thought system of love that is always present to teach us Who we are in truth and how we can discover our true Identity by becoming teachers of forgiveness. When we teach and learn forgiveness, we become what Jesus means by the phrase "teachers of God." In speaking of the qualifications of a teacher of God, Jesus says: "A teacher of God is anyone who chooses to be one. His qualifications consist solely in this; somehow, somewhere he has made a deliberate choice in which he did not see his interests as apart from someone else's" (M-1.1:1-2).

We conclude this section with a comprehensive statement about teaching and learning reproduced below almost in its entirety and found in the Introduction to the ACIM Manual for Teachers, the third volume of the Course:

> The role of teaching and learning is actually reversed in the thinking of the world. The reversal is characteristic. It seems as if the teacher and the learner are separated, the teacher giving something to the learner rather than to himself. Further, the act of teaching is regarded as a special activity, in which one engages only a relatively small proportion of one's time. The course, on the other hand, emphasizes that to teach *is* to learn, so that teacher and learner are the same. It also emphasizes that teaching is a constant process; it goes on every moment of the day, and continues into sleeping thoughts as well.
>
> To teach is to demonstrate. There are only two thought systems, and you demonstrate that you believe one or the other is true all the time. From your demonstration others learn, and so do you. The question is not whether you will teach, for in that there is no choice. The purpose of the course might be said to provide you with a means of choosing what you want to teach on the basis of what you want to learn. You cannot give to someone else, but only to yourself, and this you learn through teaching. Teaching is but a call to witnesses to attest to what you believe. It is a method of conversion. This is not done by words alone. Any situation must be to you a chance to teach others what you are, and what they are to you. No more than that, but also never less.
>
> The curriculum you set up is therefore determined exclusively by what you think you are, and what you believe the relationship of others is to you. In the formal teaching situation, these questions may be totally unrelated to what you think you are teaching. Yet it is impossible not to use the content of any situation on behalf of what you really teach, and therefore really learn. To this the verbal content of your teaching is quite irrelevant. It may coincide with it, or it may not. It is the teaching underlying what you say that teaches you. Teaching but reinforces what you believe about yourself. Its fundamental purpose is to diminish self-doubt. This does not mean that the self you are trying to protect is real. But it does mean that the self you think is real is what you teach. This is inevitable. There is no escape from it. How could it be otherwise?

Everyone who follows the world's curriculum, and everyone here does follow it until he changes his mind, teaches solely to convince himself that he is what he is not. Herein is the purpose of the world. What else, then, would its curriculum be? Into this hopeless and closed learning situation, which teaches nothing but despair and death, God sends His teachers. [Note that this primarily refers to those who have made some progress in being consistently right-minded, or at least consistently mindful enough to know when they are not right-minded. But it can also refer to anyone who is able to be right-minded in any situation, no matter how briefly.] And as they teach His lessons of joy and hope, their learning finally becomes complete.

Except for God's teachers [To reemphasize an important point, this phrase should not be confused as designating any formal teaching status or conferring any kind of mantle of special recognition upon anyone, regardless of their worldly status.] there would be little hope of salvation, for the world of sin would seem forever real. The self-deceiving must deceive, for they must teach deception. And what else is hell? This is a manual for the teachers of God. They are not perfect, or they would not be here. Yet it is their mission to become perfect here, and so they teach perfection over and over, in many, many ways, until they have learned it. And then they are seen no more, although their thoughts remain a source of strength and truth forever... (M-IN.1-5; brackets mine).

Ability and Willingness to Learn

To readers and students of his course who complain that it is too difficult and/or that they lack the ability to learn it, Jesus repeatedly says not only that the Course is simple, but that our mind's ability to learn is really quite remarkable. Look what we have learned! Jesus tells his students that their difficulties in unlearning what they have learned do not come from a lack of ability, but from fear and a lack of willingness.

Interestingly, the following statements occur in the *last* chapter of the 669 page ACIM Text, where one might assume that the student is fairly well along in the learning process. Of course, these remarks initially were made in response to protests from the scribe and her colleague, who were the first students of *A Course in Miracles*. Nevertheless, these statements are quite likely to apply to every other reader and student of the Course who has encountered its radical, mind-bending message which basically tells us that everything we have learned and come to believe—the very basis for our lives—is wrong! Resistance and protest in the face of that message is both understandable and almost inevitable. In response to such complaints, at the beginning of the thirty-first and last chapter of the first volume to be channeled, Jesus says:

How simple is salvation! All it says is what was never true is not true now, and never will be. The impossible has not occurred, and can have no effects. And that is all. Can this be hard to learn by anyone who wants it to be true? Only unwillingness to learn it could make such an easy lesson difficult. How hard is it to see that what is false can not be true, and what is true can not be false? You can no longer say that you perceive no differences in false and true. You have been told exactly how to tell one from the other, and just what to do if you become confused. Why, then, do you persist in learning not such simple things?

There is a reason. But confuse it not with difficulty in the simple things salvation asks you learn. It teaches but the very obvious. It merely goes from one apparent lesson to the next, in easy steps that lead you gently from one to another, with no strain at all. This cannot be confusing, yet you are confused. For somehow you believe that what is totally confused is easier to learn and understand. What you have taught yourself is such a giant learning feat it is indeed incredible. But you accomplished it because you wanted to, and did not pause in diligence to judge it hard to learn or too complex to grasp.

No one who understands what you have learned, how carefully you learned it, and the pains to which you went to practice and repeat the lessons endlessly, in every form you could conceive of them, could ever doubt the power of your learning skill. There is no greater power in the world. The world was made by it, and even now depends on nothing else. The lessons you have taught yourself have been so overlearned and fixed they rise like heavy curtains to obscure the simple and the obvious. Say not you cannot learn them. For your power to learn is strong enough to teach you that your will is not your own, your thoughts do not belong to you, and even you are someone else.

Who could maintain that lessons such as these are easy? Yet you have learned more than this. You have continued, taking every step, however difficult, without complaint, until a world was built that suited you. And every lesson that makes up the world arises from the first accomplishment of learning; an enormity so great the Holy Spirit's Voice seems small and still before its magnitude. The world began with one strange lesson, powerful enough to render God forgotten, and His Son an alien to himself, in exile from the home where God Himself established him. You who have taught yourself the Son of God is guilty, say not that you cannot learn the simple things salvation teaches you!

Learning is an ability you made and gave yourself. It was not made to do the Will of God, but to uphold a wish that it could be opposed, and that a will apart from it was yet more real than it. And this has learning sought to demonstrate, and you have learned what it was made to teach. Now does your ancient overlearning stand implacable before the Voice of truth, and teach you that Its lessons are not true; too hard to learn, too difficult to see, and too opposed to what is really true. Yet you will learn them, for their learning is the only purpose for your learning skill the Holy Spirit sees in all the world. His simple lessons in forgiveness have a power mightier than yours, because they call from God and from your Self to you....

The lessons to be learned are only two. Each has its outcome in a different world. And each world follows surely from its source. The certain outcome of the lesson that God's Son is guilty is the world you see. It is a world of terror and despair. Nor is there hope of happiness in it. There is no plan for safety you can make that ever will succeed. There is no joy that you can seek for here and hope to find. Yet this is not the only outcome which your learning can produce. However much you may have overlearned your chosen task, the lesson that reflects the Love of God is stronger still. And you will learn God's Son is innocent, and see another world. (T-31.I.4-7).

So, Jesus says that the ability of his students to learn is not in question. It is sufficient, and in fact, having accepted the idea of separation and placed our mind under the influence of the ego, *we* invented learning. Recognizing his student's difficulties as well as their strengths, Jesus went on to deliver through his scribe a 488 page Workbook containing 365 lessons in undoing, one for each day of a calendar year.

While ability to learn is not in question, a vitally necessary condition for making progress with Jesus' curriculum is *willingness* to learn it. We invented the ability to learn and then used it to deceive ourselves, producing a hellish death camp in our pursuit of a paradise apart from Heaven. Our willingness has brought us here, and now, for those who have come to a point of exasperation with what we have invented, Jesus offers a way out of hell. But his way will be useless unless one shares the desire for "a better way" that helped to give birth to the Course. Throughout the Course Jesus emphasizes the importance of willingness in order that our minds can learn what he would teach, pointing out that our basic problem is that we have been willing to listen to lies and unwilling to listen to the truth.

This willingness involves humility; the humility of recognizing that we lack knowledge and are therefore really incapable of understanding anything. Such willingness would say to Jesus: "Teach me brother, for I do not understand." With that willingness and humility we can be taught how to allow the Holy Spirit to undo what we have learned so that it can be replaced with the truth of oneness that He remembers for us.

You do not know the meaning of anything you perceive. Not one thought you hold is wholly true. The recognition of this is your firm beginning. You are not misguided; you have accepted no guide at all.

> Instruction in perception is your great need, for you understand nothing. Recognize this but do not accept it, for understanding is your inheritance. Perceptions are learned, and you are not without a Teacher. Yet your willingness to learn of Him depends on your willingness to question everything you learned of yourself, for you who learned amiss should not be your own teacher (T-11.VIII.3).

Willingness also involves coming to understand that our own will and God's are not different. That is because we are not separate in truth. The ego fears the Will of God and has taught us to fear it, but Jesus points out that all our misery comes from attempting to oppose the Will of God which in truth is our own will. Thus, we attempt to oppose our true Self and our mind is in conflict; and "a conflicted teacher is a poor teacher and a poor learner" (T-7.VIII. 3:4).

> ...what you will you do not know. This is not strange when you realize that to deny is to "not know." God's Will is that you are His Son. By denying this you deny your own will, and therefore do not know what it is. You must ask what God's Will is in everything, because it is yours. You do not know what it is, but the Holy Spirit remembers it for you.

> Ask Him, therefore, what God's Will is for you, and He will tell you yours. It cannot be too often repeated that you do not know it. Whenever what the Holy Spirit tells you appears to be coercive, it is only because you have not recognized your will (T-11.I.8).

Reinforcement and Practice

In order for learning to occur, reinforcement is necessary. It is a principle of conventional psychology that human learning proceeds most efficiently if the student is rewarded, therefore reinforced, for his successes rather than punished for his failures. Repeated trials, or practice, with positive feedback for successes, or even approximations of success, are helpful. The same principles apply at the level of mind where forgiveness is truly its own reward, and therefore powerfully reinforcing when experienced, however fleetingly. Such reinforcement encourages continued study and effort. Also reinforcing for a student of ACIM is growing understanding, insight and perspective at the intellectual level, along with the removal of punishment for failure to forgive that accompanies right-minded, non-judgmental observing of self.

The ACIM Workbook is structured in such a way as to provide reinforcement both through growing insight and perspective as well as through experiences derived from practice. Throughout the lessons, the voice of Jesus is consistently loving, encouraging, reassuring, understanding and non-judgmental about failures, which he obviously anticipates. For instance:

> Let us...be determined, particularly for the next week or so, to be willing to forgive ourselves for our lapses in diligence, and our failures to follow the instructions for practicing the day's idea. This tolerance for weakness will enable us to overlook it, rather than give it power to delay our learning. [In other words, overlooking and not judging failure avoids making oneself guilty, thus not giving power to guilt.] If we give it power to do this, we are regarding it as strength, and are confusing strength with weakness.

> When you fail to comply with the requirements of this course, you have merely made a mistake. [An important point of the Course is to see mistakes which can be corrected rather than sins which call for guilt and condemnation. Here, Jesus is teaching that principle by instruction as well as modeling.] This calls for correction, and for nothing else. To allow a mistake to continue is to make additional mistakes, based on the first and reinforcing it. [In other words, for learning purposes it is important to correct mistakes as well as not use them to reinforce guilt.] It is this process that must be laid aside, for it is but another way in which you would defend illusions against the truth.

> Let all these errors go by recognizing them for what they are. They are attempts to keep you unaware you are one Self, united with your Creator, at one with every aspect of creation, and limitless in power and in peace [i.e., these mistakes represent resistance to achieving the goal of the Course.] This is the truth, and nothing else is true. Today we will affirm this truth again, and try to reach the place in you in which there is no doubt that only this is true (W-pI.95.8:3-10:4; brackets mine).

Another aspect of reinforcement found in the structure of the ACIM Workbook is that of review and repetition. Throughout the first part of the Workbook consisting of 220 lessons there are six review and reinforcement sections, each comprised of some instructional comments followed by several review lessons. Of the 220 total lessons in the first part, 70 of them are review lessons and each review section is carefully structured for its particular form of reinforcing learning. That learning is directed at the mind using the brain as an instrument for the purpose of going beyond the brain and its wordy-worldly preoccupations to reach the observer/decision maker in the mind. The decision maker, who is in truth the Son of God, is the real student of the Course, and incorporates all minds as one, though experienced by us as many.

Study of the entire Course as well as practice of the Workbook lessons becomes reinforcing as progress with forgiveness is experienced. At the same time, the non-judgmental observation of one's difficulties, resistance and failures can be reinforcing as it validates what Jesus teaches about the ego. In order for *un*learning to occur, it must be recognized that what the ego offered as reinforcement for learning its lessons actually was not rewarding but painful. The ego has to accomplish its teaching by deception, preventing us from knowing the difference between pleasure and pain. In fact, as long as the focus is upon bodily experience, pleasure and pain are the same in purpose, because both reinforce body identification, separation and guilt.

Jesus and the Holy Spirit teach by contrasting the ego thought system and its results with the thought system of the Atonement and its results. This is done through teaching concepts as well as inviting the direct experience that comes from willingness to look honestly upon one's life and the thought content of one's mind. So, ironically, the path to peace through *A Course in Miracles* involves coming to recognize how unpeaceful and unhappy ego life really is:

> The Holy Spirit needs a happy learner, in whom His mission can be happily accomplished. You who are steadfastly devoted to misery must first recognize that you are miserable and not happy. The Holy Spirit cannot teach without this contrast, for you believe that misery *is* happiness. This has so confused you that you have undertaken to learn to do what you can never do [i.e., separate; achieve specialness], believing that unless you learn it you will not be happy. You do not realize that the foundation on which this most peculiar learning goal depends means absolutely nothing. Yet it may still make sense to you. Have faith in nothing and you will find the "treasure" that you seek. Yet you will add another burden to your already burdened mind. You will believe that nothing [i.e., illusion] is of value, and will value it. A little piece of glass, a speck of dust, a body or a war are one to you. For if you value one thing made of nothing, you have believed that nothing can be precious, and that you *can* learn how to make the untrue true (T-14.II.1; brackets mine).

The experience of inner peace that comes from genuine forgiveness is reinforcing, but so too is relief from pain. It is not genuine forgiveness and inner peace that come from less often behaving in ways that produce fear and guilt, yet there is positive reinforcement as pain is diminished. This is the reward of beginning to question and let go of defensiveness, judgment and attack. It is easy to confuse this relief from pain with the "peace of God," but in truth it represents only a beginning. Jesus says:

> ...how can the peace of God be recognized? God's peace is recognized at first by just one thing; in every way it is totally unlike all previous experiences. It calls to mind nothing that went before. It brings with it no past associations. It is a new thing entirely. There is a contrast, yes,

between this thing and all the past. But strangely, it is not a contrast of true differences. The past just slips away, and in its place is everlasting quiet. Only that. The contrast first perceived has merely gone. Quiet has reached to cover everything (M-20.2).

We have been reinforced for maintaining our ego identification because we have been deceived about the nature of real reward, and so we have persevered in the ways of pain, deluded about what real pleasure is. The Course states: "All real pleasure comes from doing God's Will. This is because *not* doing it is a denial of Self" (T-1.VII.1:4-5). Forgiveness is the way we do God's Will within the world and the process of learning forgiveness is reinforcing within itself. However, that process is not without fear and difficulty because it involves questioning our accepted reality and discovering the hatred in what we thought was love; the lack of justification for attack and defense we thought to be justified and necessary.

The student who elects to proceed with Jesus' curriculum is lovingly encouraged, supported and reinforced along the way, but ego identity is not undone without a fight, which means there will be conflict. There would be no conflict except for the fact that we have bought the ego's pig in a poke. We think we like being separate and that specialness is rewarding. And so the process of undoing ego identification requires coming to recognize the pain involved in specialness. It is that pain and resistance to letting go of self that results in what St. John of the Cross called, "the dark night of the soul".[1]

In the ACIM Manual for Teachers, Jesus discusses how the student of his course progresses through six stages of what he calls the "Development of Trust" (M-4.I.A). This refers to development of trust in the Holy Spirit or the student's right mind. Development of this trust is part of progress in learning the lessons of the Course's curriculum. Of the six stages, four are identified as difficult, with the fifth stage being roughly equivalent to "the dark night of the soul." Were it not for the positive reinforcement experienced previously in the learning process, conflict and discomfort born of the ego might discourage the student from continuing. However, positive reinforcement throughout the process is powerful, and once the Holy Spirit's thought system is sufficiently understood and experienced, there really is no going back, though there may be delay. After the fourth stage, Jesus says the student will proceed with "mighty companions" (M-4.I.A. 6:11), which is a way of describing the reinforcement that comes from experiencing forgiveness. Forgiveness demonstrates that those perceived as

[1] St. John of the Cross. *Dark Night of the Soul*. Trans. by Mirabai Starr. New York: Riverhead Books, The Berkely Publishing Group, a division of Penguin Putnam, Inc., 2002.

separate others are actually brothers in the truth of oneness. Jesus likewise is among the "companions" with whom the student will continue the process; a companion who is a consistent source of reinforcement and whom the student is learning to trust.

In describing the last two stages of the development of trust, Jesus points to the fact that learning progress in his curriculum is "heavily reinforced," and mentions the subject of learning transfer which we shall discuss in the next and final section of this chapter under the subject of generalization:

> The next stage is indeed "a period of unsettling." Now must the teacher of God understand that he did not really know what was valuable and what was valueless. All that he really learned so far was that he did not want the valueless, and that he did want the valuable. Yet his own sorting out was meaningless in teaching him the difference.
> The idea of sacrifice, so central to his own thought system, had made it impossible for him to judge. He thought he learned willingness, but now he sees that he does not know what the willingness is for. And now he must attain a state that may remain impossible to reach for a long, long time. He must learn to lay all judgment aside, and ask only what he really wants in every circumstance. Were not each step in this direction so heavily reinforced, it would be hard indeed!
>
> And finally, there is "a period of achievement." It is here that learning is consolidated. Now what was seen as merely shadows before become solid gains, to be counted on in all "emergencies" as well as tranquil times. Indeed, the tranquility is their result; the outcome of honest learning, consistency of thought and full transfer. This is the stage of real peace, for here is Heaven's state fully reflected. From here, the way to Heaven is open and easy. In fact, it is here. Who would "go" anywhere, if peace of mind is already complete? And who would seek to change tranquility for something more desirable? What could be more desirable than this? (M-4.I.A.7-8)

Generalization

Conventional ideas about learning emphasize the value of transferring what is learned in specific situations to other similar specific situations. For instance, learning arithmetic in the school setting is only valuable if the skills involved can be generalized for use in other similar specific situations requiring arithmetical skills, such as balancing a checkbook and planning a budget. The same is true of reading and writing skills. In the Course, however, transferring the mind training which represents the goal of the curriculum involves applying the general principle of the Atonement to *all* situations; and in the world all situations are special relationships.

Thus, specific situations represent lessons in forgiveness which require application of the Holy Spirit's Atonement principle that states we are separate from nothing and no one. So the goal of Jesus' curriculum is that the student's mind would come to accept the Atonement and apply it in *all* situations. In the previously cited Workshop, "Rules for Decision,"[1] Wapnick clarifies this in his discussion of "Setting the Goal" (T-17.VI):

> **The setting of the Holy Spirit's goal is general. Now He will work with you to make it specific, for application is specific (T-17.VI.1:4-5).**

By *general* Jesus means *abstract*— in other words, it is universal, it is in our minds, it is not specific. "Application" means that we do something on a behavioral level: apply it to our everyday lives; use these circumstances and relationships of our lives as a laboratory. This means moving from the general principle of the Atonement, which says that the separation never happened and there is nothing and no one outside us, to the application to specific situations. You—the person I'm living with, or the person that I am working—with are not outside me. You and I are not separate. We have to practice in specific situations, in the circumstances of our personal lives. We must apply the abstract or general principle to specific situations. That is what the whole Course is about. That is what the whole curriculum is about.

> **There are certain very specific guidelines He provides for any situation [i.e., the seven rules for decision (T-30.I)] but remember that you do not yet realize their universal application (T-17.VI.1:6).**

Statements like this make it clear once again that Jesus conceives of this as a process. "You do not yet realize" obviously implies that there is growth we haven't gone through yet, steps we haven't taken yet. We still think there are specific things we have to do in this world, specific relationships we have to forgive; and therefore, because we *think* in terms of specifics, he will give us specific guidelines. We will eventually realize that they are all part of the *one* lesson, and we will then generalize. But we are not there yet.

> **Therefore, it is essential at this point to use them [the guidelines] in each situation separately, until you can more safely look beyond each situation, in an understanding far broader than you now possess (T-17.VI.1:6).**

---

[1] "Rules for Decision," op. cit. For these particular comments and their context see Part VI of the transcribed series.

....What this passage is saying is that until we are ready to generalize these principles to everything, we first have to practice specifically. The same instructions are found in the workbook. In fact, in the Introduction to Review VI, he says that if you really did one lesson, you would have done them all. But until you generalize, you have to practice each lesson separately:

> Each [lesson] contains the whole curriculum if understood, practiced, accepted, and applied to all the seeming happenings throughout the day. One is enough. But from that one, there must be no exceptions made. And so we need to use them all and let them blend as one, as each contributes to the whole we learn (W-pI.rVI.2:2-5).

That is why there are 365 lessons, not one lesson. Each lesson is exactly the same as every other lesson if it is really understood. They all contain the same teaching message. But because we are so terrified of this universality, what we do instead is fragment. We apply a teaching in one situation and decide we are not ready to apply it to another. Or we forgive *this* person, but not *that* person. Or we ask Jesus for help in *this* situation, but say we can handle *that* one on our own. What we have to realize is that they are all the same, and until we realize they are all the same we must practice with each one separately.

So the mind training of the Course is teaching one general principle which undoes the single false idea that has produced the "vast illusion" (W-pI.158. 4:1) of space, time and biological life. The way this principle is accepted, implemented and eventually generalized to all situations is for the decision maker in the mind to learn how to choose the Holy Spirit or, better, how to make way for the Holy Spirit: "I will step back and let Him lead the way" (W-pI.155).

The Atonement principle which is the basis for the Holy Spirit's thought system applies in every aspect of the illusion of separation. Since we believe in a separated reality made up of specifics, then it is with specific situations that we have to practice until our mind comes to fully recognize the truth of the first miracle principle presented at the beginning of Chapter 1 in the Text: "There is no order of difficulty in miracles. One is not 'harder' or 'bigger' than another. They are all the same. All expressions of love are maximal" (T-1.I.1). This principle is true because all the specifics in the illusion are the same *in content*. They are all aspects of separation. Hence, the corollary of the first miracle principle is that there is no hierarchy of illusions (T-23.II.2); they are all undone in the same way and it is not more difficult to undo some than others. All that is needed is for the mind to implement the miracle and choose love rather than fear—choose the Holy Spirit as teacher rather than the ego.

Remember, the miracle is what makes a change of mind from ego to Holy Spirit possible; therefore makes forgiveness possible. Jesus teaches that "mind is the mechanism of decision" (T-8.IV.5:7; T-12.III.9:10) and "The Holy Spirit is the mechanism of miracles" (T-1.I.38:1). Therefore, another way of stating the learning goal of the Course is to say that it is for the student to become a "miracle worker," which means for the mind to learn how to choose the Holy Spirit as its teacher and guide in all things. It is by allowing the Holy Spirit to lead the way in every situation that the principle of the Atonement is generalized, or mind training transferred; and it is because of this that Jesus can say that every lesson in the Workbook "contains the whole curriculum."

Several passages from the Course will illustrate and clarify these points:

> Miracles demonstrate that learning has occurred under the right guidance, for learning is invisible and what has been learned can be recognized only by its results. Its generalization is demonstrated as you use it in more and more situations. You will recognize that you have learned there is no order of difficulty in miracles when you apply them to all situations. There is no situation to which miracles do not apply, and by applying them to all situations you will gain the real world [i.e., the world seen from a consistently right-minded perspective]. For in this holy perception you will be made whole, and the Atonement will radiate from your acceptance of it for yourself to everyone…In every child of God His blessing lies, and in your blessing of the children of God is His blessing to you (T-12.VII.1; brackets mine).

> Problems are not specific but they take specific forms, and these specific shapes make up the world. And no one understands the nature of his problem [i.e., the belief in separation]. If he did, it would be there no more for him to see. Its very nature is that it is *not*. And thus, while he perceives it he can not perceive it as it is. But healing is apparent in specific instances, and generalizes to include them all. This is because they really are the same, despite their different forms. All learning aims at transfer, which becomes complete within two situations that are seen as one, for only common elements are there. Yet this can only be attained by One Who does not see the differences you see. The total transfer of your learning is not made by you. But that it has been made in spite of all the differences you see, convinces you that they could not be real (T-27.V.8; brackets mine).

> Leave, then, the transfer of your learning to the One Who really understands its laws, and Who will guarantee that they remain unviolated and unlimited. Your part is merely to apply what He has taught you to yourself, and He will do the rest. And it is thus the power of your learning will be proved to you by all the many different witnesses it finds. Your brother first among them will be seen, but thousands stand behind him, and beyond each one of them there are a thousand more.

Each one may seem to have a problem that is different from the rest. Yet they are solved together. And their common answer shows the questions could not have been separate (T-27.V.10).

One brother is all brothers. Every mind contains all minds, for every mind is one. Such is the truth. Yet do these thoughts make clear the meaning of creation? Do these words bring perfect clarity with them to you? What can they seem to be but empty sounds; pretty, perhaps, correct in sentiment, yet fundamentally not understood nor understandable. The mind that taught itself to think specifically can no longer grasp abstraction in the sense that it is all-encompassing. We need to see a little, that we learn a lot (W-pI.161.4-8).

To sum this up, the learning of the Course is directed toward accepting only one general principle. This is learned in specific situations until generalization is complete when the general principle of the Atonement is applied in all situations by the Holy Spirit Who knows that all situations are the same. This can only be accomplished by 1) discovering the mind; 2) finding the "Inner Teacher," and; 3) learning how to place the mind under the direction of the Inner Teacher, which means to have become consistently right minded.

An excerpt from the introduction to the ACIM Workbook serves as an excellent example of how generalization is the goal of the Course as well as being a principle of learning implemented by Jesus in the design of his curriculum:

The purpose of the workbook is to train your mind in a systematic way to a different perception of everyone and everything in the world. The exercises are planned to help you generalize the lessons, so that you will understand that each of them is equally applicable to everyone and everything you see.

Transfer of training in true perception does not proceed as does transfer of the training of the world. If true perception has been achieved in connection with any person, situation or event, total transfer to everyone and everything is certain. On the other hand, one exception held apart from true perception makes its accomplishments anywhere impossible.

The only general rules to be observed throughout, then, are: First, that the exercises be practiced with great specificity, as will be indicated. This will help you to generalize the ideas involved to every situation in which you find yourself, and to everyone and everything in it. Second, be sure that you do not decide for yourself that there are some people, situations or things to which the ideas are inapplicable. This will interfere with transfer of training. The very nature of true perception is that it has no limits. It is the opposite of the way you see now.

The overall aim of the exercises is to increase your ability to extend the ideas you will be practicing to include everything. This will require no effort on your part. The exercises themselves meet the conditions necessary for this kind of transfer. (W-pI.IN.4-7)

Previously we have discussed another way in which the principle of generalization is recognized in the Course. Both generalization and reinforcement are involved in the law of mind that *giving and receiving are the same*; *teaching and learning are the same*. All that we can truly give and teach is thought or idea, because what we truly are is mind. The thoughts we teach, we strengthen or reinforce in our mind, and thus they are generalized as we continue to teach them. When we teach with the ego,—i.e., teach guilt, fear, specialness and attack—we are actually giving and receiving nothing. So, by teaching with the ego we are teaching ourselves that we are not Who we are; that we are nothing. Nevertheless, within the illusion, the thought system of illusions is reinforced and generalized through teaching. Thus, guilt, fear, specialness and attack are pervasive throughout the dream.

Likewise, when we teach with the Holy Spirit or Jesus, we are strengthening the thought system of the Atonement, thus teaching and learning our true Identity as Christ, the one non-separate creation of God; the extension of Love within the Mind of God. Within the dream, forgiveness is the way we teach and strengthen this idea of truth. When forgiveness has finally cleared away all thoughts of separation and guilt in our mind, then our mind is free to awaken to the truth of Christ. Along the way, by being teachers of forgiveness we teach others and ourselves that we are one, and thus we gather within our mind "mighty companions" to share the journey of awakening.

As we have already emphasized, every idea begins in the mind of the thinker. Therefore, what extends from the mind is still in it, and from *what* it extends it knows itself. The word "knows" is correct here, because the Holy Spirit still holds knowledge safe in your mind through His impartial perception. By attacking nothing, He presents no barrier to the communication of God. Therefore, being is never threatened. Your Godlike mind can never be defiled. The ego never was and never will be part of it, but through the ego you can hear and teach and learn what is not true. You have taught yourself to believe that you are not what you are. You cannot teach what you have not learned, and what you teach you strengthen in yourself because you are sharing it. Every lesson you teach you are learning.

That is why you must teach only one lesson. If you are to be conflict-free yourself, you must learn only from the Holy Spirit and teach only by Him. You are only love, but when you deny this, you make what you are something you must learn to remember. I said before that the message of the crucifixion was, "Teach only love, for that is what you are." This is the one lesson that is perfectly unified, because it is the only lesson that is one. Only by teaching it can you learn it. "As you teach so will you learn." If that is true, and it is true indeed, do not forget that what you teach is teaching you. And what you project or extend you believe....

Since you cannot *not* teach, your salvation lies in teaching the exact opposite of everything the ego believes. This is how you will learn the truth that will set you free, and will keep you free as others learn it of you. The only way to have peace is to teach peace. By teaching peace you must learn it yourself, because you cannot teach what you still dissociate. Only thus can you win back the knowledge that you threw away. An idea that you share you must have. It awakens in your mind through the conviction of teaching it. Everything you teach you are learning. Teach only love, and learn that love is yours and you are love (T-6.III.1-2, 4).

Summary

Because of the nature of the Course itself as a teaching-learning program, there is considerably more about the subject of learning in the Course than has been covered for purposes of this book. Indeed, an entire book could be written about teaching and learning from the point of view of A Course in Miracles. In this chapter we have addressed the primary topics of relevance for our purposes. Perhaps at this point it will be obvious to readers that the voice of Jesus as it speaks from the pages of the Course itself represents a wonderful model of a wise and loving teacher. Jesus himself manifests all ten of the characteristics of "God's teachers" which are discussed in chapter four of the Manual for Teachers. And by now it must be evident to the reader that the primary point of teaching and learning in the context of the Course's curriculum is forgiveness. We will further clarify that subject in the next chapter.

Chapter 10

Psychotherapy, Healing and Forgiveness

"What's wrong with me?" "People tell me I need help." "My child's teacher says my child needs counseling." "How can I get help with my problems?" "How can someone I know get help for their emotional problems?"

"How can I help?"

The last of these questions is frequently asked by those engaged in the mental health (or "helping") professions as well as lay persons; and in fact has become the title of a book,[1] and earlier was the title of a section in one of Carl Rogers' most popular books.[2] Rogers, a well known and very influential leader in the field of psychotherapy during the second half of the twentieth century, was quoted in an obituary tribute by his friend and colleague Dr. Eugene Gendlin as saying: "I didn't want to find a *client-centered* way [i.e., a system of psychotherapy]. I wanted to find a way to help people."[3]

The first of the "Four Noble Truths" of Buddhism is that life is suffering. Pain and suffering unite humanity in a common bond. Indeed, the special relationships that make up our ego way of life *require* suffering. Who among us has not felt the need for help at some point? And how many of us have wished at one time or another that we knew how to be of help to someone else? Jesus would have us understand that we who believe we are separate individuals alive in bodies have seriously impaired the functioning of our mind and are painfully mentally disordered—insane and desperately in need of help. He would also have us understand that help is available. The truth of God's oneness has insured that the Help we need is present in our mind.

Interestingly, one of the two supplementary pamphlets which extend the principles of the Course is addressed directly to the "helping" professions, specifically to the profession of psychotherapy. Many of Jesus' words to be quoted in the following discussion are taken from that little pamphlet, which we have already mentioned and drawn upon to a limited extent:

---

[1] Dass, Ram and Paul Gorman. *How Can I Help?* New York: Alfred A. Knopf, Inc., 1985.

[2] Rogers, Carl R. *On Becoming a Person*, p. 29. Cambridge, MA: The Riverside Press, 1961.

[3] Gendlin, Eugene. "Carl Rogers (1902-1987)." In the *American Psychologist*, Vol. 43, 2, February, 1988.

Psychotherapy: Purpose, Process and Practice.[4] Helen Schucman actually began the scribing of this pamphlet in January of 1973, before the Course itself was published. However, she set the work aside without completing it until certain circumstances in company with Kenneth Wapnick's encouragement led her to finish the work in 1975. It was then published in 1976, the same year that the Course itself was published. As an aside comment, the story of this little pamphlet is illustrative of how the channeling worked for Helen. The inspiration of Jesus and the words for the material she "scribed" were always available in Helen's mind, but her cooperation in choosing her right mind and joining with Jesus was necessary in order for those inspired words to be written down. Helen, exercising the power of her mind to choose, was able to turn the inspiration on and off at will, so to speak. For purposes of this Primer, we are fortunate to be able to draw upon the *Psychotherapy Pamphlet*, but as it turns out, and as one might expect, while the profession of psychotherapy provides a framework for Jesus' commentary in the pamphlet, the basic content of his message is identical to that found in the Course itself. In fact, the pamphlet is a wonderful summary of the central teachings of *A Course in Miracles*, but, because of its condensed and sophisticated nature, a background of understanding the Course teachings is necessary in order to fully appreciate the message of the pamphlet.

What Is Illness? What Is It That Needs Help?

According to the Course, all forms of illness have the same cause, and it is guilt; guilt that comes from taking the idea of separation seriously and then pursuing it:

> Once God's Son is seen as guilty, illness becomes inevitable. It has been asked for and will be received. And all who ask for illness have now condemned themselves to seek for remedies that cannot help, because their faith is in the illness [i.e., faith in the reality of separation, therefore of the body] and not in salvation. There can be nothing that a change of mind cannot affect, for all external things are only shadows of a decision already made. Change the decision, and how can its shadow be unchanged? Illness can be but guilt's shadow, grotesque and ugly since it mimics deformity. If a deformity [i.e., guilt] is seen as real, what could its shadow be except deformed?

> The descent into hell follows step by step in an inevitable course, once the decision that guilt is real has been made. Sickness and death and misery now stalk the earth in unrelenting waves, sometimes together and sometimes in grim succession. Yet all these things, however real they seem, are but illusions. Who could have faith in them once this is realized?

---

[4] *Psychotherapy*, op. cit. (See our chapter nine.)

And who could not have faith in them until he realizes this? Healing is therapy or correction, and we have said already and will say again, all therapy is psychotherapy. To heal the sick is but to bring this realization to them (P-2.IV.2-3; brackets mine).

Fear is the symptom of guilt which presumes that the Son of God is vulnerable to attack; and all illness represents a form that fear has taken in an attack on self:

> Everyone who needs help, regardless of the form of his distress, is attacking himself, and his peace of mind is suffering in consequence (P-1.IN.3:1).

> Illness of any kind may be defined as the result of a view of the self as weak, vulnerable, evil and endangered, and thus in need of constant defense [because fear is warranted]. Yet if such were really the self, defense would be impossible. Therefore, the defenses sought for must be magical. They must overcome all limits perceived in the self, at the same time making a new self-concept into which the old one cannot return. In a word, error is accepted as real and dealt with by illusions. Truth being brought to illusions, reality now becomes a threat and is perceived as evil. Love becomes feared because reality is love. Thus is the circle closed against the "inroads" of salvation. Illness is therefore a mistake and needs correction. And as we have already emphasized, correction cannot be achieved by first establishing the "rightness" of the mistake and then overlooking it. If illness is real it cannot be overlooked in truth, for to overlook reality is insanity. Yet that is magic's purpose; to make illusions true through false perception. This cannot heal, for it opposes truth. Perhaps an illusion of health is substituted for a little while, but not for long. Fear cannot long be hidden by illusions, for it is part of them. It will escape and take another form, being the source of all illusions (P-2.IV.6-7; brackets mine).

So, what needs help, or healing, is the mind's belief in separation. Guilt inevitably arises from that belief, because if separation were a real, accomplished fact then the Son of God would have destroyed his Father Whose essence is oneness, thus destroying his own true Self. The presenting symptom of the mind's belief in separation and guilt is some form of fear which will foster attack on self or others, whether acted out or harbored within.

Approaches to Illness and Healing through Psychotherapy

While the need of help is universal from the point of view of the Course, yet using the diagnostic criteria of conventional psychology, only a proportion of the population is officially identified with a "mental disorder." For instance, on the Web site of the U.S. National Institute of Mental Health one finds the following:

> Mental disorders are common in the United States and internationally. An estimated 26.2 percent of Americans ages 18 and older—about one in four adults—suffer from a diagnosable mental disorder in a given year. When applied to the 2004 U.S. Census residential population estimate for ages 18 and older, this figure translates to 57.7 million people.[1]

In most cases in the U.S., a person who seeks help from a licensed professional psychologist or psychiatrist, and most probably from other mental health professionals, will have to complete an intake interview for purposes of establishing a diagnosis. This is required in cases where a third party, such as an insurance company, will be paying at least part of the fee. The diagnosis may identify one or more psychological disorders according to criteria listed in the *Diagnostic and Statistical Manual* (DSM-IV)[2] developed and published by the American Psychiatric Association. As with everything else of traditional psychology which we have considered, establishing a diagnosis of "mental disorder" according to the DSM-IV is a complex undertaking. A complete diagnosis would have five different "axes" or dimensions associated with personal functioning, Axis I, being the "clinical syndrome" which might be, for example, some form of problem associated with depression or anxiety. All in all, there are 300 different specific psychiatric disorders listed in the DSM-IV and research is continuing to identify more each year, while, as views and understanding change, others are reclassified. An underlying assumption with this standard approach is that some forms of treatment are more appropriate for certain disorders than for others, so the diagnosing professional or agency is expected to come up with a treatment plan listing certain objective criteria for determining when and whether treatment has achieved its goal. This entire approach is often referred to as the "medical model" for psychological diagnosis and treatment. Not every person engaged in mental health counseling and therapy subscribes to this model (Carl Rogers opposed it vigorously), but it is the prevailing standard in the U.S. and elsewhere, and is the one to which third party payers adhere.

Some examples of the broad categories of mental disorder found in the DSM-IV are: Adjustment Disorders, Anxiety Disorders, Dissociative Disorders, Eating Disorders, Impulse-Control Disorders, Mood Disorders, Sexual Disorders, Sleep Disorders, Psychotic Disorders, Sexual Dysfunctions, Somatoform Disorders, Substance Abuse Disorders, and Personality Disorders. Within each of these broad categories are several subcategories.

---

[1] Statistics, National Institute for Mental Health Web site: http://www.nimh.nih.gov/healthinformation/statisticsmenu.cfm

[2] *Diagnostic and Statistical Manual on Mental Disorders, Fourth Ed. (DSM-IV).* Washington, DC: American Psychiatric Press, 1994.

As a service to the public as well as professionals and others interested in psychology, the AllPsych.com Web site contains a relatively complete discussion of the DSM-IV and its various disorders:

> AllPsych includes in these pages the etiology (how it develops), symptoms, treatment options, and prognosis for over 60 adult psychiatric disorders and 8 personality disorders, as well as the names and DSM Codes for over 150 disorders....
>
> There is a good deal of overlap among the different diagnoses listed in the DSM IV, which you may notice by browsing these pages. The reason for this is the same as for the overlap in medical diagnoses... rarely is a symptom exclusive of anything, and rarely can a diagnosis be made without a pattern or cluster of symptoms. For example, Depression includes feelings of sadness, but anxiety can lead to sadness, as can phobias, psychosis, and many other disorders. Keep this in mind when reading about specific diagnoses or you may find yourself saying way too frequently, "Oh my Gosh, I have that."[3]

In contrast, there are no diagnostic categories in Jesus' system of psychology. Everything we regard as illness—mental *or* physical—is an illusion in our split and damaged mind where there is only one basic problem: the mistaken belief in separation. Likewise, there is only one underlying psychodynamic: guilt. And there is only one presenting symptom: fear. We have elaborated already on the fact that guilt and fear take many forms—for instance the many categories of mental disorder found in the DSM-IV—but the psychology of *A Course in Miracles* is about *content*, not form; about *cause*, not effect. The underlying content, or cause, of all symptoms of distress is guilt, because it is the cause of all the many forms of fear that one may observe; and every mental disorder is an expression of fear in some form, however indirect and unapparent.

In his classes, Kenneth Wapnick has often quipped that as far as Jesus is concerned there is only one DSM diagnosis: *Son of God, Separated Type*. To establish this diagnosis one need only identify fear in any form, and of course the underlying cause of fear would be guilt over the belief in separation which manifests in some form of selfishness (what the ego calls "sin" and Jesus identifies as specialness). So, the prescribed treatment would address the underlying guilt, and that treatment is forgiveness.

To carry the comparison with the DSM-IV diagnostic system a little further, consider what we have learned about the condition of the separated mind as described by Jesus in his course. It is a mind which is split, having

---

[3] AllPsych.com, op. cit. (See our chapter eight.)

denied and dissociated truth, repressing enormous guilt over an imagined murder. The ego defenses employed by this mind include not only denial and dissociation, but require the ongoing use of projection wherein one's own denied sin and guilt is seen in others who are always perceived as enemies, or potential enemies, competing for specialness and quite capable of murder. Not only that but, "God is out to get me!" This separated, split mind believes that illusions are real, hence suffers from hallucinations, while its thought system of fear is delusional. In the DSM-IV, these characteristics would qualify for a diagnosis of *schizophrenia, paranoid type*. Jesus is telling us that the overarching, insane condition of humanity is that of a paranoid schizophrenic! Unlike the view of the DSM-IV, where this diagnosis has no real cure and for which prognosis of any improvement is poor, Jesus offers the hope and the possibility of healing. But from our perspective within the dream, where we believe in orders of difficulty in cure and hierarchies of significance in illusions, it does seem that we make of ourselves a *most* difficult population of patients who require a very skillful therapist indeed— one with a fully healed mind who has accepted the Atonement for himself. Of course, "Jesus" is the name of one of those therapists:

> There are those who have reached God directly, retaining no trace of worldly limits and remembering their own Identity perfectly. These might be called the Teachers of teachers because, although they are no longer visible, their image can yet be called upon. And they will appear when and where it is helpful for them to do so. To those to whom such appearances would be frightening, they give their ideas. No one can call on them in vain. Nor is there anyone of whom they are unaware. All needs are known to them, and all mistakes are recognized and overlooked by them. The time will come when this is understood. And meanwhile, they give all their gifts to the teachers of God [e.g. psychotherapists who accept healing for themselves] who look to them for help, asking all things in their Name and in no other (M-26.2; bracket mine).

Given Jesus diagnosis for the human condition, it is quite understandable that the entire history of *Homo sapiens* (an amusing self description which derives from the Latin and literally means "wise or rational man") is that of a murderous Bedlam.[4] And it is no wonder that under the ego's guidance humanity has been unable to develop the psychological insights and systems necessary to bring about meaningful, long-term improvement in the overall human situation. For one thing, patients and therapists all are equally insane!

---

[4] The word *bedlam* is defined in the American Heritage Dictionary as, "a place or situation of noisy uproar." However, the word was first used as a popular designation for the Hospital of St. Mary of Bethlehem, or the Bethlehem Royal Hospital, in London, which is the oldest institution for the severely mentally ill, having been established in 1247.

It should be noted at this point that everything the Course has to say about the subject of learning is applicable to the subject of psychotherapy. As with conventional psychology, in Jesus' psychology the principles of learning apply to the psychotherapeutic process. Also, just as teaching and learning are the same, so does healing take place for therapist and patient, counselor and client, alike: "Teacher and pupil, therapist and patient, are all insane or they would not be here" (P-2.II.5:6).

Likewise, just as teaching and learning are directed toward the one goal of accepting the Atonement for both teacher and student, so too is acceptance of the Atonement the goal of psychotherapy for both therapist and patient. And accepting the truth of the Atonement principle results in the recognition that not only is the perception of separate persons with separate interests an illusion, but in truth there are no separate minds. Hence, though there are superficial differences in form, such as in amount of education, professional skill and experience, still student and teacher, patient and therapist, are fundamentally the same. At the level of content—as mind—they are brothers in Christ. Jesus makes this emphatically clear in the *Psychotherapy Pamphlet*:

> Who, then, is the therapist, and who is the patient? In the end, everyone is both. He who needs healing must heal. Physician, heal thyself. Who else is there to heal? And who else is in need of healing? Each patient who comes to a therapist offers him a chance to heal himself. He is therefore his therapist. And every therapist must learn to heal from each patient who comes to him. He thus becomes his patient. God does not know of separation. What He knows is only that He has one Son. His knowledge is reflected in the ideal patient-therapist relationship. God comes to him who calls, and in Him he recognizes Himself.

> Think carefully, teacher and therapist, for whom you pray, and who is in need of healing. For therapy is prayer [because, "the only meaningful prayer is for forgiveness" (T-3.V.6:3)], and healing is its aim and its result. What is prayer except the joining of minds in a relationship which Christ can enter? (P-2.VII.1-2:3; bracket mine).

To "heal thyself" is to accept the truth of the Atonement in one's own mind. Although acceptance of the Atonement is relevant for both patient and therapist, student and teacher, still the only responsibility that anyone can reasonably accept within the dream of separation is for one's own mind. Thus, the therapist is not responsible for the patient's acceptance of the Atonement, but only for his or her own acceptance:

> The sole responsibility of God's teacher [in this case, a psychotherapist] is to accept the Atonement for himself. Atonement means correction, or the undoing of errors. When this has been accomplished, the teacher of God

> becomes a miracle worker [i.e., one who can offer forgiveness to everyone]
> by definition. His sins have been forgiven him, and he no longer condemns
> himself. How can he then condemn anyone? And who is there whom his
> forgiveness can fail to heal? (M-18.4:5-10; bracket mine)

The last sentence quoted above is based on the truth of non-separation (the
Atonement principle, oneness) that there is no one else to heal, because
all minds are joined, and in truth there is no separated mind. To accept
the Atonement in one's own mind is to accept it for the one mind we all
share. Psychotherapy is simply one form of a special relationship which
can be transformed so that this can be accomplished. We cannot begin to
understand the gift to the Sonship (i.e., the seemingly separated Sons of God)
that our own acceptance of the Atonement represents. But the Holy Spirit
and Jesus understand, and it is Their responsibility to extend throughout the
mind of the Sonship what seem to be our individual gifts of forgiveness. In
fact, acceptance of the Atonement is identical to accepting the Holy Spirit
and His thought system as our guide:

> What Comforter can there be for the sick children of God except His power
> through you? Remember that it does not matter where in the Sonship He
> is accepted. He is always accepted for all, and when your mind receives
> Him the remembrance of Him awakens throughout the Sonship. Heal your
> brothers simply by accepting God for them [i.e., accepting the Atonement,
> or the truth of oneness]. Your minds are not separate, and God has only
> one channel for healing because He has but one Son. God's remaining
> communication link [i.e., the Holy Spirit] with all His children joins them
> together, and them to Him. To be aware of this is to heal them because it
> is the awareness that no one is separate, and so no one is sick (T-10.III.2;
> bracket mine).

Again, a reminder: this paragraph is talking about a process in the *mind*. It
has nothing to do with what seems to take place in the dream of bodies and
a world, except as the illusion reflects what is taking place in the mind. Jesus
is using language metaphorically here so one needs to grasp the *content*
of what is being communicated and not become sidetracked by matters of
form or semantics. Language is symbolic and can never fully communicate
the truth of mind. As for the psychotherapeutic relationship, all that matters
for the therapist is acceptance of the Atonement in his or her own mind
which enables the ability to extend forgiveness. The patient may or may not
be consciously aware of this and may or may not accept the Atonement. But
the separation only needs healing in what seems to be one's own mind where
the illusion of separation and relationships resides.

The forgiveness principle that there is no hierarchy of illusions applies to
therapy as well as learning. All illusions serve the same purpose and all are

dissolved by the Holy Spirit in the same way. For this reason, one miracle—one lesson in forgiveness—is not more difficult than another, and one human problem is not fundamentally different from another.

> Everyone in this world seems to have his own special problems. Yet they are all the same [i.e., the belief in separation], and must be recognized as one if the one solution [the Atonement] that solves them all is to be accepted (W-pI.79.2:1-2; brackets mine).

> Only be certain you do not forget that all problems are the same. Their many forms will not deceive you while you remember this. One problem, one solution (W-pI.80.3:3-5).

As far as the DSM-IV is concerned, while it may have practical utility in the world of magic and illusions, still, in truth, all 300 diagnostic categories represent forms of the same underlying problem—a problem in the mind, not brain—and, according to Jesus, the solution will always be the same, no matter what form therapy might take. Real healing depends upon this recognition and requires the therapist's understanding that he or she is in need of healing as much as the patient. Each therapeutic undertaking requires the help of right-mindedness—the Holy Spirit—to be truly effective in healing the *one* mind that therapist and patient share.

There are some other important points of relevance regarding Jesus' approach to psychotherapy. First of all, his psychotherapy might be said to equate to the idea that *there is no psychotherapy*, at least not as the world understands it. One separate individual does not heal another separate individual; one body does not heal another body; one brain does not contain the knowledge which heals another brain; one mind does not have something that another mind lacks. All healing of all symptoms (and all symptoms are of the mind, therefore can be understood as psychological symptoms) takes place in the mind and requires that there be a process of learning that minds are joined. Since a true therapist would be a "teacher of God," the same basic qualification holds for the therapist as applies for a teacher of God: "His qualifications consist solely in this; somehow, somewhere he has made a deliberate choice in which he did not see his interests as apart from someone else's" (M-1.1:1-2).

So the questions which opened this chapter are really misdirected in the sense that they do not ask for help with the one basic problem at the level of mind. Instead, they ask for help with symptoms identified by a separate self: help with non-existent problems for a separate self which does not exist. The belief in a separate self *is* the problem! Further, those questions presume a source of help outside the mind, and assume that the one who helps is separate from the one being helped. Sincere and egalitarian as he was, Carl Rogers asked the right question in the wrong way, because underlying the question, "How can I be of help?" was the premise of separation. Certainly his emphasis upon the person-to-person approach had within it an element of recognizing that perceived differences are inconsequential, but Dr. Rogers never got beyond the illusory world of separate, individual persons to the truth of spirit, the causal nature of mind, and the unity of mind. Jesus' answer to his question, "How can I be of help?" is: "Physician, healer, therapist, teacher, heal thyself" (P-3.III.8:1). By this, however, Jesus does not mean heal thyself as a person, but as a mind.

This brings us to a second point. Sigmund Freud, Carl Rogers and all other psychologists concerned with therapy and healing have either developed or make use of theories of personality. But in a certain sense there is no theory of personality in Jesus' psychology. Instead, there is a theory of mind and a description of the ego thought system which underlies the idea of personalities and personal differences. Personalities are organized around the ego's goal of specialness. Specialness serves as the template for *all* personalities which share *all* of the elements of specialness discussed in chapter five. The belief in personalities—i.e., in separate selves—is one form that the belief in separation takes. It is the belief in specialness and is yet another way in which we see the ego's emphasis upon form to the exclusion of content. The ego is always concerned with persons and personalities, thus the popularity of tabloid journalism and the widespread fascination with celebrities. Politics, too, is primarily focused upon personalities as opposed to objective issues. In the pursuit of political campaigns one easily sees the ego's game of specialness with its characteristic strategies of attack and defense.

Forms seem to differ. Perception depends upon the appearance of differences. In fact, one of the topics typically addressed in conventional psychology, and often related to personality theory, is that of "individual differences." There are professional organizations and journals dedicated to study of this subject, which therapists and teachers are taught to respect. Rather than a psychology of personality and individual differences, Jesus offers a psychology of mind and sameness. There is only one mind. All seemingly separated minds are joined. They are actually one mind sharing the same basic content: the wrong-minded thought system of separation, the right-minded thought system of the Atonement, and the function of decision.

Of course, in terms of Jesus' Level One metaphysical teachings, there is really no separated mind divided within itself. In truth, there is only the one

Mind of God, whole and indivisible. Certainly there are no personalities in that Mind, nor does it make any sense to say that God has a personality. The only god that has a personality is that which the ego has invented in various cultures throughout the world. Those gods know all about personalities. To them some personalities are special and others are not; some are sinners and others innocent; and they hate all other gods who seem to differ from themselves, so they justify and encourage killing the followers of those other gods variously defined as blasphemers, infidels, idolaters, evil doers and devil worshippers. In this regard, Voltaire observed: "If God created man in his own image, we have more that reciprocated."[1]

To the ego differences are holy, and so the ego fosters not only killing in the name of differences, but psychologies which study and reinforce the idea of differences. In Jesus' course, what is holy is oneness, both the Oneness of Heaven, and the oneness of the mind that suffers from the illusion of separation, but where the holiness of Heaven is still remembered. It can be said that Jesus' approach to both psychotherapy and teaching asserts that these are processes by which those who initially seem to be separate and different may come to forgive their differences in light of the truth that they are one, finally to awaken to the One. To paraphrase Tolkien in the interest of a meaning quite different from his original:

> One Mind to rule them all,
> One Mind to find them,
> One Mind to bind them all and in resplendence bring them
> To the Light of Heaven where no shadows lie.[2]

One Process, Many Terms: Aspects of Sickness and Healing

As he teaches about the processes of sickness and healing that seem to take place in the mind, many of the terms Jesus uses have overlapping meanings. Thus, he helps his students to understand their mind by showing them many dimensions of what is essentially the same process, much like one might study a many-faceted gemstone from different angles and under different conditions of light. So it is that all of the terms used in the title of this

[1] From the so-called *Leningrad Notebook*, also known as *Le Sottisier*; one of several posthumously published notebooks of Voltaire.

[2] Paraphrased from J. R. R. Tolkien's original as found in Book II, Chapter 2, "The Council of Elrond" from *The Fellowship of the Ring*, Vol. I of the trilogy, *The Lord of the Rings*. Collector's Edition. New York: Houghton Mifflin, 1974:
> One Ring to rule them all,
> One Ring to find them,
> One Ring to bring them all and in the darkness bind them
> In the Land of Mordor where the Shadows lie.

chapter are basically equivalent: *psychotherapy, healing* and *forgiveness* each describes the process in time that is necessary for the mind to awaken from the nightmare dream of separation and specialness. The basic dynamic of this process is decision making—mind changing—but Jesus uses these and other terms interchangeably to help us understand different aspects of what is involved. This can be seen in the opening paragraphs of the ACIM supplementary *Psychotherapy Pamphlet*:

> Psychotherapy is the only form of therapy there is. Since only the mind can be sick, only the mind can be healed. Only the mind is in need of healing. This does not appear to be the case, for the manifestations of this world seem real indeed. Psychotherapy is necessary so that an individual can begin to question their reality. Sometimes he is able to start to open his mind without formal help, but even then it is always some change in his perception of interpersonal relationships that enables him to do so. Sometimes he needs a more structured, extended relationship with an "official" therapist. Either way, the task is the same; the patient must be helped to change his mind about the "reality" of illusions....

> Very simply, the purpose of psychotherapy is to remove the blocks to truth. Its aim is to aid the patient in abandoning his fixed delusional system, and to begin to reconsider the spurious cause and effect relationships on which it rests. No one in this world escapes fear, but everyone can reconsider its causes and learn to evaluate them correctly. God has given everyone a Teacher Whose wisdom and help far exceed whatever contributions an earthly therapist can provide. Yet there are times and situations in which an earthly patient-therapist relationship becomes the means through which He offers His greater gifts to both.

> What better purpose could any relationship have than to invite the Holy Spirit to enter into it and give it His Own great gift of rejoicing?...For psychotherapy, correctly understood, teaches forgiveness and helps the patient to recognize and accept it. And in his healing is the therapist forgiven with him (P-IN.1; P-1.IN.1-2).

To repeat once again, the central practical Level Two teaching of *A Course in Miracles* is about forgiveness. Fundamentally, the goal of all teaching and learning is forgiveness. Likewise, according to Jesus' psychology of mind, the fundamental goal of psychotherapy is forgiveness; forgiveness of the guilt that accompanies the belief in separation and is projected on to others seen as different. Forgiveness is the need of *both* therapist and patient just as it is for both teacher and student. In fact, the same can be said of all relationships, whether professional or informal, casual or long-term and familial. In this world *all* relationships *begin* as special with differences perceived as important, and if the goal of Jesus' psychology is accepted, then all relationships are in need of healing through forgiveness. This means to resolve our mind's one problem that has split us asunder, both within and without: to heal the belief in separation that has lead us to believe we are here and that our differences really matter. In the presence of this belief, guilt lurks in darkness poised to attack, ever ready to pounce in judgment and condemn.

By way of further elaborating on the central concept of forgiveness, we will now explore several different terms used in the Course with an eye to their similarities as well as the nuances of their different perspectives on forgiveness and the basic process of decision making, or mind changing.

The miracle: this concept is primary in Jesus' psychology of mind, being the dynamic which serves as the underpinning of forgiveness and is virtually identical with it. It is that function of mind which makes correction possible. It is the gift of oneness that saves our shattered, hallucinating and delusional mind from being completely isolated from Love in spite of its dedication to the ego's separation and specialness. We already have presented the *Glossary* definition of *miracle* in chapter eight, but will repeat it here because of its centrality to our current discussion:

> the change of mind that shifts our perception from the ego's world of sin, guilt, and fear, to the Holy Spirit's world of forgiveness; reverses projection by restoring to the mind its causative function, allowing us to choose again; transcends the laws of this world to reflect the laws of God; accomplished by our joining with the Holy Spirit or Jesus, being the means of healing our own and others' minds. (Note: not to be confused with the traditional understanding of miracles as changes in external phenomena.)

Chapter 1 of the ACIM Text begins with a discussion of fifty "miracle principles" which expand upon this important concept. The interested reader will find a thorough discussion of those principles, as well as an excellent overview of the Course itself, in Kenneth Wapnick's little book, *The Fifty Miracle Principles of A COURSE IN MIRACLES.*[3] Obviously, we cannot provide an exhaustive discussion here since, as its title indicates, the entire Course is about this concept. But let us recognize that the *miracle* is not a Level One concept. It is not an element of God's Mind. There is no need of miracles in Heaven; only in the diseased mind that has substituted perception for knowledge. The miracle is the gift of knowledge that makes a change of perception possible, therefore it makes psychotherapy, healing and forgiveness possible.

---

[3] Wapnick, Kenneth. *The Fifty Miracle Principles of A Course in Miracles*, 3rd Edition. Temecula, CA. Foundation for *A Course in Miracles*, 1992.

The miracle is the means by which our mind is restored to sanity; the means by which we reclaim the power of choice; and the means by which we remember our true Identity by sharing it.

In the *Glossary* definition we see that the miracle has to do with changing perception through changing the mind, and that it serves to undo the ego's reversal of cause and effect. The ego has assigned cause to the body and world, as well as blinding us to the reality of mind, therefore disabling the power of the mind to choose. The miracle undoes all of that. And what could be more central to psychotherapy than for patient and therapist to discover the mind and its power of decision? The way in which that power is exercised determines how we will be affected by our experiences in the world; therefore whether we will use our perceptions to attack ourselves with some form of distress, or to heal our minds of the beliefs in separation and guilt which produce the need of distress and attack. In the *Psychotherapy Pamphlet* Jesus comments on this. To repeat and expand upon a previously quoted sentence:

> Everyone who needs help, regardless of the form of his distress, is attacking himself, and his peace of mind is suffering in consequence. These tendencies are often described as "self destructive," and the patient often regards them in that way himself. What he does not realize and needs to learn is that this "self," which can attack and be attacked as well, is a concept he made up. Further, he cherishes it, defends it, and is sometimes even willing to "sacrifice" his "life" on its behalf. For he regards it as himself. This self he sees as being acted on, reacting to external forces as they demand, and helpless midst the power of the world.
>
> Psychotherapy, then, must restore to his awareness the ability to make his own decisions. He must become willing to reverse his thinking, and to understand that what he thought projected its effects on him were made by his projections on the world. The world he sees does therefore not exist. Until this is at least in part accepted, the patient cannot see himself as really capable of making decisions. And he will fight against his freedom because he thinks that it is slavery (P-1.IN.3-4).

The introduction to Wapnick's *Fifty Miracle Principles* contains a helpful discussion of the miracle, further explaining the overlapping meaning of some ACIM terms. An excerpt from that introduction follows:

> The best definition of what a miracle is, then, is that it is a correction for a misthinking or a misperception, and therefore *A Course in Miracles* will never advocate that you do anything about changing your behavior...This does not mean, by the way, that the Course would...[advocate against] doing something to shift your behavior. All that it would say is that you not believe that by changing your behavior you have changed the problem.

It could be a useful step towards changing a problem, but the basic problem is never out in the world or the body—it is in the mind. This idea, of course, is absolutely essential to everything that the Course teaches and everything that we will be talking about. Certainly it is essential for understanding what the miracle is. The simplest definition of a miracle is that it is a correction for how we perceive or for how we think.

One of my favorite lines in the Course, which really is a perfect definition of a miracle even though it does not use the word, says that "the holiest of all the spots on earth is where an ancient hatred has become a present love" (T-26. IX.6:1). Someone whom we hate, hatred being the ego's way of looking, becomes someone whom we love, and that vision of love is given to us by the Holy Spirit. What we are talking about are two different ways of looking at the world and, more specifically, looking at the relationships in our lives. One is the ego's way of looking, which is a way of seeing more and more separation, anger and guilt, justifying our anger, and making sickness real here in the body. All these perceptions really reinforce the basic ego premise that we are separate from each other and from God. The correction for that is to go from the ego's way of looking to the Holy Spirit's way of looking, and it is that shift from the ego to the Holy Spirit that is the miracle. The identical word for that process of shifting from the ego's perceptions of someone else to the Holy Spirit's is "forgiveness."

When we do forgive, what we are really doing is healing the problem, because the basic source of the problem is our interpretation of it, and this is based on our guilt. So all of our problems—whether they be physical, financial, or social—are not found out here in the world of the body but are found, rather, in our minds, and they all can be traced back to a problem of guilt. Another term for guilt would be "lack of forgiveness." It is when we forgive that our problems are healed, so we can then say that the words "miracle," "forgiveness," and "healing" represent basically the same process.

We can see, therefore, that a miracle is the answer to the problem, which is guilt, and we can define this even further and say that all of guilt comes from the belief that we are separate. So, these two words, "separation" and "guilt," are also virtually synonymous, because one comes from the other.[1]

Forgiveness and the miracle, then, are at the heart of Jesus' approach to psychotherapy. As with teachers and teaching, it is not the form that matters, but the content of the therapist's mind. Forms of therapy vary, as the DSM-IV anticipates that they should in order to treat the various diagnosed psychological disorders, and according to the background, training and preferences of the therapist. These forms include such diverse approaches

---

[1] ibid.

as hypnotherapy, behavioral therapy, cognitive therapy, person-centered therapy, psychoanalytic therapy, family systems therapy, etc. All of these forms have their uses in addressing human problems, but none of them will be truly healing according to Jesus' view unless the therapist practices his or her art from the right-minded perspective of forgiveness. And it is critically important to realize that forgiveness is not some behavior or technique that the therapist does, but has to do with the way he or she thinks, whether with the ego or the Holy Spirit. As a central element in Jesus' psychology, forgiveness is not just another pretty face that the ego can wear. Forgiveness is not about the illusory relationship of one body to another, but about one's mind and the relationship with one's idea of self. Therefore, it is about one's inner relationship to specialness.

The definition of *forgiveness* in Wapnick's *Glossary* is:

> looking at our specialness with the Holy Spirit or Jesus, without guilt or judgment; our special function that shifts perception of another as "enemy" (special hate) or "savior-idol" (special love) to brother or friend, removing all projections of guilt from him; the expression of the miracle or vision of Christ, that sees all people united in the Sonship of God, looking beyond the seeming differences that reflect separation: thus, perceiving sin [and guilt] as real makes true forgiveness impossible; the recognition that what we thought was done to us we did to ourselves, since we are responsible for our scripts, and therefore only we can deprive ourselves of the peace of God: thus, we forgive others for what they have *not* done to us, not for what they have done. (See: looking at the ego.)

This definition is based on all of the relevant passages from *A Course in Miracles*, as are all of the definitions in Wapnick's *Glossary*. Given our ordinary understanding, this is really quite an unusual and surprising definition that has been condensed from Jesus' teachings. The basic point, again, is that forgiveness has to do with *how* one *perceives*, therefore *interprets*, what happens in one's dream of separated life. That is what is meant by the statement that we are responsible for our scripts. As figures in the dream, we are not responsible for what other dream figures do, but as mind we *are* responsible for perceiving what is done either wrong-mindedly with the ego or right-mindedly with Jesus or the Holy Spirit. At a higher level of abstraction, we are also responsible for what happens in our dream, since we are seeming fragments of the mind that chose all scripts of separation, and since it can be said that we chose to come into our particular version of the dream. But forgiveness, being practical, does not ask us to live out of that level of understanding or to take responsibility for what other people do, only for how we interpret and react to what they do, which again goes back to the thought system in our mind we choose to follow.

In order to exercise our power of choice we must practice the non-judgmental *looking* that Jesus emphasizes throughout the Course: the honest looking which represents the heritage of Socrates, Plato and Freud.

So, rather surprisingly, forgiveness is not really about forgiving anyone else, but is about ourselves as mind and forgiving the guilt we harbor within. What seem to be "others" are projections in our mind, and are the screen upon which our own selfishness (sin) and guilt are projected. So psychotherapy is first and foremost about the mind of the therapist. Addressing this point in the *Psychotherapy Pamphlet* Jesus says:

> Sickness takes many forms, and so does unforgiveness [i.e., guilt]. The forms of one but reproduce the forms of the other, for they are the same illusion. So closely is one translated into the other, that a careful study of the form a sickness takes will point quite clearly to the form of unforgiveness that it represents. Yet seeing this will not effect a cure [in other words, insight alone is not enough]. That is achieved by only one recognition; that only forgiveness heals an unforgiveness, and only an unforgiveness can possibly give rise to sickness of any kind.

> This realization is the final goal of psychotherapy. How is it reached? The therapist sees in the patient all that he has not forgiven in himself, and is thus given another chance to look at it, open it to re-evaluation and forgive it. When this occurs, he sees his sins as gone into a past that is no longer here. Until he does this, he must think of evil as besetting him here and now. The patient is his screen for the projection of his sins [i.e., forms of specialness, selfishness and guilt], enabling him to let them go. Let him retain one spot of sin in what he looks upon [i.e., let him continue to project guilt onto another in any form], and his release is partial and will not be sure.

> No one is healed alone. This is the joyous song salvation sings to all who hear its Voice. This statement cannot be too often remembered by all who see themselves as therapists. Their patients can but be seen as the bringers of forgiveness, for it is they who come to demonstrate their sinlessness to eyes that still believe that sin is there to look upon. Yet will the proof of sinlessness, seen in the patient and accepted in the therapist, offer the mind of both a covenant in which they meet and join and are as one (P-2.VI.5-7; brackets mine).

These paragraphs are remarkable for the fact that they say virtually nothing about the patient except that he or she offers the therapist a mirror in which to see the therapist's guilt, or unforgiveness, thus offering lessons in forgiveness for the therapist! There is nothing in these passages about diagnoses or treatment modalities. The simple point of this is that, regardless of what the therapist and patient talk about and do together, true healing—healing the mind of the ego thought system—will only occur if there is forgiveness, and for the therapist that must take place in the therapist's mind. The same is true of any relationship, therefore of medical practice or any other form of professional practice that intends to be of service to people. For instance, for years many in the medical professions have recognized that the nature of the relationship between doctor and patient is a very important part of healing, hence the importance given in the past to the physician's "bedside manner." In more recent years Dr. Bernie Siegel wrote a book about this entitled, "Love, Medicine and Miracles."[2] While Dr. Siegel's understanding of "mind," "love" and "miracles" is not consistent with that of *A Course in Miracles*, still the experiences he reports and the phenomena he addresses can be understood from within the frame of reference of Jesus' psychology. Jesus did not invent the idea of forgiveness and its healing power, but in the Course he offers a thoroughgoing explanation which is applicable to understanding all human situations, as well as offering a very practical way to implement this understanding, albeit a most radical and unconventional one. The reason Jesus' psychology is so radically unconventional is that, by and large, humanity has remained mindless under the sway of the ego. And that mindless state is the result of a purposeful strategy on the part of the ego thought system designed to maintain itself—a strategy in which we are complicit because we so value separation, specialness and selfhood, oblivious to the pain that results. But when a cry for help is issued forth and heard, then a classroom in forgiveness becomes available.

In this chapter we are concerned with that specific form of forgiveness classroom that is psychotherapy, but it is only one of a vast number, since any relationship can become such a classroom. Any relationship can become a classroom in forgiveness, because guilt, too, needs a classroom, and all relationships begin in the classroom of guilt. As we pointed out in chapter five, the ego is the author of the idea of relationships. Therefore every relationship in this world *begins* as a special relationship: "...every relationship on which the ego embarks *is* special" (T-15.VII.1:7). That means that every relationship will be a classroom in which guilt is taught and learned through projection, attack and defense; and it will remain so until one mind—one decision-maker/observer—begins to *look* at what is going on and to question it. It is this looking and questioning that the ego fears, because it is an act of mindfulness, thus a threat to the ego's strategy of mindlessness, which serves its purpose of keeping us unaware of mind and choice. The ego must fear forgiveness, because that is its undoing. Therefore *we* must

---

[2] Siegel, Bernie S. *Love, Medicine and Miracles: Lesson Learned about Self-Healing from a Surgeon's Experience with Exceptional Patients*. New York: Harper Collins Publishers, 1988.

fear genuine forgiveness and the placing of our specialness motivations and manipulations under careful, objective examination. This is one place where resistance to psychotherapy comes from: the ego's fear to look within where it whispers to us we will find the horror of that "seething cauldron" of guilt that it has denied into unconsciousness. So the ego has taught us to fear our mind, and even more, to fear any step in the direction of the Atonement truth that means the dissolution of separate selfdom altogether.

Looking at the ego was discussed in chapter four. It is obviously a central principle in Jesus' teaching about forgiveness. This idea is so important, and so often mentioned in the Course, that Wapnick gives it a definition in his *Glossary*:

> the essence of forgiveness: looking with the Holy Spirit's or Jesus' nonjudgmental gentleness and patience at our ego thought system; since it is guilt that prevents us from looking at our specialness, thus sustaining the ego and keeping its true nature hidden, it is looking without judgment at our attack thoughts that undoes the ego: thus, looking at the ego without guilt and fear is the essence of the Atonement. (see: bringing darkness (illusions) to the light (truth))

Remember that the phrase, "the Atonement," refers to what is sometimes called the Holy Spirit's, or God's "plan" for coming to accept the principle that separation is not true, therefore sin, guilt and fear are without foundation in truth and all of perception is illusion. Thus, the ideas of Atonement and an "Atonement plan" represent yet another aspect from which to consider the many-faceted jewel of forgiveness. To repeat what we said in chapter eight:

> It can be said that the miracle involves accepting the "Atonement principle" that the separation never happened since that principle is the foundation stone of forgiveness and the Holy Spirit's right-minded thought system. In the Course, the term *Atonement* refers both to this principle and to what is called "God's plan" or the "Holy Spirit's plan" for undoing the belief in separation (i.e., sin). Here again, Jesus is using metaphor to communicate with us, and elsewhere in the Course points out that in truth God does not plan, nor does it make sense to speak of a "plan" in terms of the Holy Spirit's *knowledge* which includes the truth that there is no future to plan for, nor any past which could inform an effort to plan. All that the miracle and Atonement do is restore to our minds the eternal truth that the ego had us dissociate. So, neither the miracle nor the Course's Atonement "do" anything. They simply remove the barriers to the Memory of God and our true Identity that was always present. The idea of an "Atonement plan" simply refers to the *seeming process* of forgiveness in time...

Note in Wapnick's definition the emphasis upon looking at the ego *without judgment*, therefore without reinforcing guilt. In this regard it is interesting that one of Carl Roger's necessary conditions for psychotherapeutic success was non-judgment on the part of the therapist. Rogers had no understanding of *guilt*, *mind* and *right-minded* as discussed in Jesus' psychology, but, like Dr. Siegel, he observed something of profound importance based on his own experience and understanding. What is crucial here from Jesus' perspective is that observing one's ego thought system without guilt and judgment is not possible unless one looks from the position of right-mindedness, therefore looks with Jesus or the Holy Spirit who know the truth of the Atonement principle and have retained it in our mind. The ego has dissociated our right mind, but forgetting is not the same as annihilating, so the truth remains available to us; therefore non-judgmental self examination is possible, but only if we invite Jesus or the Holy Spirit in: only if we discover how to be right-minded, whatever symbols one wants to use in talking about that. What is important are not the symbols, but actually discovering how to access the mind and allow the miracle of right-mindedness. That can be likened to learning how to enter a parallel universe, which seems like a mysterious and almost impossible feat, but in truth requires less than a fraction of a step aside. Knowledge is ever present, but our addiction to perception keeps us blind:

> See how the body's eyes rest on externals and cannot go beyond. Watch how they stop at nothingness, unable to go beyond the form to meaning. *Nothing so blinding as perception of form.* For sight of form means understanding has been obscured (T-22.III.6:5-8; italics mine).

> Those who seek the light are merely covering their eyes. The light is in them now. Enlightenment is but a recognition, not a change at all. Light is not of the world, yet you who bear the light in you are alien here as well. The light came with you from your native home, and stayed with you because it is your own. It is the only thing you bring with you from Him Who is your Source. It shines in you because it lights your home, and leads you back to where it came from and you are at home (W-pI.188.1:2-8).

Bringing darkness (illusions) to the light (truth) is another way of characterizing looking at the ego, therefore is also central to the process of forgiveness. This represents another facet of forgiveness—one more angle from which to gain a better appreciation. Wapnick's definition is:

> the process of undoing denial and dissociation, expressing the decision to bring our guilt to the light of the Holy Spirit to be looked at and forgiven, rather than fearfully keeping it in the darkness of our unconscious minds where it could never be seen and undone; living in illusions brings sickness and pain, bringing them to truth is healing and salvation.

This definition requires little elaboration, but notice here that the process of forgiveness involves undoing two of the ego's major defenses: denial and dissociation. And we might reiterate what was said in the definition of *forgiveness*, that it also involves undoing the third major ego defense of projection.

This brings us to consider the three-step process involved in forgiveness, which Wapnick has discussed at length in his book *Forgiveness and Jesus*.[1]

Three steps of forgiveness are outlined in ACIM Workbook Lesson 23, "I can escape from the world I see by giving up attack thoughts." Paragraph five of that lessons states:

> The idea for today introduces the thought that you are not trapped in the world you see, because its cause can be changed. This change requires, first, that the cause be identified and then let go, so that it can be replaced. The first two steps in this process require your cooperation. The final one does not. Your images have already been replaced. By taking the first two steps, you will see that this is so (W-pI.23.5).

These could also be called the three steps of psychotherapy and are implicit in the second paragraph previously quoted from the *Psychotherapy Pamphlet* (see page 239). They require the looking within that we have emphasized; and in that looking one must be able to recognize one's projections of guilt. Remember that "projection makes perception," and it is the projection of guilt that made the ego's world, therefore is the *cause* of the "world you see." These projections will always involve some form of attack thinking, and may or may not be acted out in the body. The most common form of attack thinking is that form of judgment which condemns another for being guilty of some sin—some act of selfishness that has encroached upon one's self-defined "rights" to specialness. Our example of "road rage" in chapter five is an excellent case in point. So, the first step in the *process* of forgiveness is to recognize one's projection and be willing to take responsibility for it; be willing to take it back. With regard to psychotherapy, this is indicated in the following sentences from the *Psychotherapy Pamphlet* previously cited on page 239: "The therapist sees in the patient all that he has not forgiven in himself..." (P-2.VI.6:3). "The patient is his screen for the projection of his sins, enabling him to let them go" (P-2.VI.6:6).

The second step in the process which is forgiveness or psychotherapy is to realize that the underlying cause of projection is one's own guilt. In some cases it may be starkly apparent that what one condemns in another is some

---

[1] Wapnick, Kenneth. *Forgiveness and Jesus: the Meeting Place of A COURSE IN MIRACLES and Christianity*, 6th Edition. Temecula, CA: Foundation for *A Course in Miracles*, 1994.

form of something one feels guilty about in oneself. Other times it may not be so apparent, but what would be evident in all forms of judgmental attack thinking is that one accuses another according to one's own ego-based value system. Since guilt is the basis for the ego's value system, guilt is the source of judgment and attack thoughts, whether projected onto others or onto one's self. These projections take the form of some kind of symptom, whether physical of psychological: e.g., whether in the form of a cancer or of anxiety and depression. In ACIM Workbook lesson 134, "Let me perceive forgiveness as it is," Jesus says:

> There is a very simple way to find the door to true forgiveness, and perceive it open wide in welcome. When you feel that you are tempted to accuse someone of sin in any form, do not allow your mind to dwell on what you think he did, for that is self-deception. Ask instead, "Would I accuse myself of doing this?" (W-pI.134.9).

An honest answer to this question would always be "yes." The reason the answer would be "yes" is that only guilt harbored within—only our ego identity—impels us to accuse someone else of sin in any form. And of course, it is only our belief in separation, sin and guilt that impels us to attack ourselves in some form. Ultimately, in fact, any attack is an attack on self, because perceived others are projections of our own mind; they are our brothers in oneness.

So the second step in the forgiveness process involves recognizing our own guilt and then understanding that the belief in guilt represents a *choice*. It represents our choice to believe in separation and identify with the ego. And because it is a choice, it can be "let go," which, in practical terms, means to mentally step back from the ego. The same two sentences previously cited from the *Psychotherapy Pamphlet* also pertain to this second step: "The therapist sees in the patient all that he has not forgiven in himself, and is thus given another chance to look at it, open it to re-evaluation and forgive it" (P-2.VI.6:3). "The patient is his screen for the projection of his sins, enabling him to let them go" (P-2.VI.6:6).

Finally, the third step in the forgiveness process is *not* our responsibility. It is not the therapist who forgives. We do not *do* forgiveness. Our part is to *make way* for it; to undo; to remove "the blocks to the awareness of love's presence" (T-IN.1:7); to accept the Atonement so that the Holy Spirit can take the third step in the process of forgiveness, shining away the darkness of guilt with His light-filled knowledge; to "step back and let Him lead the way" (W-pI.155). The ultimate psychotherapist is the Holy Spirit. All that the human therapist can do is to make it possible for Him to do his work through the therapist. One could say the same of Jesus, since he is

244

a manifestation of the Holy Spirit, but he can also be thought of as the therapist's teacher, or the therapist's therapist ("supervisor," if you like).

Now a practical word is appropriate. While Jesus teaches that what is central to psychotherapy, or any relationship which would become the home of forgiveness, is the *content* of the mind of the one who would forgive, this does not relieve the therapist, or any other helping or healing professional, from the responsibility to be a competent practitioner at the level of form. The behavioral therapist must still accept responsibility for understanding the theory and practice of behavioral therapy and for implementing professional knowledge as competently as he or she is able. A surgeon must still accept responsibility for being a well informed and skillful surgeon. It is true that when forgiveness takes place in the practitioner's mind, it then extends to the mind of the patient and the minds of all others who are in truth joined as one. This is true healing. But it does not abrogate worldly responsibilities, as we have seen in other examples. The world is our classroom and we must be faithful to its requirements, while at the same time learning to be "in the world, but not of it." It is not loving to decide on one's own to take a casual, irresponsible attitude toward worldly responsibilities simply because one has the understanding that the world is an illusion and love heals all things. Humility and willingness make the best of our worldly abilities and talents, and then offer them to be used by Jesus and the Holy Spirit for Their purposes of forgiveness. That's what the third step in the forgiveness process is about, and that is why Jesus says to his students, whether psychotherapists or not:

> What you behold as sickness and as pain, as weakness and as suffering and loss, is but temptation to perceive yourself defenseless and in hell. Yield not to this, and you will see all pain, in every form, wherever it occurs, but disappear as mists before the sun. A miracle has come to heal God's Son, and close the door upon his dreams of weakness, opening the way to his salvation and release. Choose once again what you would have him be, remembering that every choice you make establishes your own identity as you will see it and believe it is.

> Deny me not the little gift I ask, when in exchange I lay before your feet the peace of God, and power to bring this peace to everyone who wanders in the world uncertain, lonely, and in constant fear. For it is given you to join with him, and through the Christ in you unveil his eyes, and let him look upon the Christ in him.

> My brothers in salvation, do not fail to hear my voice and listen to my words. I ask for nothing but your own release. There is no place for hell within a world whose loveliness can yet be so intense and so inclusive it is but a step from there to Heaven. To your tired eyes I bring a vision of a different world, so new and clean and fresh you will forget the pain and

sorrow that you saw before. Yet this a vision is which you must share with everyone you see, for otherwise you will behold it not. To give this gift is how to make it yours. And God ordained, in loving kindness, that it be for you.

Let us be glad that we can walk the world, and find so many chances to perceive another situation where God's gift can once again be recognized as ours! And thus will all the vestiges of hell, the secret sins and hidden hates be gone. And all the loveliness which they concealed appear like lawns of Heaven to our sight, to lift us high above the thorny roads we travelled on before the Christ appeared. Hear me, my brothers, hear and join with me. God has ordained I cannot call in vain, and in His certainty I rest content. For you *will* hear, and you *will* choose again. And in this choice is everyone made free (T-31.VIII. 6:2-9:7).

For this alone I need; that you will hear the words I speak, and give them to the world. You are my voice, my eyes, my feet, my hands through which I save the world. The Self from Which I call to you is but your own. To Him we go together. Take your brother's hand, for this is not a way we walk alone. In him I walk with you, and you with me. Our Father wills His Son be one with Him. What lives but must not then be one with you? (W-pI.rV. IN.9:2-9).

In reading these moving passages, one must keep in mind that Jesus often speaks in metaphor. Everything he speaks of is about *mind, not behavior.* When our mind is joined with Jesus or the Holy Spirit, whatever behavior is most loving in any particular set of worldly circumstances will ensue. *No one can know what is most loving ahead of time,* before the miracle and the third step of forgiveness. Hearing Jesus' words and giving them to the world does not mean that one would necessarily say anything. Taking a brother's hand means to join with him in your mind, not necessarily that bodies would hold hands; further, the brother whose hand you hold may no longer be present in a body, or his body may be located thousands of miles away. Again, the Course is always and ever about the mind, and psychotherapy is always and ever about the mind of the therapist.

Salvation, healing, sickness and *pain* were all mentioned in the brief definition of *bringing the darkness to the light,* and they have been mentioned frequently throughout the material quoted in this book. These are all terms with overlapping meanings which are directly related to forgiveness. We will now give them further consideration.

Salvation is basically a synonym for forgiveness. It is a term with religious connotations that may not seem relevant for psychology, but it is simply a term representing yet another way of considering what forgiveness represents. Wapnick's definition is:

> the Atonement, or undoing of the separation; we are "saved" from our *belief* in the reality of sin and guilt through the change of mind that forgiveness and the miracle bring about.

Some people can relate easily to the idea of needing salvation and being saved, but it may be a foreign and uncomfortable notion for others, particularly the more scientifically inclined or those who have been alienated by blood-of-the-cross, born-again evangelists. As can be seen from the definition, *salvation* is just a term that relates to the sense of needing help and the pleas for help which we discussed at the beginning of this chapter. The only help we need, according to Jesus' psychology, is to accept the Atonement in our own mind, which equates to the miracle, forgiveness and all that is entailed as we have been discussing:

> Salvation's single doctrine is the goal of all therapy. Relieve the mind of the insane burden of guilt it carries so wearily, and healing is accomplished [i.e., healing is accomplished through forgiveness]. The body is not cured. It is merely recognized as what it is. Seen rightly, its purpose can be understood. What is the need for sickness then? Given this single shift, all else will follow. There is no need for complicated change. There is no need for long analyses and wearying discussion and pursuits. The truth is simple, being one for all (P-2.IV.11; bracket mine).

Healing is yet another term that is synonymous with forgiveness, but which represents another angle of perspective on it, this time emphasizing the phenomenon of illness of all sorts, both mental and physical. In fact, all illness *is* mental illness, because it is of the mind. Jesus says in the *Psychotherapy Pamphlet*: "As all therapy is psychotherapy, so all illness is mental illness" (P-2.IV.1:1). "Sickness is insanity because all sickness is mental illness, and in it there are no degrees" (P-2.IV.8:1). Again, the principle that there is no hierarchy of illusions is seen in tandem with the principle that there is no order of difficulty among miracles—no order of difficulty in forgiveness or healing: "Once the professional therapist has realized that minds are joined, he can also recognize that order of difficulty in healing is meaningless" (P-3.II.8:1). "To understand there is no order of difficulty in healing...[the therapist] must also recognize the equality of himself and the patient" (P-3.II.9:4; bracket mine).

The definition of the term *healing* as used in the Course is given by Wapnick in his *Glossary*:

the correction in the mind of the belief in sickness that makes the separation and the body seem real; the effect of joining with another in forgiveness, shifting perception from separate bodies—the source of all sickness—to our shared purpose of healing in this world; since healing is based on the belief that our true Identity is spirit, not the body, sickness of any kind must be illusory, as only a body or ego can suffer; healing thus reflects the principle that there is no order of difficulty in miracles.

An important point about the fact that both sickness and healing are of the mind and in the mind, is that a healed mind may yet be associated with a sick body. It is possible that forgiveness would result in the alleviation of certain symptoms, but not necessarily so. A patient may die of cancer, yet do so with a healed mind, and therefore be at peace in spite of the body's condition. In any case, all bodies seem to die. Forgiveness does not prevent that. However the death of bodies is just as illusory as the appearance that bodies live and become ill. A completely healed mind does not need a body. It is only the mind that suffers from the sickness of believing in separation and guilt which projects a body and seems to inhabit it. And it is only the sick mind suffering from guilt that needs to attack bodies; one's own or that of perceived others.

Likewise, a person may be "cured" of a symptom at the level of form, yet not healed at the level of mind. Therefore, the recovered heart attack patient may continue to be an unpleasant, attacking person whose mind remains infected with the ego thought system. Similarly, a patient may experience the alleviation of certain symptoms of anxiety or depression from psychotherapy which employs techniques focused upon change at the level of form, yet continue in the ways of judgment and attack, now projecting guilt onto others rather than onto self. Such a situation cannot be said to represent true healing from the point of view of Jesus' psychology. Some people get ulcers and other people give them. There's no difference: guilt is guilt; attack is attack, no matter where it is focused.

So, when Jesus talks about healing, he is always talking about the mind with the understanding that the body is irrelevant, because it is not real. As with other practical considerations, this does not mean that one can go from merely having an intellectual understanding of this concept to completely disregarding health and hygiene, but it does mean that a mind at peace can go about the necessary care of the body, its relationships and responsibilities, without fear and without projecting guilt.

> Healing is the change of mind that the Holy Spirit in the patient's mind is seeking for him. And it is the Holy Spirit in the mind of the giver Who gives the gift to him (M-6.4:3-4).

248

It is not the function of God's teachers [e.g., "healers"] to evaluate the outcome of their gifts. It is merely their function to give them. Once they have done that they have also given the outcome, for that is part of the gift. No one can give if he is concerned with the result of giving. That is a limitation on the giving itself, and neither the giver nor the receiver would have the gift. Trust is an essential part of giving; in fact, it is the part that makes sharing possible, the part that guarantees the giver will not lose, but only gain. Who gives a gift and then remains with it, to be sure it is used as the giver deems appropriate? Such is not giving but imprisoning (M-6.3; brackets mine).

This next set of illustrative passages about healing from the *Psychotherapy Pamphlet* concludes with a paragraph that might be regarded as the therapist's prayer. Actually, it could be the prayer of anyone who asks, "How can I help?" It has been placed in italics to distinguish it as a prayer:

Healing is holy. Nothing in the world is holier than helping one who asks for help. And two come very close to God in this attempt, however limited, however lacking in sincerity. Where two have joined for healing, God is there. And He has guaranteed that He will hear and answer them in truth. They can be sure that healing is a process He directs, because it is according to His Will. We have His Word to guide us, as we try to help our brothers. Let us not forget that we are helpless of ourselves, and lean upon a Strength beyond our little scope for what to teach as well as what to learn.

A brother seeking aid can bring us gifts beyond the heights perceived in any dream. He offers us salvation, for he comes to us as Christ and Savior. What he asks is asked by God through him. And what we do for him becomes the gift we give to God. The sacred calling of God's holy Son for help in his perceived distress can be but answered by his Father. Yet He needs a voice through which to speak His holy Word; a hand to reach His Son and touch his heart. In such a process, who could not be healed? This holy interaction is the plan of God Himself, by which His Son is saved....

Somewhere all gifts of God must be received. In time no effort can be made in vain. It is not our perfection that is asked in our attempts to heal. We are deceived already, if we think there is a need of healing. And the truth will come to us only through one who seems to share our dream of sickness. Let us help him to forgive himself for all the trespasses with which he would condemn himself without a cause. His healing is our own. And as we see the sinlessness in him come shining   through the veil of guilt that shrouds the Son of God, we will behold in him the face of Christ, and understand that it is but our own.

> *Let us stand silently before God's Will, and do what it has chosen that we do. There is one way alone by which we come to where all dreams began. And it is there that we will lay them down, to come away in peace forever. Hear a brother call for help and answer him. It will be God to Whom you answer, for you called on Him. There is no other way to hear His Voice. There is no other way to seek His Son. There is no other way to find your Self. Holy is healing, for the Son of God returns to Heaven through its kind embrace. For healing tells him, in the Voice for God, that all his sins have been forgiven him* (P-2.V.4-5, 7-8; italics mine).

Sickness is, of course, the idea which makes healing seem necessary. We have seen that in the Course all sickness is of the mind, and in the mind there is basically only one sickness: the belief in separation which spawned the entire ego thought systems and all of its manifestations. One of those manifestations is the body, so it can be said that the body itself is a symptom of a sickness in the mind. And the belief that the body can be sick, whether psychologically or physically, serves to further reinforce the belief in separation, therefore reinforces the seeming reality of the ego, our self, and the self-importance of our specialness. That is why there is a lesson in the ACIM Workbook entitled, "Sickness is a defense against the truth" (W-pI.136).

In the Wapnick *Glossary*, sickness is defined as follows:

> a conflict in the mind (guilt) displaced onto the body; the ego's attempt to defend itself against truth (spirit) by focusing attention on the body; a sick body is the *effect* of the sick or split mind that is its *cause*, representing the ego's desire to make others guilty by sacrificing oneself, projecting responsibility for the attack onto them. (see: suffering)

A rather surprising aspect of sickness suggested in this definition is that we *want* to be sick: sickness is a *choice* which serves ego purposes that we want served. It serves the purpose of making the body and the self seem real, but also serves the purpose of projecting guilt. In conventional psychology this is referred to as "secondary gain"—that is, the seeming benefit to the self that accrues from being able to use one's own pain and suffering for purposes of attack in an attempt to inspire guilt and sympathy in others. This is a common enough form of attack and manipulation that most people will have observed it, if not in themselves then in others who use their sickness both to punish as well as manipulate. Thus, the sick person attacks as well as seeks to elicit sympathy and bind friends and family members to them in service through guilt. Nursing homes are often a show place for this kind of victimization drama.

250

Inevitably, guilt-inspired service to the ill and infirm carries resentment with it. In turn, such resentment easily becomes a reason to display suffering which the "unappreciated and unjustly treated" ministering person will use to wear the face of victim, just as the patient has, and for the same purposes of manipulation and projecting guilt. When these charades of guilt are seen through right-minded eyes, they do not become a reason for judgment and resentment, but are recognized as cries for love and forgiveness which issue forth from minds in pain; minds which believe they are separate and have forever lost their innocence as Christ.

In the ACIM Manual for Teachers there is an excellent summary of sickness and healing presented in sections five through six: "How is Healing Accomplished?" (M-5), "Is Healing Certain?" (M-6), and "Should Healing Be Repeated?" (M-7). Below is a series of excerpts from the first of these sections. These will serve to both elaborate upon and integrate the concepts of sickness and healing as they relate to Jesus' psychology, and particularly as they relate to psychotherapy. In some sentences found in these passages we have substituted the word "therapist" for "teacher of God" and "physician" in order to make them more directly relevant to the current discussion. In so doing, we are assuming that the therapist is willing to undertake responsibility for accepting the Atonement in his or her own mind, and further understands that psychotherapy, healing and forgiveness are the same process; a process of changing thought systems in the mind. An effective therapist, according to Jesus, would be a "teacher of God"—a teacher of forgiveness by example. Again, the therapist is responsible only for his or her own mind:

> Healing involves an understanding of what the illusion of sickness is for [so Jesus is returning to the fundamental question of motivation: "What is the *purpose*?"]....
>
> Healing is accomplished the instant the sufferer no longer sees any value in pain. Who would choose suffering unless he thought it brought him something, and something of value to him? He must think it is a small price to pay for something of greater worth. For sickness is an election; a decision....
>
> Healing must occur in exact proportion to which the valuelessness of sickness is recognized. One need but say, "There is no gain at all to me in this" and he is healed. But to say this, one first must recognize certain facts. First, it is obvious that decisions are of the mind, not of the body... The resistance to recognizing this is enormous, because the existence of the world as you perceive it depends on the body being the decision maker.

Terms like "instincts," "reflexes" and the like represent attempts to endow the body with non-mental motivators. Actually, such terms merely state or describe the problem. They do not answer it. [The problem here is the ego's reversal of cause and effect wherein the body is assigned the power of cause and the mind is the effect of the body. This is identical to the widespread and very common assumption that the mind is somehow a function of the brain, which we have discussed in chapter two and subsequently throughout.]

The acceptance of sickness as a decision of the mind, for a purpose for which it would use the body, is the basis of healing. And this is so for healing in all forms...Who is the... [therapist]? Only the mind of the patient himself. [But note that therapists themselves are patients. When they allow their own minds to be healed, that healing extends to all minds.]....

What is the single requisite for this shift in perception? It is simply this; the recognition that sickness is of the mind, and has nothing to do with the body. What does this recognition "cost"? It costs the whole world you see, for the world will never again appear to rule the mind. For with this recognition is responsibility placed where it belongs; not with the world, but on him who looks on the world and sees it as it is not. He looks on what he chooses to see. No more and no less. The world does nothing to him. He only thought it did. Nor does he do anything to the world, because he was mistaken about what it is. Herein is the release from guilt and sickness both, for they are one. Yet to accept this release, the insignificance of the body must be an acceptable idea....

If the patient must change his mind in order to be healed, what does the... [therapist] do? Can he change the patient's mind for him? Certainly not. For those already willing to change their minds he has no function except to rejoice with them, for they have become teachers of God with him. He has, however, a more specific function for those who do not understand what healing is. These patients do not realize they have chosen sickness. On the contrary, they believe that sickness has chosen them. Nor are they open-minded on this point. [In other words, resistance to therapy is inevitable.] The body tells them what to do and they obey. They have no idea how insane this concept is. If they even suspected it, they would be healed. Yet they suspect nothing. To them the separation is quite real.

To them God's teachers come, to represent another choice which they had forgotten. The simple presence of a teacher of God is a reminder. His thoughts ask for the right to question what the patient has accepted as true. As God's messengers, His teachers are the symbols of salvation. They ask the patient for forgiveness for God's Son in his own Name [i.e., they ask the patient to accept forgiveness for himself, thus restoring his innocence as God's Son]. They stand for the Alternative. [In other words, the therapist is a teacher by example, and what is taught that is of importance is the *content* of accepting the Atonement, regardless of the form, or techniques of therapy.] With God's Word [the Holy Spirit; the Atonement] in their minds they come in benediction, not to heal the sick but to remind them of the remedy God has already given them. It is not their hands [e.g., techniques] that heal. It is not their voice that speaks the Word of God. They merely give what has been given them [i.e., forgiveness]. Very gently they call to their brothers to turn away from death: "Behold, you Son of God, what Life [God, Oneness, spirit] can offer you. Would you choose sickness in place of this?"

Not once do the advanced teachers of God consider the forms of sickness in which their brother believes. To do this is to forget that all of them have the same purpose, and therefore are not really different. They seek for God's Voice [i.e., the Holy Spirit] in this brother who would so deceive himself as to believe God's Son can suffer. And they remind him that he did not make himself, and must remain as God created him. They recognize illusions can have no effect. The truth in their minds reaches out to the truth in the minds of their brothers, so that illusions are not reinforced. They are thus brought to truth; truth is not brought to them. [This is the same as bringing the darkness to the light rather than attempting to bring the light of truth—Jesus or the Holy Spirit—out of the mind into the world of illusions; it is rising up to the level of mind as cause rather than according the body reality; recognizing that the miracle changes the mind, not the body and the world]. So are they dispelled, not by the will of another [i.e., by magic], but by the union of the One Will with Itself. And this is the function of God's teachers; to see no will as separate from their own, nor theirs as separate from God's (M-5.1:1; M-5.I.1:1-4; M-5.II.1:1; 2:1-2, 5-6; III.1-3; brackets mine).

There is a curious and difficult-to-understand twist in Jesus view of sickness and healing which arises out of his non-dualistic view of mind, with the understanding that sickness is basically the mind's idea that duality is truth. Since even the split mind is *one*, healing is accomplished when only one *seemingly* separate mind joins with another in a shared purpose, thus overcoming the illusion of separation. But the idea of sickness (separation) is maintained when two seemingly separated minds agree that sickness (separation) is real. The following passages address this rather difficult point of understanding. In reading them, as always, it is important to remember that Jesus teaches sickness is in the mind, not in the body, which is merely an out-picturing of the basic mental illness of believing in separation. The focus of the following passages is upon sickness as manifested in physical symptoms, but it is equally applicable to symptoms of "mental illness:"

No mind is sick until another mind agrees that they are separate. And thus it is their joint decision to be sick. [i.e., sickness is separation and all symptoms arise from the guilt and fear which follow separation].

253

If you withhold agreement and accept the part you play in making sickness real, the other mind cannot project its guilt without your aid in letting it perceive itself as separate and apart from you. [Hence, the therapist must take responsibility for his or her own mind and for healing the belief in separation therein.] Thus is the body not perceived as sick [i.e., interpreted as real, with suffering seen as real] by both your minds from separate points of view. Uniting with a brother's mind prevents the cause of sickness and perceived effects [i.e., overcomes separation and guilt]. Healing is the effect of minds that join, as sickness comes from minds that separate.

The miracle does nothing just *because* the minds are joined, and cannot separate. Yet in the dreaming has this been reversed, and separate minds are seen as bodies, which are separated and which cannot join. Do not allow your brother to be sick, for if he is, have you abandoned him to his own dream by sharing it with him [in other words, do not support a brother's belief that he is sick (separate) by sharing it with him through "false empathy," a concept we will discuss a little later). He has not seen the cause of sickness where it is [i.e., in the mind], and you have overlooked the gap between you, where the sickness has been bred [i.e., the gap of believing that you are separate]. Thus are you joined in sickness, to preserve the little gap unhealed, where sickness is kept carefully protected, cherished, and upheld by firm belief, lest God should come to bridge the little gap that leads to Him. [Remember that the ego fears God and fears oneness.] Fight not His coming with illusions, for it is His coming that you want above all things that seem to glisten in the dream.

The end of dreaming is the end of fear, and love was never in the world of dreams. The gap *is* little. Yet it holds the seeds of pestilence and every form of ill, because it is a wish to keep apart and not to join. And thus it seems to give a cause to sickness which is not its cause [i.e., the belief that the body and world are the cause of sickness]. The purpose of the gap is all the cause that sickness has. For it was made to keep you separated, in a body which you see as if it were the cause of pain.

The cause of pain is separation, not the body, which is only its effect [i.e., the body is itself a symptom of sickness in the mind] (T-28.III. 2-5:1; brackets mine).

To simplify this difficult set of passages in a practical way, the point is again to take responsibility for your own mind and your belief in separation. When you react in a way that makes the other's suffering seem real—for instance with panic or suffering of your own—you merely make matters worse for both of you. When you minister to another's suffering from that place of peace in your mind that knows the body, self, separation and death are not real, *then* you can be truly helpful. This involves having a kind of double vision that on the one hand sees the body and its suffering, and on the other hand knows that what you see is a projection of your own mind; knows that the body and suffering are not the truth. Thus, one can be at peace; having at least temporarily healed one's own belief in separation and sickness while, at the same time, acting at the level of the world to minister in a peaceful, kind and loving way to one who suffers. Since everything we perceive is a projection of our own mind, and our interpretation of what we see is the result of the thought system we choose, any distress we experience at the perceived plight of others is a reflection of our own inner distress. That distress is a form of guilt over the belief in separation. Seeing and understanding this, one is then in a place to step back and ask for the miracle of right-mindedness. Forgiveness knows that pain and suffering are unreal and that we would not be reacting emotionally to them unless we harbored the pain and suffering of guilt within. In other words, we have projected our interpretation of what we see based on what we believe, and then we identify with our projection. In the case of a sick and suffering person, we can either join him in sickness and suffering, making matters worse and reinforcing separation, or we can allow our perception of sickness and suffering to be undone. In the latter case, we are at peace, and can then act out of peace and forgiveness in the world. That is why Jesus says the following things about the miracle:

> The miracle does nothing. All it does is to undo (T-28.I.1:1-2).

> A miracle is a correction. It does not create, nor really change at all. It merely looks on devastation, and reminds the mind that what it sees is false. It undoes error, but does not attempt to go beyond perception, nor exceed the function of forgiveness (W-pII.13.1:1-4).

Another way to get a practical handle on this is to ask oneself: What sort of person do I want present when I am sick and suffering? Do I want someone who believes I am only a body and who gets upset at my discomfort, acting out of pity with a sense of crisis and panic? Or, do I want to be cared for by someone who knows the truth of spirit and that we are joined as one mind and spirit; who is peaceful and loving, helping and joining with me, but who does not make a big deal out of my distress even if I am very depressed and suicidal, or suffering from an illness that threatens the life of my body?

Yet another question one might ask in attempting to understand this point is: "How would Jesus respond to suffering of any kind?" And then recall how Jesus responded when his person was under attack and his own body was mortally wounded and dying:

I have made it perfectly clear that I am like you and you are like me, but our fundamental equality can be demonstrated only through joint decision. You are free to perceive yourself as persecuted [e.g., victimized, sick and suffering] if you choose. When you do choose to react that way, however, you might remember that I was persecuted as the world judges, and did not share this evaluation for myself. And because I did not share it, I did not strengthen it. I therefore offered a different interpretation of attack [and sickness of any kind *is* attack, because it comes from the belief in separation which equates to attack], and one which I want to share with you. If you will believe it, you will help me teach it (T-6.I.5; brackets mine).

Suffering was discussed in chapter five, but since it is a term referenced under *sickness*, we will discuss it again in the context of psychotherapy, healing and forgiveness. In the Course, sickness, suffering and pain are equivalent terms which denote not only an inevitable component of the ego thought system, but a *requirement* of that thought system. Belief in the ego *demands* suffering and death. In our identification with the ego, we must *want* suffering. As with sickness, suffering and pain are expressions of guilt which follow from the mind's acceptance of the belief in separation. They serve the purpose of making the body, therefore separation, seem real, as well as serving the purpose of attack: the projection of guilt onto something or someone other than self.

To repeat the definition of *suffering* found in the Wapnick *Glossary*:

one of the basic ego witnesses to the reality of the body and the non-existence of spirit, since the body appears to experience suffering or pain; to be in pain, therefore, is to deny God, while being aware of our true invulnerability as God's Son is to deny the reality of pain. (Note -- suffering and pain are used as virtual synonyms.)

Pain and suffering are symptoms—expressions of the fear of God which follows guilt over the "sin" of separation—and can be experienced as either physical or emotional. They are different forms of the same underlying belief and purpose, and they represent a choice which psychotherapy (forgiveness) must undo. The above definition refers to the following passages, which provide a comprehensive view of suffering and pain from the perspective of *A Course in Miracles*:

Pain is a wrong perspective. When it is experienced in any form, it is a proof of self-deception. It is not a fact at all. There is no form it takes that will not disappear if seen aright. For pain proclaims God cruel. How could it be real in any form? It witnesses to God the Father's hatred of His Son, the sinfulness He sees in him, and His insane desire for revenge and death.

Can such projections be attested to? Can they be anything but wholly false? Pain is but witness to the Son's mistakes in what he thinks he is. It is a dream of fierce retaliation for a crime that could not be committed; for attack on what is wholly unassailable. It is a nightmare of abandonment by an Eternal Love, Which could not leave the Son whom It created out of love.

Pain is a sign illusions reign in place of truth. It demonstrates God is denied, confused with fear, perceived as mad, and seen as traitor to Himself. If God is real, there is no pain. If pain is real, there is no God. For vengeance is not part of love. And fear, denying love and using pain to prove that God is dead, has shown that death is victor over life. The body is the Son of God, corruptible in death, as mortal as the Father he has slain.

Peace to such foolishness! The time has come to laugh at such insane ideas. There is no need to think of them as savage crimes, or secret sins with weighty consequence. Who but a madman could conceive of them as cause of anything? Their witness, pain, is mad as they, and no more to be feared than the insane illusions which it shields, and tries to demonstrate must still be true.

It is your thoughts alone that cause you pain. Nothing external to your mind can hurt or injure you in any way. There is no cause beyond yourself that can reach down and bring oppression. No one but yourself affects you. There is nothing in the world that has the power to make you ill or sad, or weak or frail. But it is you who have the power to dominate all things you see by merely recognizing what you are. As you perceive the harmlessness in them, they will accept your holy will as theirs. And what was seen as fearful now becomes a source of innocence and holiness (W-pI.190.1-5).

Another surprising aspect of Jesus' view of pain is that it serves the same purpose as physical and emotional pleasure: the "pleasures" of specialness. Those pleasures, like pain, serve to keep us focused upon our personal self and identified with the body to the exclusion of our identity as mind and the presence of the Holy Spirit in our mind. Recall that Jesus teaches true pleasure is spiritual in nature: "All real pleasure comes from doing God's will" (T-1.VII.1:4):

Pain demonstrates the body [therefore the individual self] must be real. It is a loud, obscuring voice whose shrieks would silence what the Holy Spirit says, and keep His words from your awareness. Pain [which includes such emotional pain as depression] compels attention, drawing it away from Him and focusing upon itself [and your self]. Its purpose is the same as pleasure, for they both are means to make the body [and the separate self] real. What shares a common purpose is the same.

This is the law of purpose, which unites all those who share in it within itself. Pleasure and pain are equally unreal, because their purpose cannot be achieved. Thus are they means for nothing, for they have a goal without a meaning. And they share the lack of meaning which their purpose has.

Sin [e.g., self centeredness; seeking special status and special love] shifts from pain to pleasure, and again to pain. For either witness is the same, and carries but one message: "You are here, within this body, and you can be hurt. You can have pleasure, too, but only at the cost of pain." These witnesses are joined by many more. Each one seems different because it has a different name [or form], and so it seems to answer to a different sound. Except for this, the witnesses of sin are all alike. Call pleasure pain, and it will hurt. Call pain a pleasure, and the pain behind the pleasure will be felt no more. Sin's witnesses but shift from name to name, as one steps forward and another back. Yet which is foremost makes no difference. Sin's witnesses hear but the call of death (T-27.VI.1-2; brackets mine).

An excellent example of the compelling and luxurious nature of emotional pain and pleasure in service of the ego can be found in soap operas. Those televised dramas invite the viewer to identify with the characters through projection and then to become caught up in the self-serving "luxuries" of specialness: special love and special hate. In fact, news programs and all other forms of media entertainment serve the same purpose, which means that they can also serve the purpose of self observation and forgiveness. Anything on television that elicits any form of emotional response from the viewer is evidence of some aspect of unforgiven guilt within the mind of the viewer. This is the same point that Jesus was making about psychotherapists in P-2.VI.5 quoted on page 239 where he says: "The patient is his screen for the projection of his sins, enabling him to let them go" (P-2.VI.5:6).

In the following paragraphs from the *Psychotherapy Pamphlet*, the strong attraction of guilt which motivates clinging to pain and resistance to change—resistance to letting go of ego identity—is addressed in the context of therapy. Again, the point is that sickness, pain and suffering serve an ego purpose, and as long as ego identity seems desirable, the individual will cherish his or her sickness, pain and suffering. All that is expected of the therapist, then, is that the patient would be made a little more comfortable as a separated self dedicated to specialness. Indeed, that is the purpose that most worldly psychotherapists attempt to serve, but ultimately it is impossible to serve that purpose, as should be apparent from our previous descriptions of the ego thought system and its specialness way of life. Note that the three steps of forgiveness are again implied in this excerpt:

The process of psychotherapy, then, can be defined simply as forgiveness, for no healing can be anything else. The unforgiving are sick, believing they are unforgiven [i.e. guilty]. The hanging-on to guilt, its hugging-close and sheltering, its loving protection and alert defense,—all this is but the grim refusal to forgive. "God may not enter here" the sick repeat, over and over, while they mourn their loss and yet rejoice in it [because suffering and guilt seem to establish the reality of separation and the self]. Healing occurs as a patient begins to hear the dirge he sings, and questions its validity [e.g., the first step in forgiveness: being willing to look at one's projection and take responsibility for it]. Until he hears it, he cannot understand that it is he who sings it to himself. To hear it is the first step in recovery. To question it must then become his choice [e.g., the second step in forgiveness: recognizing that guilt represents a choice].

There is a tendency, and it is very strong, to hear this song of death only an instant, and then dismiss it uncorrected [i.e., to stop before the second forgiveness step is completed thus preventing the third]. These fleeting awarenesses represent the many opportunities given us literally "to change our tune" [i.e., change our mind]. The sound of healing can be heard instead. But first the willingness to question the "truth" of the song of condemnation [i.e., projection] must arise. The strange distortions woven inextricably into the self-concept, itself but a pseudo-creation, make this ugly sound seem truly beautiful [i.e., the ego is attracted to guilt because it serves to sustain the ego thought system in our mind: *we* are attracted to guilt for its exquisite proof of body and self]. "The rhythm of the universe," "the herald angel's song," all these and more are heard instead of loud discordant shrieks [and so forgiveness—therapy—may not yet succeed; an example here of resistance] (P-2.VI. 1-2; brackets mine).

The subjects of healing, sickness, suffering and pain naturally lead to the subject of empathy, which has been regarded as an important dimension in psychotherapy ever since the work of Carl Rogers. We will next discuss Jesus' approach to this subject.

Empathy

A little known work of Carl Rogers, which must nevertheless have taken considerable time and effort on his part, was published in 1959 in the third volume of a collection edited by Sigmund Koch: *Psychology: the Study of a Science.*[1] Rogers titled this writing, "A Theory of Therapy, Personality, and Interpersonal Relationships as Developed in the Client-Centered Framework." In writing this, he attempted to flesh out a rather complete

---

[1] Rogers, Carl R. "A Theory of Therapy, Personality and Interpersonal relationships, As Developed in the Client-Centered Framework." In *Psychology: A Study of a Science: Formulations of the Person and the Social Context.* Sigmund Koch, ed. New York: McGraw-Hill Book Company, 1959.

statement of theory and derivative hypotheses in terms that would lend themselves to scientific investigation. While this work has received very little attention, it provides some useful, succinct definitions of terms and concepts related to Client-Centered Theory. In it, Rogers defines *empathy* as follows:

> The state of empathy, or being empathic, is to perceive the internal frame of reference of another with accuracy, and with the emotional components and meanings which pertain thereto, as if one were the other person, but without ever losing the "as if" condition. Thus it means to sense the hurt or the pleasure of another as he senses it, and to perceive the causes thereof as he perceives them, but without ever losing the recognition that it is *as if* I were hurt or pleased, etc. If this "as if" quality is lost, then the state is one of identification.[2]

In general, therapists recognize the difference between sympathy and empathy, as well as the distinction Rogers' makes between empathy and losing one's self in identification with the patient. Actually however, speaking in terms of Jesus' psychology, that is exactly what the ego tries to do: identify with the ego in another and thereby strengthen itself. In the Course, Jesus makes a distinction between "true empathy" and what can be called "false empathy," a term Jesus does not use, but which is implied by his use of its opposite. The opening paragraphs of the ACIM Text section entitled "True Empathy" follow:

> To empathize does not mean to join in suffering, for that is what you must *refuse* to understand. That is the ego's interpretation of empathy, and is always used to form a special relationship in which the suffering is shared. The capacity to empathize is very useful to the Holy Spirit, provided you let Him use it in His way. His way is very different. He does not understand suffering, and would have you teach it is not understandable. When He relates through you, He does not relate through your ego to another ego. He does not join in pain, understanding that healing pain is not accomplished by delusional attempts to enter into it, and lighten it by sharing the delusion.

> The clearest proof that empathy as the ego uses it is destructive lies in the fact that it is applied only to certain types of problems and in certain people. These it selects out, and joins with. And it never joins except to strengthen itself. Having identified with what it thinks it understands, the ego sees itself and would increase itself by sharing what is like itself. Make no mistake about this maneuver; the ego always empathizes to weaken, and to weaken is always to attack. You do not know what empathizing means. Yet of this you may be sure; if you will merely sit quietly by and let the Holy Spirit relate through you, you will empathize with strength, and will gain in strength and not in weakness (T-16.I.1-2).

---

[2] ibid, p. 210-11

Jesus' basic point is that it is not helpful to empathize with a person in a way that reinforces both the therapist's and patient's sense of a separate self and identification as a body. Therapy which strengthens the patient's ego would only be regarded as useful in the context of *A Course in Miracles* if it were regarded as a temporary magical expedient necessary to help an individual function in the world so that he or she might then be in a better position to transcend the self through forgiveness. The therapist is capable of knowing the difference between magic and miracles—true empathy and false empathy—so that healing the body or strengthening the ego of the patient can be done with a genuine attitude of love rather than special love. This is similar to the situation with children that we discussed in chapter three; and also similar to the point about the importance of content versus form in teaching, which was addressed in chapter nine. In medicine as well as psychotherapy this would mean practicing the magic necessary to alleviate certain symptoms through some form of treatment, but with the understanding that true healing is of the mind. The physician or therapist can engage in the practice of magic with an attitude of forgiveness and true empathy. This involves offering the miracle of forgiveness in a way that the patient can understand and accept—what might be called a loving "bedside manner:"

> The value of the Atonement [i.e., forgiveness] does not lie in the manner in which it is expressed. In fact, if it is used truly, it will inevitably be expressed in whatever way is most helpful to the receiver. This means that a miracle, to attain its full efficacy, must be expressed in a language [or some form] that the recipient can understand without fear. This does not necessarily mean that this is the highest level of communication of which he is capable. It does mean, however, that it is the highest level of communication of which he is capable *now* (T-2.IV.5; brackets mine).

What Jesus means by "true empathy" is to identify with the strength of Christ, our True Identity, in both the therapist and patient. False empathy basically identifies with the weakness of the ego. This does not mean that it is unimportant for the therapist to deeply hear and understand the patient's concerns—what Rogers called accurately perceiving the internal frame of reference of the patient—but it means that such understanding would come from a detached, right-minded perspective that knows pain and suffering are illusion. They do not represent who the patient is in truth, but result from the patient's choice for the ego. No therapist can listen in this way without having set his or her own ego aside, which is what it means to be right-minded. That is why, in terms of *A Course in Miracles*, the therapeutic relationship constitutes a classroom in forgiveness for the therapist.

261

In ACIM Workbook Lesson 92 there is a clear statement contrasting what it means to join with another out of strength or weakness. This is the same lesson which earlier asserts that our senses do not sense nor does our brain actually think. It is the mind that senses and thinks, hence in order for there to be true empathy, the therapist must think with Jesus or the Holy Spirit Who represent what Jesus sometimes calls the "Christ Mind." To think with the Holy Spirit and perceive from His thought system of the Atonement is to be able to look past the weakness of the ego to the strength of Christ in a brother, which is the reflection of Christ's strength in one's own mind. Thus, the principle that "projection makes perception" applies to right-mindedness where projection becomes a worldly form of extension—a *reflection* of creation, which is the extension of the Love of God in Heaven:

> It is your weakness that sees through the body's eyes, peering about in darkness to behold the likeness of itself; the small, the weak, the sickly and the dying, those in need, the helpless and afraid, the sad, the poor, the starving and the joyless. These are seen through eyes that cannot see and cannot bless.

> Strength overlooks these things by seeing past appearances. It keeps its steady gaze upon the light that lies beyond them. It unites with light, of which it is a part. It sees itself. It brings the light in which your Self appears. In darkness you perceive a self that is not there. Strength is the truth about you; weakness is an idol falsely worshipped and adored that strength may be dispelled, and darkness rule where God appointed that there should be light (W-pI.92.3:3-4:7).

To relate to another out of true empathy is to recognize that he or she is not a body but is mind, and has the same right mind, and the same capacity to choose right-mindedness, that I have. It is to recognize that minds are joined. The love in my mind seeks to join with itself in the mind of what appear to be others. This has nothing to do with bodies. Jesus is clear that bodies cannot join. At the same time, the ego always seeks to join with itself, so when we look out from the ego thought system in our mind, we look to join with weakness and suffering, and to make separation real. What the ego calls joining or empathy is concern for bodies and suffering, pity, sympathy and compassion for pain which has its roots in guilt. The empathy of the world as directed by the ego is some form of special love, which is a great temptation for therapists, and why Jesus emphasizes that they must heal their own mind lest they not help but hinder by reinforcing specialness and making the error of separation seem even more real.

To further clarify Jesus' view of empathy, as well as the contrast between true empathy and false empathy, following are presented some excerpted remarks from Kenneth Wapnick's workshop entitled "True Empathy"[3] which is based on the first section in ACIM Text Chapter 16 with the same title. In these excerpts we have elided some words and phrases, and inserted some bracketed words by way of editorial clarification:

> Sickness works just as effectively [as a defense] whether I believe I'm the one who's sick, or I believe someone else is sick. Dynamically, they are exactly the same, whether I identify with your pain and suffering, or I feel it in myself. It doesn't matter, because either way the body and suffering have been made real, which the ego interprets as punishment from God. All suffering that the body experiences, whether we personally experience it or other people experience it and we identify with it, the ego interprets as proof that God has broken through our defenses, found us out and is now going to take back what we stole from Him....

> ...false empathy... [is] when we identify with someone's weakness instead of someone's strength. The weakness is not of the body; the seeming weakness of the body is the reflection of the weakness of the ego thought system, which is weak because it opposes the strength of God. The strength of Christ in ourselves and in each other is the reflection of the presence of the Holy Spirit. That is what true empathy is: we empathize with the strength of Christ in each other rather than with the weakness of the ego....

> Another way of explaining the ego thought system is to say that the ego has made victimization real in the mind. The original victim from the ego's point of view is God, and we are the victimizer. We have victimized God. We have stolen from Him. Then the ego turns it around: God is hurt. God is angry. God is wrathful. God is going to victimize us. We become the innocent victims, and He is the mean victimizer. Since that is the original ego thought that was projected out into the world, the world then becomes a place of victimization....

> What is really important to understand is the motivation behind our perceiving pain and suffering and injustice in the world. And the ego never tells us what its ultimate purpose is. Its ultimate purpose is always murder (T-24.II.12:6). The ego would never let us recognize that "what is not love is murder" (T-23.IV.1:10), and nothing here is love. So it tells us its version of love. Its version of love is compassion, concern, pity, feeling sorry for people, taking care of people, ministering to people, taking away people's pain, etc., and we call that love. The ego never tells us its ultimate purpose, which is to kill.

[3] A transcript of this workshop on "True Empathy" may be read on the World Wide Web at: http://www.facim.org/excerpts/s2e1.htm The original cassette tape set is available from the Foundation for *A Course in Miracles*, Temecula, CA.

Instead it makes up a world of pain and suffering, and tells us we will be the good people, and we will undo pain and suffering in the world. These are the do-gooders in the world. That is why Jesus says, "Trust not your good intentions. They are not enough" (T-18.IV.2:1-2)....

This does not mean that, on a behavioral level, I don't do something for someone in the world. It means that if I do, I don't do it out of weakness or pity. I don't do it out of feeling sorry for the person. I do it because I am answering that person's call for love on the level that that person can accept it. Whenever anybody is in pain, that person is saying, "I have turned the Love of God into an enemy, and I am being punished. I now need a happy dream which ends that pain." And so I join with that person seemingly to end the...pain, which I may have the power to do. But what I am really doing by ending another's...pain is giving a message that says God is not angry at you, and by my love and my peace I am reflecting for you the love and peace that is inside you. Just as I was able to make a choice not to make your error real, not to make guilt or sin real, so can you make the same choice. On the level of form or behavior I may do exactly what someone else does, but my motivation will be different. I will be doing it from a place of strength, not weakness. It is not my heart that goes out to you; it is the light in my mind that calls to the light in your mind. It is not that I identify with your weakness. The strength of Christ in me calls to your mind to make the same choice I did, which is to join with the strength of Christ in you. That is the joining. I do not join with you on the level of the body. That is not joining. I join with you in my mind, which means part of my mind is able to look beyond the appearances and sees whatever is going on in this world as an expression of the call for the Love of God that you believe you have separated from....

To the ego joining always means joining with itself. We discussed how in the original ontological instant when the decision maker had to make his choice, he joined with the ego instead of with the Holy Spirit. From that joining, which is really a pseudo-joining, because it is joining with nothing, the whole world is made. We continually join with this limited and separated self that is the ego. In the world, the limited and separated self is no longer in the mind but is in the body, and so joining for us in the world is joining with other people. There is an important line in the text that says "Minds are joined; bodies are not" (T-18.VI.3:1). Bodies do not join. When we find ourselves in sympathy and empathizing with people who are in pain, or identifying with a particular group against another group, we are identifying and joining with their bodies. That is not joining, because we are joining with an illusion. We are joining with weakness instead of strength.

In true joining, we change our minds and move away from the ego and back to the Holy Spirit. That is the meeting place that the lesson talked about, the meeting place of the little "s" self with the capital "S" Self. The capital "S" Self is represented for us in the dream by the Holy Spirit, Who reminds us of the Self we are as Christ....

..."I Need Do Nothing"...is probably the most important theme in the Course—that we don't have to do anything. We simply have to accept truth and reality for what they are. In the context of... [true empathy], this means we do not have to do anything about people's problems. We do not have to feel bad for people and try to solve their problems, because it is always the ego that wants to do something. We can see how nicely this fits into the whole ego trap. Right at the beginning the ego told us that we have to do something. A real problem exists in the mind, which has been transformed into a battleground. The real problem is God's wrath and vengeance, and we must do something about it. The "doing" took the form of having a defense against that fear, and the world became that fortress....

You know you are involved with false empathy rather than true empathy when you feel impelled to do something: You *have* to comfort somebody; you *have* to solve the problem; you *have* to remedy the situation; you *have* to relieve the pain; you *have* to do something. What we are talking about is not what you do on a behavioral level, but the impetus that you feel within you, the *need* that you have to do something. In true empathy you do not do anything. The Love of God simply does it through you, but you do not have a *need* to help anybody else.[4]

We conclude this discussion of empathy with another selection from "True Empathy" found in Text Chapter 16. These words apply to anyone, but can be thought of as being addressed directly to a psychotherapist:

Your part is only to remember this; you do not want anything you value to come of a relationship. You choose neither to hurt it nor to heal it in your own way. You do not know what healing is. All you have learned of empathy is from the past. And there is nothing from the past that you would share, for there is nothing from the past that you would keep. Do not use empathy to make the past real, and so perpetuate it. Step gently aside, and let healing be done for you. Keep but one thought in mind and do not lose sight of it, however tempted you may be to judge any situation, and to determine your response *by* judging it. Focus your mind only on this:

> I am not alone, and I would not intrude the past
> upon my Guest.
> I have invited Him, and He is here.
> I need do nothing except not to interfere.

True empathy is of Him Who knows what it is. You will learn His interpretation of it if you let Him use your capacity for strength, and not for weakness. He will not desert you, but be sure that you desert not Him (T-16.I.3-4:3).

---

[4] ibid, selections from Parts I-IV of the on-line transcript.

What Is Required for a Relationship to Be Truly Helpful?

Before continuing to examine various issues related to this question, let us point out that throughout the *Psychotherapy Pamphlet* Jesus emphasizes one primary element which is necessary for psychotherapy to be truly healing: the willingness of the therapist to set separate, personal interests aside in favor of sharing a common goal and purpose with the client. We already have seen that the single requirement of a teacher of God is that, "...somehow, somewhere he has made a deliberate choice in which he did not see his interests as apart from someone else's" (M-1.1:2). A truly helpful psychotherapist is just another version of what Jesus means by the term "teacher of God." One illustrative statement from the *Psychotherapy Pamphlet* about this central requirement follows:

> What must the teacher do to ensure learning? What must the therapist do to bring healing about? Only one thing; the same requirement salvation asks of everyone. Each one must share one goal with someone else, and in so doing, lose all sense of separate interests. Only by doing this is it possible to transcend the narrow boundaries the ego would impose upon the self. Only by doing this can teacher and pupil, therapist and patient, you and I, accept Atonement and learn to give it as it was received (P-2.II.8).

Note that this passage regards sharing a common interest as the means of accepting the Atonement. We have seen that accepting the Atonement is another way to understand what is involved in forgiveness and that forgiveness is the essence of psychotherapy, according to Jesus. Therefore, in order to facilitate a "truly helpful" relationship the therapist need only be concerned with accepting the Atonement, or identifying with the Holy Spirit, in what seems to be his or her own mind. And the shared purpose— the common interest—between therapist and client is that both are in need of healing; both are in need of accepting the Atonement:

> We go together, you and I" (S-1.IV.1:8).

> Take your brother's hand, for this is not a way we walk alone. In him I [Jesus, but also the Holy Spirit and Christ] walk with you, and you with me. Our Father wills His Son be one with Him. What lives but must not then be one with you?" (W-pI.rV.IN.9:6-9).

There is more to be said about this subject of what is necessary to be truly helpful, which has been a central preoccupation with therapists and those who conduct research on psychotherapy. Carl Rogers explored this question in one of his most well known writings entitled "The Characteristics of a Helping Relationship," published first as an article in a 1958 issue of the *Personnel and Guidance Journal*.

Later, in 1961, this article was reproduced as a chapter in Part II of his famous book, *On Becoming A Person.*[1] He also distilled these characteristics into six "Conditions of the Therapeutic Process" published in the previously mentioned outline of theory found in Koch's volume III of *Psychology: A Study of a Science.* While Rogers was entirely concerned with the world of perception and strengthening the ego self, therefore unwittingly reinforcing separation, he nevertheless identified at least two important characteristics of the therapist's state of mind that have a direct relationship to Jesus' teachings about healing and what is helpful. As listed in the Koch volume, these two characteristics are:

> That the therapist is *experiencing unconditional positive regard* toward the client
>
> That the therapist is *experiencing* an *empathic* understanding of the client's *internal frame of reference*[2]

Rogers, his colleagues and others who conduct research on psychotherapy, have hoped to be able to measure these characteristics, or inner experiences, reducing them to the behavioral level for purposes of operational definition and objective, scientific study. Then, assuming that it could be shown that these characteristics contribute to a truly helpful relationship (some research results do seem to have shown this), discover how a therapist might learn or develop them. As it turned out, therapists tend to develop such characteristics by being exposed to them on the part of others; in other words, by undergoing some kind of therapeutic relationship themselves.

We have seen already that Jesus makes a distinction between true and false empathy, and that true empathy comes from right-mindedness, or from identification with the Holy Spirit at the level of mind. It is not a behavior to be taught, but an attitude of mind that follows naturally when the ego is set aside. The way in which this is achieved is not too dissimilar from the answer Rogers and his colleagues discovered; that is, that true empathy can be facilitated through a relationship with one who is right-minded. But that "one" might be Jesus and not any person who seems to be living in a body. The teacher of importance is the "Internal Teacher" in the mind. Ultimately, the underlying metaphysics of the two approaches (person-centered therapy and Jesus' therapy of forgiveness) are so dissimilar that it leads to confusion to try to carry this comparison very far. Rogers and his followers assume that there really are separate persons and that something

---

[1] Rogers, Carl R., op.cit.

[2] Rogers, Carl R. "A Theory of Therapy…," p.213, op. cit.

important is happening between them. Thus, they focus on the illusion as the ego directs in the interest of keeping us unaware of mind. Jesus is basically saying that the perception of separate persons and attempting to heal them is both illusory and misdirected. All that matters is becoming aware of mind and then healing what is experienced as one's own mind. The illusion then becomes a classroom for learning how to heal one's own mind: to escape from illusions. Speaking in terms of Level Two, since all minds are joined, a contribution is made to the healing of all minds when one seemingly separated mind is healed, if only for an instant.

> Physician, healer, therapist, teacher, heal thyself. Many will come to you carrying the gift of healing, if you so elect. The Holy Spirit never refuses an invitation to enter and abide with you. He will give you endless opportunities to open the door to your salvation, for such is His function. He will also tell you exactly what your function is in every circumstance and at all times (P-3.III.8:1-5).

In his own way, Carl Rogers came close to discovering the truth of that statement. In "Characteristics of a Helping relationship" he stated:

> One way of putting this [i.e., how to create a helping relationship] which may seem strange to you is that if I can form a helping relationship to myself—if I can be sensitively aware of and acceptant toward my own feelings—then the likelihood is great that I can form a helping relationship toward another.

> Now, acceptantly to be what I am, in this sense, and to permit this to show through to the other person, is the most difficult task I know and one I never fully achieve. But to realize that this *is* my task has been most rewarding because it has helped me to find what has gone wrong with interpersonal relationships which have become snarled and to put them on a constructive track again. It has meant that if I am to facilitate the personal growth of others in relation to me, then I must grow, and while this is often painful it is also enriching.[3]

Of course Rogers was speaking from within the framework of the ego thought system of specialness. He had no understanding of mind, right-mindedness and forgiveness as we have been discussing those concepts in the context of Jesus' psychology. Rogers, like all others who pursue psychology and psychotherapy within the metaphysical tradition of dualism, thought that the development of the individual self was preeminent, and that human persons could love by and of themselves. They had only to resolve their conflicts, and become self-actualizing. From the perspective of Jesus' psychology, one

---

[3] Rogers, Carl R. *On Becoming a Person*, p.51, op. cit.

might say that the actualization of self equates to the first act of separation; basically an attempt at destruction on a cosmic scale that would amount to the murder of God or Oneness. In Jesus' psychology, self actualization is the equivalent of self-creating; the ego's attempted replacement for God-creating. And in Jesus' view, the systems and theories of psychology that envision the goal of psychotherapy to be self-actualization or a "fully functioning person," confuse specialness with the true worth of spirit, while special love is confused with genuine Love. That genuine Love, which is of God, is reflected within the illusion of relationships through the Holy Spirit in the form of forgiveness. But again, forgiveness is only possible if one understands the reality and the potential of *mind* as opposed to the illusion of self and its potential. The potentialities of self—the so-called "human potential"—can be only to foster illusions of destruction, because the idea of self begins with the belief in destruction. The history of human kind on this planet witnesses to this. And now we come to another point of comparison.

Rogers, Maslow and other "humanistic psychologists" have assumed that human beings are fundamentally good; that their aggressive and destructive behavior is the result of inner conflicts which can be resolved, in which case they become more loving and more inclined toward the spiritual or transpersonal aspects of existence. They disagreed with Freud and his followers who saw the destructive, murderous nature of basic id instincts and believed those would always lurk in the unconscious, requiring some kind of control. At the same time, they agreed with the view that the perceptual world is real, as are the separate selves which inhabit it.

Humanistic psychologists have sought to unleash the potentialities of the person, or the self, without any recognition of what Jesus identifies as the ego thought system and the viciousness that pertains to it. Freud and others have sought to employ the ego in constructive self service which can yet exist in peace with other self-serving selves. But there never can be peace and love in a world dominated by self-interest. Shared interests derive from oneness, not from separation. And oneness is only apparent at the level of mind, not at the level of the body, which is the level of the illusion of separation; the level of differences with separate and competing goals.

While Freud "knew a bad thing when he saw it," Rogers and others of the humanistic bent basically saw nothing fundamentally bad in the human being; they "saw no evil," so to speak. Freud saw the destructive, murderous impulses of the id, differentiated them from the ego, and sought to control them through the ego. Humanistic psychologists see destructive behavior, but deny anything so basic in human nature as what Freud called the id. To them, following Maslow, destructive behavior is the result of frustrated human needs and potentials, which are basically either neutral or positive. In Jesus' psychology, the id and the ego are not differentiated, but are aspects of the same thought system, as is what Freud called the superego. In Jesus' system of psychology, the ego ("human nature") is completely destructive right from its core. There is no point in trying to use the ego to control the ego, or in attempting to somehow bring love out of what is essentially a thought system of hate. As we have seen, Jesus' answer lies with the reality of spirit and of mind wherein the ego represents a choice to believe a lie; to believe in an impossibility that could never lead to anything but dreams and illusions of separation and conflict. Jesus' answer is to awaken our mind from dreams and illusions by undoing that mistaken choice at the level of mind. That means to reject the ego altogether, not to seek somehow to strengthen it or find in it constructive potentials which it does not have.

In sum, in order for psychotherapy to be successful according to the Freudian tradition, id impulses must be recognized and then controlled through constructive channeling by the ego. Successful psychotherapy in the humanistic tradition requires a belief in the fundamental goodness of human nature, with efforts directed toward either fostering it or releasing it from the bonds of frustration and inner conflict. In Jesus' system, successful therapy is basically forgiveness, which is a process of undoing the ego at the level of mind. And, as far as therapists are concerned, that process begins in the therapist's mind. Jesus' approach to psychotherapy is about recognizing and undoing the negative, not about affirming the positive. What is positive will manifest in the mind once the barriers to it have been removed through forgiveness.

What Jesus has to say is that the ego which motivates the vast majority of humanity is thoroughly evil, but that in truth it does not exist. However, as long as we identify with the ego thought system and believe in separation,— as long as we cherish the status of being a separate self, value individuality, specialness and personhood—then we have made evil real for ourselves and mere intellectual understanding of the metaphysical truth does not get us off the hook. The answer to evil does not lie in trying to make a better ego, either as Freudians would attempt or as Maslow and Rogers would attempt. The answer lies in discovering that we are mind, not body and self; that we are a dreaming mind whose salvation lies in awakening, but before awakening can have a happy dream rather than a nightmare dream of separation and conflict. Jesus' answer lies in forgiveness, as we have seen, but that answer will only work when we rise up to mindfulness out of the obscuring spell of mindlessness that the ego has cast. *A Course in Miracles* can be thought of as an invitation to take the journey from mindlessness to mindfulness. While there are many forms of transportation for that journey, Jesus would have us know that there is no other way out of our pain and suffering—no other way to escape human evil—except to take the journey. And, paradoxically to our limited understanding, the journey is already complete. But we cannot know that until we take the journey. Timelessness—eternity—was never disrupted by time, but we who dream of time must now allow right-mindedness to make use of time to help us discover that.

With regard to the optimistic view voiced by Maslow, Rogers and others, because it assumes the reality of the world and of separate human beings, and is unaware of *mind* as Jesus explains it, it is a view which focuses exclusively upon changing the world and behavior. In terms of Jesus' psychology, this means that Maslow and his followers have focused on effects, or symptoms, without understanding the underlying cause; therefore with no way to address human problems at the causal level. They have bought into the ego thought system hook, line and sinker. So, what is offered is essentially a mind-less psychology which supports and fosters mindlessness. People like to hear that they do not have to be concerned about their selfish, murderous motivations, but only about how to satisfy their needs and build upon their innate human potentials. That is because they, too, have bought into the ego thought system with its self-centered specialness, its dependence upon guilt and fear, and its purpose of keeping us unaware of mind. So, the optimistic humanism of Maslow amounts to an invitation *not* to look—exactly the opposite of Jesus' approach.

In terms of the non-dualistic thought system of *A Course in Miracles*, nothing good can come of separation, or the thought system of duality. But it is separation that humanistic and other psychologists seek to build upon and encourage, because they assume the dualistic reality of separate individuals and the world of perception they seem to inhabit. Consequently, they celebrate the seeming potentials of separation (i.e., specialness), naively assuming that love and brotherhood can come from a thought system that is dedicated to guilt, fear and attack: underlying dynamics that they do not recognize and assiduously seek *not* to see, because that is how the ego directs them. If one understands and accepts Jesus' psychology, one must see that the only potential separation has is to produce more separation; therefore more fragmentation and conflicts of interest, more fear and defensiveness, more guilt, more projection and attack—on and on in the very cycle of viciousness that is so apparent when one looks upon the nature of humanity and human life with the same keen eye as Freud.

Back, now, to our question which can be regarded as one of asking how an illusory relationship in the mind can be truly helpful for awakening the mind from its illusions. The second major characteristic of a helping relationship identified by Rogers—unconditional positive regard—is again not too far off the mark as understood in the Course. But remember that the mark is in the mind, not in persons.

Interestingly, Bill Thetford was at one time a graduate assistant for Carl Rogers when both were at the University of Chicago in 1945. Later, Bill would be Helen Schucman's colleague in scribing the Course and the one who uttered the plea for a "better way" that helped open the door to Jesus in Helen's Mind. In a 1984 interview with Bill conducted by James Bolen and published in *New Realities* magazine, Bill commented about Rogers and the concept of "unconditional positive regard":

> **New Realities:** What would you say was your philosophical or spiritual outlook then?
>
> **Thetford:** I would describe myself as an agnostic. I was not really concerned with whether spiritual reality was a fact or not.
>
> Freud regarded religion as an illusion, and I think many of the graduate students and faculty with whom I associated at the time saw religion as something that lacked intellectual respectability.
>
> **New Realities:** Given your agnostic outlook at the time, was there anything you were involved with that might have set the stage for your being the catalyst for *A Course in Miracles*?
>
> **Thetford:** Not as such, although I was one of Carl Rogers' first graduate students after he came to the University of Chicago in 1945. He taught that "unconditional positive regard" was an essential prerequisite for client-centered therapists. I now realize what Rogers was really emphasizing was that total acceptance in our relationships meant expressing perfect love. Although I recognized how far I was from being able to practice this concept in my life, I grew to appreciate its contribution to my own spiritual development.[4]

Before coining the term "unconditional positive regard," Rogers had discovered the importance in psychotherapy and counseling of a non-judgmental attitude on the part of the therapist, in company with the communication of interpersonal warmth and acceptance. Clearly, these therapist attitudes can be equated to expressions of forgiveness as taught in the Course.

---

[4] Bolen, James. "An Exclusive, Candid Conversation with William Thetford, Ph.D." In *New Realities*, Larkspur, CA. October, 1984. (*New Realities* magazine is no longer in publication, however Mr. Bolen retains copyright in this article.)

Unconditional positive regard might be a synonym for forgiveness. But in discussing forgiveness, Jesus is not talking about techniques and behaviors. He is talking about what occurs in the mind through looking at the ego and being willing to step back from it in confidence that there is a Presence of love which can be extended in relationships. Neither was Rogers talking about techniques and behaviors. He continually emphasized that both empathy and unconditional positive regard had to represent genuine attitudes of the therapist; attitudes which could not be imitated or learned by rote and practice, but which could develop organically within. And these attitudes were not seen as static, therefore not easily defined behaviorally, but became part of a dynamically developing relationship wherein the therapist's goal was to be helpful.

Just as non-judgment on the part of the therapist was an important element in Rogers' "helping relationship," so is it an important aspect of forgiveness and the truly helpful psychotherapeutic relationship as understood in Jesus' psychology. A line from the *Psychotherapy Pamphlet* emphasizes this point: "It is in the instant that the therapist forgets to judge the patient that healing occurs" (P-3.II.6:1).

There are two other important and commonly used terms in the Course which pertain to this question of the truly helpful relationship: *holy relationship* and *holy instant*.

Holy relationship is defined in Wapnick's *Glossary* as:

> the Holy Spirit's means to undo the unholy or special relationship by shifting the goal of guilt to the goal of forgiveness or truth; the process of forgiveness by which one who had perceived another as separate joins with him in his mind through Christ's vision.

The most important point of difference between the holy relationship and what conventional therapists regard as a truly helpful relationship is that it is entirely a matter of thought at the level of mind and has nothing to do with the perceived relationship between persons. We have already discussed the concept of the holy relationship in connection with our consideration of special relationships in chapter five where the definition was given in a footnote. For our purposes here, in terms of Jesus' psychology, a truly helpful relationship would be a holy relationship. Further, as previously discussed, it is not the case that there can be one or more holy relationships while other relationships in the mind remain special. You cannot concurrently have a little bit of the ego thought system and a little bit of the Holy Spirit. It is just a fact of the split mind that it's either one thought system or the other, and when it is the Holy Spirit's thought system of the Atonement, then *all* relationships are holy—all are forgiven, no longer serving the purposes of guilt and specialness. So it is that there is really only one holy relationship; and *all* perceived as other, *without exception*, are embraced in the love and holy oneness that is the thought content of the holy relationship. It is a truly helpful relationship, but cannot be confined to just one set of circumstances, such as psychotherapy. This is not to say that, within the illusion of linear time, the mind does not switch back and forth between holiness and specialness, but in the moment of holiness there are no exceptions; which brings us to the *holy instant*, another term mentioned previously, primarily by Dr. Wapnick in his discussion of the present memory found in chapter eight.

Holy instant is defined by Wapnick as:

> the instant outside time in which we choose forgiveness instead of guilt, the miracle instead of a grievance, the Holy Spirit instead of the ego; the expression of our little willingness to live in the present, which opens into eternity, rather than holding on to the past and fearing the future, which keeps us in hell; also used to denote the ultimate holy instant, the real world, the culmination of all the holy instants we have chosen along the way.

Obviously, the holy relationship takes place in the holy instant, a moment in the mind which is outside of time and space. Once again, the thought system of the Course invites us to heights beyond our mundane world of perception and specialness. In psychotherapy, but in any relationship where forgiveness is the goal, Jesus invites us out of ourselves to a view which he describes in one place in the Text as "above the battleground:"

> The lovely light of your [holy] relationship is like the Love of God. It cannot yet assume the holy function God gave His Son, for your forgiveness of your brother is not complete as yet, and so it cannot be extended to all creation. Each form of murder and attack that still attracts you and that you do not recognize for what it is, limits the healing and the miracles you have the power to extend to all. Yet does the Holy Spirit understand how to increase your little gifts and make them mighty. Also He understands how your relationship is raised above the battleground, in it no more. This is your part; to realize that murder [i.e., separation] in any form is not your will. The overlooking of the battleground is now your purpose.

> Be lifted up, and from a higher place look down upon it. From there will your perspective be quite different. Here in the midst of it, it does seem real. Here you have chosen to be part of it. Here murder is your choice. Yet from above, the choice is miracles instead of murder.

> And the perspective coming from this choice shows you the battle is not real, and easily escaped. Bodies may battle, but the clash of forms is meaningless. And it is over when you realize it never was begun. How can a battle be perceived as nothingness when you engage in it? How can the truth of miracles be recognized if murder is your choice?....
>
> Who with the Love of God upholding him could find the choice of miracles or murder hard to make? (T-23.IV.4-5; 9:8; brackets mine)

The word "murder" may seem unnecessarily gruesome and harsh, but at this point in our primer it ought to be clear that Jesus really means it when he says, "What is not love is murder" (T-23.IV.1:10). Remember that the ego thought system to which we cling out of our infatuation with self and specialness begins with a murderous attack on God—on the truth of oneness. All that follows is built on that germinal idea of attack and murder. It is not difficult to see this acted out in the affairs of mankind, and if one accepts the invitation of "looking at the ego," it is not difficult to see the covert murder in the thought content of one's own mind. Again, this must be seen without judgment and is not meant to terrify or to inspire guilt; but "freedom lies in looking at it" (T-16.IV.1:1). If we seek to be "truly helpful," then we must be willing to see within ourselves what is not truly helpful, and that unhelpfulness—that murderous specialness—surely will enter into the "helping relationship" if the therapist is not aware of it in his or her own mind.

The counterpart for the holy relationship is the *unholy relationship*, which is another term for the special relationship. There are but two choices. Likewise, the counterpart for the holy instant is the *un*holy instant of ego acceptance and pursuit of separation through specialness. There are but two choices; and so it is with the helping relationship. If it is not truly helpful in any given instant, then it will be unhelpful: therapist heal thyself, if only for an instant. Your ability to be "truly helpful" in any instant of therapy depends on it.

At Level Two, the level of time, there is a *process* involved in forgiveness and therapy, and there is a process involved in becoming a truly helpful therapist. So, while what has been said above may sound like being truly helpful is an all-or-nothing proposition, within the illusion of linear time—the seeming progression of instants—this is not so. The process of forgiveness and of becoming truly helpful can be thought of as *gradually* learning, through vigilant *looking*, to undo the ego with its guilt and judgment. Likewise, some moments in therapy will be truly helpful and others not, but Jesus reassures us that no truly loving moment of forgiveness is lost:

Somewhere all gifts of God [i.e., all thoughts of love and forgiveness] must be received. In time no effort can be made in vain. It is not our perfection that is asked in our attempts to heal. We are deceived already, if we think there is a need of healing. And the truth will come to us only through one who seems to share our dream of sickness. Let us help him to forgive himself for all the trespasses with which he would condemn himself without a cause. His healing is our own. And as we see the sinlessness in him come shining through the veil of guilt that shrouds the Son of God, we will behold in him the face of Christ, and understand that it is but our own (P-2.V.7; brackets mine).

Ideally, psychotherapy is a series of holy encounters [i.e., holy instants] in which brothers meet to bless each other and to receive the peace of God. And this will one day come to pass for every "patient" on the face of this earth, for who except a patient could possibly have come here? The therapist is only a somewhat more specialized teacher of God. He learns through teaching, and the more advanced he is the more he teaches and the more he learns. But whatever stage he is in, there are patients who need him just that way. They cannot take more than he can give for now. Yet both will find sanity at last (P-2.I.4).

Healing is limited by the limitations of the psychotherapist, as it is limited by those of the patient. The aim of the process, therefore, is to transcend these limits. Neither can do this alone, but when they join, the potentiality for transcending all limitations has been given them. Now the extent of their success depends on how much of this potentiality they are willing to use. The willingness may come from either one at the beginning, and as the other shares it, it will grow. Progress becomes a matter of decision; it can reach almost to Heaven or go no further than a step or two from hell.

It is quite possible for psychotherapy to seem to fail. It is even possible for the result to look like retrogression. But in the end there must be some success. One asks for help; another hears and tries to answer in the form of help. This is the formula for salvation, and must heal. Divided goals alone [i.e., the failure to join in a common purpose, thus any form of a specialness goal which enters in] can interfere with perfect healing (P-2.III.2-3:6; brackets mine).

The Unhealed Healer

It is quite *un*likely that a healed mind would choose to stay in a body and the world, or to manifest as a body in the world. If it did so, it would be to serve as a symbol and messenger of love in some form. Jesus is an example, and even he no longer takes form in a body. So, at least according to the thought system of *A Course in Miracles*, it is a very safe bet that all who experience themselves as bodies in the world perceived as real are images projected by an unhealed mind. We all have unhealed minds, thus when we attempt to be helpers or healers we can just assume that we are unhealed healers. Knowing that, one can then enter into a psychotherapeutic relationship with the understanding that it represents an opportunity for healing and forgiveness. Mindful of one's unhealed state, one is in a position to exercise the vigilance of looking at the ego, hence to facilitate the potential to "choose a miracle instead of murder" (T-23.IV.6:5). Thus, psychotherapy can become truly helpful, or truly healing for the mind of the therapist, which then can extend healing to the mind of the patient. The therapist who is in the process of accepting the Atonement through forgiveness can become for the patient a teacher by example.

When Jesus talks of the "unhealed healer" in his course, he is basically talking about those who seek to heal in any form or context without having a clue as to what Jesus means by forgiveness and healing; those who are essentially mindless and in no position to exercise the vigilance of looking at the ego. In other words, the unhealed healer is one who seeks to heal others out of the motivations of specialness. He or she seeks to nourish his or her own separate self identity, and to heal at the level of form rather than content, having no understanding of the reality of mind. Certainly healing seems to take place at that level, but it is all magic and illusions, not true healing as Jesus speaks of it in *A Course in Miracles*. The unhealed healer lives the unexamined life, and certainly has a lot of company in whatever profession he or she might be engaged.

Jesus does not speak of unhealed healers in a condemning way, but in a very forthright way which points to the futility of their efforts. And he often speaks of the unhealed healer in the context of psychotherapy. In fact, there is an entire section of Chapter 9 in the ACIM Text devoted to this subject, and five direct references to it in the *Psychotherapy Pamphlet*. We will examine some of this material by way of further elucidating the concept as it applies to the subject we are considering here.

The Text section entitled "The Unhealed Healer" (T-9.V) begins as follows (references to healers other than psychotherapists have been elided):

> The ego's plan for forgiveness is far more widely used than God's. This is because it is undertaken by unhealed healers, and is therefore of the ego. Let us consider the unhealed healer more carefully now. By definition, he is trying to give what he has not received...If he is a psychotherapist, he is...likely to start with the...incredible belief that attack is real for both himself and the patient, but that it does not matter for either of them (T-9.V.1:1-4, 6).

277

The ego's plan of forgiveness is called "forgiveness-to-destroy" in the supplementary pamphlet entitled *The Song of Prayer: Prayer, Forgiveness and Healing*,[1] and is alluded to elsewhere in the Course as it is here. This approach first sees sin as real. That is, it assumes the reality of separation and all that follows from it, which of course will include attack. In fact, forgiveness-to-destroy *is* an attack which seeks to substitute special love for true forgiveness; seeks to destroy brotherhood and our true Identity. Thus, forgiveness-to-destroy not only attacks forgiveness, but attacks truth by seeing as real separation and attack in some. Therefore, guilt is warranted, but then is "forgiven" by one who deigns to overlook the sin even though it is real and deserving of punishment. God and the Holy Spirit, as understood in the Course, do not enter into this kind of forgiveness. If there is a god in it at all it is the ego's god of vengeance who believes sin is real and demands that it be atoned for through suffering and sacrifice. Of course, the ego's plan of forgiveness is designed to establish the special status of the one who "forgives" in spite of seeing a "real," and perhaps "grievous," error. An excerpt from the thoroughgoing discussion of this topic in the *Song of Prayer* pamphlet follows:

> Forgiveness-to-destroy has many forms, being a weapon of the world of form. Not all of them are obvious, and some are carefully concealed beneath what seems like charity. Yet all the forms that it may seem to take have but this single goal; their purpose is to separate and make what God created equal, different. The difference is clear in several forms where the designed comparison cannot be missed, nor is it really meant to be.
>
> In this group, first, there are the forms in which a "better" person deigns to stoop to save a "baser" one from what he truly is. Forgiveness here rests on an attitude of gracious lordliness so far from love that arrogance could never be dislodged. Who can forgive and yet despise? And who can tell another he is steeped in sin, and yet perceive him as the Son of God? Who makes a slave to teach what freedom is? There is no union here, but only grief. This is not really mercy. This is death [because it denies true life, which is our shared identity as spirit, or Christ; further, the specialness of the "forgiver" can only be established by killing off the other, whether figuratively or literally, who is seen as a competitor for specialness] (S-2.II.1-2; bracket mine).

Thus, the unhealed healer who attempts to practice psychotherapy easily winds up engaging in some form of forgiveness-to-destroy which must then deny the brotherhood of patient and therapist, defeating any possibility of a shared purpose. And such a therapist will not understand the nature and importance of mind, thus emphasizing causal factors in the world of

[1] *The Song of Prayer*, op. cit. (See our chapter seven.)

special relationships, unaware of the present cause of fear which comes from choosing in the present to believe in separation and guilt. Linear time is accepted as real, thus the patient's symptoms are assigned to a cause that is real and irretrievably lost in the past, therefore not really able to be healed and let go, but only compensated for somehow. Jesus comments on this:

> If the way to counteract fear is to reduce the importance of the mind, how can this build ego strength? Such evident inconsistencies account for why no one has really explained what happens in psychotherapy. Nothing really does. Nothing real has happened to the unhealed healer, and he must learn from his own teaching. His ego will always seek to get something from the situation. The unhealed healer therefore does not know how to give, and consequently cannot share. He cannot correct because he is not working correctly. He believes that it is up to him to teach the patient what is real, although he does not know it himself.
>
> What, then, should happen? When God said, "Let there be light," there *was* light. Can you find light by analyzing darkness, as the psychotherapist does... Healing is not mysterious. Nothing will change unless it is understood, since light *is* understanding. A "miserable sinner" cannot be healed without magic, nor can an "unimportant mind" esteem itself without magic (T-9.V.5-6).

To round out the picture of the unhealed healer, following are a series of excerpts from the *Psychotherapy Pamphlet*. What is most important about this picture is that it might assist the would-be therapist to look at the nature of his or her own ego and the specialness motivations that are involved in the desire to be of help, but which must inevitably interfere with successfully fulfilling that desire. The basic point of this is not that the therapist can immediately avoid being an unhealed healer, or should feel guilty, or should fight against his or her specialness, but that simply by being *willing* to look, one begins the process of forgiveness—takes the first step in the forgiveness process. In this way, the unhealed healer enters into the process of healing and is thus able to share it with the patient or client. In what seems paradoxical to us, Jesus' approach to forgiveness and healing asks not that we attempt on our own to become loving and forgiving healers, but that we *look with him* at how we are *not* loving and forgiving and don't really want to be; *look with our right mind* at how we really don't share the common purpose of healing with others and in fact don't truly care about others, only about ourselves. It is that first step of looking honestly and without judgment that prepares the way for the second and third steps in the forgiveness process, which can follow very quickly—in a holy instant. Thus, the unhealed healer becomes healed and healing, at least for an instant; and in that instant can somehow communicate to the patient (not necessarily with words), "that all his sins have been forgiven him along with his [the therapist's] own" (P-2.VII.3:1; brackets mine).

279

The fact of being unhealed does not deny hope, because hope is eternal, being of God:

> "Something good must come from every meeting of patient and therapist [simply because of the desire to help and be helped]. And that good is saved for both, against the day when they can recognize that only that was real in their relationship" (P-3.II.5:1-2; bracket mine).

We turn now to a lengthy series of excerpts concerning the unhealed healer who remains caught up in specialness, but in whom the potential for healing is ever present:

> What could be the difference between healing and forgiveness? Only Christ forgives, knowing His [own] sinlessness. His vision heals perception and sickness disappears. Nor will it return again, once its cause has been removed. This, however, needs the help of a very advanced therapist, capable of joining with the patient in a holy relationship in which all sense of separation finally is overcome.

> For this, one thing and one thing only is required: The therapist in no way confuses himself with God. All "unhealed healers" make this fundamental confusion in one form or another, because they must regard themselves as self-created rather than God-created. This confusion is rarely if ever in awareness, or the unhealed healer would instantly become a teacher of God, devoting his life to the function of true healing. Before he reached this point, he thought he was in charge of the therapeutic process and was therefore responsible for its outcome. His patient's errors thus became his own failures, and guilt became the cover, dark and strong, for what should be the holiness of Christ. Guilt is inevitable in those who use their judgment in making their decisions. Guilt is impossible in those through whom the Holy Spirit speaks.

> The passing of guilt is the true aim of therapy and the obvious aim of forgiveness. In this their oneness can be clearly seen. Yet who could experience the end of guilt who feels responsible for his brother in the role of guide for him? Such a function presupposes a knowledge that no one here can have; a certainty of past, present and future, and of all the effects that may occur in them. Only from this omniscient point of view would such a role be possible. Yet no perception is omniscient, nor is the tiny self of one alone against the universe able to assume he has such wisdom except in madness. That many therapists are mad is obvious. No unhealed healer can be wholly sane.

> Yet it is as insane not to accept a function God has given you as to invent one He has not. The advanced therapist in no way can ever doubt the power that is in him. Nor does he doubt its Source.

He understands all power in earth and Heaven belongs to him because of who he is. And he is this because of his Creator, Whose Love is in him and Who cannot fail. Think what this means; he has the gifts of God Himself to give away. His patients are God's saints, who call upon his sanctity to make it theirs. And as he gives it to them, they behold Christ's shining face as it looks back at them.

The insane, thinking they are God, are not afraid to offer weakness to God's Son. But what they see in him because of this they fear indeed. The unhealed healer cannot but be fearful of his patients, and suspect them of the treachery he sees in him [self]. He tries to heal, and thus at times he may. But he will not succeed except to some extent and for a little while. He does not see the Christ in him who calls. What answer can he give to one who seems to be a stranger; alien to the truth and poor in wisdom ...

Think what the joining of two brothers really means. And then forget the world and all its little triumphs and its dreams of death. The same are one, and nothing now can be remembered of the world of guilt. The room becomes a temple, and the street a stream of stars that brushes lightly past all sickly dreams. Healing is done, for what is perfect needs no healing, and what remains to be forgiven where there is no sin?

Be thankful, therapist, that you can see such things as this, if you but understand your proper role. But if you fail in this, you have denied that God created you, and so you will not know you are His Son. Who is your brother now? What saint can come to take you home with him? You lost the way. And can you now expect to see in him an answer that you have refused to give? Heal and be healed. There is no other choice of pathways that can ever lead to peace. O let your patient in, for he has come to you from God. Is not his holiness enough to wake your memory of Him? (P-2.VII. 3-7:6; 8-9; bracket mine).

The unhealed healer may be arrogant, selfish, unconcerned, and actually dishonest. He may be uninterested in healing as his major goal. Yet something happened to him, however slight it may have been, when he chose to be a healer, however misguided the direction he may have chosen. That "something" is enough. Sooner or later that something will rise and grow; a patient will touch his heart, and the therapist will silently ask him for help. He has himself found a therapist. He has asked the Holy Spirit to enter the relationship and heal it. He has accepted the Atonement for himself.

... neither a perfect therapist nor a perfect patient can possibly exist. Both must have denied their perfection, for their very need for each other implies a sense of lack. A one-to-one relationship is not One Relationship. Yet it is the means of return; the way God chose for the return of His Son. In that strange dream a strange correction must enter, for only that is the call to awake.

281

> And what else should therapy be? Awake and be glad, for all your sins have been forgiven you. This is the only message that any two should ever give each other.
>
> Something good must come from every meeting of patient and therapist. And that good is saved for both, against the day when they can recognize that only that was real in their relationship. At that moment the good is returned to them, blessed by the Holy Spirit as a gift from their Creator as a sign of His Love. For the therapeutic relationship must become like the relationship of the Father and the Son. There is no other, for there is nothing else. The therapists of this world do not expect this outcome, and many of their patients would not be able to accept help from them if they did. Yet no therapist really sets the goal for the relationships of which he is a part. His understanding begins with recognizing this, and then goes on from there (P-3.II.3:2-5:8).

There is one place in all of the Course material where Jesus refers to a "healed healer." This is in the *Psychotherapy Pamphlet*. Following is the passage containing that reference in a context which further explains the goal and process of psychotherapy according to Jesus' system of psychology:

> It is in the instant that the therapist forgets to judge the patient that healing occurs. In some relationships this point is never reached, although both patient and therapist may change their dreams in the process [i.e., the patient may change his or her self concept or life view a bit; the therapist likewise, or have a somewhat changed view of therapy]. Yet it will not be the same dream for both of them, and so it is not the dream of forgiveness in which both will someday wake [thus a truly shared interest has not been served]. The good is saved; indeed is cherished. But only little time is saved. [Elsewhere, in the pamphlet and throughout the Course Jesus says that the goal of forgiveness is to save time in salvation or awakening.[2]] The new dreams will lose their temporary appeal and turn to dreams of fear, which is the content of all dreams. Yet no patient can accept more than he is ready to receive, and no therapist can offer more than he believes he has. And so there is a place for all relationships in this world, and they will bring as much good as each can accept and use.
>
> Yet it is when judgment ceases that healing occurs, because only then it can be understood that there is no order of difficulty in healing. This is a necessary understanding for the healed healer. He has learned that it is no harder to wake a brother from one dream than from another. No professional therapist can hold this understanding consistently in his mind, offering it to all who come to him....

---

[2] In Wapnick's *Glossary*, "awakening" is defined as follows: "the Course speaks of the separation as being a dream from which we need to awaken; salvation therefore consists of hearing the Holy Spirit—the Call to awaken—in ourselves and in our brothers: thus accepting the oneness with each other that undoes the separation which gave rise to the dream in the beginning."

Once the professional therapist has realized that minds are joined, he can also recognize that order of difficulty in healing is meaningless. Yet well before he reaches this in time he can go towards it. Many holy instants can be his along the way. A goal marks the end of a journey, not the beginning, and as each goal is reached another can be dimly seen ahead. Most professional therapists are still at the very start of the beginning stage of the first journey. Even those who have begun to understand what they must do may still oppose the setting-out. Yet all the laws of healing can be theirs in just an instant. The journey is not long except in dreams. (P-3.II.6-7:4; 8; brackets mine).

In concluding this discussion of the unhealed healer, let us return to a little further consideration relevant to the truth we discussed at the end of our section on sickness: "No mind is sick until another mind agrees that they are separate. ...Uniting with a brother's mind prevents the cause of sickness and perceived effects (T-28.III.2:1, 5). The following paragraph is a nice summary of the "double vision" of the healed mind, thus how the healed healer perceives in this world. In addition, this passage offers a succinct statement of Jesus' view of healing:

The body's eyes will continue to see differences. But the mind that has let itself be healed will no longer acknowledge them. There will be those who seem to be "sicker" than others, and the body's eyes will report their changed appearances as before. But the healed mind will put them all in one category; they are unreal. This is the gift of its Teacher [i.e., the Holy Spirit]; the understanding that only two categories are meaningful in sorting out the messages the mind receives from what appears to be the outside world. And of these two, but one is real. Just as reality is wholly real, apart from size and shape and time and place—for differences cannot exist within it—so too are illusions without distinctions. The one answer to sickness of any kind is healing [i.e., forgiveness]. The one answer to all illusions is truth [i.e., the Atonement principle] (M-8.6; brackets mine).

Resistance

Finally, before we end this chapter let us consider what it is that stands in the way of healing—i.e., let us take a further look at "the blocks to the awareness of love's presence" (T-IN.1:7) that psychotherapy, healing and forgiveness will encounter and must remove. It was another contribution of Freud's keen insight to observe the phenomenon of resistance to healing on the part of those who had asked for help. And it would be surprising if the reader who has persisted this far in our primer had not already encountered some form of resistance to Jesus' psychology as we have been describing and explaining it; also not surprising if resistance had led many others to put this book down or aggressively discard it before reaching this chapter. In the history of the Course, at least one early reader attempted to flush its pages down the toilet, many have thrown it across the room in violent rejection, and no doubt there is more than one copy resting on the bottom of Tennanah Lake in the Catskill mountains of New York where the Foundation for *A Course in Miracles* used to conduct classes at its former retreat center.

We would not be in the predicaments of our lives had we not *chosen* resistance as a way of life in the first place. The ego *is* resistance: resistance to God and an attempt to flush the truth of oneness down the toilet of oblivion in the very way that the early Course student attempted to be rid of it. In the *Psychotherapy Pamphlet* Jesus says of the ego:

> "Resistance" is its way of looking at things; its interpretation of progress and growth. These interpretations will be wrong of necessity, because they are delusional. The changes the ego seeks to make are not really changes. They are but deeper shadows, or perhaps different cloud patterns [i.e., strengthening the ego; improving the self concept; eliminating certain behaviors; "self actualization"]. Yet what is made of nothingness cannot be called new or different. Illusions are illusions; truth is truth.
>
> Resistance as defined here can be characteristic of a therapist as well as of a patient. Either way, it sets a limit on psychotherapy because it restricts its aims (P-2.I.2:4-3:2; brackets mine).

And the aim of psychotherapy, or forgiveness, is the complete undoing of resistance; i.e., of the ego thought system, therefore of our specialness and cherished self identity. So, we resist the very process that would help us. Years ago, in the late 1950s, a brief account of children's elementary school writings appeared in a monthly issue of the *Saturday Review of Literature*. In that little article it was reported that one third-grade child had written: "I have a little kitty. Sometimes he scratches me. But he's still *my* cat." That's how it is with us. We have this little self and it not only sometimes scratches us, it is absolutely dreadful when closely observed—murderous and shrouded in guilty self hatred at its root; entirely the source of our suffering of any kind—but it is still *ours*. The idea of "me and mine" is what we cherish in our special love of specialness. And so we do not want to give it up, willingly remaining blind to the unhappiness it costs us; terrified of the *looking at the ego* which psychotherapy and Jesus invite, because the ego has counseled fear of the mind. It subliminally whispers that our mind is very dangerous, "the home of evil, darkness and sin" (W-pI.93.1:1), and, "all is black with guilt within you" (T-13.IX.8:2): **do not look!**

In our confusion about the nature of love, we fear love. That fear is at the bottom of resistance to psychotherapy: our resistance to true forgiveness and healing. As we have said before, identified with the ego we *must* fear the Love of God, because finally that does mean the end of our tiny illusion of self which will disappear in the grandeur of our true Self. Light dispels darkness. But within the illusion of time we can keep the opaque shades of guilt and fear drawn against the light in our mind as long as we fear it. That light is of the Holy Spirit and is the key to forgiveness. So we draw the shades and resist forgiveness.

It is very helpful to know of our ego's fear of love because that knowledge allows us to understand our self defeating ways and why it is that we ask for help, but then reject it when it appears. Of course, Jesus knows that we fear his love which represents the Love of God. But his love—the love of the Holy Spirit and a reflection of God's Love—does not attack our ego and our fear. That love is infinitely patient, because: "Those who are certain of the outcome can afford to wait, and wait without anxiety. Patience is natural to the teacher of God" (M-4.VIII.1:1). Therefore, that love in our mind symbolized by the name "Jesus" is infinitely patient because it knows that time is an illusion and forgiveness (therapy) "is a journey without distance to a goal that has never changed" (T-8.VI.9:7); "...the outcome is as certain as God" (T-2.III.3:10; T-4.II.5:8). The therapist who takes Jesus as his model, therefore accepts the Holy Spirit as his Guide, becomes a "teacher of God" to whom patience is natural. It is this patience that can smile at the fear of love and accept the resistance it inspires while gently working to undo it in both patient and therapist. *Looking at the ego* with gentle non-judgment and patience is the key to undoing resistance.

Kenneth Wapnick has written and taught extensively about the subject of resistance as it relates to study and practice of *A Course in Miracles*. We conclude this section with an extensive excerpt from the article, "Resistance: How One Studies *A Course in Miracles* Without Really Learning It," which he wrote in company with his wife Gloria for the June, 1999 issue of *The Lighthouse*, the quarterly newsletter of the Foundation for *A Course in Miracles*:

> Although the term *resistance* appears infrequently in *A Course in Miracles*, it is nonetheless a key concept in the process of students learning the mind-changing lessons of forgiveness that are the Course's central teaching. Indeed, it is the only concept that can satisfactorily explain a phenomenon experienced by most (if not all) students of the Course at some point or another in their work with it. This is the seeming paradox, on the one hand, of consciously and most sincerely attempting to learn, live, and practice the

Course principles under the guidance of Jesus or the Holy Spirit, while on the other hand, experiencing the ongoing frustration of *not* doing just that. Most spiritual seekers are familiar with the famous words of St. Paul, who exclaimed out of this same sense of frustration: "For the good that I would I do not: but the evil which I would not, that I do" (Romans 7:19). This article explores the issue of resistance in Course students' efforts to put into practice its principles of forgiveness as taught by their Inner Teacher, the Holy Spirit.

As with so many other areas that touch on the *process* of healing in *A Course in Miracles,* the work of Sigmund Freud offers us many parallels which underscore the importance of understanding the dynamics of the problem and its solution. Very early in his psychoanalytic work, Freud observed that his patients were not improving, despite the insights he was offering them as to the cause of their neurosis. It eventually dawned on him that the problem lay in the fact that the patients did not *want* to get better, a dynamic he termed *resistance:*

> ...the [therapeutic] situation led me at once to the theory that *by means of my psychical* [i.e., psychological] *work I had to overcome a psychical force in the patients which was opposed to the pathogenic ideas becoming conscious....* This work of overcoming resistances is the essential function of analytic treatment.... (*Studies on Hysteria* (with J. Breuer), 1893, Vol. II, p. 268; *Introductory Lectures on Psychoanalysis*, 1917, Vol. XVI, p. 451).[1]

Indeed, in several places in *A Course in Miracles* Jesus lets us know that *he* knows that we will experience resistance to his teachings. We present a few of these, beginning with this statement from the "Rules for Decision" in Chapter 31 of the text:

> And if you find resistance strong and dedication weak, you are not ready. *Do not fight yourself* (T-30.I.1:6-7).

Repeatedly throughout the workbook for students, Jesus alerts us to our potential resistance to the radical ideas he is teaching. In fact, in the Introduction itself he states:

> Some of the ideas the workbook presents you will find hard to believe, and others may seem to be quite startling. This does not matter.... Remember only this; you need not believe the ideas, you need not accept them, and you need not even welcome them. Some of them you may actively resist (W-pI.in.8:1-2; 9:1-2).

---

[1] All references to Freud in this article are taken from *The Standard Edition of the complete Psychological Works of Sigmund Freud* (London: Hogarth Press, 1953).

One other example from the workbook:

> Your mind is no longer wholly untrained. You are quite ready to learn the form of exercise we will use today, but you may find that you will encounter strong resistance. The reason is very simple. While you practice in this way, you leave behind everything that you now believe, and all the thoughts that you have made up. Properly speaking, this is the release from hell. Yet perceived through the ego's eyes, it is loss of identity and a descent into hell (W-pI.44.5).

In the Manual for Teachers we find a similar statement from Jesus, alerting his students to the fear involved in accepting his teachings; in this case it is the principle that the cause of sickness is found in the mind and not the body:

> The resistance to recognizing this is enormous, because the existence of the world as you perceive it depends on the body being the decision maker (M-5.II.1:7).

The resistance referred to in the above passages is directly related to the fear of losing our personal specialness and individual uniqueness, the letting go of which is the final step before one can awaken from this dream of separation.

Resistance—the unconscious attempt to sabotage what alone will help—is so surprising as to be almost unbelievable, as Freud himself observed in this clever, quasi-Platonic dialogue with himself, taken from *The Question of Lay Analysis*, written in 1926:

> It will then be your fate to make a discovery for which you were not prepared.
>
> "And what may that be?"
>
> That you have been deceived in your patient; that you cannot count in the slightest on his collaboration and compliance; that he is ready to place every possible difficulty in the way of your common work -- in a word, that he has no wish whatever to be cured.
>
> "Well! that is the craziest thing you have told me yet. And I do not believe it either. The patient who is suffering so much, who complains so movingly about his troubles, who is making so great a sacrifice for the treatment -- you say he has no wish to be cured! But of course you do not mean what you say."

> Calm yourself! I *do* mean it. What I said was the truth -- not the whole truth, no doubt, but a very noteworthy part of it. The patient wants to be cured -- but he also wants not to be.... They [the patients] complain of their illness but exploit it with all their strength; and if someone tries to take it away from them they defend it like the proverbial lioness with her young (*The Question of Lay Analysis*, 1926, Vol. XX, pp. 221-22).

This phenomenon, which is so clear to the psychoanalyst or psychotherapist, is not always recognized in discussions of the spiritual life. And yet how could it *not* be just as present in spiritual seekers as in psychotherapeutic patients, since undoing the thought system of guilt, anxiety, and fear is common to both disciplines? And how could the undoing of this resistance *not* be among the most significant aspects to anyone's spiritual path, since the ego with which we all identify *is* the impediment to our progress?

Thus we see that an important component of our resistance to learning the teachings of *A Course in Miracles* is our need to suffer and be guilty, what in the pamphlet *Psychotherapy: Purpose, Process and Practice* Jesus refers to as "the hanging-on to guilt, its hugging-close and sheltering, its loving protection and alert defense" (P-VI.1:3), or in Freud's words below, the "powerful need for punishment":

> ...the impression derived from the work of analysis [is] that the patient who puts up a resistance is so often unaware of that resistance. Not only the fact of the resistance is unconscious to him, however, but its motives as well. We were obliged to search out these motives or motive, and to our surprise we found them in a powerful need for punishment....The practical significance of this discovery is not less than its theoretical one, for the need for punishment is the worst enemy of our therapeutic efforts. It is satisfied by the suffering which is linked to the neurosis, and for that reason holds fast to being ill....[It is the] "need to be ill or to suffer"...The patient must not become well but must remain ill (*New Introductory Lectures on Psychoanalysis*, 1933, Vol. XXII, p. 108; *An Outline of Psychoanalysis*, 1940, Vol. XXIII, pp. 178-80).

This attraction to guilt in ourselves is central to *A Course in Miracles'* teachings on the ego thought system, for guilt witnesses to the seeming reality of the separation. The experience of punishment—real or imagined—justifies our belief in guilt and therefore reinforces the fundamental premise of the ego's existence. To let it go would be tantamount ultimately to letting go of the belief in the reality of a personal self, and thus we *resist* doing so, not to mention *resist* the one (or One) helping us to do just that. Jesus comments on this phenomenon, referring to his own life:

> Many thought I was attacking them, even though it was apparent I was not. An insane learner learns strange lessons. What you must recognize is that when you do not share a thought system, you are weakening it. Those who believe in it therefore perceive this as an attack on them. This is because everyone identifies himself with his thought system, and every thought system centers on what you believe you are (T-6.V-B.1:5-9).

Needless to say, when we believe we are being attacked, we feel justified in attacking back, and almost always *do*, literally in *self*-defense. And so we are led to another significant effect of a student's resistance to *A Course in Miracles*: the need to prove the Course wrong. Underlying this dynamic is the hope that if it is wrong then we do not have to do what it says and change from our ego's way of thinking. Freud, too, in his monumental *The Interpretation of Dreams*, remarked on this interesting phenomenon in his patients: the need to prove the analyst wrong:

> One of the two motive forces leading to such dreams is the wish that I may be wrong. These dreams appear regularly in the course of my treatments when a patient is in a state of resistance to me; and I can count almost certainly on provoking one of them after I have explained to a patient for the first time my theory that dreams are fulfillments of wishes. Indeed, it is to be expected that the same thing will happen to some of the readers of the present book: they will be quite ready to have one of their wishes frustrated in a dream if only their wish that I may be wrong can be fulfilled (*The Interpretation of Dreams*, 1900, Vol. IV, pp. 157-58).

This form of resistance as it is expressed in students of *A Course in Miracles*, can take the form of arguing with the material, especially focusing on the *form* as a means of ignoring the *content*. Readers of Kenneth's *Absence from Felicity: The Story of Helen Schucman and Her Scribing of A Course in Miracles* may recall the story he tells there (pp. 255-57) of Helen's attempts to do just that during the early weeks of the dictation....

Therefore, when students of *A Course in Miracles* are *not* experiencing the positive effects "promised" by Jesus in his Course, it is not because *A Course in Miracles* has failed them. Rather it is because of their unconscious resistance to what it is truly saying. When Helen complained to Jesus that she was not being helped by his teachings, he responded in the following words, presented here in the edited form of the published Course:

> You may complain that this course is not sufficiently specific for you to understand and use. Yet perhaps you have not done what it specifically advocates. This is a not a course in the play of ideas, but in their practical application (T-11.VIII.5:1-3).

289

As Cassius said to Brutus:

> The fault, dear Brutus, is not in our stars,
> But in ourselves.... (Julius Caesar, I,ii).

Or as Jesus so emphatically states near the end of Chapter 27 of the text:

> The secret of salvation is but this: That you are doing this unto yourself (T-27.VIII.10:1).

It was clear to Freud, just as Jesus makes it clear in *A Course in Miracles*, that a mere intellectual understanding of one's problem is not enough. Rather, it is essential that the resistance to letting go of the problem be uncovered and looked at:

> It is true that in the earliest days of analytic technique we took an intellectualist view of the situation....It was a severe disappointment when the expected success was not forthcoming....Indeed, telling and describing his [the patient's] repressed trauma to him did not even result in any recollection of it coming into his mind....After this, there was no choice but to cease attributing to the fact of knowing, in itself, the importance that had previously been given to it and to place the emphasis on the resistances which had in the past brought about the state of not knowing and which were still ready to defend that state. *Conscious knowledge...was powerless against those resistances...*(Freud, *On Beginning the Treatment,* 1913, Vol. XII, pp. 141-42).

> *How do we remove the resistance?...by discovering it and showing it to the patient....*If I say to you: "Look up at the sky! There's a balloon there!" you will discover it much more easily than if I simply tell you to look up and see if you can see anything. In the same way, a student who is looking through a microscope for the first time is instructed by his teacher as to what he will see; otherwise he does not see it at all, though it is there and visible (Freud, *Introductory Lectures on Psychoanalysis,* 1917, Vol. XVI, pp. 437; italics mine).

This is the heart of Jesus' teaching message in *A Course in Miracles*: uncovering the ego so that we may see our identification with it. Indeed, this process of looking at the ego is the essence of forgiveness:

> Forgiveness...is still, and quietly does nothing....It merely looks, and waits, and judges not (W-pII.1.4:1, 3).[2]

---

[2] Wapnick, Gloria and Kenneth. "Resistance: How One Studies *A Course in Miracles* Without Really Learning It." In *The Lighthouse,* Vol.10, 2. Temecula, CA: Foundation for *A Course in Miracles,* 1999. A transcript of this article may be read on the World Wide Web at: http://www.facim.org/acim/lh991002.htm

Summary

In spite of the lengthy consideration we have given to the subject of this chapter, the basic points can be to be stated quite simply and succinctly. First, *psychotherapy, healing and forgiveness* are synonymous terms that designate a *process* of change at the level of mind. Secondly, the therapist need only be concerned with that process in what is experienced as his or her own mind. Third, the process of mind changing *requires* objective, non-judgmental *looking* at one's own ego. Fourth, resistance to the process of mind changing is inevitable in both therapist and patient. Fifth, when the therapist is able to allow right-mindedness, the Holy Spirit becomes the therapist and what follows will be truly helpful to both therapist and patient, who are actually projections in one shared mind, thus share one fundamental goal: awakening the mind from its nightmare ego dream of separation and conflict.

> A therapist does not heal; *he lets healing be.* He can point to darkness but he cannot bring light of himself, for light is not of him. Yet, being *for* him, it must also be for his patient. The Holy Spirit is the only Therapist. He makes healing clear in any situation in which He is the Guide. You can only let Him fulfill His function. He needs no help for this. He will tell you exactly what to do to help anyone..., and will speak to him through you if you do not interfere. Remember that you choose the guide for helping, and the wrong choice will not help. But remember also that the right one will. Trust Him, for help is His function, and He is of God. As you awaken other minds to the Holy Spirit through Him, and not yourself, you will understand that you are not obeying the laws of this world. But the laws you are obeying work. "The good is what works" is a sound though insufficient statement. Only the good *can* work. Nothing else works at all.

> This course offers a very direct and a very simple learning situation, and provides the Guide Who tells you what to do. If you do it, you will see that it works. Its results are more convincing than its words. They will convince you that the words are true (T-9.V.8-9:4).

> You can do much on behalf of your own healing and that of others if, in a situation calling for help, you think of it this way:

>> *I am here only to be truly helpful.*
>> *I am here to represent Him Who sent me.*
>> *I do not have to worry about what to say or what*
>>   *to do, because He Who sent me will direct me.*
>> *I am content to be wherever He wishes, knowing*
>>   *He goes there with me.*

>> *I will be healed as I let Him teach me to heal (T-2.V(A).18)*

Chapter 11

Final Summary and Conclusion: *The course is simple*

> While truth is simple, it must still be taught to those who have
> already lost their way in endless mazes of complexity (C-IN 3:8)

Throughout the Course Jesus repeatedly says that his teachings are simple. While that is true, it is also the case that his teachings are so radically different from our usual understandings of ourselves and life that they are difficult to accept and easily forgotten or distorted. That is why in this primer we have repeated the same basic psychological principles over and again in various forms and contexts. Now, we can sum up the simple truth of *A Course in Miracles* and of Jesus' system of psychology with the following four points:

1. We are not separate bodies and there is no world. Everything we think is real and important is taking place in our mind which is outside of time and space, though ever present. Mind is the cause of everything we experience—everything!

2. Our true Identity is as Christ at one with the Mind of God, but we dream of a mind apart from Mind and other minds. As such, we still have the power to choose between which of two thought systems will be the source of our dreaming. Basically that is a choice between having a nightmare dream of guilt and fear which leads to continued conflict and mindless sleep, or to a happy dream of peace and forgiveness leading to mindfulness and awakening.

3. The two thought systems which can serve as the basic cause of our dream are that of the Holy Spirit which begins with the premise of the Atonement truth that we are not separate in any way at any level; and that of the ego which begins with the belief that separation is possible and true.

4. In truth—in the truth of eternity and the Mind of God—there never was a dream of separation. Since that truth does not help us who grope in mindless darkness, Jesus offers us the shining gift of forgiveness as a way to dispel the darkness and awaken from the dream of separation.

Following are some instructive examples from the ACIM Text where Jesus asserts the simplicity of his course:

Have faith in nothing and you will find the "treasure" that you seek. Yet you will add another burden to your already burdened mind. You will believe that nothing is of value, and will value it. A little piece of glass, a speck of dust, a body or a war are one to you. For if you value one thing made of nothing, you have believed that nothing can be precious, and that you *can* learn how to make the untrue true.

The Holy Spirit, seeing where you are but knowing you are elsewhere, begins His lesson in simplicity with the fundamental teaching that *truth* is true. This is the hardest lesson you will ever learn, and in the end the only one. Simplicity is very difficult for twisted minds. Consider all the distortions you have made of nothing; all the strange forms and feelings and actions and reactions that you have woven out of it. Nothing is so alien to you as the simple truth, and nothing are you less inclined to listen to. The contrast between what is true and what is not is perfectly apparent, yet you do not see it. The simple and the obvious are not apparent to those who would make palaces and royal robes of nothing, believing they are kings with golden crowns because of them....

If you would be a happy learner, you must give everything you have learned to the Holy Spirit, to be unlearned for you. And then begin to learn the joyous lessons that come quickly on the firm foundation that truth is true. For what is builded there *is* true, and built on truth. The universe of learning will open up before you in all its gracious simplicity. With truth before you, you will not look back (T-14.II.1:7-2:7; 6).

The reason this course is simple is that truth is simple. Complexity is of the ego, and is nothing more than the ego's attempt to obscure the obvious. You could live forever in the holy instant, beginning now and reaching to eternity, but for a very simple reason. Do not obscure the simplicity of this reason, for if you do, it will be only because you prefer not to recognize it and not to let it go. The simple reason, simply stated, is this: The holy instant is a time in which you receive and give perfect communication.[1] This means, however, that it is a time in which your mind is open, both to receive and give. It is the recognition that all minds are in communication. It therefore seeks to change nothing, but merely to accept everything (T-15.IV.6).

---

[1] In Wapnick's *Glossary* the term *communication* is defined at two different levels of meaning. The meaning which applies here is that which refers to "true perception," or perception cleansed of the need to project guilt. That definition states: "we experience communication in our right minds through the Holy Spirit, allowing His Love to be shared through us." Thus, we become channels for the love of the Holy Spirit which is both received in our open minds and then shared, or given through our mind to other minds."

We have noted already that the *last* chapter in the ACIM Text begins this way:

> How simple is salvation! All it says is what was never true is not true now, and never will be. The impossible has not occurred, and can have no effects. And that is all. Can this be hard to learn by anyone who wants it to be true? Only unwillingness to learn it could make such an easy lesson difficult. How hard is it to see that what is false can not be true, and what is true can not be false? You can no longer say that you perceive no differences in false and true. You have been told exactly how to tell one from the other, and just what to do if you become confused. Why, then, do you persist in learning not such simple things? (T-31.I.1)

Finally, two selections from the ACIM Workbook which again emphasize the simplicity of the lessons Jesus hopes to teach:

Let me recognize the problem so it can be solved.

> Let me realize today that the problem is always some form of grievance that I would cherish. Let me also understand that the solution is always a miracle with which I let the grievance be replaced. Today I would remember the simplicity of salvation by reinforcing the lesson that there is one problem and one solution. The problem is a grievance; the solution is a miracle. And I invite the solution to come to me through my forgiveness of the grievance, and my welcome of the miracle that takes its place (W-pI.rII.90.1).

Forgiveness offers everything I want.

> What could you want forgiveness cannot give? Do you want peace? Forgiveness offers it. Do you want happiness, a quiet mind, a certainty of purpose, and a sense of worth and beauty that transcends the world? Do you want care and safety, and the warmth of sure protection always? Do you want a quietness that cannot be disturbed, a gentleness that never can be hurt, a deep, abiding comfort, and a rest so perfect it can never be upset?...

> Here is the answer! Would you stand outside while all of Heaven waits for you within? Forgive and be forgiven. As you give you will receive. There is no plan but this for the salvation of the Son of God. Let us today rejoice that this is so, for here we have an answer, clear and plain, beyond deceit in its simplicity. All the complexities the world has spun of fragile cobwebs disappear before the power and the majesty of this extremely simple statement of the truth (W-pI.122.1; 6).

The teachings of *A Course in Miracles* may seem outrageous, preposterous, and too ridiculous to be believed. But in the Course Jesus implores his readers to *look*! Look closely at life as you experience it. Look at what so many of the world's illustrious writers and thinkers have pointed to throughout the centuries. Look at the thought content of your own mind. The Course is not an isolated, crazy bunch of words dreamed up by a hallucinating and delusional woman. It speaks to the core of life. Look! Just look. And as we look, Jesus invites us to consider whether somewhere within us there is at least a whispering suspicion that, "There must be a better way"?

> The world you see is the delusional system of those made mad by guilt. Look carefully at this world, and you will realize that this is so. For this world is the symbol of punishment, and all the laws that seem to govern it are the laws of death. Children are born into it through pain and in pain. Their growth is attended by suffering, and they learn of sorrow and separation and death. Their minds seem to be trapped in their brain, and its powers to decline if their bodies are hurt. They seem to love, yet they desert and are deserted. They appear to lose what they love, perhaps the most insane belief of all. And their bodies wither and gasp and are laid in the ground, and are no more. Not one of them but has thought that God is cruel.
>
> If this were the real world, God *would* be cruel. For no Father could subject His children to this as the price of salvation and *be* loving. *Love does not kill to save.* If it did, attack would be salvation, and this is the ego's interpretation, not God's. Only the world of guilt could demand this, for only the guilty could conceive of it. Adam's "sin" could have touched no one, had he not believed it was the Father Who drove him out of paradise. For in that belief the knowledge of the Father was lost, since only those who do not understand Him could believe it.
>
> This world *is* a picture of the crucifixion of God's Son. And until you realize that God's Son cannot be crucified, this is the world you will see. Yet you will not realize this until you accept the eternal fact that God's Son is not guilty. He deserves only love because he has given only love. He cannot be condemned because he has never condemned.
>
> The Atonement is the final lesson he need learn, for it teaches him that, never having sinned, he has no need of salvation (T-13.IN.2:2-4:6).

Jesus' system of psychology can be understood as a psychology of forgiveness. Forgiveness is the central theme that runs throughout and is the companion of the miracle which gives the Course its title. Forgiveness is offered by Jesus as the saving illusion for a mind lost in the darkness of illusions. It is offered as a light to illuminate the way to Light. It is the way to awaken from the misery and crimson, bleeding horror of a dream that there could be a life apart from Heaven and from the Love of God. We conclude with the hopeful promise of the following passages from the ACIM Workbook:

Forgiveness is the key to happiness.

Here is the answer to your search for peace. Here is the key to meaning in a world that seems to make no sense. Here is the way to safety in apparent dangers that appear to threaten you at every turn, and bring uncertainty to all your hopes of ever finding quietness and peace. Here are all questions answered; here the end of all uncertainty ensured at last.

The unforgiving mind is full of fear, and offers love no room to be itself; no place where it can spread its wings in peace and soar above the turmoil of the world. The unforgiving mind is sad, without the hope of respite and release from pain. It suffers and abides in misery, peering about in darkness, seeing not, yet certain of the danger lurking there.

The unforgiving mind is torn with doubt, confused about itself and all it sees; afraid and angry, weak and blustering, afraid to go ahead, afraid to stay, afraid to waken or to go to sleep, afraid of every sound, yet more afraid of stillness; terrified of darkness, yet more terrified at the approach of light. What can the unforgiving mind perceive but its damnation? What can it behold except the proof that all its sins are real?

The unforgiving mind sees no mistakes, but only sins. It looks upon the world with sightless eyes, and shrieks as it beholds its own projections rising to attack its miserable parody of life. It wants to live, yet wishes it were dead. It wants forgiveness, yet it sees no hope. It wants escape, yet can conceive of none because it sees the sinful everywhere.

The unforgiving mind is in despair, without the prospect of a future which can offer anything but more despair. Yet it regards its judgment of the world as irreversible, and does not see it has condemned itself to this despair. It thinks it cannot change, for what it sees bears witness that its judgment is correct. It does not ask, because it thinks it knows. It does not question, certain it is right.

Forgiveness is acquired. It is not inherent in the mind, which cannot sin. As sin is an idea you taught yourself, forgiveness must be learned by you as well, but from a Teacher other than yourself, Who represents the other Self in you. Through Him you learn how to forgive the self you think you made, and let it disappear. Thus you return your mind as one to Him Who is your Self, and Who can never sin.

Each unforgiving mind presents you with an opportunity to teach your own how to forgive itself. Each one awaits release from hell through you, and turns to you imploringly for Heaven here and now. It has no hope, but you become its hope. And as its hope, do you become your own. The unforgiving mind must learn through your forgiveness that it has been saved from hell. And as you teach salvation, you will learn. Yet all your teaching and your learning will be not of you, but of the Teacher Who was given you to show the way to you (W-pI.121.1-7).

297

APPENDIXES

Appendix A

Preface to *A Course in Miracles*

Reproduced with permission of the Foundation for A Course in Miracles

PREFACE

This Preface was written in 1977, in response to many requests for a brief introduction to *A Course in Miracles*. The first two parts—*How It Came, What It Is*—Helen Schucman wrote herself; the final part—*What It Says*—was written by the process of inner dictation described in the Preface.

How It Came

A Course in Miracles began with the sudden decision of two people to join in a common goal. Their names were Helen Schucman and William Thetford, Professors of Medical Psychology at Columbia University's College of Physicians and Surgeons in New York City. They were anything but spiritual. Their relationship with each other was difficult and often strained, and they were concerned with personal and professional acceptance and status. In general, they had considerable investment in the values of the world. Their lives were hardly in accord with anything that the Course advocates. Helen, the one who received the material, describes herself:

> *Psychologist, educator, conservative in theory and atheistic in belief, I was working in a prestigious and highly academic setting. And then something happened that triggered a chain of events I could never have predicted. The head of my department unexpectedly announced that he was tired of the angry and aggressive feelings our attitudes reflected, and concluded that, "there must be another way." As if on cue I agreed to help him find it. Apparently this Course is the other way.*

Although their intention was serious, they had great difficulty in starting out on their joint venture. But they had given the Holy Spirit the "little willingness" that, as the Course itself was to emphasize again and again, is sufficient to enable Him to use any situation for His purposes and provide it with His power.

To continue Helen's first-person account:

> *Three startling months preceded the actual writing, during which time Bill suggested that I write down the highly symbolic dreams and descriptions of the strange images that were coming to me. Although I had grown more accustomed to the unexpected by that time, I was still very surprised when I wrote, "This is a course in miracles." That was my introduction to the Voice. It made no sound, but seemed to be giving me a kind of rapid, inner dictation which I took down in a shorthand notebook. The writing was never automatic. It could be interrupted at any time and later picked up again.*

303

It made me very uncomfortable, but it never seriously occurred to me to stop. It seemed to be a special assignment I had somehow, somewhere agreed to complete. It represented a truly collaborative venture between Bill and myself, and much of its significance, I am sure, lies in that. I would take down what the Voice "said" and read it to him the next day, and he typed it from my dictation. I expect he had his special assignment, too. Without his encouragement and support I would never have been able to fulfill mine. The whole process took about seven years. The Text came first, then the Workbook for Students, and finally the Manual for Teachers. Only a few minor changes have been made. Chapter titles and subheadings have been inserted in the Text, and some of the more personal references that occurred at the beginning have been omitted. Otherwise the material is substantially unchanged.

The names of the collaborators in the recording of the Course do not appear on the cover because the Course can and should stand on its own. It is not intended to become the basis for another cult. Its only purpose is to provide a way in which some people will be able to find their own Internal Teacher.

What It Is

As its title implies, the Course is arranged throughout as a teaching device. It consists of three books: a 622-page Text, a 478-page Workbook for Students, and an 88-page Manual for Teachers. The order in which students choose to use the books, and the ways in which they study them, depend on their particular needs and preferences.

The curriculum the Course proposes is carefully conceived and is explained, step by step, at both the theoretical and practical levels. It emphasizes application rather than theory, and experience rather than theology. It specifically states that "a universal theology is impossible, but a universal experience is not only possible but necessary." (Manual, p. 77). Although Christian in statement, the Course deals with universal spiritual themes. It emphasizes that it is but one version of the universal curriculum. There are many others, this one differing from them only in form. They all lead to God in the end.

The Text is largely theoretical, and sets forth the concepts on which the Course's thought system is based. Its ideas contain the foundation for the Workbook's lessons. Without the practical application the Workbook provides, the Text would remain largely a series of abstractions which would hardly suffice to bring about the thought reversal at which the Course aims.

The Workbook includes 365 lessons, one for each day of the year. It is not necessary, however, to do the lessons at that tempo, and one might want to remain with a particularly appealing lesson for more than one day. The instructions urge only that not more than one lesson a day should be attempted. The practical nature of the Workbook is underscored by the introduction to its lessons, which emphasizes experience through application rather than a prior commitment to a spiritual goal:

> Some of the ideas the workbook presents you will find hard to believe, and others may seem to be quite startling. This does not matter. You are merely asked to apply the ideas as you are directed to do. You are not asked to judge them at all. You are asked only to use them. It is their use that will give them meaning to you, and will show you that they are true.

> Remember only this; you need not believe the ideas, you need not accept them, and you need not even welcome them. Some of them you may actively resist. None of this will matter, or decrease their efficacy. But do not allow yourself to make exceptions in applying the ideas the workbook contains, and whatever your reactions to the ideas may be, use them. Nothing more than that is required (Workbook, p. 2).

Finally, the Manual for Teachers, which is written in question and answer form, provides answers to some of the more likely questions a student might ask. It also includes a clarification of a number of the terms the Course uses, explaining them within the theoretical framework of the Text.

The Course makes no claim to finality, nor are the Workbook lessons intended to bring the student's learning to completion. At the end, the reader is left in the hands of his or her own Internal Teacher, Who will direct all subsequent learning as He sees fit. While the Course is comprehensive in scope, truth cannot be limited to any finite form, as is clearly recognized in the statement at the end of the Workbook:

> This Course is a beginning, not an end...No more specific lessons are assigned, for there is no more need of them. Henceforth, hear but the Voice for God...He will direct your efforts, telling you exactly what to do, how to direct your mind, and when to come to Him in silence, asking for His sure direction and His certain Word (Workbook, p. 487).

What It Says

Nothing real can be threatened.
Nothing unreal exists.
Herein lies the peace of God.

This is how *A Course in Miracles* begins. It makes a fundamental distinction between the real and the unreal; between knowledge and perception. Knowledge is truth, under one law, the law of love or God. Truth is unalterable, eternal and unambiguous. It can be unrecognized, but it cannot be changed. It applies to everything that God created, and only what He created is real. It is beyond learning because it is beyond time and process. It has no opposite; no beginning and no end. It merely is.

The world of perception, on the other hand, is the world of time, of change, of beginnings and endings. It is based on interpretation, not on facts. It is the world of birth and death, founded on the belief in scarcity, loss, separation and death. It is learned rather than given, selective in its perceptual emphases, unstable in its functioning, and inaccurate in its interpretations.

From knowledge and perception respectively, two distinct thought systems arise which are opposite in every respect. In the realm of knowledge no thoughts exist apart from God, because God and His Creation share one Will. The world of perception, however, is made by the belief in opposites and separate wills, in perpetual conflict with each other and with God. What perception sees and hears appears to be real because it permits into awareness only what conforms to the wishes of the perceiver. This leads to a world of illusions, a world which needs constant defense precisely *because* it is not real.

When you have been caught in the world of perception you are caught in a dream. You cannot escape without help, because everything your senses show merely witnesses to the reality of the dream. God has provided the Answer, the only Way out, the true Helper. It is the function of His Voice, His Holy Spirit, to mediate between the two worlds. He can do this because, while on the one hand He knows the truth, on the other He also recognizes our illusions, but without believing in them. It is the Holy Spirit's goal to help us escape from the dream world by teaching us how to reverse our thinking and unlearn our mistakes. Forgiveness is the Holy Spirit's great learning aid in bringing this thought reversal about. However, the Course has its own definition of what forgiveness really is just as it defines the world in its own way.

The world we see merely reflects our own internal frame of reference—the dominant ideas, wishes and emotions in our minds. "Projection makes perception" (Text, p. 445). We look inside first, decide the kind of world we want to see and then project that world outside, making it the truth *as we see it*. We make it true by our interpretations of what it is we are seeing.

If we are using perception to justify our own mistakes—our anger, our impulses to attack, our lack of love in whatever form it may take—we will see a world of evil, destruction, malice, envy and despair. All this we must learn to forgive, not because we are being "good" and "charitable," but because what we are seeing is not true. We have distorted the world by our twisted defenses, and are therefore seeing what is not there. As we learn to recognize our perceptual errors, we also learn to look past them or "forgive." At the same time we are forgiving ourselves, looking past our distorted self-concepts to the Self That God created in us and as us.

Sin is defined as "lack of love" (Text, p. 11). Since love is all there is, sin in the sight of the Holy Spirit is a mistake to be corrected, rather than an evil to be punished. Our sense of inadequacy, weakness and incompletion comes from the strong investment in the "scarcity principle" that governs the whole world of illusions. From that point of view, we seek in others what we feel is wanting in ourselves. We "love" another in order to get something ourselves. That, in fact, is what passes for love in the dream world. There can be no greater mistake than that, for love is incapable of asking for anything.

Only minds can really join, and whom God has joined no man can put asunder (Text, p. 356). It is, however, only at the level of Christ Mind that true union is possible, and has, in fact, never been lost. The "little I" seeks to enhance itself by external approval, external possessions and external "love." The Self That God created needs nothing. It is forever complete, safe, loved and loving. It seeks to share rather than to get; to extend rather than project. It has no needs and wants to join with others out of their mutual awareness of abundance.

The special relationships of the world are destructive, selfish and childishly egocentric. Yet, if given to the Holy Spirit, these relationships can become the holiest things on earth -- the miracles that point the way to the return to Heaven. The world uses its special relationships as a final weapon of exclusion and a demonstration of separateness. The Holy Spirit transforms them into perfect lessons in forgiveness and in awakening from the dream. Each one is an opportunity to let perceptions be healed and errors corrected. Each one is another chance to forgive oneself by forgiving the other. And each one becomes still another invitation to the Holy Spirit and to the remembrance of God.

Perception is a function of the body, and therefore represents a limit on awareness. Perception sees through the body's eyes and hears through the body's ears. It evokes the limited responses which the body makes. The body appears to be largely self-motivated and independent, yet it actually responds only to the intentions of the mind. If the mind wants to use it for attack in any form, it becomes prey to sickness, age and decay. If the mind accepts the Holy Spirit's purpose for it instead, it becomes a useful way of communicating with others, invulnerable as long as it is needed, and to be gently laid by when its use is over. Of itself it is neutral, as is everything in the world of perception. Whether it is used for the goals of the ego or the Holy Spirit depends entirely on what the mind wants.

The opposite of seeing through the body's eyes is the vision of Christ, which reflects strength rather than weakness, unity rather than separation, and love rather than fear. The opposite of hearing through the body's ears is communication through the Voice for God, the Holy Spirit, which abides in each of us. His Voice seems distant and difficult to hear because the ego, which speaks for the little, separated self, seems to be much louder. This is actually reversed. The Holy Spirit speaks with unmistakable clarity and overwhelming appeal. No one who does not choose to identify with the body could possibly be deaf to His messages of release and hope, nor could he fail to accept joyously the vision of Christ in glad exchange for his miserable picture of himself.

Christ's vision is the Holy Spirit's gift, God's alternative to the illusion of separation and to the belief in the reality of sin, guilt and death. It is the one correction for all errors of perception; the reconciliation of the seeming opposites on which this world is based. Its kindly light shows all things from another point of view, reflecting the thought system that arises from knowledge and making return to God not only possible but inevitable. What was regarded as injustices done to one by someone else, now becomes a call for help and for union. Sin, sickness and attack are seen as misperceptions calling for remedy through gentleness and love. Defenses are laid down because where there is no attack there is no need for them. Our brothers' needs become our own, because they are taking the journey with us as we go to God. Without us they would lose their way. Without them we could never find our own.

Forgiveness is unknown in Heaven, where the need for it would be inconceivable. However, in this world, forgiveness is a necessary correction for all the mistakes that we have made. To offer forgiveness is the only way for us to have it, for it reflects the law of Heaven that giving and receiving are the same. Heaven is the natural state of all the Sons of God as He created them. Such is their reality forever. It has not changed because it has been forgotten.

Forgiveness is the means by which we will remember. Through forgiveness the thinking of the world is reversed. The forgiven world becomes the gate of Heaven, because by its mercy we can at last forgive ourselves. Holding no one prisoner to guilt, we become free. Acknowledging Christ in all our brothers, we recognize His Presence in ourselves. Forgetting all our misperceptions, and with nothing from the past to hold us back, we can remember God. Beyond this, learning cannot go. When we are ready, God Himself will take the final step in our return to Him.

Appendix B: *Glossary-Index* Part I, Theory

From the *Glossary-Index for A COURSE IN MIRACLES*, 5th Edition Revised,
by Kenneth Wapnick, Ph.D. Temecula, CA:
Foundation for *A Course in Miracles*, 1999

THEORY

A Course in Miracles distinguishes two worlds: God and the ego, **knowledge** and **perception, truth** and **illusion**. Strictly speaking, every aspect of the post-separation world of perception reflects the **ego**. However, the Course further subdivides the world of perception into wrong- and right-mindedness. Within this framework the Course almost always uses the word "ego" to denote wrong-mindedness, while right-mindedness is the domain of the Holy Spirit, Who teaches forgiveness as the correction for the ego. Thus, we can speak of three thought systems: **One-mindedness**, which belongs to knowledge, and **wrong-** and **right-mindedness** which reflect the world of perception. Our discussion will follow this tripartite view of **mind**.

The accompanying chart summarizes the Course's description of the mind. It should be examined in conjunction with the following references from the Course which deal with the relationship of spirit to mind, spirit to ego, and the three levels of mind:

T-1.V.5
T-3.IV.2-6
T-4.I.2-3
T-7.IX.1-4
W-pI.96.3-5
C-1

A Course in Miracles, therefore, is written on two levels, reflecting two basic divisions. The first level presents the difference between the One Mind and the separated mind, while the second contrasts wrong- and right-mindedness within the separated mind. On this first level, for example, the world and body are illusions made by the ego, and thus symbolize the separation. The second level relates to this world where we believe we are. Here, the world and the body are neutral and can serve one of two purposes. To the wrong-minded ego they are instruments to reinforce separation; to the right mind they are the Holy Spirit's teaching devices through which we learn His lessons of forgiveness. On this level, illusions refer to the misperceptions of the ego; e.g., seeing attack instead of a call for love, sin instead of error.

Thus, the Course focuses on our thoughts, not their external manifestations which are really projections of these thoughts. As it says: "This is a course in cause and not effect" (T-21.VII.7:8).

We are urged not to seek to change the world (effect), but to change our mind (cause) about the world (T-21.In.1:7). When lesson 193 states: "I will forgive, and this will disappear" (W-pI.193.13:3), what is meant is that our perception of the problem and any pain that comes to us from this perception disappear, not necessarily the physical expression of the problem. For example, if rain threatens proposed plans and brings upset or disappointment, we should not pray for sunshine, but rather for help in looking at the inclement weather as an opportunity we have chosen to learn a lesson in forgiveness the Holy Spirit can teach us. This is not to deny that the ego can make or affect a physical world. However, as this physical world is inherently illusory, a result of our thoughts, the Course's emphasis is on correcting these mistaken or miscreative thoughts, which are always the true source of any problem. This correction then allows the Holy Spirit's Love to direct our behavior in the world.

Diagram: Level One – Level Two

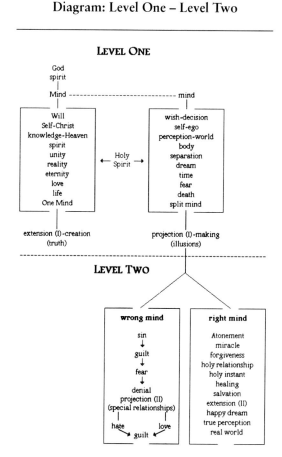

One-mindedness

The One-mindedness of Christ is the world of **Heaven** or knowledge: the pre-separation world of **spirit**, **love**, truth, eternity, infinity, and reality, where the **oneness** of God's **creation**—the sum of all His **Thoughts**—is unbroken. It is the natural state of direct **communication** with God and His creation that existed before the mind of God's Son thought of separation. In this state the perfect unity of the **Trinity** is maintained.

The Trinity consists of: 1) **God**, the Father; 2) His **Son, Christ**, our true **Self**; and 3) the **Holy Spirit**, the **Voice for God.** Included in the Second Person of the Trinity are our **creations**, the extensions of our Self or spirit. The Second Person of the Trinity is not exclusively identified with **Jesus**, who is part of Christ, as we all are.

Wrong-mindedness

The ego consists of three fundamental concepts: **sin:** the belief that we have separated ourselves from God; **guilt:** the experience of having sinned, of having done something wrong which emanates from our belief that we have attacked God by usurping His role as First Cause, making ourselves our own first cause; and **fear:** the emotion that inevitably follows guilt, coming from our belief in sin and based on our thought that we deserve to be punished by the ego's made-up god of vengeance.

To ensure its survival, the ego continually attracts guilt to itself, since guilt proves sin's reality and it is sin that gave the ego birth. Once it has established guilt as real the ego teaches us never to approach or even look at it, for it says we would either be destroyed by an angry, vengeful god—a god that the ego made, in fact, to suit its purpose—intent on punishing us for our sin against him, or else annihilated in the oblivion of our own nothingness. This fear keeps the guilt and sin intact, for without seeing them as decisions of our minds we can never change our belief in them.

Left with the anxiety and terror brought on by the fear of God, our only recourse is to turn to the ego for help, since God has become our enemy. The ego's plan of salvation from guilt has two parts: the first is **denial**, wherein we push our guilt out of awareness, hoping that by not seeing the problem it will not be there. Second, after the guilt is denied, we project it out from us onto another, **magically** hoping to be free from the guilt by unconsciously placing it outside ourselves.

Projection has two principal forms: **special hate** and **special love relationships**. In special hate relationships our self-hatred or guilt is transferred onto others, making them responsible for the misery we feel. Our **anger** or **attack** attempts to justify the projection, reinforcing others' guilt for the sins we projected from ourselves. Special love relationships have the same goal of projecting guilt, though the form differs greatly. Our guilt teaches we are empty, unfulfilled, incomplete, and needful, all aspects of the **scarcity principle**. Believing this lack can never be corrected, we seek outside ourselves for those people who can complete us. Special love, thus, takes this form: I have certain special needs that God cannot meet, but you, a special person with special attributes, can meet them for me. When you do, I shall love you. If you do not, my love will turn to hate.

The ego's world becomes divided into enemies (special hate) or savior-**idols** (special love), and the true Identity of Christ in others is obscured. **Judgment**, always based on the past rather than acceptance in the present, is the ego's guiding principle. Through special relationships the ego sustains its existence by maintaining guilt, since using others to meet our needs constitutes an attack, and attack in any form reinforces guilt. This sets into motion the guilt-attack cycle, wherein the greater our guilt, the greater the need to project it by attacking others through special relationships, which merely adds to the guilt, increasing the need to project it.

The ego's wrong-mindedness is a **dream** of **separation**, most clearly expressed in the physical **world** which was made as "an attack on God" (W-pII.3.2:1). The **body's** existence is one of **sickness, suffering,** and **death**, which witness to the seeming reality of the body as opposed to spirit, which can never suffer pain, or die. **Crucifixion** is the Course's symbol of the ego, representing the belief in attack and **sacrifice**, where one's gain depends on another's loss. All aspects of the separated world are illusions, since what is of God can never be separate from Him, and therefore what seems separate from God cannot be real. This is expressed by the Course principle **"ideas leave not their source"**: we are an Idea (or Thought) in the **Mind** of God that has never left its Source.

Right-mindedness

God's **Answer** to the separation is the Holy Spirit, and His plan to undo the ego is called the **Atonement**. *A Course in Miracles* employs many terms that reflect the Holy Spirit's plan, and each is a virtual synonym for the other.

They include: **miracle, forgiveness, salvation, healing, real world, true perception, vision, face of Christ, reason, justice, holy instant, holy relationship, function, happy dream, Second Coming, Word of God, Last (Final) Judgment, resurrection, redemption, correction, awakening,** and **undoing.**

These terms, belonging to the separated world of perception, refer to the **process** (the miracle) that corrects our misperceptions, shifting from hearing the ego's voice of sin, guilt, and fear, to the Holy Spirit's Voice of forgiveness. In this way, special or unholy relationships become holy. Without these relationships we would have no way of being freed from the guilt the ego has taught us to bury through denial, and retain through projection. The Holy Spirit turns the tables on the ego by changing its purpose for projection into an opportunity to see this denied guilt in another, thereby bringing it back within which allows us finally to change our minds about it.

While the practice of forgiveness, or undoing guilt, is usually experienced as complex and long term, it can be understood essentially as a three-step process (see, e.g., T-5.VII.6; W-pI.23.5; W-pI.70.1-4; W-pI.196.7-11). The first step reverses the projection as we realize that the guilt is not in another but in ourselves. Second, now that the guilt has been brought to our attention and we recognize that its source is in us, we undo this **decision** by choosing to see ourselves as guiltless Sons of God, rather than guilty sons of the ego. These two steps are our responsibility; the final one is the Holy Spirit's, Who is able to take the guilt from us now that we have released it to Him, **looking** at it with His Love beside us, and thus without judgment and guilt. This looking without judgment, in gentle **laughter**, is the meaning of forgiveness. Using the workbook as our guide, we become trained over time to hear the Holy Spirit's Voice, learning that all things are opportunities to learn forgiveness (W-pI.193).

Illustrative of this process-aspect of forgiveness are the references under **periods of unsettling** and **bringing darkness (illusions) to the light (truth)**, as well as workbook lesson 284. These reflect the almost inevitable difficulty that results when one begins to take the Holy Spirit's lessons seriously, and allows the deeply denied guilt to begin to surface in one's consciousness.

When our guilt is finally undone, right-mindedness having corrected wrong-mindedness, the **bridge** to the real world is complete. The **memory of God** dawns within our minds, as all interferences to it have been removed and we see the face of Christ in all people. This world of illusion and separation ends as God takes the **last step**, reaching down and lifting us unto Himself. Restored to the One-mindedness of Christ, "we are home, where ... [God] would have us be" (T-31.VIII.12:8).

Terms

Several words, especially those pertaining to One-mindedness, have no precise meaning in this world and their definition can only be approximated here.

As *A Course in Miracles* says: "words are but symbols of symbols. They are thus twice removed from reality" (M-21.1:9-10). It should be noted that many of the terms have different meanings or connotations outside the Course, and these should not be confused with the Course's usage. Moreover, some words have differing uses in *A Course in Miracles* itself, reflecting knowledge or perception (e.g., extension), right- or wrong-mindedness (e.g., denial). Some terms, incidentally, appear in more than one listing.

The capitalization used in the Course is followed here. Thus, the Persons of the Trinity—God, Christ (Son of God), Holy Spirit—are always capitalized, as are all pronouns referring to Them. Pronouns referring to the Son of God in his separated state are lower case. Words that directly relate to the Trinity, such as Love, Will, Heaven, etc., are capitalized, though their pronouns are not.

One-mindedness

abundance	judgment
Christ	knowledge
communication	Last (Final) Judgment
communion	laws of God
creation	light
creations	love
extension	mind
function	Mind of God
gift	Name of God
God	One-mindedness
gratitude	oneness
Great Rays	Self
Heaven (Kingdom of God, Heaven)	Son of God
Holy Spirit (Answer, Voice for God)	spirit
"ideas leave not their source"	Thoughts of God
innocence	Trinity
invulnerability	Will of God

Wrong-mindedness

anti-Christ	innocence
attack (anger)	judgment
body	magic
crucifixion	means-end
death	perception
defenses	projection
denial	sacrifice
devil	scarcity principle
dissociation	separation
dream	sicknes
ego	sin
fear	sleep
gap	Son of God
goft	special relationship
giving-receiving	split
guilt	suffering (pain)
hell	temptation
"ideas leave not their source"	time
idol	world
illusion	wrong-mindedness

Right-mindedness

accepting the Atonement	last step
a little willingness	laughter
Atonement	laws of God
awakening	light
body	looking at the ego
communication	love
death	means-end
defenses	memory of God
denial	miracle
extension	no order of difficulty in miracles
face of Christ	not to make the error real
forgiveness	oneness
free will (1)	peace
freewill (2)	perception
function	prayer
gift	process
giving-receiving	projection
grace	real world
Great Rays	reason
gratitude	resurrection
happy dream	revelation
healing	right-mindedness
holy instant	salvation
holy relationship	Second Coming
"I am as God created me"	Son of God
"ideas leave not their source"	teacher of God
innocence	Thoughts of God
invulnerability	time
joining	true perception
joy (happiness, gladness)	vision
judgment	Word of God
justice	world
Last (Final) Judgment	

Related Terms

A Course in Miracles	humility-arrogance
bringing darkness (illusions) to the light (truth)	jesus
cause-effect	make-create
Christmas	periods of unsettling
decision	questions
Easter	senseless musings
faith	teaching-learning
form-content	truth-illusion
having-being	wish-will

Symbols

altar	song of Heaven
angels	star
bridge	thorns
child	toys
lilies	war

WORKS CITED

ACCEL TEAM. UK (Cumbria): http://www.accel-team.com/productivity/index.html

AllPsych Online, The Virtual Psychology Classroom, http://allpsych.com/dictionary/m.html

American Heritage Dictionary of the English Language, Fourth Edition. New York: Houghton Mifflin Company, 2000.

Bolen, James. "An Exclusive, Candid Conversation with William Thetford, Ph.D." In *New Realities*, Larkspur, CA. October, 1984.

Becker, Ernest. *The Denial of Death*. New York: The Free Press, 1973.

Breuer, Joseph and Sigmund Freud, *Studies on Hysteria*. Trans. by James Strachey. New York: U.S. publication by Basic Books, Inc. in arrangement with Hogarth Press, 1957.

Brown, G. Spencer. *Laws of Form*. New York: Julian Press, 1972.

College of Pharmacy, University of Texas at Austin, material dated August 4, 2004, http://www.utexas.edu/pharmacy/general/experiential/practitioner/effective/motv.html

Conroy, Susan. *Mother Teresa's Lessons of Love and Secrets of Sanctity*, p.199. Huntington, Indiana: Our Sunday Visitor, Inc., 2003.

Course in Miracles, A. Glen Ellen, CA: Foundation for Inner Peace, 1992.

Dass, Ram and Paul Gorman. *How Can I Help?* New York: Alfred A. Knopf, Inc., 1985.

Diagnostic and Statistical Manual on Mental Disorders, Fourth Ed. (DSM-IV). Washington, DC: American Psychiatric Press, 1994.

Encyclopedia of Psychology: http://www.psychology.org/links/Environment_Behavior_Relationships/Learning/

Freud, Anna. *The Ego and the Mechanisms of Defence*. London: Hogarth Press and Institute of Psycho-Analysis, 1937.

Freud, Sigmund. *Beyond the Pleasure Principle*. Trans. by James Strachey. New York: W. W. Norton & Co., 1961. (First published in German in 1920.)

____. *New Introductory Lectures on Psychoanalysis*. Trans. by James Strachey. New York: W. W. Norton & Co., 1964, 1965. (First published in German in 1933.)

Gendlin, Eugene. "Carl Rogers (1902-1987)." In the *American Psychologist*, Vol. 43, 2, February, 1988.

Humphry, Nicholas. *A History of the Mind*. New York: Simon & Schuster, 1992.

Jampolsky, Gerald G. *Teach Only Love: The Seven Principles of Attitudinal Healing*. Revised. Hillsboro, Oregon: Beyond Words Publishing, Inc., 2000.

Kelly, Walter Crawford Jr. *The Pogo Papers*. New York: Simon and Schuster, 1953.

Keyes, Ken Jr. *Handbook to Higher Consciousness*. Coos Bay, Oregon: Love Line Books.

Khayyam, Omar. *Rubaiyat of Omar Khayyam*, pp.45-47. Trans. by Edward FitzGerald. New York: St. Martin's Press, 1983.

Krishnamurti, J. *Choiceless Awareness: A Selection of Passages from the Teachings of J. Krishnamurti*. Ojai, CA: Krishnamurti Foundation of America, 1992 (Revised, 2001).

____. *Freedom from the Known*, p.39. Ojai, California: Krishnamurti Foundation, 1969.

Kubler-Ross, Elizabeth. *On Death and Dying*. New York: Touchstone, 1997. (Originally published in 1969.)

Maslow, Abraham. *Motivation and Personality*, 3rd ed. New York: Addison-Wesley, 1987. (Originally Published in 1954 and revised in 1970.)

McGinn, Colin. "Can We Solve the Mind-Body Problem?" *Mind* 98 (1989), pp. 349-66.

National Institute for Mental Health Web site, Statistics: http://www.nimh. nih.gov/healthinformation/statisticsmenu.cfm

Psychotherapy: Purpose, Process and Practice, An Extension of the Principles of A Course in Miracles. Mill Valley, CA: Foundation for Inner Peace, 1989.

Revelle, William. "Individual Differences in Personality and Motivation: 'Non-cognitive' Determinants of Cognitive Performance." In *Attention: Selection, Awareness and Control: A Tribute to Donald Broadbent*. Baddeley, A. & Weiskrantz, L., eds. Oxford, UK: Oxford University Press, 1993.

Rogers, Carl R. *On Becoming a Person*, p. 29. Cambridge, MA: The Riverside Press, 1961

____. "A Theory of Therapy, Personality and Interpersonal relationships, As Developed in the Client-Centered Framework." In *Psychology: A Study of a Science: Formulations of the Person and the Social Context*. Sigmund Koch, ed. New York: McGraw-Hill Book Company, 1959.

Shakespeare, W. *As You Like It*, II, vii,139-142.

____. *Hamlet*, III,i,62

____. *Macbeth*, V, v, 19.

____ .*Sonnet 64*, l.1

Schucman, Helen. *The Gifts of God*, p.115. Mill Valley, California: The Foundation for Inner Peace, 1982.

Siegel, Bernie S. *Love, Medicine and Miracles: Lesson Learned about Self-Healing from a Surgeon's Experience with Exceptional Patients*. New York: Harper Collins Publishers, 1988.

Song of Prayer: Prayer, Forgiveness and Healing: An Extension of the Principles of A COURSE IN MIRACLES, The. Mill Valley, CA: Foundation for Inner Peace, 1978

Stevenson, Robert Louis. "Playthings," in *Elbert Hubbard's Scrapbook*, p. 47. New York: American Book Co., 1943.

St. John of the Cross. *Dark Night of the Soul*. Trans. by Mirabai Starr. New York: Riverhead Books, The Berkely Publishing Group, a division of Penguin Putnam, Inc., 2002.

Tennyson, Alfred Lord. "A letter to Mr. B. P. Blood" in *Alfred Lord Tennyson: A Memoir by His Son*, V2. Basingstoke Hampshire, England: Macmillan Publishers Limited, 1899.

Thomas, Dylan. "In my craft or sullen art" in *The Collected Poems of Dylan Thomas*. New York: New Directions Books, 1939, 1942, 1946.

Tolkien, JRR. *The Fellowship of the Ring*, Vol. I of the trilogy, *The Lord of the Rings*. Collector's Edition. New York: Houghton Mifflin, 1974:

Voltaire. From the so-called *Leningrad Notebook*, also known as *Le Sottisier*; one of several posthumously published notebooks. See: Besterman, Theodore. *Voltaire's Notebooks*. Geneva: Institute et Musee Voltaire Les Delices, 1952.

Wapnick, Gloria and Kenneth. "Resistance: How One Studies *A Course in Miracles* Without Really Learning It." In *The Lighthouse*, Vol.10, 2. Temecula, CA: Foundation for *A Course in Miracles*, 1999.

Wapnick, Kenneth. *A Vast Illusion: Time According to A Course in Miracles*. Third Edition. Temecula, CA: Foundation for *A Course in Miracles*, 2006.

_____. *All Are Called*, Volume One of *The Message of A Course in Miracles*. Temecula, CA: Foundation for *A Course in Miracles*, 1977.

_____. *The Fifty Miracle Principles of A Course in Miracles*, 3rd Edition. Temecula, CA. Foundation for *A Course in Miracles*, 1992.

_____. *Forgiveness and Jesus: the Meeting Place of A Course in Miracles and Christianity*, 6th Edition. Temecula, CA: Foundation for *A Course in Miracles*, 1994.

_____. *Glossary-Index for A Course in Miracles*, 5th Ed. Revised. Temecula, CA: Foundation for *A Course in Miracles*, 1982, 1986, 1989, 1993, 1999.

_____. "Identify With Love." *The Lighthouse*, Vol. 16, 3. Temecula, CA: Foundation for *A Course in Miracles*, 2005.

____. "Rules for Decision." Temecula, CA: Foundation for *A Course in Miracles*, 1993.

____. "True Empathy." Temecula, CA: Foundation for *A Course in Miracles*, 1990.

Wilber, Ken. *The Spectrum of Consciousness*, 2nd Ed., pp.96-106. Wheaton, IL: The Theosophical Publishing House, 1977.

Wikipedia®, *The Free Encyclopedia*. St. Petersburg, FL: Wikimedia Foundation, Inc.

INDEX

331

Began reading 20th March 2018
Finished reading 2nd June 18

Lightning Source UK Ltd.
Milton Keynes UK
UKOW01f0039030816

279839UK00001B/70/P